Contents

BUILDING BRIDGES

The Life & Times of
Richard Charles Lee
Hong Kong: 1905-1983

Richard Charles Lee, 1964.

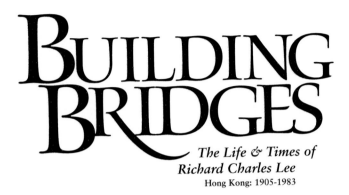

BUILDING BRIDGES

The Life & Times of
Richard Charles Lee
Hong Kong: 1905-1983

CALYAN
PUBLISHING LTD.

VIVIENNE POY

First Published in Canada by

Calyan Publishing Ltd.
4151 Sheppard Avenue East, 2nd floor
Scarborough, Ontario
Canada M1S 1T4

ISBN 1-896501-04-4

Poy, Vivienne
   Building Bridges, The Life & Times of Richard Charles Lee
      Hong Kong, 1905-1983

English Editors: Mary Adachi
                Philippa Campsie
Chinese Editor: Simon S.H. So 蘇紹興

Production and Design: Justin Poy Media

Photograph of Author: Dr. Neville G. Poy

By the same author: A River Named Lee

All inquiries regarding the motion picture, television and dramatic rights for this book should be addressed to the Author's representative:

Calyan Publishing Ltd.
4151 Sheppard Avenue East, 2nd floor
Scarborough, Ontario
Canada M1S 1T4
Representations as to the disposition of these rights are strictly prohibited without express written consent.

Printed and bound in Canada   First printing September 1998

To those whose lives have been touched by my father

ACKNOWLEDGEMENTS

I was able to write this biography of my father because of the generous help of many. In particular, I would like to thank Hon Chiu Lee, Chairman of Hysan Development Co., without whose help this book could not have been written. Yao Kang, Advisor of the Swire Group, Hong Kong, and director of many Swire subsidiaries; Sir Quo Wai Lee, Chairman of the Hang Seng Bank; Anna Li, Father's former secretary; David K.P. Li, Chairman of the Bank of East Asia; Professor Ma Lin, Chairman of Shaw College, The Chinese University of Hong Kong; Shinishi Shiraishi, former deputy president of Yamaichi Securities Co. Ltd., Japan; C.T. Wu, Father's old friend and former employee of the Lee family; Peter Yeung, Director of the Canada-Hong Kong Resource Centre, University of Toronto-York University, Joint Centre for Asia Pacific Studies; and Yoshiyuki Yoshioka, Secretary of the Japanese Club, Hong Kong, must be thanked for their patience in answering my many questions and for giving me a great deal of information.

I would also like to thank the following who contributed significantly to the content of this book: Barbara Bennett, Sir Jack and Lady Peggy Cater, Dr. Chi Chao Chan, Chen Jixuan, Chieko Kato, Josephine Chu, Professor Ruth Hayhoe, He Mingsi, He Jianli, Jenny Hoo, Huang Maolan, Per Jorgensen, Albert Kwan, Chien Lee, J.S. Lee, Peter T.C. Lee, Raymand Lee, Violet Lee, Professor Arthur K.C. Li, Aubrey K.S. Li, Greta Li, Lian Weilin, Professor Paul Lin, Donald Liu, Percy O'Brien, Reiko Ogata, William Poy, Lady May Ride, Elizabeth Ride, Dr. Ray Rook, Ronald Ross, Sir Evelyn de Rothschild, Sing Sheng, Joseph and Jeanne Tam, George Todkill and Wang Kuang.

In my research, I was greatly helped by: Vincent Chen of the Campus Planning and Building Committee of The Chinese University of Hong Kong; Chen Rongsheng, Cultural Consul of the People's Republic of China in Toronto; Frank Ching, Senior Editor at the *Far Eastern Economic Review*; Y.C. Wan, Curator of the Hung On-To Memorial Library of the University of Hong Kong Libraries; Johnson Li of the Canada-Hong Kong Resource Centre; Sam-Chin Li, librarian of the Cheng

Yutung East Asian Library of the University of Toronto; Anne Cheng, lawyer at the Bank of East Asia, Hong Kong; Tiffany K.W. Chan, graduate of the University of Hong Kong; T.W. Chu, librarian of the University of Hong Kong Libraries; Wandy Wong, secretary to the Chairman of Hysan Development Company; and Karen Diensdale, secretary of the Pontifical Institute of Medieval Studies of St. Michael's College, University of Toronto.

I am grateful to University Professor Julia Ching, of the University of Toronto, whose patience and guidance helped me clarify the form of this manuscript and organize the massive amount of information; to Professor Bernard Luk, co-chair of the Joint Centre for Asian Pacific Studies, University of Toronto and York University, for his comments and guidance; to Ku Hanzhao, scholar, and Kan Chung Yuen, a retired civil servant of the former government of Hong Kong, who were kind enough to read the manuscript and offer advice.

My special thanks to Peggy Ku for her tireless assistance, her skill in drawing all the maps, and for the translation of this book into Chinese. Special mention and thanks to my husband, Neville, who reshot many of the old photographs as well as taking new ones, and to our son Justin, who designed the cover, and oversaw its layout and publication.

FOREWORD

By any standard, Dr. Richard Charles Lee led an incredible and remarkable life. He lived through the tumultuous events of modern Chinese history and played a major role in the making of Hong Kong as we know it today — a vibrant international city.

Born into an aristocratic Hong Kong family, Oxford educated and for his time, widely travelled, he took charge of a dynastic business empire at a very young age. His vision of a modern China, including the need for international ties and friendships and the role that Hong Kong should play, is as relevant for the future as it was in his day. His love for the people of Hong Kong and the many significant major contributions that he made to improve their lives, in housing, education, welfare as well as in many other areas are well documented here in this personal account by his daughter Vivienne Poy. She shares with us the story of a gifted and intelligent man whose life was not without personal tragedies, like the untimely loss of both his father and his son. Dr. Lee was compassionate without being sentimental, and maintained a simple lifestyle despite his wealth.

Dr. Lee was a decisive man of very strong principles. Few people have ever resigned, as he did, from the Executive Council of the Hong Kong Government. He believed in justice and righteousness, blending Confucianism with the best from the West.

As Vivienne playfully remarks, when people speculated long ago that Dr. Lee would be the first Chief Executive of Hong Kong after the resumption of Chinese sovereignty in 1997, little did they realise that he would have been 92 years old! However, the serious point is that speculation stemmed from hope, admiration and a yearning for someone of his stature and proven track record to take charge of Hong Kong. Perhaps, Dr. R.C. Lee was the best Governor or Chief Executive that Hong Kong never had.

Arthur K.C. Li
Vice-Chancellor
The Chinese University of Hong Kong
March 1998

PROLOGUE

What kind of a man was Richard Charles Lee, my father? He was a stern man, rather set in his ways, punctual, disciplined. He always expected a lot of himself. He was a typical Chinese father who never put us on his knees and cuddled us as children, but he always showed that he cared and he always made sure we were well looked after. People who didn't know him were often afraid of him because he looked so solemn when he was not smiling. He was actually very affable and laughed a lot. However, his self-image was that of a very serious man, so he almost never smiled when he knew a photograph was being taken of him. He was honest, intelligent, inquisitive, hard-working and kind, and he would go out of his way to help others. He was a man of great generosity to others, but was very frugal towards himself. He was a man of integrity and principle who was willing to die for his beliefs. He was public-spirited and cared for the people and the society he lived in. As I could see at his funeral, those who came to pay their respects to him reflected the life he had lived.

Father was a civil engineer by training. He was a builder both literally and metaphorically. He built two kinds of bridges in his life: those made of steel and concrete and those made of human kindness. Of the two, the most important were the human bridges he built for Hong Kong and for China.

Except for one year, I have been away from Hong Kong since 1956 and because of that, I missed a great deal of what went on in his life. I realize that he belonged not just to his family, but to Hong Kong, its society and its people. He was a part of the history of Hong Kong. For some time I have been very curious about his life, and now I am ready to write about it.

This is an account of Father's life based on my parents' recollections and their correspondence, research and interviews with those close to Father, my own observations and personal experience, and my relationship with him. We are a family of four children, two boys and two girls. Each of us, because of our diverse personalities, had a very different kind of relationship with our father. In this book, I am speaking from my own perspective. In order to protect the privacy of the rest of my family, I will mention them from time to time, but they will not play a major role in this account.

Vivienne Poy, Toronto, 1997

A FAREWELL

July 11, 1983, was one of Hong Kong's typical hot summer days. By early morning, the sun was blazing. Mother, my brother, sister and I, the in-laws and the grandchildren were all up very early. We dressed in black and headed for the Hong Kong Funeral Home. It was the day of Father's funeral.

We had spent the previous few days at the funeral home where more than three thousand people came to pay their last respects. In accordance with Chinese custom, when guests approached the casket and the altar where the photograph of Father was displayed, they bowed three times, and our entire family, in black mourning robes provided by the funeral home, rose and bowed in unison to thank them. One day, we had to be at the funeral home unusually early because some of the Legislative and Executive Council members wanted to pay their respects before flying to Beijing for talks with China. On the morning of July 11, guests started arriving at eight in the morning, and many stayed for the service scheduled to start at ten.

It was obvious to anyone present that Father was not an ordinary man. On one side of his photograph was the largest wreath in the hall, from China's newly elected president, Li Xiannian; on the other side was the wreath from the governor of Hong Kong, Sir Edward Youde. Other prominently displayed wreaths were from the vice-chairman of the Military Commission, Yang Shangkun; vice-premier of the State Council, Gu Mu; Ji Pengfei, standing committee member of the Central Advisory Commission; member of the Central Committee of the Communist Party Xi Zhongxun; Ren Zhongyi, first secretary of the Guangdong Provincial Committee; the political commissar of the People's Liberation Army, Yu Qiuli; the governor of Guangdong, Liang Lingguang; the chief secretary of the Hong Kong government, Sir Philip Hadden-Cave; and many prominent citizens of Hong Kong.

The guests coming down the aisle represented a cross-section of the population. Among the many friends and family who came to pay their last respects were dignitaries from Hong Kong and China, including the chairman of the Hong Kong and Shanghai Bank, Michael Sandberg; the managing director of Hong Kong Land, Trevor Bedford; Financial Secretary Sir John Brembridge; Chairman of the Urban Council, Hilton

Cheongleen; Executive Councillors Dr. Harry Fang and T.S. Lo; Legislative Councillors Francis Tien and Dr. Rayson Huang; as well as Sir Shiukin Tang and film magnate Sir Run Run Shaw. Two former directors of the local branch of the Xinhua News Agency, Wang Kuang and Lian Weilin, came from Beijing and Guangzhou to attend the funeral. What I remember most of all was the sight of many ordinary people there. Some were our former employees; I knew some of them but not all. They were there because their lives had in some way been touched by Father.

The ten pallbearers were: Fei Yiming, publisher of *Ta Kung Pao*; Chusei Yamada, Japanese Consul-General; Sir Yuetkeung Kan, Executive Councillor; Professor Ma Lin, Vice-Chancellor of The Chinese University of Hong Kong; friends P.C. Woo and F.S. Li; Arthur Gomes, the most senior mason of the Irish Constitution in the Far East; N.J. Gillanders, long-time Bursar of the University of Hong Kong; Shum Waiyau, publisher of *Wah Kiu Yat Po*; and Xinhua News Agency chief Xu Jiatun, who obtained special permission from Beijing to be a pallbearer.

The funeral was attended by fifteen hundred people. The service was conducted according to Christian rites by Canon Frank Lin of St. Mary's Church in Causeway Bay, where Father had been a member for more than twenty years. Before the sermon, an old friend of our family, P.C. Woo, gave a short account of Father's life, a life that was not only successful, but interesting, unusual and most of all, filled with kindness.

In a tribute to Father on behalf of Sir Edward Youde, the governor, who had left for talks in Beijing early that morning, acting governor Sir Philip Hadden-Cave said that with Father's passing, Hong Kong had lost "one of the major public figures of its post-war history."[1] Professor Ma Lin, vice-chancellor of The Chinese University of Hong Kong, said that Father's death was a great loss to the university, since he was involved in its foundation well before the university came into being. In fact, Father had always considered The Chinese University as one of his "children." Friends and business associates described Father as "a man of vision," "a sound man with great influence" and "the backbone" of the Lee family. China's leaders referred to Father as an "old friend" and a "patriot."[2]

The man on the street lamented the loss of a good man who cared about the ordinary people of Hong Kong. And I lost a loving father.

BUILDING BRIDGES

The Life & Times of
Richard Charles Lee
Hong Kong: 1905-1983

1

The Young Man:
From Hong Kong To
Oxford

Hong Kong, at the turn of the century, was a city of palaces and more magnificent than the hillside Italian city of Genoa. Above the city of Victoria was a suburb hanging in the clouds of the Peak where the wealthy British lived. This was how American Eliza Ruhamah Scidmore described Hong Kong in her book *China: Long lived Empire*, published in 1900. A new hospital for Europeans had just opened on the Peak, and a newspaper, the *South China Morning Post*, had been launched. Only Europeans were permitted to live on the Peak, with the exception of Sir Robert Hotung's family.

At the foot of the hill, the first trams were put into service in 1904, all single-deckers, open to the elements. The carriages that used to fill the streets had vanished, and the coach houses of great mansions stood empty. Everyone went about by rickshaw or sedan chair, and carts were pulled by oxen or water buffalo. One could hear the sighs of coolies as they made their way along the streets, shoulders straining under their heavy loads on bamboo poles. The motor car had yet to reach Hong Kong.

The population of the Colony had reached over 325,000, the majority being Chinese. Water shortages were a perennial problem and new and bigger reservoirs were being planned. In 1901, the drought was so severe that water had to be shipped from the New Territories to Victoria.

The port of Hong Kong was expanding, and huge warehouses, known as godowns, lined the Kowloon waterfront. The number of ships entering the harbour increased 60 per cent from the previous ten years. Industries such as sugar refineries, flour mills, cotton mills and cement works had sprung up. Hong Kong Land was progressing with its land reclamation in Central (commercial section of Victoria), and the area was dotted with new four or five-storey buildings. Businesses were controlled by the hongs, such as Jardine Matheson and Butterfield & Swire in shipping, the Hong Kong and Shanghai Bank in banking, and John Swire's *Taikoo* in sugar refinery.

While the hongs were investing their opium fortunes in legitimate businesses, the government derived an annual revenue of about $2 million from the sale of the opium monopoly to the highest bidders, despite the strong opposition to the drug in Britain. Opium smoking was so popular among the Chinese that it was estimated that one in ten men was an opium smoker. Even though there was a gradual reduction of divans (establishments where Chinese men gathered to smoke opium) and no new licences were sold by the Hong Kong government after 1910, the sale of opium remained legal until 1945, and licences continued to be sold to the highest bidder by the Portuguese government in Macao.

The population of Hong Kong lived in two separate communities, the Chinese and the non-Chinese, each having very little to do with the other except at work. The Chinese men wore their hair in queues (pigtails) in Manchu style, and few dressed in Western clothes. Most of them wore mandarin jackets and pants or long gowns, with soft black shoes. They did not take part in foreign sport and none went swimming. The vast majority of them had no contact with Europeans at all. The old men spent time taking their caged birds for an airing outdoors, and the youngsters liked to kick a shuttlecock or fly a kite. In the evening, one could hear the clatter of mah jong, the favourite game of the Chinese.

As for the Chinese women, with the exception of petty hawkers, sampan women, scavengers and seamstresses, none went out onto the streets. The upper-class women had bound feet and never left their family compounds. The poorer classes wore cotton clothes like pyjamas, while the upper-class ladies wore beautifully embroidered pants, skirts and mandarin jackets.

Despite the description of Hong Kong as a city of palaces, it was, for the Chinese population, a very unhygenic place in which to live. Plague was endemic and malaria was widespread. Officers of the sanitary teams charged with rat-proofing houses and spraying mosquito breeding grounds were discovered, by an enquiry in 1907, to have made small fortunes by evading the law, in collusion with property owners and building contractors. Sanitary problems magnified racial prejudice, and demands were made for separate residential areas to be set aside for Westerners and Chinese. Following the creation of the Peak reservation, an ordinance in 1902 set aside an area in Kowloon for the Europeans, since the government believed the Chinese could not be trusted to keep the mosquito population down. However, exceptions were made by Foreign Secretary Joseph Chamberlain, who, on approval of a separate area for "people of clean habits," added that Chinese of good standing should be permitted residence there.

The Chinese population had come a long way since Hong Kong became a British colony in 1841. Many of its enterprising members had become wealthy. This new merchant class was recognized by the colonial government as leaders in their community due to their commercial success and their leadership in organizations such as the Tung Wah Hospital, a charitable organization which became the centre of Chinese power in the Colony. Despite the segregation in most schools, Queen's College encouraged the enrollment of boys of different nationalities. Chinese students from this school had the advantage of learning Western culture and the Western way of doing business.

This was the Hong Kong into which Father was born.

Childhood

On March 7, 1905, concubine Cheung Mun Hee (Second Lady) of Grandfather Lee Hysan, gave birth to a son, Ming Chak, my father. He was not only the eldest son, but also the first surviving child in the family, as an older sister born to Grandfather's wife (Grandmother) died soon after birth. When Second Lady became pregnant, there was great excitement because Grandfather had been married for seven years and still did not have a child. A European midwife was arranged for the delivery, since Grandfather didn't feel that he could take any more chances after the death of his first child. It was believed that European midwives were cleaner and more knowledgeable than their Chinese counterparts.

When Father was born, Grandfather was delighted that he finally had an heir. Father's birth was also regarded as a lucky omen for the family, for from then on, Grandfather's import-export business flourished. His company, Nam Hung Shipping Co., carried goods from China to Hong Kong, Singapore, Malaya and Rangoon. He became a well-known and respected merchant of the Nam Pak Hong Business Association in Hong Kong, an association of merchants who traded between China and Southeast Asia.

According to Chinese custom, when a concubine has a son and the wife does not, the son is taken from his birth mother to live with the wife, in order to bring her luck and fertility. This was the case with Father, who grew up in Grandmother's household. He did indeed bring her luck, for after the birth of a second son by Second Lady, Grandmother gave birth to two sons and two daughters.

Father had a very special relationship with Grandmother because he grew up in her household, and she came to treat him as her own. She respected his judgment and that became important for the entire family after Grandfather died.

Father was a healthy child, alert and sturdy, with a narrow face and a small stature like his mother, Second Lady. He had strong, square hands, and his skin was as dark and shiny as Grandfather's. He probably wore his hair in a queue when he was very young, as Grandfather did, since it wasn't until the Revolution of 1911 that Chinese men abandoned this custom.

As a small child, Father lived in Hong Kong and sometimes visited his grandparents, my great-grandparents, in China. At the time, Great-grandparents lived in our ancestral village, Garlieu, in the south of Guangdong province. Father once told me that Great-grandparents used to have only two meals a day, one early in the morning and the other between four or five in the afternoon. It seemed very strange to me, but that was the habit of the Chinese people who lived in the countryside. I'm sure it was also because food was scarce. As Grandfather became more prosperous, it was rumoured that bandits intended to kidnap his parents, so he built a house for them in Sunwui city, not far from Garlieu.

Being the eldest son, Father was not only important to Grandfather, he was doted on by Great-grandparents. As a show of affection, Great-grandfather used to feed Father all the time when they were together, and even stuffed chicken legs in his mouth when he was asleep! He also told Father about the dreadful trip in a sailing ship across the Pacific to the Golden Mountain (San Francisco) during the gold rush, and the life of Chinese people in America. Even though Grandfather was the second son of Great-grandparents, Father's position in the family was considered so important that, when Great-grandfather died, and his body travelled in a boat along the river that ran past Garlieu village, Father sat in the front of the boat and Grandfather sat at the back, with the coffin in the middle. This was how the body was transported to the burial place according to our village custom.

Because of repeated outbreaks of plague in Hong Kong, Grandfather moved his family to Macao when Father was five years old. Most of the family remained there until 1918, although Grandfather continued to work in Hong Kong. As a well-educated man, he was concerned about the education of his children, both sons and daughters, so he hired a well-known Chinese teacher, Chen Zibao, to teach them.

As time went on, Grandfather invested in many successful businesses, and became one of the wealthiest men in the Colony. He took a second and later on a third concubine (Third Lady and Fourth Lady). According to Chinese custom in those days, it was considered a sign of wealth to have many concubines and children. The number of children in the family increased, and Grandfather was good to them all. Realizing the importance of an English education for his children in the British Colony, Grandfather brought Father back to Hong Kong from Macao, and enrolled him in Queen's College, one of the best-known colonial schools at that time, regarded as the Harrow or Eton of the Far East.

Grandfather had learned English in San Francisco as a child, during the years he lived there with his father. After they returned to China, Great-grandfather had the foresight to enroll Grandfather in Queen's College in Hong Kong in order to continue his English education, where he was able to make friends who became important to him in later life. He wanted the same advantages for his children.

Studies in Oxford

Since he was well acquainted with the English educational system, Grandfather thought it best for his children to send them to school in England so that they could be totally immersed in the English tradition. At the same time, they would have the opportunity to make friends who could help them later on in life. In 1917, at the age of twelve, Father and his third brother were sent to study in England with a governess. They lived at the home of a Mr. Churchill, and were tutored there in preparation for university entrance. It was then that they acquired their English names: Father became Richard Charles and Third Uncle[1] became Harold. Several years later, two younger sisters were also sent to England for schooling. Once the children went to England, they were expected to stay until they finished their education. The boys were told before they left that if they married non-Chinese while they were away, they would be automatically disinherited.

Father was fond of Mr. Churchill, whom he referred to as "Old Man Churchill" to us, and with whom he continued to correspond until Mr. Churchill died. Even when Mr. Churchill began to lose his sight, he continued to write to Father, with some help, I am sure. I remember seeing his scribbles.

By the 1920s, it was fashionable for the more adventurous and wealthy Chinese parents to send their children abroad to school — to France, Germany, England and Japan. These students were usually of university age. Most of the Chinese students from Hong Kong went to England. The only mode of travel was by ship via the Suez Canal, and the long trip took weeks.

In a letter to his old friend and neighbour in Macao, Father wrote about the Chinese he met:

> Since my arrival in England, I have been well. Generally, the climate and life here are quite suitable to the Chinese ... In the town of Oxford, there were less than ten Chinese students including myself ... There are two Chinese in town, by the names of Zhou and Chen, from the village of Hoiping,[2] who are to be admired. They arrived here, by mistake, eleven years ago. They wanted to go to London, Ontario, Canada, to make a living. However, the tickets that were bought for them were incorrect, and neither knew that there were two Londons in the world. When they arrived in London, England, no relatives came to meet their boat, and they knew something was wrong. Not knowing whether to laugh or to cry, they realized they had arrived in a different part of the world, with no friends and with very little money. A few days later, they made their way to Oxford, and opened a laundry establishment. They worked hard and had become very well known for the best laundry service. Almost all the students in Oxford send their laundry to them. It shows that, for those who are abroad, with hard work, they will succeed. Being very busy, I am sorry I don't see them as often as I would like, and have forgotten their first names. These two can put many present-day overseas Chinese students to shame.

He went on to say that despite the importance the parents put on education, many of the Chinese students in England were not really interested in studying:

The majority of the present-day overseas Chinese students have no idea how difficult it is to make a living. They are generally lazy, and are constantly complaining how difficult the subjects are, so they often skip the examinations. But, fearing rebukes from their parents, they enroll into colleges that do not have examinations and anyone can be accepted. There are many such colleges in both towns of Oxford and Cambridge. These students will write home to say that they have entered Oxford or Cambridge Universities, and their parents would not know any better. Their parents will send them money which they will spend lavishly. In three years' time, they will buy a degree to return to China. There is usually a lot of fanfare when these students return home, but if they are ever asked, by someone who knows, which university they graduated from, Oxford or Cambridge, they would be in trouble ...

China is so weak among so many strong nations, if the younger generation has no ability, how can we save China? These students are not capable of thinking. There are so many in China who want to study, but their families cannot afford to send them abroad. Those who have the chance to go abroad and not study hard are to be pitied.

And he concluded on a personal note:

Oxfordshire has the climate that makes people tired. Many go to the seaside during the summer to avoid illness. I will be going away and will return to Oxford at the end of the summer.[3]

We can tell from this letter that Father's lifelong wish to help China and the Chinese people was already emerging.

In 1923, Father entered Pembroke College, Oxford, to study Civil Engineering, where he was known to the other undergraduates as Dickie Lee. Percy O'Brien, who entered Pembroke in 1924 to read Chemistry, remembers Father as a sprightly individual who was always happy and smiling. He walked quickly, was always in a hurry, and very punctual. He was well dressed and carried a watch chain across his waistcoat. Father studied excessively hard and spent hours reading in the Radcliffe Science Library. At times he showed O'Brien some of his studies on the mathematics of engineering which O'Brien found very obtuse and difficult to understand.[4]

By the time he entered Pembroke, Father was already used to life in England, but life in the colleges was a different experience. Undergraduate behaviour was still controlled by the statute *de Moribus Conformandis* of 1636, even though rules had been modified. Colleges exacted small gate fines from those who were not back in college by a certain hour in the evening. Although tobacco could be purchased (its sale having been banned in 1636), no undergraduate was allowed to smoke in academic dress. A rule prohibiting students from keeping motor cars had been rescinded, and so Father was able to own one. Students were not allowed to play billiards before one o'clock in the afternoon or after ten o'clock at night, and they were forbidden to loiter at stage doors, attend public race meetings or take part in shooting and other sports. Their opportunities for dancing, drinking and dining were carefully regulated. A male undergraduate was not allowed to enter the room of a female undergraduate, but a female student was allowed to enter the room of a male with a chaperone, with special leave from the head of her college.[5]

Pembroke had some well-established customs that no longer exist. Undergraduates were obliged to attend college chapel daily at eight o'clock in the morning under the threat of a fine of two shillings and sixpence. Less onerous was the penalty for talking "shop" in the hall. The perpetrator could be challenged to drink one or more pints of beer without pause from a tankard marked by pegs within, to bring the ego down a peg or two.[6]

Father was privileged to have lodgings in the Old Quadrangle, regarded as superior by the students. His rooms were on the ground floor, with a bedroom, a small pantry and a fairly large sitting/dining/study room with a fireplace. The communal rooms were in the back of the Quadrangle, and the undergraduates sometimes had to trudge through snow and ice in the winter to reach them. There was no college nurse or doctor in those days; the undergraduates were supposed to be tough. In the evening, the gates were closed at nine o'clock when the Old Town clock chimed. Latecomers were fined, so the students found ways of climbing into the residences without being caught.[7]

The residences were taken care of by "scouts," who were essential to college life. Each scout was in charge of a "staircase," meaning a set of rooms that branched off from a staircase. In some respects, a scout was like a servant, but in many ways, he was more like a "wife and parent" to his men. He cared for their general welfare, looked after them when they were ill, advised them, got them out of trouble and put them to bed when they were drunk. Father was very fortunate to have a fine scout named Fred. Fred would light Father's fire, clean his room, make his bed and do his laundry. It was also Fred's duty to make Father's breakfast and lunch and look after his parties.[8]

The Master of Pembroke during Father's time was Dr. Holmes Dudden, a man of great distinction and ability, a very good administrator and an author of some note. To be invited to dine at Pembroke was much sought after in the 1920s, because of its fine table and excellent wines.[9]

Friendships

During his university days, Father made some very good friends with whom he kept in touch all his life. Many became prominent in their own countries. One was Percy O'Brien, who later became a tutor and Fellow of Pembroke. Until he retired in 1974, he was Director of the Nuffield Department of Clinical Biochemistry in the Oxford Medical School.

Another was Qian Changzhao, who became an important official in China under the Nationalist leader Chiang Kaishek. Both Qian and Father subsequently devoted themselves to the betterment of the lives of the Chinese. While Father spent most of his life in Hong Kong, Qian remained in China. After the Nationalist government was ousted, Qian served the government of the People's Republic of China. Qian was persecuted during the Cultural Revolution. In the early 1960s, the two men were able to resume a friendship that had been interrupted during the

Chinese civil war (1945–1949) and the subsequent restrictions on its population imposed by the Chinese government.

Other schoolmates were Liu Jia, later Chiang Kaishek's representative at the United Nations in the 1950s, and Konosuke Koike, a graduate of Tokyo University, who later became chairman of Yamaichi Securities. Although Father lost contact with Koike because of the Pacific War, the two men were able to pick up where they left off in the late 1960s.

The one friend Father made who was not a student at Oxford was Ley On, whom we came to call Uncle. Ley On was adopted by a family without a son, in our ancestral village. He was badly treated, so he sold himself as an indentured labourer to North America when he was in his teens. When his contract was over, he stowed away on an ocean liner, not knowing where it was going. He arrived in France and found himself unable to communicate with anyone, so he boarded a boat to an English-speaking country, again as a stowaway, and arrived in London. This was around the same time Father and Third Uncle were in England. Ley On was an enterprising young man who started a small Chinese restaurant in London, catering mainly to overseas Chinese students.

Father and his young friends would go to Ley On's restaurant whenever they were in London. Father used to tell me that Ley On made his tofu with an ingredient that gave his patrons diarrhea! Despite that, the two young men became good friends. I am sure Father admired Ley On for his diligence and entrepreneurial spirit. Ley On went on to become a successful restaurateur in London and the owner of many racehorses. His restaurant was frequented by famous movie stars who befriended him. Probably because he had a classic Chinese face — with high cheekbones and slanted eyes — and was tall and dark-skinned, he was asked to act in small parts in Hollywood movies. I first met him when he stayed with us in Hong Kong in the early 1950s, by which time he had become an alcoholic. I remember Father telling him, "It's a custom in Hong Kong not to drink before sundown!"

All Oxford undergraduates boarded in the colleges, and they were required to have dinner with the Master and the fellows in the hall.

In fact, although undergraduates were free to choose whether they wanted to attend the lectures, they were *strictly advised* to attend the dinners. If an undergraduate's annual attendance at the dinners was not sufficient, he would lose the right to sit for examinations. At each table, ten to twelve undergraduates who had joined the college in the same year would sit together. In spite of the fact that the subjects they took were different, they usually became good friends, bonded by the habit of eating meals at the same table.

Konosuke Koike entered Pembroke College in 1923. Since he and Father both entered in the same year, they sat at the same table for dinners. They played sports together and became close friends. In winter, when the British students played rugby, Father and Koike would go to the gymnasium to box.[10] Boxing was a favourite sport of many Pembroke men. Father loved the sport even though he broke his nose doing it.

Father had high ideals and was a leader among men. He became President of the Chinese Students' Union of Europe in 1925. He already knew then that he would spend his life helping his country-men. He kept all the menus of the Union dinners on which he and his fellow students sketched their plans for a brave new China.

Grandfather's Enterprises

While Father was in England, Grandfather's businesses continued to prosper. He became one of the wealthiest men in Hong Kong and a well-respected citizen in the community. Real-estate development became his main business, and he purchased land and built row-houses, mainly for the Chinese middle class in Hong Kong. He also invested in many companies in Hong Kong, such as the China Sugar Refinery, Hong Kong Electric, the Hong Kong and Shanghai Bank, and the Dairy Farm Ice and Cold Storage Co., and he became a major shareholder and a member of the consulting team of China Light & Power Company, which supplied electricity to south China and Hong Kong. Unfortunately, he also invested in the Yue Sing firm, which held the opium monopoly from 1924 from the Portuguese govern-ment of Macao, and this caused his misfortune later.

Around the time of the First World War, while Father was in England, Grandfather purchased a large piece of land on the side of a hill on Kennedy Road with the intention of building a home for his family. Because of the war and labour problems, the house was not built until 1920. It was designed and constructed by Palmer and Turner, the same firm that designed the head office of the Hong Kong and Shanghai Bank on the Bund in Shanghai. The designs of the two buildings were rather similar. The family home, called *Dai Uk*, meaning the Big House, was one of the grandest homes in Hong Kong. Father did not see the Big House until he returned to Hong Kong in 1927.

The Big House commanded a magnificent view of Hong Kong Harbour. The beautiful gardens with their fountains, pagodas, artificial hills and caves, bamboo groves, chicken coops and vegetable plots were surrounded by high walls. At the main gate stood a guard house where a tall Sikh kept watch with a shotgun. Sikhs were traditionally hired as guards in Hong Kong because the Chinese regarded them as fierce-looking. Our guard's family lived in their own compound beside the garden of the fountain of the Goddess of Mercy.

The Big House consisted of three floors. The second and the third floors were living quarters for the family, with large balconies and a kitchen on each floor. For family meals, the men were served on the second floor, and the women and children on the third floor. The ground floor was reserved for entertaining. It consisted of an enormous front hall, the library, the bamboo room and other entertaining rooms and the main kitchen in the back. From the front hall, one walked out onto the terrace to a panoramic view of the Hong Kong harbour. The house was filled with *objets d'art* from all over the world.

Besides being grand, the Big House was also a home away from home for all the Lee relatives or visitors from our ancestral village. There were many guest rooms behind the entertainment rooms on the ground floor, and anyone who needed a place to stay or a good meal was welcomed. Grandfather was known for his generosity which extended to distant relatives. Throughout his life, he made sure that his siblings were financially secure, and that all his nieces and nephews were in good schools or were given good jobs. His sons carried on this tradition after his death.

The land where the Big House stood was so large that Grandfather decided to erect another building at the other end of the property higher up on the hill. It was a three-storey apartment built in the same style as the Big House, with a wide central staircase, and large balconies for each apartment. This was called *Lee Hong*, meaning Lee Building, and was rented to tenants during Grandfather's lifetime. I wonder whether at the time Grandfather could foresee that, as his family expanded, the Lee Building would be used by them as well. My family lived in both the Big House and the Lee Building until the beginning of the 1950s.

In 1920, experts from England went to Hong Kong to investigate land development around the harbour. In their opinion, the development in the west had reached its limits, and the Colony's future lay in the east around Kowloon Bay. Grandfather then looked into buying land in that area for housing development. Hong Kong island was difficult to build on because of the hilly terrain. In order to build row-housing, hills had to be levelled and the soil used for landfill to create more flat land. In January 1924, Grandfather made the most high-profile purchase of his life. He bought East Point Hill from John William Buchanan Jardine for the sum of $3,850,960.35. East Point Hill was the original homestead, offices and godowns of the Jardine taipans. The property also included the homes of the number one and number two taipans, with a riding stable in between. The original agreement with the government was to use the soil on East Point Hill for land reclamation in North Point, but the government reneged on the agreement, so development was stalled. In the meantime, in order to earn income from the property, Grandfather turned it into a garden and amusement park for the Chinese, called The Lee Gardens. The Chinese population needed recreation areas, since parks built by the government were restrictive. The Lee Gardens became the year-round pleasure ground for the Chinese and was financially very successful. The taipans' houses became restaurants.

Grandfather planned ahead for his family. In 1925, he established the Lee Hysan Estate Company, which owned East Point Hill and a number of other properties. He then continued to develop the areas in the vicinity of The Lee Gardens, clearing slums and building wide streets and well-constructed houses.

As an entrepreneur, Grandfather was always looking into new businesses. He loved Chinese opera, and felt that there was a need for a new type of staging that would make changing scenery in a Chinese opera easier. In 1926, he built the Lee Theatre on Percival Street and equipped it with a revolving stage which allowed the realistic touch of scenery changes as the actors walked along. Chinese opera in the Cantonese vernacular was the most popular type of entertainment, and the theatre became hugely successful. The theatre had a beautiful high dome, decorated with dragon designs and lights, and a movie screen was subsequently added. Many Chinese opera stars started their careers at the Lee Theatre.

2

From Marriage
In Hong Kong
To Work In China

Upon graduation from Oxford University in 1927, Father returned to Hong Kong at the age of twenty-two, after having been away for ten years. His plan was to go back to England to do his practical training. Grandfather was delighted to have his eldest son back, and this time, he wanted to see his son get married before leaving again. The word was out, and many girls were brought to Grandmother for her approval.

The Hong Kong Father returned to was a society that he did not remember. He had been treated as an equal in England, and now he was back in a colony where the British still believed that they were the master race of Asia. There was segregation in every facet of life in the Colony. In hospitals and the Hong Kong civil service, segregation persisted until the Second World War. An example was the Matilda Hospital on the Peak, which in 1940 refused to admit an American woman because she was married to a Chinese. It was not until 1942 that the civil service dropped the demand that all candidates for positions should be of pure European descent. As late as 1992, all senior posts in the civil service were held by British officers. It was the policy of the Hong Kong and Shanghai Bank not to have

Chinese on the board, and many British firms forbade employees to marry non-British women.

Father was a diligent student who benefited from the British liberal education that taught the equality of men. Therefore, when he returned to Hong Kong, he could not accept the stigma of being a second-class citizen. Having been used to riding in England, Father wanted to join the Hong Kong Jockey Club, but was refused entry because he was Chinese. Grandfather immediately said, "We don't need them. We will start a Chinese Jockey Club." On hearing that, Father was immediately allowed to ride there, because the Hong Kong Jockey Club depended on the income from bets placed by the Chinese population.

Hong Kong's colonial snobbery was described by Ely Kadoorie, a successful merchant in Shanghai as well as in Hong Kong, as small "shopkeeper's mentality." He was comparing international Shanghai to a very British Hong Kong. However, at least the racial chasm in business was narrowing, for the Chinese were not excluded from any commercial activities. Father realized that Hong Kong was a place to do business, but, as someone who believed in the brotherhood of men, it was not a society he would choose to live in.

Father Meets Mother

As a sociable young man, Father was always seen with a group of friends. One day that summer, not long after he returned from England, he was with his friends on a beach when two girls dropped by on their way home from a tennis game. As one of them caught his eye, he asked a girl he knew, Julia Wong, to introduce him. Julia said, "Don't bother with her, she's just my younger sister!" Father persisted, and thereby met Esther, my mother. They ended up spending the rest of the afternoon together.

Mother was only seventeen, a student at the Diocesan Girls' School, when she met Father. It was a whirlwind courtship and they fell in love. But Mother was not ready to get married; she wanted to finish school first. Father's parents were delighted that their son had found someone so suitable. When Father proposed, they went to see Mother's parents to ask for consent, but Mother stated she was just not ready. Grandfather then came up with a brilliant idea: he would send Mother to study at Oxford, where Father was to finish his practical training. Mother could study Portuguese to help in the Lee family business. Grandfather also promised to take her parents on a trip around the world to visit the young couple the following year. That did it, and Mother agreed to get married.

All this happened so quickly that my parents didn't really have time to get to know each other well. Theirs was a relationship that grew with the years together, establishing mutual trust, understanding and respect that lasted throughout their lives.

The Wongs, Mother's family, were modern and progressive. Grandfather Wong, one of the élite in the Chinese society in Hong Kong, was good friends with Hong Kong notables Sir Robert Hotung and Sir Shou Son Chau. The Wongs lived a luxurious life on Prince Edward Road. When Mother and her siblings were growing up, they not only had a large household staff and gardeners, but also four cars so that the growing children could drive themselves around.

Mother always prided herself that her father was the first person in Hong Kong to own a motor car when cars were first imported into the Colony in 1912, despite the fact that the Chinese community described cars as "coughing, spluttering, honking demons." Mother's parents, Joseph and Jeannie, had eleven children of whom eight were girls. Mother was the number-five daughter. Mother and her siblings lived a free and easy life, driving everywhere, swimming, playing tennis and dancing. Mother used to get caught by the police for speeding, probably on her way to buy sweets, of which chocolates were her favourite. Mother also took flying lessons but never got her licence.

Mother was fond and proud of her family. Her grandfather, Great-grandfather Wong, had gone to the West Indies as a young man to work as a labourer. He returned to China with a sizable fortune when he was in his early thirties and moved to Hong Kong to work as a court interpreter because of his knowledge of English. He chose a wife from a convent school run by German nuns, a girl whose father and brother were both ministers of the church. She spoke not only English and Chinese, but also German, and she wore only European clothes. That was unusual for a Chinese girl at that time. The two did not know each other well when they got married. Great-grandmother Wong later told her grandchildren she wondered on her wedding day why her wealthy husband had such rough hands.

As a court interpreter, Great-grandfather Wong was well paid. The Wongs lived on a large estate near Boundary Street in Kowloon. (The land was subsequently repossessed by the Hong Kong government, and they were relocated to present-day Prince Edward Road.)

Mother and her siblings were full of stories of the fun they had as children when they visited their grandparents. The person who was held in highest esteem by the grandchildren was the matriarch of the Wong clan, Great-grandmother Wong. She loved having them around and used to teach them to sing German songs. She was religious and encouraged the grandchildren to sing hymns to her by rewarding them each time. She spent her time doing charitable work, which continued after she was confined to a wheelchair. Her grandchildren were impressed by the fact that she chose a concubine for her husband when she was tired of bearing children. But the real reason for finding a concubine was to have someone willing to stay in the village in China to look after her in-laws, since Great-grandfather was the only son, and Great-grandmother certainly didn't want the job. There were a total of sixteen children, of which eleven were her own.

In his home village Great-grandfather Wong was regarded as the son who made good. When he returned to Dong Guan (Guangdong province) from abroad, he built a house with gun towers for the family in his ancestral village, Ho Pak Kiu. The Wongs were *Hakka*, (guests), who were later settlers on the land, and therefore got poorer land than the *Punti* (locals). They had to fight with their neighbours to protect the water supply needed for their fields.

The Wongs owned rice fields, leichee orchards and a peanut oil factory. Whenever Great-grandfather Wong or any of his sons returned from Hong Kong to check on the business, they were met at the train station by an armed brigade for protection.[1] Due to the deterioration of law and order in China, rural militarization became the norm, and armed guards were standard for the landlords, especially absentee landlords.

Traditionally, the *Punti* and the *Hakka* did not inter-marry. Father, being a *Punti*, used to tease Mother that *Hakka* women had big feet, considered ugly to the traditional Chinese. The fact was that *Hakka* women never bound their feet because they did a large share of the work in the fields, and besides, they were needed to help in the fighting and had to be able to run fast.

It was Great-grandfather Wong's wish that his descendants would one day return to the ancestral village, so at the entrance of the house he placed a large picture entitled "Hundred birds returning to the nest." However, only the eighth son, who was the first-born of the concubine, actually lived and remained in the village, looking after the rice fields and the business. The rest of the children chose to live in Hong Kong, and with the political unrest that existed over the years in China, it was at times impossible for them to return even for a visit. The only time a number of them went back was during the Second World War, after the surrender of Hong Kong. Food was scarce in Hong Kong, and there was always enough to eat in the village because of the rice fields that the family owned.

Great-grandfather Wong was well known and respected in Hong Kong. When he died, many people came to pay their respects by kow-towing all the way in from the entrance to the altar of their red house on Prince Edward Road. He had a grand funeral, with four white horses drawing the carriage that carried his coffin. The family was sent so many flowers that the colony's shops were said to have run out of flowers.[2]

Mother's father, Joseph, was the second son. He was a prosperous and well-respected member of Hong Kong society, a chartered accountant and the first president of the Chinese Association of Chartered Accountants. During the First World War, he was in the police reserve in Hong Kong, when many of the British went to fight in Europe, and the gap had to be filled. His daughters Josephine and Jennie remember him looking very handsome in his white uniform.

Whenever there was a shortage of personnel, Grandfather Wong would fill in as interpreter in the law courts. He became a Justice of the Peace in 1923, and subsequently was decorated by both King George VI and Dr. Sun Yatsen. After his first wife died childless, he married Jeannie Maxwell, my grandmother. Jeannie's nickname was Beauty, because she was a beautiful Eurasian girl. Great-grandmother Wong encouraged her sons to marry Eurasians because she wanted beautiful grandchildren, and she had many.

Grandmother Jeannie Maxwell Wong was one of four children and the only daughter of John Maxwell and a Chinese lady whose name we don't know, because she was always referred to as Grandmother by Mother and her siblings. John Maxwell went to Hong Kong from Scotland in the nineteenth century, stayed on to work and to get married. He chose a Chinese girl from an orphanage which was the precursor of the Po Leung Kuk, an institution established in 1878 by a group of wealthy and influential Chinese gentlemen to protect destitute women and children. That was really his only option, since there were very few European women of marriageable age of his own class, and no Chinese girl from a good family would consider him eligible. Great-grandfather Maxwell worked as a policeman in Hong Kong, and by all accounts, he was a fine father to his children.

In those days, Eurasians did not belong to either the Chinese or the European communities, so they had to try very hard to be one or the other. Grandmother Jeannie Maxwell Wong became more Chinese than the Chinese. She could understand and speak English, but she could read only Chinese. She was the authority on Chinese customs, and everyone in the Wong family always consulted her. I remember her in her later years looking very serene in a Chinese cheongsam, wearing her hair in a bun.

The Wedding

My parents' wedding took place on February 28, 1928, at St. John's Cathedral. Mother always said that she wished the fashion for wedding dresses that year had been long gowns instead of short, but, having to be fashionable, she had a short wedding dress of silver lace trimmed with pearls, and she carried white roses. Mother was a beautiful girl, tall for a Chinese and rather big-boned. She had to wear low-heeled shoes so that she would not look taller than Father. In fact, she kept growing after they were married and became quite a bit taller than Father. She was as fair-skinned as Father was dark, with brown hair covered by her wedding head-piece that came down to her eyebrows, according to the fashion of the day. She had a large wedding party, with her sisters and cousins in dresses of different pastel colours and decorated with rosettes. They were beautiful young women and girls, and all Great-grandmother Wong's grandchildren.

The Cathedral was filled to the brim with Chinese and European guests, and many people had to stand outside because they couldn't get in. The wedding was performed by the Very Rev. A. Swann, Dean of Hong Kong, who broke tradition by officiating at a Chinese wedding for the first time. Hong Kong society was so divided between the Chinese and the Europeans that it was only on occasions like these that the two groups were brought together.

The reception was held at The Lee Gardens where a huge matshed (a structure of bamboo and straw) was erected, because the taipans' houses were not large enough to accommodate the two thousand guests. Hong Kong Hotel, which was one of Father's favourite hotels, catered the affair. A dais was erected to support a six-tier wedding cake. Sir Robert Hotung toasted my parents and speeches were made by Sir Robert, Dr. Robert H. Kotewall and Father.

After the wedding, my parents went on their honeymoon by boat to Europe. They sailed through the Suez Canal and did what most tourists do in Egypt, riding camels and visiting the Sphinx. Their first stop in Europe was Switzerland, where Mother met Third Uncle for the first time. He was attending school there. Subsequently, they went to England, where Mother met Father's sisters Doris and Ansie (Second and Third Aunts), who were in a boarding school for girls.

Grandfather's Murder

During Father's visit to Hong Kong, Grandfather got embroiled in what became a court case over the Yue Sing firm's opium licence with the government of Macao. The Yue Sing firm had had the opium monopoly since 1924. A third of the company was owned by the Lee family, and Grandfather was the general manager. In March 1927, the Portuguese government announced in the *Boletim Oficial* that the monopoly system under which opium had been imported, prepared, sold and distributed would come to an end; therefore its contract with the Yue Sing firm would be terminated, to be replaced by a government monopoly under the superintendence of the Inspector of Consumption Taxes. It established an Opium Administration and Pedro Jose Lobo was appointed as Administrator. By 1927, a quarter of the original investment of $3 million had been returned to the subscribers of Yue Sing, but the winding-up proceedings in the courts in Macao would mean that the rest of the investment would be lost. This was something the subscribers to the firm had to accept.

Then Grandfather discovered that the Macao government had not taken back the licence, but had given it to another company, the Yau Sing Company, for a payment of $120,000. The company opened an account at a branch of the Mercantile Bank of India in Hong Kong, and the comprador of the bank confirmed that the opium monopoly had been obtained by the Yau Sing Company by tender from the government of Macao. The Company was opened for subscription. A friend of Grandfather's was approached to buy shares, and he came to Grandfather for advice.

Grandfather believed that since the contract with Yue Sing had been terminated by the Macao government, no other firm should legally be given a new contract by the same government. He sent a petition to the governor of Macao, requesting fair treatment for his firm and for an enquiry into the matter, as well as the return, in due course, of the original deposit by Yue Sing to the Portuguese government. The petition was also sent to the Legislative Councillors, sixteen lawyers and the Consul-General of Macao. In his petition, the name of Pedro Jose Lobo was implicated.

In the spring of 1928, during the preparation of my parents' wedding, Pedro Jose Lobo sued Grandfather for libel and asked the Hong Kong court for an injunction to prevent him from sending further petitions to the governor of Macao. During the period leading up to the trial, Grandfather received letters threatening his life, saying also that bombs would be thrown at my parents' wedding. These letters were ignored by Grandfather even though friends and relatives advised him to be careful and change his routine. The wedding went smoothly, my parents left for Europe, and the threats were forgotten. On April 17, Chief Justice Gollan of the Supreme Court in Hong Kong gave judgment in Grandfather's favour. And Grandfather believed that it was all over.

On April 30, at one o'clock in the afternoon, as Grandfather was entering the Chinese Yue Kee Club on Wellington Street for tiffin, which was his routine, he was shot in the corridor. He called out a couple of times, "*gau meng*," meaning save my life, and members at the Club heard the shots and his cries. When a *foki* (waiter), Law Lau, reached the corridor, he saw Grandfather injured, holding on to the wall, and looking very pale. Instead of stopping to help, he followed a man in white trousers and a short jacket who darted through the passage from the Club. By the time the members of the club reached Grandfather, he was already dead. He was forty-seven years old.

The family offered a reward of $10,000 for information leading to the arrest of the assassin, but despite the police having many leads and some arrests, the murderer was never caught. The entire family was in shock. Grandfather left behind a wife, three concubines, seven sons and six surviving daughters, with daughter number-eight on the way.

My parents and three of Father's siblings were in England when the news reached them. They immediately began their return journey, but travel by boat through the Suez Canal was so slow, they missed the Buddhist funeral service. On May 25, Grandfather was buried in a beautiful site overlooking the ocean in the Permanent Cemetery in Aberdeen.

Later, at Lady Clara Hotung's suggestion, a matshed was specially built in The Lee Gardens. Buddhist services were held for seven days to pacify Grandfather's ghost and to raise his soul from suffering in the next world.[3]

Father as Head of the Family

At the age of twenty-three, Father became the head of the family. Mother, at eighteen, was no longer a student, but his partner. Since Grandmother was illiterate, it was up to Father to make sure the huge family was taken care of. In order to raise money for death duties, he arranged for the sale of many of Grandfather's shares. Father suffered insulting experiences, which he never forgot, when some of Grandfather's "friends" refused to open the door when he called on them. One of the exceptions was Arthur Morse, chief accountant of the Hong Kong and Shanghai Bank, to whom he went to borrow money. It was very intimidating for Father, but the kindness and consideration shown to him by Morse made them fast friends for the rest of their lives.

Grandfather had mortgages on many of his properties, the largest of which was East Point Hill (now The Lee Gardens), which was held by Jardine. This meant that if we reneged on the payment, the property would be repossessed. Father borrowed money from the Hong Kong and Shanghai Bank to pay off the mortgage.

Many people approached Grandmother to buy our properties, but with Father's encouragement, she refused to part with any of it. From then on, and for many years, the entire family lived on a tight budget in order to pay off the mortgages on our extensive holdings from the rents collected.

When Grandfather's estate duties were settled, Father remained in Hong Kong, working for the Lee & Orange Architectural firm to complete his practical training. One of his projects was the lengthening of the No.1 Dock of the Whampoa Dockyard in Kowloon.[4] Today, in the same location, is a shopping centre in the shape of an ocean liner.

My parents lived in the Big House with Grandmother and the rest of the family. With all the mortgage and loan payments, there was very little money to go around, and Grandmother held the purse strings. While Father was completing his training, he had no income. Mother, at the age of eighteen, found herself trapped in an old-fashioned, traditional household which was totally different from her own, and because Father was not earning an independent income, she had no psychological or financial freedom. She began to lose weight and became depressed, so her mother decided to take her to Lushan for a complete change of scenery.

Lushan, in Jiangxi province in the county of Jiujiang, not far from Poyang Lake, is famous for the beauty of its scenery and the wonderful mountain air. It was well known as a spot for patients to recuperate from their illnesses. It used to be (and still is) a retreat for the wealthy, and spotted along the mountainside were many villas owned by West-erners and wealthy Chinese. Later on, both Chiang Kaishek and Mao Zedong had villas there. Mother called it the Switzerland of China.

At that time, the only way to reach the town at the top of Lushan was by walking or being carried in a sedan chair. Mother told me that she was so thin when they arrived that the chair-coolies fought to carry her up the mountain. However, by the time she came back down, she had gained so much weight, no chair-coolie wanted to carry her. Mother never said how long she stayed, but she slept and ate well until Father went to bring her home.

Work in Guangzhou

When Father finished his practical training with Lee & Orange in 1931 and became a qualified engineer, he wanted to pursue his pro-fessional career. The various businesses of the Lee family were looked after by employees, and Father felt that it was not necessary for him to remain in Hong Kong as long as he was close by.

The 1930s were the years when the Chinese Republic needed a great deal of help to build a new country. Like many young Chinese at the time, Father was filled with hope for the future, and he want-ed to do his part for China.

Being Cantonese, he went to Guangzhou, also known as Canton, to work in the government of Mayor Liu Jiwan. He occupied differ-ent posts over a number of years. He was Chief Secretary for the city, Chief Engineer, a member of the Department of Water Works, and also an auditor in the Ministry of Audit.

At the beginning, Mother remained living on the third floor of the Big House in Hong Kong while Father worked in Guangzhou. The children in the Lee family were Sixth Uncle, Seventh Uncle, Seventh Aunt, Eighth Aunt and cousin Hon Chiu, son of Second Uncle and the eldest grandson. Hon Chiu remembers that they were always hungry, not only because the family was cash poor, but also because Grandmother was very frugal. They used to visit Mother on Sundays at teatime and she would bake a cake as a treat for them. By that time, Father had an independent income, and Mother was no longer cash-strapped. Those were memorable times for the children. Mother was the modern and fashionable sister-in-law, and was looked up to by all of Father's siblings. The younger girls who did not have the opportunity to go to England before Grandfather died wanted to have English names, and Mother named them Dione, Joyce and Amy.

When Father was more settled in his post in the Guangzhou government, Mother moved there. They lived in Dongshan, which was a pleasant residential area in the suburb of Guangzhou. They had by then become good friends with Mayor Liu Jiwan and his family. They socialized a great deal with government officials, and Mother was expected to keep company with their wives. One day, a group of ladies went to a fortune-teller, who told the officials' wives that their futures were not rosy, but that Mother's was very good. Mother found that embarrassing, being the wife of the most junior person in the hierarchy of the Guangzhou government. The other ladies were very displeased. Of course, at that time, no one foresaw the change of government in China from Nationalist to Communist, when all the government officials became refugees.

My parents commuted to Hong Kong every weekend by train, back to the Big House to see Grandmother and the family. By that time, as the Lee family expanded, many members had moved into the Lee Building, up the hill from the Big House. My parents stayed in the Big House during their weekend visits.

Since Grandmother was the only person in the family with a motor car, in order for the children to go swimming at South Bay, where the family owned a cabin, all the children would go to the Big House after half-day school on Saturdays to have lunch, and wait to see who would take them swimming. It was usually Father or Third Uncle (who had returned from Oxford by then) or Second Aunt. It was a much anticipated outing for the youngsters who enjoyed their afternoon picnic of tea sandwiches at the cabin, and a swim. Cousin Hon Chiu was just learning to swim then, so he mainly played on the beach. After their swim, Father always treated all of them to ice cream sold by a vendor for Dairy Farm. [5]

During the years when my parents commuted between Hong Kong and Guangzhou, they had friends who also made the same return trip each week, so the group usually played bridge during the journey.

During this period, Father worked closely with Yuen Menghong, Director of Public Works in Guangzhou. Yuen's cousin Yuen Yaohong used to tease Father that, as a foreign graduate, he would know only theory, and not anything about the practical side of building. Yuen Yaohong himself first started work in construction as a carpenter. However, the two men became good friends, and he became Uncle Yuen to us.

In the mid 1930s, Yuen Yaohong moved to Hong Kong and started to work for the Lee family as the general manager of International Entertainment Enterprises Ltd., the company which leased the Lee Theatre. This company was formed because one of Grandfather's brothers was in the habit of taking money from the till in the theatre, and no employee dared to challenge him. Since he was an elder, Father and his brothers were not in a position to stop him, even though the theatre belonged to them. The employees could then tell Grandfather's brother that the Lee Theatre was leased by another company, which meant he could no longer help himself to the till. From then on, if he needed money, he had to go Lee Hysan Estate Co. or to Lee Tung, the rental office.

When my parents' lives became more settled in Guangzhou, they bought a piece of land in Conghua, where there were natural hot springs. They built a small house on a beautiful hillside. The rest of the land was planted as orchards with many different fruit trees. The house, designed by Father, was built in the typical Chinese style with red walls and a green tiled roof which housed a tank fed by hot spring water. The kitchen was open to the outside. Aside from my parents' bedroom, there were no separate rooms. It was an open concept where all the guests slept on tatamis on the floor.

My parents spent many happy hours there with their siblings, friends and relatives. They often went swimming in a small lake which had a waterfall at one end. One day Mother's sister Jenny swam a little too close to the fall and almost drowned. The water in Conghua is well known for its medicinal qualities, and Mother's sister Sarah often brought her son Jay, who was having skin problems, to bathe in the hot springs.[6]

The house in Conghua turned out to be such a wonderful country retreat that Mayor Liu Jiwan and many of the officials of Guangdong went there too. Later, the leaders of the Chinese Communist Party also built their villas there. The area became a favourite resort for the well-to-do.

After the Second World War, because of political unrest in China, my parents had no plans to use it any more, so they asked the caretaker, who had been looking after the house and grounds, to move into the house. I met the caretaker when he came to Hong Kong at the end of the 1940s to report the condition of the property to Father, and Father asked him in particular how the fruit trees were doing.

I didn't see this house myself until the late 1980s, when my husband, Neville, and I went to Conghua with Mother and her friend Daisy Li. The garden was completely overgrown with weeds, and it was difficult to distinguish the trees. The house was altered and in a terrible state of disrepair. Mother was so disappointed to see it painted white instead of the original red and green. A nondescript house had been built close to it, and a public dining hall was located in the area which used to be set aside for parking their cars. It saddened Mother to see the property in that condition.

Pioneers in Hainan

In 1934 Father left his employment with the Guangzhou government to do something very different in Hainan Island. Situated between the South China Sea and the Gulf of Tonkin, it is about the same size as the island of Taiwan. Except for the Paracel Islands, which had troops stationed by China, Taiwan and Vietnam, Hainan Island is the most southern territory of China.

Why did an Oxford graduate take his young wife to a backward place like Hainan Island? I never thought to ask Father, but I guess he had a sense of curiosity and of adventure. After all, he was an inquisitive person all his life. But I think the main reason was his desire to help China, by working in a remote and backward place. He believed that one person could make a difference even in a country with a population of hundreds of millions.

Hainan Island was just beginning to attract the attention of the Chinese government in the 1930s. Minister T.V. Soong visited the island and expressed the opinion that it should be developed. Industrialists and educators began to realize the economic importance of the area known as the "larder of China," where rice crops can be harvested up to three times a year. It was also known as "the paradise of China" because flowers bloom year round and delicious fruits and magnificent trees grow everywhere. Ancient Indian writers referred to Hainan as "The Island of Palms" because at least six types of palm grow luxuriantly on the island, producing considerable income. On this tropical island, the sun is so intense during the day that people cannot go out without hats or umbrellas. The humidity is usually high. In summer, the temperature goes up to as high as 98°F, and in winter, drops to 45°F. However, along the mountain range, Limu Ling, that runs through the middle of the island, the temperature is always cool.

Hainan became known to the Chinese at the time of the first emperor, Qin Shihuangdi (245–210 B.C.). The island, inhabited by aborigines known as the Li tribe, attracted about 23,000 Chinese colonists from the mainland during the Early Han Dynasty (206 B.C.–A.D. 24.) By the end of the Later Han Dynasty (A.D. 25–219), the entire island was subjugated and the Li tribes were pushed into the centre of the island. The name Hainan, meaning "south of the sea," came from the Yuan Dynasty.

In 1921, the island officially became part of Guangdong province. By the late 1920s, there were already more than two million Chinese living on the island. Chinese settlements were founded along the northern part of the island, where close contact could be maintained with the mainland. Haikou, the major city, was located at the northern tip of the island and was not only the home of the governor but also the headquarters of the Garrison Commander.[7]

Hainan Island was known as Qiongya province to the Chinese government. In the 1920s, the Chinese government started to build highways in order to open up the island for development. Besides shops, restaurants, hotels and banks that catered to the population, there were some Chinese investments, mainly in rubber and sugar cane plantations. Some of these companies were later abandoned because of problems with bandits in the area.[8] In the 1930s, it was divided into thirteen counties, two of which were exclusively inhabited by Chinese. The Li tribe and the Chinese lived in separate communities even if they were geographically in the same areas.[9]

The Li aborigines physically and culturally resemble the Tai people who lived in Thailand, Burma, Yunnan province in China and Indo-China. They are stout, of medium stature, with yellowish-brown skin, straight black hair and dark brown eyes. Their facial features are quite different from those of the Chinese. (For centuries, Chinese scholars referred to them as the tattooed race of the south who knew no civilization.) The women are tattooed (in a practice known as *tantan*), apparently to make it easier to identify their own descendants. They have their own native costumes, but in the summer, the adult males usually wear only loin cloths and turbans. In the 1930s, they lived on hunting and farming.

Since Father wanted to help open up a primitive part of China for agriculture and trade, he and Mother moved to Hainan to work as pioneers in ranching, with the idea of selling cattle to Europe. The weather and the topography in parts of Hainan are known to be good for cattle farming.[10] He bought land "as far as the eye can see," according to the description in his land deed, and imported the best cattle from Europe for breeding.

Being adventurous, Father crossed the island through the Limu Ling mountains to the area known as the Li Country, where the aborigines lived. He was warned by the local Chinese not to go into the interior because of the danger of malaria and other diseases; nine out of ten people who went in, did not come out alive. Father had faith in modern science, and believed that as long as he had quinine and other medicines with him, he would be all right. And he was.

While in Hainan, Father also became a plantation owner, growing flax and sugar cane. In 1936, Father, together with other investors, bought Bao Cheng Company. Bao Cheng, which had been established in 1928 by two partners, owned 5,000 acres where flax was grown as a cash crop. The cost to produce a ton of processed flax was seven pounds sterling, but it could fetch thirty pounds in the London market. It was a profitable business, but again, due to bandits in the area, the company closed between 1930–1931.[11]

After Father's group bought the company, he renamed it Lee Hing Plantation Company, and later changed the name to Lee Hing Agricultural Company Ltd. The company was situated on the north coast of Hainan near Ling Gao county (west of Haikou). The size of the farm was increased to 15,000 acres, growing flax and sugar cane. By January 1937, more land was purchased, and the size was increased to 20,000 acres. The company was well established with its own flax-processing machines and storage buildings, forty-five horse-power generators, gasoline storage, a garage for cars, an office building and residences for workers.[12]

My parents brought Second Uncle with them, as well as a young man named Leung Kwong Wing, who continued to be in the employ of the Lee family, eventually becoming one of our gardeners in the Big House. Men from the Li tribe were hired to clear the land and look after the cattle.

In the mountain streams in Limu Ling were gold nuggets, which the Li collected for use as jewellery, or for barter with outsiders. Father told me that he bartered with them using glass beads, mirrors and soap. They were fascinated by seeing themselves in the mirrors. They loved making soap suds in the river. Glass beads were a lot more colourful than gold nuggets.

Father had firearms for hunting, and perhaps also for protection against bandits, but issued strict instructions that guns were not to be given to or even handled by the Li aborigines. One day, he was beside himself when he found out that Second Uncle had used some of the guns for bartering with the aborigines.

Father used to say that because Hainan Island was so far out of the way one could always come across something unusual on the island and in its waters. One day, while my parents were at the coast, a fishing boat came back to shore dragging a garouper ten feet long. There was great astonishment because no one had ever seen a garouper that large before. The entire village, my parents and their entourage included, celebrated with a meal from that one fish. We were very impressed by this story.

Father often went hunting for wild boars. It was a dangerous sport because the boars, if wounded, would charge at the hunter. Sometimes Mother would go along, riding a small horse. She was not a good rider, and was frightened whenever the horse jumped at the sound of gunfire. However, riding was necessary because it was the only way to travel in the interior.

My parents lived the lives of pioneers, hunting and growing their own food. Since there was no electricity, Father built his own generators with wind power.[13] My parents made friends there, mostly with other pioneers and missionaries, and with some of the local village headmen. They would sometimes go into town and stay in small hotels and meet their friends, and at times they took visitors to various parts of the island. They both loved living there. Tanned by the strong tropical sun, Father became almost as dark as the Li people. He often talked about Hainan Island with nostalgia, because it was a part of his life that he treasured but something that could never be repeated. The best souvenirs he had from Hainan were mango forks and knives which he had designed and crafted there, and which I still use and treasure.

But important events were happening elsewhere. On July 7, 1937, Japanese and Chinese troops collided at the Marco Polo bridge in the Lugouqiao region near Beijing. It was the beginning of the undeclared Sino-Japanese war. Father felt it was time for him to go back to mainland China to help. Mother told me, "Even if China had not been at war, when the war broke out in Europe in 1939, it would not have been possible to ship cattle or agricultural products there anyway."

Return to Hong Kong

At the end of 1937, my parents moved back to Hong Kong and Father again commuted to China, this time to help the Nationalist government. Mother began to feel unwell, and a visit to the doctor confirmed that she was pregnant. In February 1938, ten years after their wedding, my eldest brother, Richard, was born.

Father thought the return to Hong Kong was just an interruption from his life in Hainan. He had left the plantations in the care of others, not realizing that future events would prevent him from going back, and that eventually all the land would be repossessed by the Chinese government. Although Mother told me that the land deed was kept in her safe deposit box, we couldn't find it after she passed away.

During the 1930s, the Central Chinese government under Chiang Kaishek enjoyed the support of many well-educated, highly qualified persons with high ideals about building a new and progressive China.[14] With the Japanese invasion of Manchuria in 1931, and the subsequent Marco Polo bridge incident in 1937, China's problems became urgent. In Hong Kong, a group of brilliant engineers gathered to discuss the rebuilding of China after the war and in 1938, the Chinese Institute of Engineers, Hong Kong Chapter, was established. The membership was restricted to qualified engineers who had more than seven years of practical experience. The first president was Huang Boqiao[15] who was Director of the Jinghu Railroad Bureau, and Father was the vice-president. As a young man, Ching Tong (C.T.) Wu was hired as secretary for the Institute, and that was how he and Father first met.[16] He became a lifelong friend and confidant, and an important source for this book.

In 1938, Japan invaded south China, and in October, Guangzhou was occupied by the Japanese. Father commuted between mainland China and Hong Kong frequently during the years before the fall of Hong Kong. He was involved not only as an engineer, but also in many other aspects in the war effort against the Japanese. He was an advisor and the purchasing manager for the China Tea Company, which was one of the most important branches under the Finance Ministry of the Chinese Central government. A large proportion of the country's foreign exchange income came from the sale of tea.[17] In later years, Mother explained to me the importance of selling Chinese tea for foreign exchange in order to buy equipment for the defence of China against the Japanese invasion. The head office of the China Tea Company was in Chongqing, and Father frequently commuted there from Hong Kong.

Father was also asked by the Chinese government to look after the distribution of sea salt.[18] In certain parts of the interior of China, the local population lacked iodine in their diet and goitre was prevalent. It was, therefore, important to make sea salt available to them. I remember the adults talking about this problem during the war, and in the interior of China we saw people suffering from goitre.

In October 1939, Mother gave birth to my older sister, Deanna.

Father's enthusiasm and reputation got him elected in 1940 as president of the Institute of Chinese Engineers, Hong Kong Chapter. His connections in Hong Kong made it possible for him to arrange visits for the engineers to various companies and factories, because he was trusted not to allow any stealing of trade secrets. An example was the Tian Chu Weijing factory (The Heavenly Kitchen Monosodium Glutamate Factory), owned by Wu Yunchu. At that time, monosodium glutamate was mostly manufactured in Japan. Under normal circumstances, Wu would never allow visitors to his factory, but Father was able to organize a tour for the engineers.[19] Dinners for the Institute were always held at the Big House. C.T. Wu said he was at times mistaken for one of the members because he was dressed in a suit and following Father around.

As the secretary of the Chinese Institute of Engineers, C.T. Wu made thirty dollars a month. Father took a liking to him and promised to find him a higher paying job. At the beginning of 1941, Father called up his friend Zhu Baiying, who was head of the research department of the China Tea Company, to recommend that he hire C.T. Wu. Even as a clerk, Wu's salary tripled. Wu's mother declared that he could get married since he was making so much money.[20]

3

Storm Clouds Gather: Hong Kong Falls To The Japanese

The Japanese invasion of China began in 1937, and between 1937 and 1941 the population of Hong Kong increased from 700,000 to 1.5 million as refugees flooded in. Horrible tales of massacre, rape and starvation circulated in the colony, but Britain was powerless against Japanese military might. Since it could not count on the help of the Americans, it tried to placate the Japanese government in the hope of avoiding war. The more virulent anti-Japanese literature in Hong Kong was censored by the colonial government.[1] The British government misjudged the importance of Hong Kong to Japan as a centre for the movement of troops and war materials, and British military intelligence was unaware of troop preparations across the Chinese border and of Japanese spies who infiltrated Hong Kong.

Under the command of Major-General Takeo Ito, Japanese Intelligence officers worked in Hong Kong as bartenders, barbers, masseurs and waiters in establishments frequented by the British military, offering cold beers, exotic food, accommodating women, generous credit facilities, and listening to their conversations. In fact, the best men's hairdresser in Hong Kong, who over a seven-year period cut the hair

36

of two successive governors, generals, the Commissioner of Police, the officer in charge of Special Branch and the chairman of the Hong Kong and Shanghai Bank, presented himself to his employer after the capitulation of Hong Kong on Christmas Day 1941, in the uniform of a Commander of the Imperial Japanese Navy.[2]

After the fall of Guangzhou in October 1938, the Japanese amassed troops north of the Hong Kong border. The 38th Army was training daily at Baiyunshan in Guangzhou, which had the same topography as the area at Gin Drinker's Line, in the southern part of the New Territories. Nightly, they prepared for a border attack on Hong Kong from Shenzhen.[3]

Defence of Hong Kong

In 1939, while the Second World War was raging in Europe, the War Office in London was well aware of the military deficiencies in Hong Kong, but the Colony was regarded as expendable and in fact, militarily indefensible. When Lord Hastings Ismay, Prime Minister Winston Churchill's Chief of Staff, proposed at the War Office conference to demilitarize Hong Kong, he was accused of being a defeatist. Sir Geoffrey Northcote, Governor of Hong Kong, believed that Lord Ismay was a realist and wrote to Whitehall in October 1940 to urge the withdrawal of the British garrison "in order to avoid the slaughter of civilians and the destruction of property that would follow a Japanese attack."[4] No one listened. Besides, Northcote was about to retire due to ill health, and would be replaced by Sir Mark Young.

Both Whitehall and many Hong Kong residents wanted to believe Major-General Edward Grasett, the Toronto-born commander of the British troops in Hong Kong, who did not believe that the Japanese would declare war on the British or the Americans. However, he still felt that the garrison in Hong Kong should be reinforced, but his request was denied by the War Office. In 1941, Air Chief Marshall Sir Robert Brooke-Popham, Commander-in-Chief of the Far East, believing that Hong Kong could endure a siege of six months or more, requested an increase in the garrison. He too was denied because Churchill believed that there was not the slightest chance of holding Hong Kong.

In the meantime, Major-General Grasett continued to campaign for reinforcements even after he knew of Churchill's decision. When he retired from the Hong Kong command in July 1941, he stopped off in Ottawa en route to England, where he met with Canada's Chief of General Staff, H.D.G. (Harry) Crerar, his old schoolmate. They discussed how long Hong Kong could withstand an extended siege if it had an addition of one or two battalions. He did not suggest to Crerar that Canada should supply the manpower, but he did make that proposal to the British Chiefs of Staff.[5]

So the defence of Hong Kong was dealt with half-heartedly. A single RAF squadron was diverted to Malaya, leaving five obsolete fighters as Hong Kong's air defence. Sea defence depended on the H.M.S. *Prince of Wales* and the H.M.S. *Repulse*, which were supposed to come from the South Seas to relieve Hong Kong when necessary. It was also assumed that the U.S. Pacific Fleet in Pearl Harbor would be able to contain the Japanese in the event of a major conflict.[6] On land, the defence of the Colony depended entirely on a garrison of 11,000 regular British and Indian troops, and a citizen force of 1,387 Hong Kong Volunteers. Batteries were put on the island of Hong Kong at the entrances to the harbour. Gin Drinker's Line was to be the first line of defence. Tunnels and bomb shelters were built all over the city in preparation for an attack.

The population of Hong Kong did have drills in case of a bombing attack, and students in middle schools were given uniforms and trained as air raid wardens.[7] As the news became more alarming, black-out practices became more frequent. Young civilian men were asked to join the Hong Kong Volunteer Defence Corps. Among them was Bill Poy, who was married to Mother's cousin Ethel Lam, and who later became my father-in-law. However, the reality of war was not taken too seriously, because, as Poy told me, it was considered "fun for young men to be with their friends in a motorcycle squadron." Some actually joined because they would be given motorcycles.[8] Poy owned his own motorcycle at the time and he used to take my future husband, Neville, on it to go to school at Ling Ying, at the top of The Lee Gardens. Poy, an Australian-born Chinese, was working for the Canadian Trade Commissioner in Hong Kong.

No one wanted to believe that Hong Kong would be attacked, even with the appearance of many refugees in the Colony. Overnight, Hong Kong became the cultural capital of the Chinese world because of the arrival of refugee artists, scholars and writers. The economy boomed when the population tripled, and a thriving smuggling trade with inland China, across Japanese-controlled territories, was making some people very rich. Manufacturing in the colony flourished.

In May 1941, in the midst of all this, I was born.

In July 1941, all Japanese assets in Hong Kong were frozen, following similar action in Britain and the United States. However, Britain still did not believe Japan would invade Hong Kong, and Japanese nationals in the Colony were not kept under close surveillance. When Colonel Suzuki, a Japanese intelligence officer, was exposed by a British agent, the Foreign Office did not expel him from Hong Kong because Britain and Japan were not at war. When he departed of his own accord at the end of November, barely two weeks before Japan attacked Hong Kong, he had with him the complete details of the British defence plan.

On September 19, 1941, the Dominions Office in London dispatched a secret telegram to William Lyon Mackenzie King's government, asking Canada to provide one or two battalions for the defence of Hong Kong.[9] On November 19, the population of Hong Kong welcomed the arrival of the two Canadian battalions. However, no one knew that the troops had no battle training, and no knowledge of the Colony or of local transportation. The information about these matters had been sent to Australia by mistake.

Life in our family went on as usual. No one was considering leaving the colony since conditions in China were much more serious. It was at this time that Father met Liao Chengzhi,[10] Secretary of the South China Bureau of the Chinese Communist Party Central Committee, and they became good friends. Liao was engaged in activities in Guangdong and Hong Kong until the fall of Guangzhou in 1938, when he escaped to Hong Kong. There he organized forces to send to

Huipo, which became the progenitor of the East River Detachment, an anti-Japanese guerrilla force in South China and Hong Kong. Father and Liao tried to negotiate with the British government to provide ammunition for the Hong Kong-Kowloon Brigade guerrillas to help to defend the island against the Japanese, but the talks failed because the British did not want ammunitions to fall into the hands of the pro-Communist guerrillas.[11]

The two men, along with an English friend, planned the sabotage of the electric plant in expectation of a Japanese invasion, but the Japanese attack took everyone by surprise.[12]

The one thing the Lee family did in preparation for a Japanese attack was to stockpile rice in the Big House. Some people in the Wan Chai district, just below us, knew of our rice reserve and this resulted in looting during and after the Japanese invasion.

On the evening of December 6, 1941, Governor Sir Mark Young attended a charity ball at the Peninsular Hotel. The following day, Sunday, at midday, the mobilization call went out and a state of emergency was announced over the radio. Many who heard it thought it was just another preparedness test. Bill Poy reported for duty, but he told me that many volunteers did not when they realized that there was real danger of war. Poy and Willy Eu, the son of Eu Tongsan, a very wealthy gentleman in Hong Kong, reported to Kowloon Railway station because they were attached to the Field Engineers. They had to mobilize to blow up roads and bridges in the New Territories in predetermined areas in case of an invasion. That day, Mother's youngest sister, Jenny, was preparing for her wedding scheduled for the following day. She and her husband were to sign the register in the City Hall in Hong Kong, and the wedding and reception were to take place in Kowloon.

The Battle of Hong Kong

At eight-thirty on Monday morning, December 8, my future husband, Neville, who was in Grade One at the time, was told not to go to school. He went to the rooftop with one of his family's servants to take down the dry laundry, and they saw planes in the sky. Just as someone said, "It's only another practice," bombs started falling on the urban area of Kowloon and on Kai Tak airport.

My Aunt Jenny and her husband had just gone to the City Hall to register. That was the end of the wedding since they could not get back to Kowloon for the ceremony. Until her husband's death, Aunt Jenny wondered whether their marriage was legal since there were no witnesses, and the ceremony never took place.

Grandparents Wong were living in Shouson Hill Road in Aberdeen at that time, next door to their good friend, Sir Shou Son Chau. The British military commandeered their house because it was in a strategic position and they were told to leave within four hours. With no time to pack anything, they came to stay with us.

The bombs on Kai Tak destroyed the five old fighter planes. Within a few hours, the people of Hong Kong heard about the destruction by the Japanese of the U.S. Fleet in Pearl Harbor, of the first bombs on Manila and Singapore, and of the sinking of the H.M.S. *Prince of Wales* and H.M.S. *Repulse*.[13]

The Big House was hit by shrapnel, and a bomb created a huge hole on one side of the Lee Building. We were very easy targets because we were so high up on the hill. Members of the Lee family gathered their essentials and moved to the backstage area of the Lee Theatre. We were grateful to Grandfather for building the theatre as strong as a fortress so that his descendants could use it in times of war. Along with our Wong Grandparents, we moved into the rooms behind the backstage area which also had a kitchen. We were crowded, but safe. We were not able to bring enough rice, so we had to make do with congee, a type of gruel. The older children were given crispy rice to ease their hunger between meals. As a seven-month-old baby, I immediately started getting sick and could not drink the powdered milk my mother brought along. Mother blamed it on the lack of clean water, because we used well water at the Lee Theatre. From then on until the end of the war, my health was poor.

During the period of fighting, whenever there was an air-raid signal, everyone would go to the bomb shelters. The one near the Lee

Theatre was at Leighton Road. During one of the bombing raids, Grandfather Wong did not enter the shelter fast enough and was hit on his shoulders by shrapnel.

Once the Japanese took control of Kowloon, artillery was stationed along the waterfront facing Hong Kong. Mother's younger sister Josephine's home in Tsim Sha Tsui was commandeered by the Japanese for that purpose.

At the Queen Mary Hospital, Joseph Tam was a nurse in training on his early morning shift that started at 6 o'clock. The moment the bombs started to drop, all in-patients were discharged to make room for war casualties. Those who still needed care were transferred to St. Stephen's Girls' College, which was converted into a relief hospital with camp beds set up for the patients. Female nurses were sent home, with the exception of those who wished to stay, and the male nurses took on most of the responsibility. By afternoon, many injured soldiers were brought in. Tam, as a nurse-in-training, had to look after twenty-four patients, most of whom were Canadians. Some of the doctors left for China and some were conscripted to stay to help in Hong Kong. Two of the Chinese doctors Tam worked with were Sik Nin Chau and Han Suyin.[14] Many of the Irish doctors stayed, because Ireland was a neutral country.[15]

The doctors' offices and the nursing school at the Queen Mary Hospital were converted into dormitories and some government officials moved in. Among them were Governor Sir Mark Young. Father T.F. Ryan, leader of the Irish Jesuit priests in Hong Kong, and some professors of Hong Kong University also stayed in the hospital.[16]

On December 10, 1941, at three o'clock in the morning, there was a loud banging on the door at villager Chung Poon's house in Wong Chuk Shan in the New Territories. Thinking that it might be bandits, he approached the door with a knife in his hand. He opened the door to find several guns pointing at him. For Chung and the rest of the population in Sai Kung, in the New Territories, the occupation had begun. Two days earlier, the Japanese army had overrun Tai Po and Shatin, and the day before had taken Shingmun Redoubt, which was part of Gin Drinker's Line. British forces were withdrawing from the New Territories to the island of Hong Kong, and a contingent of

Sepoy soldiers were covering the retreat at Devil's Peak. The Japanese soldiers had come over from Shap Sze Heung, intending to find their way to Kowloon, and had probably strayed into the village of Wong Chuk Shan by mistake. The soldiers were knocking at every door to force villagers to act as their porters. On December 11, the Japanese cavalry passed the Sai Kung Market. There was no disturbance or fighting, since the police had been withdrawn before the Japanese arrived. The villagers just stayed indoors.[17]

The British defensive positions on the New Territories and Kowloon had been prepared with a view to a delaying action that would allow consolidation on the island of Hong Kong. However, within forty-eight hours, the Japanese had broken this defence line, capturing the Jubilee Redoubt at Shing Mun Dam. (Jubilee Redoubt on Gin Drinker's Line overlooked the Sing Mun Dam of the Jubilee Reservoir, just north of the range of hills separating Kowloon from the New Territories.) The Volunteers retreated to the island of Hong Kong and reported to Headquarters. The Japanese fired mortars at the British defences, but there was no bombing. By December 12, enemy guns were lined up along the Kowloon wharves. At nine o'clock the next morning, a Japanese staff officer crossed to Victoria Pier in a launch bearing a flag of truce, and presented to Governor Mark Young a demand for the surrender of the Colony, under threat of heavy artillery and bombardment from the air. The Governor rejected the offer and the blitz began.

During the night of December 18 to 19, the Japanese landed at three different points on the island — North Point, Braemar Point and Shau Kei Wan — cutting the island into eastern and western halves. The Japanese who landed in North Point took over the electrical generating station which was guarded by civilian volunteers, a group of older men, all of whom were killed.[18] The Japanese troops crossed the island and there was a great deal of fighting towards Repulse Bay and Stanley. Bill Poy saw a Canadian general killed in a bunker in Wong Nai Chung Gap while he was delivering messages between Headquarters and the troops. On December 21, the governor was given further instructions from Churchill that "there must be no thought of surrender."[19]

Father was in Chongqing, China, when the Japanese invaded Hong Kong. He immediately flew back on one of the China Tea Company planes and had actually reached Hong Kong air space but the plane could not land. It was diverted to Huizhou. It was fortunate for Father, for he used to tell us that if he had been there and had been captured by the Japanese troops, he would have been executed because of his involvement in the resistance movement.

By Christmas Eve, the British and Canadian troops had retreated to the Peak because they believed the Japanese had taken over the Gap. Bill Poy was sent to take a look, but didn't see anyone, so the troops moved back into the Gap. By then, news had come to the troops that negotiations were in progress with the Japanese who had occupied half of the island. They had not yet moved into the city of Victoria.

Under Japanese Occupation

On Christmas Day 1941, at 6:30 in the evening, Governor Sir Mark Young surrendered to the Japanese. He was removed to the Peninsular Hotel, and subsequently to Taiwan and then to Mukden (both under Japanese rule at the time). The survivors of the garrison and the non-Chinese members of the Hong Kong Volunteer Defence Corps. were sent to POW camps — North Point, Shum Shui Po, Argyle Street and Ma Tao Chung. Many of the POWs were shipped to labour camps in Japan and other Japanese-occupied territories. The Chinese Hong Kong Volunteers were given permission to take off their uniforms and return home. The internment of civilians classified as enemies at Stanley camp was a slower process, and they remained there until the end of the war. There were many stories of heroism, treachery, great suffering and survival during these times.

When Bill Poy heard of the surrender, and before orders were given, he asked the senior officer what they, the Volunteers, were supposed to do, and he was told to wait for instructions from the Japanese. Poy said, "I'm not going to wait, I must join my wife and children." He then turned to Willy Eu and said, "Let's go!" They went to the Portuguese Volunteers Unit, where they left their revolvers and their motorcycles. They changed out of their uniforms into Chinese clothes which they always carried with them, just in case, and walked to Eu Yan Sang, a Chinese medicine shop owned by Willy's father, Eu Tongsan. From there, they phoned Willy's mother at Euston on Bonham Road, one of the Eu castle-style homes in Hong Kong. She told them everything was all right, and that the Japanese had allowed them to stay. That night, Poy and Eu could hear the Japanese troops moving in and cordoning off the city.

The next day, Poy and Eu decided to go up to Euston, but when they looked out of the medicine shop they saw a Japanese sentry posted almost outside the door. In order to look as casual as possible, they went outside, chewing on Chinese dried plums. The next thing Poy knew, he'd been hit on the head. He didn't know that he had to bow to all Japanese soldiers. They made their way to Euston bowing all the way.

The rest of the Poy family was at home in Happy Valley. Neville was very sad that, because of the lack of food, they had to let Snow White, their Borzoi (Russian wolfhound), go. It was probably caught and eaten the moment it was let out of their sight.

For a period, there was total chaos, because the Japanese soldiers, some of whom were Taiwanese, were given a free hand to rob, rape and murder. The soldiers went from house to house looking for "flower maidens," and young women hid wherever they could. They put mud and ashes on their faces and wore tattered clothes to avoid being raped. As in all wars, there was tremendous suffering. Some were luckier than others. The entire population was gripped with fear.

The following day, the cook at Euston returned home late and was scolded by Willy Eu's mother. He said the Japanese had stopped him to do some work for them and given him a card with which he could go anywhere. The next day, Bill Poy borrowed the card which gave the name and the age of the cook, who happened to be approximately the same age as himself. He used it to pass all the sentries to get to Blue Pool Road in Happy Valley where his family was. When he arrived, he found out that there had been rapes and atrocities in their apartment building. A few people were killed and Tang Siu Kin of the Kowloon Bus Company, a well-known person in Hong Kong, had been stabbed many times by Japanese soldiers. Tang had gone there because a fortune-teller had told him that it would be a safe place to be.

Fortunately, when the Japanese soldiers came, Ethel Poy had her mother with her. She hid in the cupboard with blankets over her, while her mother took Neville and his sister, Adrienne, and sat on the floor in front of the cupboard. Her mother told the soldiers that they were alone. It was a very close call. After the Japanese soldiers left, Ethel and her mother took the children to join her brother David and his wife, Connie, downtown. The servants in the apartment told Bill Poy where they had gone.

After he found his family, Poy told his wife that he had to return to their apartment, to retrieve three diamonds which he had hidden in one of the legs of their sideboard. He used the Eu's cook's ID card again. On his way, he was stopped by a sentry, but he was able to explain, with his few words of Japanese learnt as a youth in Manchuria, that he needed to go home to fetch clothes for his children. As he was approaching their apartment, he saw their dining table on the street for sale.

When he entered the apartment with a Japanese sentry, he saw clothes strewn everywhere, some of which had been used as toilet paper. The sideboard was still there, but he had to get rid of the sentry. Fortunately, the sentry was called away for a few minutes, and Poy got the diamonds out just in time before he returned. "You've never seen anyone working so fast with a screw driver!" Poy told me. The sentry then asked him, "Are you twenty-six?" That was the age on the ID card. If the question had been, "How old are you?" he would have been in grave trouble because he had forgotten to check the cook's age on the card.

Bill Poy returned to his family downtown. He wanted to take them up to Euston, but by then it was dark and there was a curfew. Ethel said, "You go and return with help tomorrow morning."

The next morning Bill and one of the Eu's servants found the apartment empty. The walls were covered with bullet holes and smeared with blood. His neighbours told him his wife and children were hiding under the stairwell. He found Neville holding a flask, and Ethel had Adrienne on her back, with biscuits in her hands. Ethel's mother,

David and Connie had already left but Ethel and her children had waited for Bill.

Apparently, after Bill left, Japanese soldiers had come to the building to look for young women. Ethel's mother put Ethel and Connie in the cupboard and put a blanket over them. She and David put a mattress on the floor, and lay down with Neville and Adrienne, in front of the cupboard. Two Japanese soldiers came into their apartment with flashlights (there was no electricity), and fortunately, just in the nick of time, the Kempeitai (Japanese Military Police) came in and told the soldiers to leave.

With the servant carrying Adrienne, Bill, Ethel and Neville walked to Wan Chai, where they saw a big street parade with Japanese on white horses, and soldiers carrying their dead comrades in boxes. They passed a small family restaurant and went in to get something to eat. They bought a chicken for one hundred dollars, and ate it while waiting for the parade to pass. They then headed to Euston, where there was no sign of war, and there was food. When Neville went to bed that night, he asked if he could stay there forever.[20]

The Japanese army took over the Queen Mary Hospital and everyone was told to go except the mechanic Ah Law, who was needed to operate the hospital steam room and the big stove. Everything, including all the medicine, was discarded, and replaced by shipments from Japan. After some months, Ah Law was dismissed.[21]

Some of the staff of the Queen Mary Hospital served in the relief hospital that had been set up at St. Stephen's Girls' College. St. Stephen's remained a hospital for close to five years and admitted only Chinese Hong Kong citizens. A small classroom was converted for minor surgery and dressings. There were Chinese and Irish doctors, such as Dr. G.E. Griffiths. Dr. K.D. Ling and Dr. Raymond Lee. Most of the British nursing sisters and the doctors were, by then, interned, with the exception of Dr. Selwyn Selwyn-Clarke,[22] who continued to serve as Director of Medical Services. In that capacity, he was able to help many of the citizens of Hong Kong during the occupation. Joseph Tam and other medical staff were given notes by Dr. Selwyn-Clarke so that they would get employment with the British, should they get to Free China.[23]

The Hong Kong-based research department of the China Tea Company was closed. The Chinese Finance Ministry gave instructions that the money in the company in Hong Kong was to be distributed to all the employees and each received the equivalent of four months' salary. C.T. Wu volunteered to help withdraw the money from the Hong Kong and Shanghai Bank for the company, and in the distribution of the cash, took his share in ten-dollar bills, because he felt they would be much more acceptable than the larger bills in times of war. He was right, because later the Japanese banned the use of notes larger than ten dollars. With this money he went into China as a refugee.

Two days after the Poys arrived in Euston, Bill Poy went downtown to Pedder Street. He passed a French jewellery shop that he sometimes visited with Eu Tongsan, Willy's father. The shop was flying a Vichy flag (a sign of neutrality). Poy had an idea. He knew the Japanese wanted watches and so asked the owner, Mr. Walsh, if he would trust him to sell some watches to the Japanese for him. Mr. Walsh gave him ten of the ones that were more difficult to sell, and a couple of the lower line of Rolexes. Poy went straight to the headquarters of the Kempeitai where he saw sacks of flour and rice, as well as cigarettes and whisky. When the sergeant in charge asked how much the Rolex was, Poy told him, "For you, it's free." The sergeant then offered Poy goods from the station and Poy asked for a sack of flour, cigarettes, whisky and some rice. The sergeant not only gave these items to him, but had them delivered to Euston. However, the flour was found to be full of weevils. When Poy told the sergeant, he asked Poy if he could sell the remaining sacks of flour for him. Poy went to a Chinese friend who in turn sold these to the Japanese. For each sack, the sergeant got forty yen and Poy kept sixty yen. From then on, if the Japanese wanted to buy anything, Poy would go and look for them. At that time, one Japanese yen was equivalent to two Hong Kong dollars, and it was useful to have some Japanese money.

By hanging around the Kempeitai headquarters, Poy was able to help his friends get supplies such as rice and flour. Within a short time, he became friendly with more members of the Kempeitai, who visited them in Euston and sometimes brought rice. Since the Kempeitai had control of Hong Kong, the family did not suffer. Neville, only six then, remembers that the sergeant of the Kempeitai was very nice to him and Adrienne, who was three. Neville, being musical, was often asked to perform for the Japanese when they visited them. However, to his parents' great concern, he liked to sing *Qi Lai*, a Chinese revolutionary song that schoolchildren used to sing at assembly in school every morning, and to play *Colonel Bogey* on the piano. His parents had to stop him whenever he wanted to perform these pieces when the Kempeitai were around. For the rest of her life, his mother never lost her fear of or dislike for the Japanese.

Japan not only needed Hong Kong as a naval base, but also considered it as a source of income and of material wealth. Anything that could be of use in Japan was confiscated, including cars, building materials and machinery, and shipped to Japan. The Japanese helped themselves to whatever they liked. Aunt Jenny's family car was taken by the Japanese, but they were fortunate that the soldiers gave them a bag of rice in exchange. The soldiers even took their pet monkey. Hong Kong harbour was filled with heavily loaded outgoing cargo ships. Few armaments left by the British were taken by the Japanese because the guerrillas as well as the local population got there first. Some of these were smuggled into China. There was a thriving market of British armaments between December 10 and December 31, 1941, in the Kowloon City area. The buyers were Hong Kong people, Sai Kung villagers, as well as the guerrillas.

The Chinese Guerrillas

After the British surrender, the Lee family members left the Lee Theatre and went home. Mother and the three of us went to live in the Lee Building with many other members of the family. The Big House had been looted and there were many dead bodies lying around because the Japanese soldiers shot looters on sight. It was a very difficult time for Mother, being so young and with three small children. What she didn't know was that she was looked after by "agents" sent by Father, since he could not be there himself.

The "agents" were Chinese guerrillas or guerrilla sympathizers. Few people in Hong Kong knew that Chinese guerrillas and agents of various political factions had infiltrated into the New Territories by the beginning of 1941. There were official guerrillas who were paid and armed by the Nationalist government under Chiang Kaishek. However, the most active guerrilla group in Hong Kong after the British surrender on Christmas Day 1941 was that of the Hong Kong–Kowloon Brigade, a subdivision of the East River Detachment, the foundation of which was laid by Liao Chengzhi in Hong Kong after the fall of Guangzhou. The Detachment went officially under the Communist banner in December 1943, when the name changed to the Guangdong People's Anti-Japanese Guerrilla Corps.

The Chinese guerrillas in the Colony had a network for intelligence, communications and sabotage. During the initial stage of the occupation, guerrillas of different political stripes were busy smuggling important Chinese and Allied nationals out of Hong Kong. One of the first was Liao Chengzhi, who escaped on January 5, 1942.[24] Within the first seven months of occupation, more than three hundred important Chinese nationals were rescued. Among the more well-known names were: He Xiangning, Liu Yazi, Zhou Taofen, Mao Dun, Qiao Guanhua, Sa Kongliao, Liang Shuming, Hu Die, the famous movie star, and Shang-Guan Xiande, the wife of Yu Hanmou, Commander of the Seventh War Zone of the Central Chinese Army.[25] Admiral Chen Ce, the chief Nationalist intelligence agent in Hong Kong who liaised with the British, made an escape on his own. Escapees from POW camps were assisted by the guerrillas and guerrilla sympathizers, who took them across the water by sampan or overland through mountain paths. The guerrillas worked with the villagers in the New Territories to hide and feed escapees, and lead them into Free China. Children as young as nine years old were recruited into the guerrilla camp to help as runners and as spies. They were called Siugui (Little Devils).

The first plans for escape from a POW camp were made in Shum Shui Po in January 1942 by Lt.-Col. Lindsay T. Ride, of the Hong Kong Volunteer Defence Corps Field Ambulance, and Lance-Corporal Francis Lee Yiu Piu, who had originally been with No. 3 Machine Gun Company of the Hong Kong Volunteer Defence Corps, but who transferred to Field Ambulance to be with Ride. Ride was an Australian doctor and teacher who was appointed to the Chair of Physiology at the University of Hong Kong in 1928. He had served in the First World War and was twice wounded in France. Lee, a slim, bespectacled and shy clerk, worked in the Physiology department and had earned respect and admiration from Ride for his hard work. Lee was not supposed to be in Shum Shui Po camp, because Chinese members of the Hong Kong Volunteers were given permission to return home. He told Ride he remained because he wanted to know what it was like being a POW, and he also wanted to stay in case Ride needed help to escape, and he felt he would be of more use inside than outside the camp. He played a vital role in the escape.

Lee made their travel arrangements with the help of contacts inside the camp, guerrillas or guerrilla sympathizers who delivered food or supplies. Many were later killed by the Japanese for what they had done. When the escape plans were made, Ride and Lee were joined by Lieutenant D.W. Morley, a lecturer in Engineering at the University of Hong Kong, and Sub-Lieutenant D.F. Davies, a lecturer in Physics at the same university, both from the Hong Kong Royal Navy Volunteer Reserve. The group escaped on January 9, 1942.[26]

The party was picked up by sampan and let off on a beach near Castle Peak Road. From there they walked through the New Territories, dodging Japanese search parties while they made their way to the outskirts of Sai Kung. After the occupation, the Japanese had left the Sai Kung peninsula in the hands of Wang Jingwei's men. (Wang was a Nationalist minister who defected to the Japanese side. He was Chiang Kaishek's most important rival in the Nationalist party.)[27] Then bandits moved in and caused chaos. Fortunately for the escape party, on January 9, the guerrillas had taken control of the Sai Kung peninsula. When the news of the escape reached the guerrillas and Wang Jingwei's men, they raced to see who could get to the escapees first. The Hong Kong–Kowloon Brigade leader was Cai Gualiang, whom Lee brought to meet the escapees at a rendezvous. Ride described in his diary the amazing experience he had of seeing Chinese villagers appear from nowhere to help them. Without them, the escape certainly would have failed. The escape party was given food, shelter and clothing. Dressed as Chinese villagers, they arrived in Free China on January 17, 1942.[28]

In Free China, Ride was instrumental in starting the British Army Aid Group (BAAG) in order to pass much-needed medical supplies into the POW camps, plan escapes and help those who managed to escape on their own to reach safety. BAAG was established under MI9 because it was also part of British Intelligence, with the reluctant approval of the Chinese government, which did not want to have foreign Intelligence working within China. However, the British were allies in the war. The work of BAAG in Hong Kong could not have been carried out without the help of the guerrillas. In Ride's report to the War Office, the guerrillas were referred to as "our" guerrillas because they were the escapees' lifeline to Free China, and at times "red" guerrillas because of their Communist leanings. Ride considered them to be "the most active, reliable, efficient and anti-Japanese of all Chinese organizations."[29]

The Chinese guerrillas infiltrated every aspect of life in Hong Kong under Japanese occupation. They were in the city and in the villages. They worked in Japanese banks, printing presses and even in the Japanese high command. They were involved in espionage, sabotage and rescue missions. They were an important link between the people of Hong Kong and the free world.

The control in the Japanese occupation zone was actually quite porous. People were smuggled back and forth across Japanese lines between Hong Kong and mainland China. It was also possible to sail to neutral areas like Macao or the French colony of Guangzhouwan, and then into China.

Initially, the guerrillas assisted many POWs to escape, but then it became too difficult, and the punishment of the prisoners who were left behind so severe that escape was no longer worthwhile. They passed information to the Chinese High Command, some of which was passed on to the Allies. It was with this information that the U.S. Air Force was able to bomb Hong Kong during the occupation, and a number of times guerrillas rescued Allied airmen who were shot down during these bombing raids.

Father As a Resistance Fighter

Since 1937, Father had been involved both in an official and an unofficial capacity in the Chinese resistance against the Japanese. He wanted to help as many people as possible, while making sure that his family was well looked after. His "guerrilla" activities involved both the Nationalist guerrillas and the pro-Chinese Communist Party guerrillas based in the East River Basin, Guangdong province. If it had not been for the protection of the guerrillas, it would have been almost impossible for our family, during the entire duration of the war, to escape unscathed, not only from the Japanese, but also from the Chinese bandits who were just as cruel.[30]

Father did not belong to any political party, and his actions were considered beyond reproach by both the Nationalists and the Communists. Once he overheard that the Nationalist Party was going to arrest Zhou Enlai who was with the Nationalists at the time (Zhou was the Chinese Communist Party liaison officer with the Nationalist Party, under safe conduct from Chiang Kaishek), and he immediately warned Zhou to escape. Zhou never forgot that. After the war, Zhou gave an order to the Xinhua News Agency, which was in effect an unofficial Chinese consulate in Hong Kong, that Father was to be given free access anywhere in China.[31]

Father was in Huizhou, a Chinese guerrilla base in the East River Basin, when Mother and the three of us arrived in China. I don't believe he ever joined the guerrillas because the situation was very confusing. Different factions were competing with each other while working against the Japanese. There were actually two types of guerrillas, the "red" guerrillas and the official guerrillas who operated in Guangdong under General Yu Hanmou. In addition, there were spies from Wang Jingwei's group, the British Army Aid Group and others. During those years, Father became friends with Soong Chingling, the widow of Dr. Sun Yatsen, and Edgar Snow, Mao Zedong's friend, as well as many top officials from the Nationalist government of Chiang Kaishek. After the war, Edgar Snow used Father's office whenever he was in Hong Kong.[32]

Father acted as a liaison between the escapees from Hong Kong, the guerrillas and the Chinese government, and his position was that of a humanitarian. He was frequently mentioned in Lt.-Col. Lindsay Ride's diary for his help in getting supplies such as blankets and medicine to POWs in Hong Kong and the refugees who made it into China. It was likely that he was able to get these supplies because he was the treasurer of the Chinese Red Cross. Father's other wartime activities will be mentioned in a later chapter. Fourth Uncle told me that he went to see Father in Qujiang (the wartime capital of Guangdong province after the fall of Guangzhou to the Japanese), in northern Guangdong province, in 1942, where Father was with Ride at the British Army Aid Group headquarters. Fourth Uncle, who was working for the Bank of China, was fortunate enough to be transferred to London and remained there until 1947. Ride and Father earned each other's respect and became good friends. After the war, when Ride became the vice-chancellor of the University of Hong Kong, Father was on the Council.

4
A Family On The Run

The years between 1941 and 1945 were the early years of my life. As a war baby, I went with my family into China as refugees. Many events were told to me by others who were there. However, I do have some memories that remain fresh even decades later.

Under the Japanese administration, there was widespread propaganda of "A New Asia where Asians were ruled by Asians," meaning Asians ruled by the Japanese. People constantly lived in fear. The wealthier managed to buy rice at black market prices, and the rest just died of starvation.

By the beginning of 1942, the Japanese military made a public announcement of their intention to reduce the population in Hong Kong from 1,600,000 to what they deemed a "manageable" number of 500,000. They very nearly succeeded. The unfortunate were picked up in the streets and taken by truckloads to junks in the harbour. These were towed out to sea and sunk or set on fire. In 1942 alone, 83,435 burials were recorded, many being victims of war, terrorism and reprisals.[1] The rest of the population was reduced by starvation to the point where cannibalism was practised. The rice ration of 8.46 oz. per person per day was provided for those who were fortunate enough to get it and this was often mixed with sand.

The streets of Hong Kong were dreadful sights. People lying in the streets were cut up for meat before they were dead, and anyone who

forgot to bow to a Japanese soldier risked being decapitated. Whenever Joseph Tam went to visit his girlfriend's home on Bonham Road,
he would see truckloads of dead bodies being dumped into a long rec-
tangular pit on the side of the Upper-level Police Station[2] (the
present-day site of King George VI park), which was situated just
below Euston, where the Poys were staying with the Eu family. In
Central Market, Chinese tea houses were turned into gambling
places. Special red-light districts in the city, known as comfort stations, were set up for the Japanese soldiers.

Retreat from Hong Kong

The Chinese in Hong Kong were encouraged by the Japanese occupation government to return to China. Many in the Lee and the
Wong families went to different parts of China, although a few chose
to remain in Hong Kong.

The only branch of the Lee family that went to our ancestral village, Garlieu, was Second Uncle, with his wife and the three younger
children. His older son and daughter went into China with the rest of
the Lee family. Because of that, their experiences over the war years
were different from those of the rest of the family. They went by boat
through the Pearl River, then made their way to Garlieu. The two
older boys, aged three and five at the beginning of the war, attended
the village school.

Whenever there was news that the Japanese soldiers were in the
area, the entire village would hide in the little huts in the fields, or
they would all move to a neighbouring village to get out of the way.
Cousin Raymand, who was three at the beginning of the war, remembers that whenever the villagers had to go into hiding, he and his
younger sister would be put into large baskets, and carried on a bamboo pole. However, his older brother, Hon Ching, who was five at the
time, had to walk with the adults. The problems in the village were
caused not only by Japanese soldiers, but also bandits, who looted
villages at will. As a child, Raymand thought it very exciting whenever there was news of bandits approaching, because the whole
village would assemble at our ancestral home, which was large

enough to accommodate the entire village, and Second Uncle would give out guns to all adult males who defended predetermined posts, turning the house into a fortress. Cousin Raymand does not recollect any major damage done by bandits during their stay in Garlieu.[3]

Grandmother and Second Grandmother (Father's biological mother) went into China as refugees with their respective families. Helena, the older daughter of Second Uncle, followed Second Grandmother. Fourth Grandmother (concubine Ng Yuet) went to her own home town of Wuzhou in Guangxi province. All the teenaged children travelled to China together, and they attended school wherever they went. The only person who stayed was Third Grandmother (concubine So Han) who remained in Hong Kong with her son, Fifth Uncle, who worked in our rental office throughout the war years, collecting rent.[4] Our family members took two routes to enter China — by land through Sha Tau Kok or by boat to Zhanjiang, formerly known as Guangzhouwan which was under the Vichy government, and therefore neutral. Many of us met up in China.[5]

Since Father was not able to get back to Hong Kong to take charge of us, he sent an underground messenger, probably a member of the guerrilla force, with a letter to Mother, asking her to follow the man into China with all of us. Mother at first suspected a trap and refused to go. When a second letter came, she decided to leave.

Many refugees sewed bits of jewellery into the lining of their clothes, or hid them in the soles of their shoes since they were subject to body searches by the Japanese and robbery by bandits. Jewellery could be used as cash, but the value was difficult to determine. By far the most valuable form of money was gold coins, which were easily convertible for the purchase of food and other necessary items. Mother must have hidden whatever she could in our baggage and clothing. However, she buried the bulk of her jewellery in the garden of the Big House with the help of Bill Poy.

In February 1942, my family left for China together with thousands of refugees from Hong Kong. Mother took four-year-old Richard, two-year-old Deanna, and me, nine months old, two servants, and six huge bags, and headed across the harbour by boat to the train station on the Kowloon side, accompanied by Fourth Uncle and Bill Poy, and watched over by the guerrillas. Bill Poy had obtained passes from the Kempeitai sergeant by telling them that Mother was his sister. He did this to avoid the possibility of us being stopped and searched. With his connections, he was also able to exchange some money for Mother before we left. After the war, Father asked Poy for the name of the Kempeitai sergeant in order to find him to thank him.[6] Whether he was successful or not, we don't know.

The train was crowded and we had difficulty stuffing our bags in. Fourth Uncle said goodbye at the train station, and we headed for Fan Ling, still accompanied by Bill Poy. We got off at Fan Ling and Mother hired some bicycles to carry our luggage. From there, we walked with a stream of refugees towards Sha Tau Kok, one of the entry points into China. Richard and Deanna were carried by the servants on their backs, and Mother carried me. At Sha Tau Kok, Bill Poy said goodbye to us and Mother immediately destroyed the passes. Then we boarded a boat. When we got off we walked for about a day to Huiyang, and boarded another boat again to reach Father in Huizhou.

From Huizhou, we travelled by truck to Shaoguan, in the northern part of Guangdong province, and then by train to Guilin.[7] Father instructed his younger siblings and nephew Hon Chiu to follow the same route, and to meet us in Guilin. We were able to travel safely through enemy-and-bandit controlled territories probably because we had the protection of the guerrillas.

Soon after my family left, news came to Bill Poy from the Canadian Trade Commissioner's office where he was an employee, that he and his family had a chance to go to Canada. It seemed that they were fortunate enough to have been put on the list for diplomatic exchange between the United States and Japanese governments. The U.S. government was exchanging Americans captured by the Japanese for Japanese interned in America.[8] Since there were more Japanese than Americans, Canadians were allowed to make up the difference. And since all Canadian soldiers in Hong Kong were in POW camps, the deficiencies were made up by the employees of the Canadian Trade Commissioner's office.

When Bill Poy heard the news, he thought it might be a trap set by the Japanese. He went to their family doctor, who was a brother-in-law, to get his wife's X-ray which showed a scar in one of her lungs. Then he went to see the Kempeitai sergeant to sound him out to see if it was a trap. The sergeant advised him to take his family to Canada when Poy showed him the X-ray, saying that his wife really needed treatment. The sergeant didn't know that it was an old X-ray.

The Poys — Bill and Ethel, Neville and Adrienne — left Hong Kong in August 1942. To this day, the Poys don't know how their names got on the list. When they arrived in Canada, immigration officials told them they were not allowed into the country because they were Chinese, until they saw their names on the exchange list. They were permitted to stay, becoming the first Chinese refugees in history to arrive in Canada. They were given housing, and Bill Poy continued to work for the Canadian government in Ottawa in the Department of Trade and Commerce. They had originally planned to return to Hong Kong after the war, but because of conditions in Hong Kong in 1945, Poy decided that the family should stay in Canada. They were made Canadian citizens by an Order in Council in Parliament in April 1949.

Life in Guilin

On our way to Guilin, Father encountered C.T. Wu again in Liuzhou. It was here that Wu met Mother, my siblings and me for the first time, and from then on, he became very close to our family.

In Guilin, we lived in a large house outside the entrance to the Seven Star Cave, which is a well-known tourist attraction. In 1942, houses were built right in front of the cave where now a road runs through to bring tourists to the site. Whenever there was an air raid, which happened more and more often as the Japanese advanced towards Guangxi province, we went into the cave for shelter.

Cousin Hon Chiu, who was in boarding school, used to stay with us on weekends. He came to get a little more to eat, because the boarding schools provided only two meals a day, and the children were always hungry. One of our servants, Suen Zeh, who was with us in Guilin, told Hon Chiu that we had ghosts in that house. From then on, he thought he actually felt someone pressing on top of him when he slept. He never dared to mention this to my parents, but whenever he had the excuse, he slept in Second Aunt's house, which was only five minutes away on Jiangan Road.[9] Hon Chiu also said that he would go to whichever house had more food. Hon Chiu was with us, off and on, during the entire period of the war, and so was Second Grandmother.

We lived in Guilin for over a year. During our stay there, our two servants gave notice that they were going to leave. Mother thought it wise to go back to Hong Kong before the servants got there, because she was sure that they knew where her jewellery was buried. Jewellery could be used as cash, and it was necessary for our survival. She also needed to bring into China as many of our household necessities as possible.

Leaving us in the care of the servants and Father, Mother headed for Hong Kong with her sister Sarah, through Zhanjiang. However, Aunt Sarah could not get a pass to go to Hong Kong, so Mother went alone, while her sister waited for her in Zhanjiang. This meant that she had the added responsibility of getting Aunt Sarah's household belongings as well as her own.

Mother went back to the Big House to gather our belongings with the help of servants who had remained in Hong Kong. The first two floors of the Big House were covered with dead bodies. These were bodies of looters who had died from shrapnel or had been killed by Japanese soldiers who shot looters on sight. It seemed the looters never made it to the third floor where my family used to live. Mother told us how they had to walk over the dead bodies to get around. She used the third floor to pack the household belongings because the parquet floors on the ground and second floors were caked with blood. (After the war they had to be completely replaced because they could not be cleaned.) I can't even begin to imagine how Mother managed.

Mother stayed in the Lee Building, further up the hill from Wan Chai, which had not been looted. She saw her parents and her younger sister, Josephine, who visited her there. One day, Mother was with her mother when they passed someone dying in the street and the person cried out, "Please save me!" The two women were helpless themselves, but Grandmother Wong, being a religious person, said, "Pray to Jesus, and He will help you."

In Mother's later years, especially after Father died, whenever she came across any difficulties, she would tell me that since she had survived the war, she was no longer afraid of anything.

Mother stayed in Hong Kong for a couple of weeks, then left by boat for Zhanjiang to meet Sarah. Everyone was convinced that Mother was well protected by the guerrillas. She brought with her not only her jewellery, hidden in all kinds of places, but also more than twenty large bags of household necessities, some of which belonged to her sister. The most important items were warm clothing and padded silk blankets.[10]

People had the most imaginative ways of hiding things during wartime. I love the story of how one of my parents' friends, Lucy Chan, a lawyer, whom I was to meet in 1949, handled the situation. She boldly wore all her jewellery, big diamonds and all, and convinced the Japanese soldiers that they were fake.

When Mother returned to Guilin, she gave a padded silk blanket to C.T. Wu, for which he was very thankful, because throughout the war years he was always cold, but could not possibly afford to buy one himself. To this day, he has high regard for Mother as a very brave woman.

Throughout the war years, Mother sold or bartered her jewellery for our family to live on. For personal reasons, Father refused repeated offers to work as an engineer for the Americans in China, but carried on with his wartime resistance activities and was, therefore, without an income. He worked closely with the Chinese Central government, the East River guerrillas, as well as the British Army Aid Group, on a voluntary basis. He had all his light-coloured clothing dyed dark in order to cut down on laundry. Being a thrifty person, his needs were few. We were barely managing financially, but he told Mother that when the war was over, everything would be fine. She was not to worry about our lack of possessions or the disposal of her jewellery, for he would replace them, and he certainly kept his promise.

When the Japanese reached Guangxi in 1942, the repair and the completion of the Qian Qui (Guizhou Guangxi) railway lines[11] became of immediate importance for the movement of refugees. The

Central government formed a committee of four engineers,[12] headed by Hou Jiayuan, who was a Kuomingtang (Nationalist) member. However, they still needed someone capable and reliable to supervise the work, and Father was chosen for the job, and made an Honorary Kuomingtang Executive Member.[13]

At that time, C.T. Wu was the manager of the Yong Guang Coal Company[14] in Guilin. Father convinced him that he would have a better future with us, and he became Father's secretary. Father needed someone like C.T. Wu who could speak Mandarin fluently, as Father could not. Wu often had to express what Father wanted to say at meetings. The two of them represented the Central government, and neither one was a genuine Kuomingtang member.[15]

Wu accompanied our family to Yishan, in Guangxi province, where the Head Office of the Railway Administration was located. Here, Director Hou Jiayuan gave us a piece of land close to the Administration Head Office, on which Father designed and personally supervised the building of a two-storey house for us to live in. This house was built in the typical local fashion, of woven bamboo sheets patched with mud. Ours was better built than most, because Father had some concrete mixed in with the mud, and the mixture was thick enough to stop the wind coming through the walls.[16] By the time we built our house in Yishan, Second Grandmother rejoined us.

All through the war years, Father was, among other things, a volunteer treasurer for the Red Cross in China. Because of this connection, he had in his possession the drug Sulphanilamide which was not readily available in China. While in Yishan, C.T. Wu had a bad infection on his arm that was treated by this drug.[17]

From time to time, C.T. Wu had to represent Father in a supervisory capacity when Father was down with malaria.[18] In later years, Father always prided himself that he had never been sick in his life, but he had forgotten the war years. When Father's health deteriorated to a point when he felt he had to resign his post as the Honorary Kuomingtang Executive Member looking after the repair and building of the Qian Qui railway lines, he found alternative employment for Wu. Through his friends Lu Yanming,[19] Lian Yingzhou[20] and Ou-Yang Qi,[21] Father arranged a job for Wu with the Overseas Union

Bank of Singapore in Liuzhou. This bank was owned by overseas Chinese from Shantao, China, and under normal conditions, only Chinese from Shantao were trusted as employees. An exception was made for Wu because of Father's recommendation, and he was put in a position of trust, with responsibility for buying supplies for the bank.[22] However, a few months later Liuzhou fell to the Japanese, and the bank moved to Chongqing.

On the Run Again

By 1943, with Japanese troops advancing, it was too dangerous to stay in Guilin. The five teenagers — my uncles, aunts and cousin Hon Chiu — needed to move to safer areas, but train tickets were impossible to come by. Former Lee Theatre employee and friend of the family, Yuen Yaohong, came to their rescue. He knew someone high up in the Central government bureaucracy, Huang Maolan, whose father was a general. Yuen persuaded them to let the teenagers cram into the general's private carriage on the train. They arrived in Liuzhou, temporarily safe. From there, they took a train to Yishan. By that time, we had already left for Dushan in Guizhou province. Second Grandmother was still in our house in Yishan when the five of them moved in. Hon Chiu remembers that we had a garden where we planted a lot of tomatoes, and we also raised chickens. It was at this time that he learnt to kill chickens. He said if he hadn't, no one would have had chicken for dinner. They stayed in Yishan for a little while and then followed us to Dushan.

Transportation was always a problem in China, particularly during the war. Father's friend Wang Aigai, who was in charge of transportation for the Bank of China, had a fleet of trucks which provided a means of transport for our family members from Yishan to Dushan. Dushan was a hilly town and our house was on the outskirts. Conditions were primitive, and there was no running water. When the teenage uncles, aunts and Hon Chiu arrived, they attended school there; Hon Chiu was in junior high school at the time. Father would take Hon Chiu with him every day to bathe in a nearby brook with a waterfall, no matter how cold it was. My older brother was spared because he was too young to withstand the cold. Father used to tell Hon Chiu about his past, and about his engineering studies at Oxford.[23] The bonding between uncle and nephew began at this time, and Mother remembered Hon Chiu saying that he would like to be like Father when he grew up.

In Dushan I became very ill. I was just skin and bones and too weak to hold my head up. Mother said I looked like a starved kitten, I was so small and frail. I was taken to a very primitive hospital, and one day the woman missionary doctor told Mother that I was about to die, and that Father should be called to see me for the last time. My teenaged Sixth Uncle, who was with Mother at the time, hopped on his bike and rode home to fetch Father. When Father heard the news, he came, bringing with him the only "magical" drug he had in his possession — Sulphanilamide. The doctor had never heard of it, but Father asked her to give it to me, since there was nothing to lose. The drug saved my life.

I was a burden during the war because I was sick all the time, and ended up in hospital wherever we went. I started getting sick at the age of seven months, when Hong Kong surrendered to the Japanese. I had intestinal problems, dehydration, and once I had lymphangitis of the leg. My parents thought many times that they had lost me. On top of that, both my parents and my older brother had malaria. Fortunately, we all survived, and I lived to tell the tale.

As the Japanese troops were advancing into Guizhou, it was time for us to leave Dushan. By this time, I was old enough to know what was going on. After one of the bombing raids, Mother and I happened to walk past our former house. She was very surprised that I immediately recognized it even though the roof was gone, and only the thick walls were still standing.

When we left, we once again had the help of Wang Aigai's transport fleet of the Bank of China. We travelled with them, on top of the cargo, to Guiyang, the capital of Guizhou. The journey along the hilly mountain roads was treacherous, and going downhill was hair-raising, especially when the brakes didn't work very well. Along the way, the convoy was stopped several times by Nationalist troops turned bandits. Fortunately, we were not harmed.[24] As a child of two,

I can remember climbing on top of the cargo using something that resembled a rope ladder, and holding on for dear life. I also remember being very carsick and throwing up hard-boiled eggs. Wherever we travelled in the primitive unhygenic parts of China, Father would not buy any cooked food (he described all the meats as looking black because they were covered with flies), so we had to survive on hard-boiled eggs. It has taken me fifty years to get over my phobia of hard-boiled eggs.

It was a lengthy journey. When we arrived in Guiyang, it was evening, and the sky was getting dark. The trucks arrived at a theatre, and out came former Lee Theatre employee Yuen Yaohong with a bag in his hand. He said to Father, "Dick, take this. It's for you." It was a bag filled with money. Hon Chiu said that it was a moment he would never forget, he was so impressed. No one in our family had money during the war. Yuen was managing that theatre in Guiyang at the time. He also looked after our living accommodations. In a house that was not soundproof, with my family upstairs, and Second Grandmother, the teenage uncles and aunts, Hon Chiu and his sister Helena downstairs, Hon Chiu said he could hear everything that went on upstairs.

Life in Chongqing

From Guiyang we moved on to Chongqing, in Sichuan province, again by the Bank of China convoy. This part of the journey was more secure because it was better controlled by the Nationalist troops. When we entered Sichuan, we were exposed to practices and foods that were distinctly different from those in southeast China. Sichuan foods were hot with chili, and it was difficult for us to eat because we were not used to it. Mother found it rather an appalling custom that the wealthier inhabitants had their coffins made ahead of time and placed under their own beds.

Since I was just a small child, I have only interesting memories. The adults had the worries, and I was the observer — that is, when I wasn't in hospital. I had the greatest adventures with our servants all over the countryside, in my wooden clogs in the summer and cloth shoes in the winter. Leather was saved for making boots for the soldiers, so civilians didn't have leather shoes. We would walk along the rice paddies to see the farmers working and watch people picking snails. In our home snails from rice fields were never eaten because of parasites. Just the same, it was interesting to watch. One day, the servant and I heard a great commotion as we were walking, and we went to see what the excitement was all about. We saw a large catfish struggling for air, stranded in very shallow water. It would be somebody's dinner. Another time, we heard that in one of the farms in the vicinity, a cow was about to give birth. The servant took me there just in time to see the birth of the calf. It was a wonderful learning experience for a child. Sometimes we would go to buy eggs, and some of these eggs would be fertilized. I still remember the embryos when the eggs were cracked open. Once, someone had the idea of having goat's milk, so my teenaged Seventh Uncle got hold of a goat and tried to milk it. What a sight!

When we entered Chongqing, we crossed the Yangtse River. We joined Grandmother, Third Uncle and Fifth Aunt, who were fortunate enough to have flown directly from Guilin in the transport plane of the Shanghai Commercial Bank.[25] They had not experienced the hardship that we had. Sixth Uncle, sixteen years old, wanted to join the Chinese army but was turned down because of his age. He left school anyway in order to make some money, and worked for the Chinese government as a translator because his English was good. He was later sent to Burma.

In Chongqing, my family lived in Tao Yuan, a complex of houses that belonged to the Tao family, friends of my parents. The complex was built by Tao Guilin, who was the biggest contractor in China, having built some of the most important buildings in the country, especially in Nanjing and Shanghai.[26] The Tao family lived in the large house on the left as you entered the gate, and we lived in the last house on the far right.

Grandmother, Third Uncle and some of the other uncles and aunts lived in Tian Tan Xin Cun, which was owned by the Shanghai Commercial Bank. Third Uncle, being a director of the bank, had the use of one of its houses.

By the time we were in Chongqing, I was close to three years old. I remember the little bungalow we had in Tao Yuan, on the banks of the Yangtse River. It was a simple house, with the living room in front, and the bedrooms at the back. The house was perched on the bank of the river, so even though the entrance was at street level, the end of the bedrooms was high above ground, since the river-bank was steep. The interesting feature of this house was that the kitchen was in a separate building down towards the river.

My brother, sister and I used to catch fireflies after dinner. We would put them in a bottle, and watch them glow. We caught turtles along the river-bank and tied them to a string attached to the back of the sofa in the living room so that they would eat the mosquitoes.

The kitchen was so far down the river-bank that it always got flooded. Whenever the water rose, all the adults in the family would rush down to the kitchen to move everything to the house. After each flood, I would have something new to play with, because the water always brought interesting things to the shore. Once we caught a crab that I wanted to play with, but Father was afraid that the pincers would hurt me. He did not know about tying the pincers, so he crushed them and put mercurochrome on them. He obviously did not know the biological difference between a human being and a crab. He tied a string on it so that I could walk it. We had no toys in those days, and I certainly never missed them.

I had friends I played with and visited, who taught me to speak a childish version of Mandarin which I've been able to retain to a certain extent since. During our years in China I came to be called Mei Mei, for little sister, because I was the youngest of the three, and after the war, I got stuck with the name May, short for Mei Mei. It was a name I disliked because it is so common among Chinese girls.

While in Chongqing, we visited with our relatives, many of whom ended up there. In fact, with the advancing Japanese armed forces, that was the safest place to be, since it was the wartime capital of China.

On New Year's Eve 1944, my mother's younger brother Daniel, his wife, Helen, and their children were visiting us at Tao Yuan. After dinner, while the adults were chatting in the living room, the children went into my parents' bedroom to play. All of a sudden, my older brother felt sick, and he climbed up on a chair and vomited out of the window. The rest of the children clamoured up to see what was happening, and suddenly my cousin Joan fell out of the wide window. Being the youngest, I was watching on the sideline. None of the older children made a move, so I went into the living room to tell the adults that cousin Joan had fallen out of the window.

One can imagine the hysteria. It was fortunate that electric wires strung across the back of the house under the window broke her fall. Otherwise she would have fallen a distance equal to two stories. Since it was not only wartime in Chongqing, but also New Year's Eve, getting medical attention was not a simple matter. However, my uncle and aunt managed to get a couple of rickshaws to take them to the closest hospital. Fortunately, cousin Joan was not badly injured, and ended up with nothing more than a scar under her chin. Till the end of my parents' days, they talked about my presence of mind at the age of three and a half.

The Japanese Surrender

Hostilities ended in Europe in May 1945, and the war against Japan assumed a different character. The objective in the Pacific became one of bringing the war to a speedy conclusion with as few casualties as possible. On August 6, the first atomic bomb was dropped on Hiroshima, followed by another one on Nagasaki three days later. On August 14, 1945, at 23:30 Tokyo time, the Emperor of Japan formally announced an unconditional surrender to the Supreme Command of the Allied Forces.

On the same night in Chongqing, the Oversea Union Bank of Singapore was having a dinner party. Among the guests were Minister of Foreign Affairs Chen Qingyun and the former mayor of Shanghai, Wu Tiechen. Chen's family phoned the bank to let him know that the Japanese had surrendered. Bank Chairman Lian Yingzhou and general manager O-Yang Qi immediately asked C.T. Wu to buy firecrackers. Lian and Ou-Yang, who were from Chaozhou (Guangdong province), did not know that the people of Sichuan only lit firecrackers when someone had died. When the people on the street heard the firecrackers going off, they thought someone at the bank had died. That night, when the news was broadcast, no one slept. The crowds in the streets celebrated and everyone got drunk.[27]

In Hong Kong, the moment the news of the Japanese surrender came, everyone went out onto the streets to look for Japanese soldiers to beat up.[28] Chiang Kaishek claimed that Hong Kong was part of the China theatre, and therefore the Japanese forces should surrender to him. The future of Hong Kong had been discussed in earlier wartime summit meetings, and the retrocession of Hong Kong had been supported by President Roosevelt. However, Churchill was not going to let that happen. For the next few days, there was confusion as to who was going to take over from the Japanese government. A message was sent to Franklin Gimson in Stanley camp, through the British Army Aid Group agent Y. C. Leung, code-named "Phoenix," on August 23, to take control of the government. Three days later, Gimson moved out of the camp to take up office in the French Mission building in town. On August 30, Admiral Sir Cecil Harcourt arrived with the Royal Navy to begin the postwar military government of Hong Kong, which lasted until May 1, 1946.

That August, Father, Third Uncle and Grandmother, flew back to Hong Kong from Chongqing on the plane of Lieutenant-General Sir Adrian Carten de Wiarte, who was the special representative of Prime Minister Churchill in the China theatre. Having been under Japanese rule since December 1941, Hong Kong's monetary system was in disarray. As one of the first to arrive back to Hong Kong, Father was asked to hand-carry a large amount of cash for the Hong Kong and Shanghai Bank.[29]

Mother and the three of us, together with our servants, returned to Hong Kong the usual way, as did other refugees in China. Mother told us that the war was over and we were going home. Father had to go first because he was needed immediately to help Hong Kong get back on its feet. Part of our journey was on a small, crowded, flat-bottomed boat, on which we placed our bedding next to each other. The last part of our journey was by train and seats were difficult to come by. Fortunately, our family knew the stationmaster, who told Mother that, in order to get seats, we had to be at the station at four o'clock in the morning. We took his advice, and we were on our way home.

Our teenaged uncles and aunts, together with Hon Chiu, remained in Chongqing to continue their schooling. Food for the boarders in the schools in Chongqing was quite plentiful, unlike Guilin's two meals a day, so when the older members of the family left to go back to Hong Kong, they were not as badly missed. During this time, whenever the teenagers needed money for school fees and living expenses, they would go to the Shanghai Commercial Bank. Hon Chiu remembers someone by the name of Karl Wu, a friend of Third Uncle at the bank, who would invite Hon Chiu for coffee from time to time. Hon Chiu was very impressed by the beautiful mansion Wu owned.

In 1948, when Hon Chiu graduated from high school, he planned to go to Shanghai to stay with Third Aunt and her American husband, Henry Sperry, in order to take the entrance exams for Jiaotong and Qinghua universities. By that time, the Chinese Communist Party was already in control of northeast China and had reached Beijing. Father telegraphed him to return to Hong Kong immediately to take the entrance exam for Lingnan University in Guangzhou, and to wait for an opportunity to go to the United States. When Hon Chiu left Chongqing to return to Hong Kong, Wu saw him off at the airport. The following year, China was liberated by the Communists, and Hon Chiu never saw Wu again.

5

After The War:
The Society Changes

At the end of the war, Hong Kong was in shambles. Then civil war broke out in China. The ensuing tide of refugees to Hong Kong caused a population explosion from 1.6 million in 1946 to 2.36 million by the end of 1950. In the first six months of 1950 alone, 700,000 refugees poured in from the mainland. In May of that year, the government adopted a quota system, which proved to be totally ineffective. Most of the refugees were unskilled labourers who were willing to work and were determined to make their new homes in Hong Kong. Some of them did not even know where Hong Kong was before they arrived there.

Occasionally, my parents would get a phone call in the night from a relative or a friend who had escaped from China and had reached Hong Kong. The landscape became dotted with squatters. Many of the huts on the hillsides were made from boards or scrap metal from junkyards, and there were beggars everywhere.

The Chinese Communists erected loudspeakers at Lowu and Man Kam To pointing towards Hong Kong, pouring forth propaganda and abuse against the British in general and the authorities in Hong Kong in particular. Along the border stood the guards from China and Hong Kong, facing each other. The Chinese troops would shoot anyone who was caught trying to escape. However, many did escape, which contributed to the increase in Hong Kong's population.

We were lucky to have homes to return to. We even had a large garden where we had many fruit trees, a large chicken coop and a tennis court. Grandmother moved back to the Big House with her own children. Third Uncle got married and lived on the third floor as we had done before the war. Fourth Uncle, who returned from England in 1947, and Fifth Aunt lived on the second floor with Grandmother. Grandmother's other daughter, Second Aunt, was married before the war.

My family moved into the Lee Building, and occupied the top-floor apartment on the left. There were six apartments altogether, three on the right and three on the left of a wide central stairway. No one lived in the apartment below us. Father's old friend from his "guerrilla" days, Major Hector Shulwan rented the ground-floor apartment. Shulwan might have had connections with the British Army Aid Group in China. Shulwan, an English engineer who spoke fluent Mandarin, was a confirmed bachelor and his only hobby was car engines. During the day, he worked as Director of the Labour Department in Hong Kong, and after work he would put on his overalls, and we would always find him under his car. I was fascinated by this tall man in the greasy overalls whom we called Uncle Shulwan.

On the right side of the building, Second Uncle and his family lived on the top, Second Grandmother one floor below them. Fourth Grandmother lived on the bottom floor. With the children of Second Uncle, and with the frequent visits of many other cousins, we had lots of playmates.

My brother, sister and I shared a large bedroom. At night, one of the servants would set up her bed in our room to keep us company. She would tell us stories from Chinese operas, and at times, these stories were so long that they would carry on for many nights. In the summer, we all slept with mosquito nets over our beds. In the winter, our beds were warmed by brass hot-water bottles wrapped with towels and pinned with large safety pins.

Even though Father was considered well-off, and we had a nice home, we had very little money. For the first and only time in her life, Mother made some of our clothes. I remember Mother dressing quite simply and wearing costume jewellery. The first toy I owned was a doll my parents bought me for my first Christmas in Hong Kong in

1945. I was four and a half years old. It remained my favourite toy throughout my childhood.

Rationing and Shortages

The most important tasks the postwar Military Administration faced were the repatriation and resettling of prisoners of war and internees, the closure of the prison camps, and the demobilization of the armed forces and auxiliary defence services. There was a great shortage of government staff, and for the first time, local Chinese and Portuguese personnel were given much more responsibility. The credentials they were able to establish during this period could not be ignored by future Hong Kong governments.

The first years after the war were very difficult for everyone in Hong Kong. The major concern was food, which was rationed. Supplies were controlled by the United Nations. The rebuilding of a healthy, growing community was constantly under threat from sheer lack of food. On May 14, 1946, the government appointed Father as Rice Controller for Hong Kong. The following week, Father held a press conference to announce that since Hong Kong was allowed only 20,000 tons of rice by the United Nations, which was half the required amount for the population, flour and green peas would be added to the ration.[1] By the end of the month, he protested to the United Nations because of the limitation imposed on Hong Kong. By September, the rice ration had to be reduced again, so biscuits and additional flour were added. Throughout 1947, conditions remained stable, but by the beginning of 1948, prices for flour and rice began to increase. In order to control prices, Father allowed the sale of cheaper rice imported from Thailand and Vietnam, and flour, which met with public approval. On May 6, 1948, Father resigned his voluntary post, but was kept on as an advisor by the government.[2]

Father carried out his duty with such efficiency and correctness that no one, not even family and close friends were given preference with the rice ration coupons.[3] I remember one incident in school when one of the boys teased me and said, "Your father is the 'shit' Controller." When I related this to him, Father said with a smile, "Ask him what he eats."

During Father's term as Rice Controller, he became very good friends with Ma Luchen, an overseas Chinese in Thailand, frequently called the "rice king" of Southeast Asia. Since that time, the Ma family has sent us bags of Thai rice, pomolos and mangoes every year. The white flower mangoes from Thailand are, I believe, the best in the world, but because they don't transport well they are not commercially available. Yearly, my parents distributed these gifts to family members. This practice was continued by Ma Luchen's son after his father died, and it went on until my mother died in 1996.

During those early years, when there were shortages and small industries had a difficult time, Father tried his best to help. Companies such as Yu Tat Chi, which manufactured candied ginger, and the Garden Bakery, which needed sugar for baking, were grateful to Father for arranging supplies of sugar.[4] I remember the beautiful ginger jars and the wonderful candied ginger we used to have after dinner. Garden Bakery sent my parents cakes on special occasions, and they continued to do so, even after Father died. I saw the beautiful Christmas cake sent from Garden Bakery to Mother in 1995, the year before she died.

Another problem Hong Kong faced with the large increase in the refugee population was the shortage of water. Hong Kong had, up to that point, depended on rainwater, which was collected in reservoirs. The water supply became inadequate, and water rationing started. Depending on the time of year, water might be available for only a few hours twice a week. Because of the lack of water pressure, those who lived on the upper floors in high-rises might not get any water from their taps at all. It was particularly desperate in the poorer sections in the city where people had to line up at public taps with buckets and fights often broke out. The newspapers and radio stations reported many stories of woe. At least the wealthy could check themselves into a hotel when they needed a good shower, because there was no rationing for the hotels. I remember this time very well. Our lives were consumed by this problem. My parents would tell us when water was available and insisted that we be frugal with it. Our household staff used to fill the bathtubs and all available containers when the water was turned on.

A large new reservoir was built at Tai Lam Chung in the New Territories, but when it was finished, the government realized that it was not big enough. The government could not keep up with the needs of the increasing population.

Health Problems

Health was also a major government concern in postwar Hong Kong. I remember the public-health nurses coming to the school to give us typhoid and cholera injections. I often had painful reactions to these, sometimes accompanied by a fever. We also had tuberculosis tests and smallpox vaccinations, when we had to wear wire covers over the vaccination area to prevent us from scratching. I dreaded those "public-health nurse days."

With my usual inquisitiveness, I found out that Father gave blood regularly to the Red Cross. I just happened to ask one day after school because I thought he was home a little earlier than usual. He never talked about it, but it was rather unusual for a Chinese to donate blood in the years immediately after the war.

It's not possible to think of the postwar years without mentioning de-worming. Father was quite aware of the state of hygiene in China during the war, and in Hong Kong right after the war. Once a year on a weekend during the cool months, all of us would starve ourselves for one day, eating only very liquid plain rice congee. At the end of the day, Father would give us worm medicine. The idea was that any parasites living in our bodies would be hungry and would ingest the medicine. The next morning, we would be given castor oil with orange juice, a horrible mixture. Presumably, that would eliminate the worms and the eggs from our bodies. Father never planned too far ahead, because it had to be at his convenience. Our cousins always hoped to avoid this procedure, even though they loved staying over at our place, but anyone who happened to be with us that weekend would get the same treatment. Father impressed upon us that if we allowed parasites to live in our bodies, all our nutrition would be taken from us and we wouldn't grow. He was absolutely right. I did have worms in my body and I saw them being expelled.

Father also believed his children should be trained to have regular bowel movements in the evening. So every night after dinner, the three of us would troop into the washroom. My brother would sit on the toilet, my sister on a tall spittoon, and I would be on a small spittoon. Often we just talked and did nothing.

When we bought our first launch in 1947, the *Swan*, one of the crew members, Ah Gun, was scrawny and looked as though he had been affected by parasites. Father treated him with worm medicine. Over the years he worked for us, he actually grew taller and became much healthier.

Some time in the late 1940s, my parents came to the realization that my hearing was impaired. This was caused by my frequent illnesses during the war, and subsequent ear infections. A friend of Father's, Dr. Chan Yik Ping, was an eye, ear, nose and throat specialist, trained in Vienna around the same time Father was at Oxford. Like many doctors who were licensed in China, Dr. Chan was able to work only for the Hong Kong government health service,[5] and not allowed to have his own practice. However, my parents had great respect for his ability and asked him about my hearing loss. He diagnosed a perforated eardrum in my left ear. After school on a regular basis I was taken to see him by Father, who always came with me because he was so anxious and concerned. Dr. Chan inserted a thin tissue in place of my eardrum, and applied an ointment to encourage regrowth. Eventually, my eardrum did grow back, but I still notice a difference between my right and left ears.

The Refugee Families

My first personal experience with what was happening in China was when we suddenly had visitors. Sing Sheng[6] and Dorothy Chu, who was related to the Tao family we stayed with in Chongqing, arrived on the first day of Chinese New Year 1947. In January, the two had left Shanghai for Hong Kong to get visas to go to the United States. The plane in which they were travelling was diverted to Manila because of stormy weather. Then two of the four engines caught fire and the pilot ditched the plane in the China Sea. Seven of the thirty-six passengers died and the survivors stayed afloat in two rubber rafts for thirty hours until they were rescued by an American ship. After being hospitalized for two weeks, Sing Sheng and Dorothy finally arrived in Hong Kong and were welcomed by my parents.[7] They stayed for about a month, in the apartment below, and had all their meals with us, while they waited for their visas. I was six years old at the time, and just loved hearing their stories. After they obtained their visas, they returned to Shanghai to prepare to go to the United States.

Between 1948 and 1949, friends and relatives who came out from China stayed in the Lee Building. I am not sure whether it was because of a shortage of rental accommodations or because it was a temporary measure. At one time there were three families living in the same apartment below us. As children, we thought it was wonderful to have even more playmates, but I was beginning to realize the seriousness of the political upheaval in China by listening to the adults talk. I knew that the new playmates were only there temporarily and I was quite aware of the overcrowded conditions our guests were living in. Knowing that people had to leave their homes was not a comforting thought.

The apartment was divided into three sections for the three families. One of them was the family of Mother's older sister Pearl. Aunt Pearl left Shanghai with her six children while her husband, C.C. Kwong, stayed behind. Uncle C.C. was a highly qualified engineer who felt that he could stay in China to help the country. By 1950, he believed that the political situation was settling down, and he came out to Hong Kong to take his family back to Shanghai. However, they left behind their eldest son, Joseph, with us because he was of conscription age, and they did not want him to be sent to Korea to be "cannon fodder," now that the Korean War was on. Within two years, their other children escaped back to Hong Kong, one by one.

The Chans were another family — husband, wife and four children. Lucy Chan, a friend since the 1920s, was the lawyer mentioned earlier, who trained in England at the same time Father studied there. Mr. Chan was the son of an important official in China. What I remember most was the fact that Mrs. Chan, besides being a skilled lawyer, could knit a sweater in a day. She could even knit while she was having an afternoon rest.

The third family was Father's former employer in Guangzhou, Liu Jiwen, his wife and their children. Mrs. Liu, a beautiful and serene lady, was a gifted painter. During their stay with us, every day after school I would go downstairs and watch her paint. Because she knew I was so interested, she showed me how to grind traditional Chinese colours, and how to use Chinese brushes. Soon, I was sitting next to her at her table and she was teaching me Chinese painting. Mrs. Liu told Mother that I had artistic talent, and should be given painting lessons.

In 1949, the Chinese Communist Party formed the government of the Peoples' Republic of China, and the Nationalists of the Republic of China under Chiang Kaishek retreated to Taiwan.

Housing Problems

Father played a major role in helping the people of Hong Kong both privately and through the government. In 1946, Father was made a Justice of the Peace (JP). One of his duties was that of acting as a judge in the JP court, presiding over cases of minor infractions, such as hawkers who set up their stands where they were not allowed to by law. In appreciation of Father's service to the community, particularly as the Rice Controller for Hong Kong, the British government awarded him the OBE in 1949.

In 1953, Father became a member of the Urban Council. He immediately spoke out publicly on the lack of affordable housing. He encouraged large companies to work with the government to build housing for their employees by providing affordable mortgages. He knew that this would greatly improve the relationship between employers and employees. At the same time, he also brought up the subject of the lack of understanding by the general public about public health issues and suggested that the government produce brochures explaining the problems.[8]

The crisis in housing caused severe health problems. The poor lived in shacks or in the open. Others paid landlords to be allowed to build shacks on top of buildings. There were no toilets or running water.[9]

On Christmas Day 1953 there was a terrible fire in an area filled with squatters, and 53,000 people were hurt. The government finally realized that a third of the population of Hong Kong was made up of refugees who had nowhere else to go. Something had to be done to integrate them into the community. From then on, the Hong Kong government embarked on an ambitious resettlement program to provide safer housing at minimal cost. This also helped to clear the land occupied by the squatters for industrial and commercial developments. Despite the speed with which public housing was built, the squatter population grew even faster.

In 1961, as an unofficial member of the Legislative Council, Father complained that the government was working too slowly. It had promised to move 75,000 people into public housing in 1959. According to Father's information, as of February 1961, only 32,432 had been moved. He urged the government to cut the red tape to speed up the process, giving priority to those earning less than $300 a month.[10]

It took until the 1980s to solve the problems of housing. The shacks on the hillside gradually disappeared and were replaced by high-rise public housing. The majority of these refugees became the backbone of Hong Kong's industrialization.

Refugees and Industry

During the Korean War of 1950 to 1953, the United Nations placed an embargo on China, dealing a fatal blow to the entrepôt trade in Hong Kong. Fortunately for Hong Kong, some of the refugees brought with them not only money but industrial and technological know-how. According to one estimate, several billion Hong Kong dollars came with the immigrants during this period. Between 1947 and 1949, more than two hundred Shanghai enterprises transferred their registration to Hong Kong.

Industrialists arriving from northeastern China provided a boost to local industries, and were in turn aided by the established international trading networks in Hong Kong.[11] Because of its lack of natural resources, Hong Kong's most valuable resource was its manpower, much of it including the refugee population and their knowledge and skills. Hong Kong's textile industry originated with these new arrivals. The opening of factories helped to provide jobs for the masses. By the beginning of the 1950s, "Made in Hong Kong" labels began to appear on many manufactured goods, a change from the late 1940s, when "Made in Japan" labels were common. At the same time, there was a growing need for skill and knowledge so that the Colony could become competitive internationally.

As more and more factories were built, important changes in social structures occurred. The traditional Chinese family with live-in Chinese female servants gradually declined. Many of these servants were women who originally came from the silk districts of the Pearl River Delta and had worked in the silk industries near their home villages until the Great Depression. When their factories collapsed, they moved to Guangzhou (Canton), Macao and Hong Kong. Some were women who had decided they were not going to get married, others were widows who had chosen not to remarry. Since they were illiterate, their only alternative was to work as household servants. They formed a sisterhood, *zei mui*, and depended on one another for moral and sometimes financial support. They were known as women who put their hair up, *saw hai*, meaning they would never marry. They braided their hair in the back in one thick braid, and it was never cut. The older women sometimes wore their hair in a bun. I was always fascinated by the amount of hair these servants had, and loved watching them going through the ritual of hair washing, using a certain type of wood shaving, *pao far*, which they bought from the market, and which added a lovely sheen to the hair.

With the opening of more and more factories in Hong Kong, many unskilled jobs were available, and these were filled by the younger servants. The older ones remained with the families they had been with for years. Gradually, the factories absorbed all the unskilled labour in Hong Kong, and no Chinese household servants were available.

Working in a factory meant being able to have one's own home and family. Government subsidized housing had helped greatly in this respect and the standard of living for the majority improved. The positions of household servants were gradually filled by Filipino maids, and later, maids from Thailand brought by employment agencies into Hong Kong. By the 1970s, live-in household help was almost entirely from other Southeast Asian countries.

As for me, the real change in Hong Kong began when we started to hear the Shanghai dialect spoken in public, and noticed the odour of "smelly" tofu, a popular Shanghai dish. We were frequently visited by the "Shanghai Woman," a gem agent who, with private references, went to wealthy homes to sell jewels smuggled out of China by refugees. The rich smuggled whatever they could out of China into Hong Kong, and overnight there was an abundance of jewels available for sale, the proceeds of which, I was told, were used to finance factories and various other businesses. For the next few years, the "Shanghai Woman" would call on Mother whenever she had something special. She was a chubby lady who wore a plain loose cheongsam, inside which was an undergarment full of secret pockets. I used to watch in great fascination as she unbuttoned her cheongsam, and from each secret pocket of her undergarment came the most beautiful pieces of jewellery. I always hoped she would come when I was home after school, and sometimes I was lucky. With such valuables on her person, I often wondered about her safety, but I didn't think it was my place to ask.

Refugees and Education

Father became involved with grass-root organizations, such as the Szeyup Business Association (an association of people from the area of our ancestral village in China), Wan Chai Kaifong Benevolent Association (a community organization to help the needy), Tung Wah Hospital (a hospital for the poor), Po Leung Kuk (for the protection of women and children) and many others. He spent a great deal of time organizing donations of warm clothing, and helped to set up free medical and dental clinics, free primary schools and also donations of free coffins, which was very important to the Chinese. As an education enthusiast, he was often invited to different schools for prize-giving days or for new school openings. Many of these were Chinese-language middle schools catering to the refugee population that needed someone to raise their profile. Throughout his life, Father always had time for those who needed him.

Schools in postwar Hong Kong were in a state of disarray. Many of the buildings were either destroyed or so badly damaged that they could not be used. With the increasing number of people moving into Hong Kong from China,[12] there was constantly a shortage of schools. Classes were held in any available building. Between 1946 and 1948, I changed school four times. Two of the four schools soon ceased to exist.

In the 1950s Rev. R.O. Hall, Bishop of Hong Kong, set up Workers' Schools for refugee children. The Colonial government suspected these schools of communist infiltration[13] and anti-British indoctrination and closed them down, and in some cases, deported the teachers.[14] The Education Ordinance of 1953 and its subsidiary regulations prohibited any kind of political activity in schools, including discussions of contemporary Chinese politics or of colonialism.

Improvisations such as three-sessional schools had to be adopted by the government. This meant that three sessions of school were held in the same building, morning, afternoon and evening, each with its own set of teachers and students. In 1952, my older brother, Richard, and my sister, Deanna, were sent to school in England. My younger brother, Christopher, and I attended St. Paul's Co-educational College. We were very glad to be in the morning session, which started at eight o'clock.

I subsequently learnt that, because of food shortages and the disorganization of the schools in Hong Kong, the Poy family decided to stay in Canada where conditions were much better.

6
The Magical Years

From the end of the war to the early 1950s, my family lived in the Lee Building. Those were magical years for me. There were so many children living in the same building that we were never short of playmates. I loved the freedom to play in the garden, swinging on tree branches, picking fruit, and chasing chickens in the chicken coop. I constantly had scraped knees and my legs were dotted with mosquito bites. I loved the beautiful fragrance of the flowering trees and bushes. Mother used to pick the flowers to put in her hair. Whenever I hear the sound of heat bugs buzzing now, or smell the fragrance of Chinese jasmine, I am reminded of my childhood in our garden, a carefree time, full of fun.

We built a little "club" house with pieces of boards. We had small wooden benches and stools, and the most important item was a little coal burner. Every Saturday night, all the children got together to tell stories and roast sweet potatoes on the burner. I remember once Grandmother had her cook make soya sauce chicken and bring it to us in the club house. My sister had told Grandmother that she came first in class, and we deserved something for our Saturday night club. Being the youngest in the group, I was mainly a listener and observer. We were allowed to stay up as late as we liked. I was so pleased that I was allowed to join this group even though I was always frightened by the ghost stories the older children told. At the end of the evening, without fail, everyone ran upstairs calling out, "Ghosts chasing us!" I was always the last to reach the top of the stairs because I couldn't run as fast as the others.

83

One night, I woke up and saw a white shadow with long hair moving from our bedroom to the bathroom. The first thought that came to mind was what Mother had said: no one had died in the Lee Building during the war. I thought, if there was no violent death in the house, we would not be harmed.

Another night, I woke up and saw a white shadowy female figure with long hair standing between my bed and my sister's bed. I thought it had to be the servant, but when I sat up in bed to check and saw her fast asleep, I froze. I couldn't even cry out. The white figure moved closer and closer, then turned towards my sister's bed and fingered the mosquito net with her long nails. I kept saying to myself that she was not going to hurt us since we had never hurt anyone, then I passed out. The next morning, I asked the servant whether she had gotten up in the middle of the night to adjust my sister's mosquito net, and she said no. I never told my parents about this because I didn't want to worry them.

To this day, I can't explain what I saw, but I remember those images very clearly.

Even though we lived on the side of a hill and were surrounded by trees full of birds, Father loved having birds in our home. We had a parrot and a couple of canaries. Father would give the canaries water, bird seed and dried squid cartilage. The cages hung in our balcony, and sometimes, wild canaries were attracted by them. Father enjoyed hearing them sing, especially early in the morning. Our cook also liked to feed the blackbirds that flew to the window of her kitchen in the back.

There were a lot of hungry people in Hong Kong during the postwar years. Sometimes our cook would give them leftover food from our kitchen.

Very early one morning, I was awakened by the sound of Father shouting from the window. When I went to the window to see what was happening, I saw a man carrying two chickens, one under each arm, running down the slope from the Lee Building towards Wan Chai. Apparently, he had climbed into our garden, and got into our chicken coop. Father saw him just as he was getting away.

Those were the days when we were visited quite regularly by men who purchased recyclable and reusable cans and bottles. These men carried on their shoulders bamboo poles strung with huge baskets on each side. This was the postwar Hong Kong way of recycling.

Father was an early riser, unlike Mother, who liked to sleep in, so we always had breakfast with him. The first things he put in front of us were cod-liver oil, a brown thick liquid that we took with a table-spoon, as well as vitamin C, and calcium. He made sure we had a full breakfast. He retained the English habit of having bacon and eggs, or kippered herring. I used to like a piece of pan-fried fish if the cook could get it in the market early enough.

Father was always in a good mood in the morning. That was his best time of the day. He liked to drive us to school even though school in Hong Kong could start as early as eight o'clock in the morning. He liked to get to the office before everyone else, including the office boy. I asked him once why he didn't have the chauffeur drive us, and he said, "I don't want Ah Muk to have to get up so early since he lives in Kowloon. He can get the car from me at the office, and come back to drive Mommy." But I actually think he liked driving us to school.

My childhood image of Father was that of an old-fashioned, stern man on whom we could always depend, and one who commanded a great deal of respect. I was a quiet child who listened and absorbed everything around me. I don't believe Father knew how much I admired him. I was but a few years old when I realized that I was as strong-willed as he was, a quality he came to accept in me. I remember an incident when I was about five years old when he insisted that I should finish my lunch. I was not hungry and I refused. Since I was not allowed to leave the table until I finished, I sat there for hours until he relented. Ever since then, he knew I always made my own decisions.

As a child, I would rather listen than talk. We usually spoke Can-tonese at home, but during dinner time, my parents always spoke English to each other so that the servant would not understand what they were saying. In order for me to understand what was said, I had to learn very quickly. That was how I learnt English, by listening. I could understand the language before I could speak it.

It was also around this time that I was made aware that I was an inquisitive child, for Mother complained that if she told me about a person, I would always want to know everything, including what the person's intestines look like.

In 1947, since my sister was a boarder at the Diocesan Girls' School and thrived there, my parents decided that they were going to enroll me as well. My stay didn't last very long. Not only did I have nightmares, I also cried every Sunday afternoon when it was time to go back to school for the week. My parents finally gave up and enrolled me in Grade Three at St. Paul's Co-educational College, which was a day school.

I used to have to fill in forms at school. At first I would write "engineer" under Father's occupation. But then I thought, it couldn't be right, because he seemed to do so many different things, and I knew he didn't make a living being an engineer. I decided to ask him one day what I should put as "father's occupation." He was involved with so many businesses that he took a minute to think, and then said, "Just put director of companies."

In the summer, we used to go swimming in South Bay, using the Lee family's swimming shack for changing. Our car was usually driven by our chauffeur, Ah Muk, but Father liked to drive us to school himself during the week and to swim on the weekends. The summers were so hot and humid that we used to develop boils on our skin, but Father told us that the sea water was very good for our boils. Whenever we went to South Bay, the winding roads reminded me of the rides on top of the Bank of China transport trucks, and invariably, I would be carsick, and Father had to make frequent stops.

One day, while we were swimming in South Bay, Father asked me whether I would like to have our own house in that part of the island, and I was just delighted. However, what worried him was the isolation and the lack of public security during those years in Hong Kong and he changed his mind.

In 1946, I could sense something new was going to happen to our family. In May 1947, my younger brother, Christopher, was born.

Launching as Recreation

Father believed in fresh air and sunshine. In 1947, as soon as he could afford it, he bought a launch, the *Swan*. It was the first of four he owned in his lifetime. The other three were the *Mayflower*, the *Fortuna* and the *Atalanta*. Boating became a part of our lives, and I loved it. On weekends Father would take us out on our launch, and sometimes we would have dinner in one of the floating restaurants in Aberdeen. Later Aberdeen Harbour became so polluted that Father would not permit us to eat in any of the restaurants there.

We never stayed overnight on the launch in the outer islands, because Father said there were pirates around Hong Kong. However, we begged and begged, and one day he agreed. We stayed overnight in the typhoon shelter in Causeway Bay. Our sailors hung a light over the water for us that night, and we caught quite a few cuttlefish to bring back to Mother, who was home with the new baby.

We used to have spectacular sunsets in Hong Kong, particularly in the summer. That was before the Colony became overcrowded, and the atmosphere was full of pollution. I always observed the sunsets when we were on the water and tried to remember the colours and the shapes of the clouds. Because I was very young, often, at the end of a long day on the launch, I would fall asleep before we got home. Father would carry me in and tuck me in bed. The next morning when I got up, I would get out my water-colours and paint the sunset from the night before. My parents loved my paintings and my appreciation of the beauty of nature.

Spending time on the launch was the only recreation Father enjoyed. Some of our best moments were spent on our launch, out on the water, or on one of the off-islands in Hong Kong, away from the hustle and bustle of the city. It was also the time when the whole family was together, often joined by relatives or school friends. My parents rarely used the launch for entertaining, especially when we were young, because it was reserved for the family.

Father was one of the very first people in Hong Kong to own a launch, so we were able to go to many unspoiled beaches. Those were the days when the water was clear, and the beaches were so clean that we could dig clams to bring home to eat. We could observe sea life not normally accessible to city dwellers. I touched a baby octopus, watched a baby sole flapping in shallow water, saw sea-horses swim near our launch, and caught transparent shrimps with a handkerchief. We learnt the names and habits of many sea creatures from our crew, all of whom were *Tankar* people, who lived their whole lives on boats.

Being a public-spirited person, Father would clean the beaches of broken bottles and sharp rocks with the help of our crew. We were never asked to help because he wanted us to have as much time to play as possible. I taught myself to swim in shallow water. Because of my perforated eardrum, my head had to stay above water, in order to avoid an ear infection. I used to love waiting for low tide because that was when I would find interesting sea creatures that were normally under water. Even now, whenever we go to the seashore, I wait for low tide.

Once we docked in a bay where there were many jellyfish. They had claws that looked like chicken claws and poison which was hazardous to people. Father asked the crew to scoop up as many as they could and put them on the beach, where they melted in the sun and turned to water.

In the summer, because of the heat, we always went out in the afternoon for high tea and sometimes for dinner as well, returning to Hong Kong harbour when all the lights were reflected on the water. I can still feel the sea breezes on my face and smell the salty air. Those were special moments that I will always treasure. The harbour is no longer the way it was. Land reclamation has made it narrow and it is crowded with busy boat traffic.

In the winter, we would go out on the launch in the morning and have a picnic lunch. After lunch and a short rest, Father would hike with us on the islands. We saw rather primitive burial plots and jars where descendants collected the bones of their ancestors. We saw fields of sweet potatoes, and crumbling buildings that had been there for hundreds of years when these islands were first inhabited by fishermen, farmers and those who worked in the plantations of fragrant wood which was exported to mainland China. It was fascinating for me to see how the villagers lived. Their lives had not changed for generations, little touched by the progress in Hong Kong. We would always return by late afternoon before it got too cold. Even today, I like going to the off-islands to trek across the hills when we visit in the winter.

Throughout the year, when we were on one of the islands, we would see fishing boats coming back to shore late in the day. Once we were on the beach and a fisherman asked Father whether he wanted to buy some scallops shaped like half-open fans. He then opened one, and to my surprise, there were little pearls in it. The fisherman told us that they scraped these from the bottom of the ocean for the pearls as much as for the flesh of the scallops. I was disappointed Father didn't buy any.

We loved fishing with fishing-lines and often caught many colourful fish. My parents did not participate. We asked our crew many questions about the different types of fish we caught and learned a lot about marine life. At times a fishing boat would come up to our launch to sell fresh fish. From the hold in their boat where we could see many colourful fish swimming, my parents would choose one or two that we would take home to cook for dinner.

By the middle of the 1950s, we had our third launch, *Fortuna*. It was my favourite because it was so big that we were able to have large picnics with our friends and cousins, uncles and aunts. I was the most gregarious of the four children and I always enjoyed these outings. We kept our crew busy looking after us. They would watch over those who were swimming to warn us in case a jellyfish surfaced. Once, a cousin was touched by the yellow tentacles of a blue jellyfish just as he was climbing up the swim ladder. He had to be taken to the hospital immediately.

The Lee Building and the Big House

Out of our living-room window in the Lee Building, we had a beautiful view of the hill and waterfalls. One of the waterfalls flowed into a rock formation that resembled a pool, where in summer, children would swim and play. We were not allowed to go there, but I loved watching them.

We had many different fruit trees in our garden, such as papaya, logan, guava, loquat, mango, wongpei and leichee, all planted by Grandfather. As children, we loved picking fruit off the trees, or in the case of papaya, because the trees were usually too high and too straight to climb, we would knock a ripe papaya off the tree with a stick, and catch it in an old raincoat. We would open it up and eat it right there in the garden. We played on the swing and the slide, we rode our bicycles around the garden, and walked on stilts that Second Uncle had made for us. We caught tadpoles in the fish ponds and the fountains, and we watched the goldfish swim. The older children would play basketball in the basketball court.

Occasionally, we also went to the Big House to see Grandmother, who always looked solemn and always sat in the same chair. We would sometimes have a chat with the Sikh watchman in the guard house, Nam Singh, who would show us the snakes he caught. In the evening, when the servants came looking for us to have our baths, we would hide in the artificial caves Grandfather had built in the garden.

We often dropped in on Second Grandmother and Fourth Grandmother, and visited our uncles and aunts since we all lived so close together. In the Big House, we had our altar to our ancestors, to whom we paid our respect on special occasions. Second Grandmother and Fourth Grandmother had altars to Buddha in their prayer rooms. We were often at Second Grandmother's because she was Father's own mother. I was fascinated by her serenity and her faith. I liked to watch her smoke her water-pipe, making a gurgling sound and blowing puffs of smoke. At a set time every morning and every afternoon, she would go into her prayer room, light the incense, put on her coarse brown prayer robe and kneel in front of the altar to Buddha with her prayer beads in her hands. She would then recite her prayers and move the beads with her fingers as if counting them. She was always so entranced that she wouldn't notice us going in and out making faces behind her back.

Second Grandmother was thankful for what life had given her and I never once heard her complain about anything. She always spoke of Grandfather with great respect, and she would go out of her way to have harmony in the family. She was a small woman with a strong and resilient character which gained her respect in the family. After Grandmother died, Second Grandmother became the matriarch in the Lee family.

On Father's birthday according to the Chinese calendar, Second Grandmother always made a village dish of duck cooked with taro, because that had been Father's favourite childhood dish. She would not let the servants make it, but always made it herself in the old Chinese fashion, cooking it slowly on a stove in the garden with dry straws. After she moved from the Lee Building to Caroline Mansion in the 1950s, she had to do this in a more modern kitchen.

My parents entertained a great deal. With Father's involvement with the Hong Kong government and with business, Mother was kept very busy being a hostess. In 1948 and 1949, Father was Hong Kong's delegate at the 4th and 5th Sessions of the Economic Commission for Asia and the Far East. By the beginning of the 1950s, he was on many government commissions, as well as being a member of the Urban Council. For as long as we lived in the Lee Building, they entertained in the Big House. I remember my parents getting dressed up and walking down through the garden. These were catered parties, but Mother had to supervise the menus, the flowers, the guest lists and the seating. My parents' parties were known to start early and end early. Father was famous for saying, "When the guests leave, the host will regain tranquillity."

Until the beginning of the 1950s, the Big House was the focal point of our lives. All family gatherings, Christmas parties and wedding parties were held in the main hall. The first day of Chinese New Year, we would all put on our padded cheongsams, little gold rings and bracelets, and gather at the Big House to pay our respects to Grandmother. On the second day, wearing the same dresses, we would go over to the Wong Grandparents to pay our respects. Every dress I had as a child was red or pink, because these are good-luck colours for the Chinese. I got so sick of red and pink that it took me almost forty years to wear pink again. I still can't wear red.

The empty apartment below us in the Lee Building was occasionally occupied by my Grandmother Wong when she visited us. Our

Wong Grandparents lived in Kowloon, and crossing the harbour was not so convenient then. One day, when I came home from school, Grandmother Wong had just returned from the Lee Theatre after seeing a war movie starring Errol Flynn. She had a headache and asked one of the servants to get her an ice bag. By the time the servant brought it, she had passed away. She had had a stroke, although she was only in her sixties. It was my first encounter with death in the family. I always remember her as a beautiful and gentle person.

Servants and Hawkers

It was the custom at that time for well-to-do families to have many servants — a cook, a laundry *amah*, a baby *amah*, and one or two servants for general housework, besides gardeners and a chauffeur. Second Grandmother also had a *muitsai* (meaning "little girl") in her household. In China, when a father was poor and had no way of supporting his children, he would give away his young daughter to a wealthy household to become a *muitsai*. In keeping with old Chinese tradition, money was often paid to the parents. Sons were never given away. The household that took in a *muitsai* was supposed to have her as a general helper, and in return, she got her board and lodging, and learned household work. This was not always the case, and there were frequent abuses of the system. When a *muitsai* grew up, it was the duty of the family to marry her off. In my Second Grandmother's case, her *muitsai* was her masseuse, who also performed light household chores.

Even though Father was against the *muitsai* system, he did not interfere until after the war. Then he told his mother that her *muitsai* had to go. Whether Second Grandmother married her off, I really don't know, but I suspect she was sent back home, because I remember her being a rather young girl. In my own home, no one ever worked without pay, so I did not know about this custom. I merely thought the servant was called *muitsai* because she was so young.

One day after school, I met a *muitsai* of friends of my parents who came to our home to say goodbye, because she was to be married to someone in the United States. She was telling Mother about the English lessons she was taking in preparation for the journey. By listening, I began to learn more about the custom of *muitsai*.

Father was always concerned about the well-being of others, and he always had time to help people from all walks of life. What I noticed everyday was his consideration for our servants. Never was there an unkind word. He always helped them to improve their lives, even though it meant that we would lose them from our service.

We had a servant called Ah Nam, who was hired to look after my baby brother, Christopher. One day she was spitting blood and was so distraught she wanted to kill herself. Mother took her to the doctor's and found out that she had tuberculosis. She was hospitalized and went through lengthy treatment which was paid for by Father. She never worked as a servant again, but when she was better, she got married and had a family. When Caroline Mansion was built on Yun Ping Road in the early 1950s, she went to see Father because she wanted to have a small retail business. Father gave her a space, a stairwell that had a lot of walk-by traffic, to sell slippers and magazines. She did well and prospered. She always insisted on giving all of us her merchandise, but because she wouldn't take any money, we told her that we didn't read the type of magazines she sold. She insisted, however, that we could always use slippers, and she would press these into our hands. The last time I saw her was when Mother moved from Tower Court after Father died. Tower Court was just a few steps from Caroline Mansion where Ah Nam had her stand.

After we moved into Embassy Court in 1951, we had a house boy called Ah Mun who Father thought was too smart to remain in that position. Father felt that he should have an education to better himself, so he sent him to night school to learn English, and later to learn drafting. Often, dinner parties were planned around Ah Mun's school examinations. He sometimes had to miss a class if my parents really needed him to help serve. I remember him looking very smart dressed for school in a jacket and tie given to him by Father. Ah Mun sometimes practised his English by reading Mother's recipe books, and he learned to bake a very good orange chiffon cake. Once Ah Mun completed his drafting course, he left our home to seek better employment.

On one of our trips back to Hong Kong in the late 1960s, I met the new cook, Ah Wu. She had been a cleaner at Tower Court, the building we lived in. Father noticed that she was a hard worker, and he offered her a job in our home so that she could learn cooking. Ah Wu stayed with us for many years, and she is like family to me as well as our children. Over the years, Father helped her and her husband buy an apartment so that they would have security. Ah Wu's employment had interruptions because of differences with Mother, but she always came back. In fact, after Father died, and after she retired, out of gratitude to Father, she came back to help Mother near the end of Mother's life. The last time I saw her was at Mother's memorial service in October 1996.

Despite the fact that Father was considered a wealthy man, he never carried more than a few dollars in his pocket. His secretary in the 1970s and early 1980s, Anna, said that it would be a waste of time picking his pocket. This could sometimes be an inconvenience. Anna told me of an incident when Father saw a street hawker in front of one of our office buildings, One Hysan Avenue. He wanted to buy some pears from the man but didn't have enough money on him, so he went upstairs to his office, and asked Anna to buy some for him. Anna sent an office boy, who said to the hawker, "The big boss, Mr. Lee, sends me." The hawker, frightened because he should not have been selling there, said, "I'm leaving right away." When the office boy assured him that Mr. Lee only wanted to buy some pears, the hawker immediately offered them for free. It was Father's policy never to accept anything for free, so the office boy paid ten dollars. But instead of the usual eight pears for ten dollars, the hawker gave him twenty pears.[1] Father, totally unaware of the price of pears, thought it a good deal.

Embassy Court

By the beginning of the 1950s, all the refugee families who stayed with us in the Lee Building had gone their own way, and my parents were planning our new home in Embassy Court, on Hysan Avenue, which was the first high-rise owned by the Lee family.

I still remember the architectural plans Father brought home. These were drawings of the two-level penthouse we were going to live in, with the entire roof as our garden. Mother was very much involved in the planning and the decor. My parents would spend time in the side streets of Hong Kong looking for interesting artifacts and antiques. It was an exciting time for them. From then on, they would be able to entertain at home instead of in the Big House.

The building was designed with large water-storage tanks on the roof, so that when water was available, it would be piped to the tanks first in order that no one in the building would suffer from the lack of water pressure. This type of design continued with our subsequent buildings. I was aware of Father's concern, not only for us, but for all the tenants. Father had always been proud of all our buildings because they were so well built that they would never budge when typhoons hit Hong Kong, unlike many other high-rises that used to collapse with high winds or torrential rains.

After we moved to Embassy Court, Father continued to drive us to school every morning. Being a practical person, he liked to give rides to as many students as possible. A friend of mine, Miranda, who lived near us, always got a ride just outside her home. The next person we picked up was Ah Woon, who would be waiting for us outside the Big House. The daughter of Grandmother's cook, she was a student at Sacred Heart School.

My life changed dramatically after our move. I not only lost the garden to play in, I actually became a serious student. Like most students in Hong Kong, I had a tutor. Miss Chan would come after school and teach me mathematics. I had a system worked out to get a high average. It was almost impossible to get a grade higher than 80 per cent in any subject except mathematics, because of the way examinations were marked. So the only way was to try to get a 100 per cent in all three mathematics subjects.

The first year I entered secondary school I came first in a class of forty students. Actually I think Miss Chan should have been given the credit. When Mother heard the news from my principal, Miss Bobby Kotewall, she was so excited she couldn't sleep. It was generally known that St. Paul's Co-educational College had high academic standards, and to come first was extremely difficult. One of my teachers said to me the following year, "For someone with your family background, I don't understand why you work so hard!" People have been saying that to me ever since.

My parents were so pleased that they gave a luncheon for all my teachers. Subsequently, my art teacher presented my parents with a large Chinese painting he had done of peach blossoms, which complemented the pale blue colour of our dining room. This painting was treasured by my parents and remained hanging in their dining room until Mother passed away.

Once we moved into Embassy Court, I started Chinese painting lessons with a well-known artist, Boa Siu Yao, who lived not far from us. I used to walk there after school, and during the summer, I went every morning. I also took piano lessons and singing lessons. The singing lessons only lasted about a year because I soon found out that my voice was not very strong, even though I love singing. Painting was still my favourite extracurricular activity. I was kept so busy in my early teens that I wasn't even interested in going out. I had a painting table in my bedroom, quite separate from my desk so that my paints and paper never had to be put away. In the 1970s Father came across some of my paintings and sent them to me in Toronto.

The first couple of years after we moved into Embassy Court, Richard and I used to ride our bicycles to the South China Stadium after school or on weekends to fly kites. I think I was able to fly a kite properly only once and found it frustrating. In late summer we made nets to catch huge dragonflies in the partially flattened ground of The Lee Gardens right opposite us. One Chinese New Year, Richard put firecrackers in glass bottles that exploded like bombs.

In order for the Lee family to develop the land at The Lee Gardens, the hill had to be levelled. During the few years we lived in Embassy Court, I saw the hill situated on the other side of Hysan Avenue removed right before my eyes. Day after day, the hill became lower. I saw men and women carrying heavy loads of rocks and soil from the hill to the trucks, which were then driven to a dump site. Occasionally, I would hear dynamite going off to break up the rocks. During that process, beautiful rock crystals were found. Father treasured these, and had carved wood stands made for some of the large pieces. He kept some himself and gave some away.

Many interesting events occurred during the excavation of The Lee Gardens. A Goddess of Mercy or Guanyin statue was found buried in the hill. It was said that anyone who dared to remove it would become ill. Work was halted and monks and nuns were brought to the site to chant and pray. It was decided that they were the only people who could remove the Goddess of Mercy. An auspicious date was set, and with all the proper respect paid to the Goddess, the statue was removed ceremoniously to be housed in one of the Buddhist temples in the New Territories. Work on the levelling of the hill was then resumed.

During the excavation, a large iron bell was unearthed, dating back to over two hundred years. It had been donated by the Lo family to a temple on the hill in gratitude for their good fortune. "Favourable weather" was inscribed on the bell, referring to the Lo family as farmers. This was a treasure Father was very proud of. He had a beautiful large carved wood frame made to hold this bell which weighed tons. It became his prized show-piece in our living room.

Living in Embassy Court meant that I got to see how my parents entertained. The upper level of the penthouse was for entertaining, and the bedrooms were all downstairs. Whenever my parents entertained, they always had a Chinese restaurant do the catering. Catering in those days meant moving all the equipment to our entertaining kitchen upstairs (for everyday, our cook used the kitchen downstairs), and everything would be cooked there. After school, I liked to see what type of food was being served. If winter melon soup was to be one of the courses on the menu, the vegetables in it would be cut in the most beautiful stylized forms of birds, butterflies or fish. I would also check Mother's floral decorations and decide which one I was going to paint the next day. Just before I went to bed, I would look at the party from behind the Chinese screen. I loved the glitter of the silver candelabras and the crystal, the flickering candlelight and the sound of talk and laughter. Mother always used the most beautiful Chinese crocheted tablecloths with matching napkins. If the party was Chinese style, there would be three tables of eight. If it was a

European-style dinner (Chinese food served European style), it would be a long table of twenty-four. Only Chinese food was ever served in our home; my parents' Jewish friends, who could only eat Kosher food, always ate dinner at home before coming to our parties.

During these years I often saw Uncle Quo Wai (Q.W. Lee) and his wife, Aunt Helen, at my parents' parties. Uncle Quo Wai is Father's cousin who worked at the Hang Seng Bank. Father had high regard for this cousin whom he believed had great potential, so he wanted to introduce him to as many of his friends as possible. Today, Uncle Quo Wai is Sir Q.W. Lee, a prominent Hong Kong citizen. In addition to holding many other titles, he is the chairman of the Hang Seng Bank.

Father's habits became well known to everyone. Besides never going to the movies, he never danced, to Mother's dismay. He wouldn't agree to be on any company board if he had to socialize with movie stars. He never gambled, and mahjong playing was not allowed in our house. Mother had one mahjong game a year on her birthday, when she played with her siblings. Father loved his work, and his only form of relaxation was going out on the launch on Sundays, enjoying nature.

There was a story about father being invited to the opening of the May Flower, a dance hall owned by a business friend of his. Father abhorred places of that sort and was not going to attend, but Granduncle Lee Shu Yuen persuaded him to go with him. The dance hall was on the second floor of a building and could only be reached by an escalator. Apparently Father went up the escalator, turned around and came back down, and considered that as having attended the opening.[2]

After we moved into Embassy Court, the yearly Christmas party would be held at our home. It was a party for close relatives only, and they always numbered over a hundred. There were presents for each child and adolescent, and a raffle of a few gifts for the adults. I liked getting involved in planning the presents, which included a large number of Japanese toys.

For Christmas 1953 we did not have a party. Instead, my parents took Christopher and me to Bangkok, Thailand. We were invited by Father's friend, the "rice king" Ma Lushen, to travel on one of his merchant ships returning from Hong Kong to Bangkok. It was my first cruise and it was a wonderful experience. We had private cabins, and dined with the Danish captain and his officers. It was exhilarating to see flying fish sail through the air along the side of the ship.

Early one morning, Father called us up on deck so that we could watch as the ship entered the estuary towards Bangkok. The sun was just about to rise, and we saw jungle on both sides. As we approached the city, we saw the silhouettes of temples backlit by an orange sky. Then a red ball rose from behind the temples. It was absolute magic!

We stayed in the Oriental Hotel where we dined outside by the river, with mosquito coils burning on the tables. That was before the hotel was renovated and the dining room became enclosed. We were invited by the Ma family a few times to their home and to restaurants.

During our visit I learned that the young men in Thailand, at the age of eighteen, had to go either into national military service or to a monastery to become a monk for a number of years. It was a wise policy because it recognized that not all men are warlike.

We were invited to the American Embassy in Bangkok to see *This Is Cinerama*, the first seventy-mm, three-projector, three curved-screen movie. My parents also took us to see orchid farms and rice fields and we went on a river cruise to see how the local Thai people lived.

At the end of our stay in Bangkok, Father thought we were all having such a good time that he wanted to extend the holiday and to take us to Singapore. I objected, because examinations would begin the moment school started in January, and I needed to go home to study. My father accepted my reason and we all returned to Hong Kong.

7

Towards Racial Harmony: The Hong Kong Country Club

Back in 1927, when Father returned from England at the age of twenty-two, he wanted to join the Hong Kong Club, which used to be called the Hong Kong British Club until the end of the nineteenth century. He was turned down because he was Chinese. He never forgot this refusal. Later, when he was asked to join, he declined the offer. As I grew older, I came to understand his feelings.

One day after school in the 1950s, I was introduced to two visitors, Governor Sir Alexander and Lady Grantham. Lady Grantham was a friendly American who told me that I looked just like Father. Before they left, they came into my room to say goodbye, and Lady Grantham said to me that I looked just like Mother. Then she said, "Now, what am I saying? I guess you look like both your parents." After they left, Father said, "Don't mention this visit to anyone in school. The governor is not supposed to be a guest in a Chinese home." I wondered about the fact that we were, in effect, second-class citizens, in a place we called home.

A Multi-Racial Club

Soon after the war, Father and some of his friends came together to discuss forming a multi-racial family social club in Hong Kong. Historically, and well into the 1960s, access to social clubs in Hong Kong was restricted by one's race, nationality or religion. The Hong Kong Club, the Chinese Club, the Jewish Recreational Club, the Club Lusitano for Portuguese, the German Club and the American Club kept the different races separate. The exceptions were the cosmopolitan clubs that only catered to sports or special interests.

The formation of a multi-racial club was the work of Father and his friends over a period of fifteen years. In the forefront were Father, his close friend, J. R. Jones, legal advisor to the Hong Kong and Shanghai Bank, and D.F. Landale, the taipan of Jardine Matheson. Landale, who had unsuccessfully campaigned for the Chinese to be admitted to both the Hong Kong Club and the Shek-O Country Club in the late 1940s, provided two hundred dollars to cover the initial expenses of this club.[1] Landale retired in 1956, and his successor, Hugh D.M. Barton, assumed an active role in the formation of the club.

In 1947, Father and J. R. Jones submitted the original plan for the interracial club to D.M. MacDougall, the Colonial Secretary. The government was receptive to the idea of a multi-racial club. The site on Brick Hill was chosen because it was easily accessible to the residents of Hong Kong. A group that included Father, D.M. MacDougall and Sir Arthur Morse, Chief Manager of the Hong Kong and Shanghai Banking Corporation, who had been so helpful to Father when Grandfather died, held informal talks. The group estimated that $1.5 million was required to build the club. J.R. Jones sent letters to various consular representatives, heads of banks and representatives of different nationalities, setting out the broad outline of the scheme of the club.

The planning went smoothly with the informal committee, and in June 1948, a meeting was held in the boardroom of the Hong Kong and Shanghai Bank to discuss the offer from the government. The government agreed to lease approximately 7.5 acres fronting the sea to the club at an annual rent of $7,200 for twenty-one years.

A general meeting was called in April 1949. Some of the original members of the informal committee had either left Hong Kong or were on leave, and the composition of the membership changed. At this meeting, the original name of the International Club was replaced by the name Hong Kong Country Club. It was interesting to note that of the fifty-six representatives from the various national communities in the Colony, only two Chinese attended, Father and M.W. Lo. The two confirmed the interest of the Chinese to join once the club was formed. Three sub-committees were formed — Legal, Financial and Building. The Financial Committee, working through a wider Appeal Committee, was able to obtain a total pledge of $2 million from companies and individuals.

Negotiations with the government continued through 1949, although the formation of the People's Republic of China by the Chinese Communists caused a general feeling of uncertainty in the colony. In 1950, when war broke out in Korea and the United Nations imposed an embargo on shipments from Hong Kong, the committee decided to postpone the development of the club.

In May 1951, the committee wrote to the government, requesting that the site for the club be reserved pending a more favourable outlook. By this time, D.M. MacDougall was no longer the Colonial Secretary, and the government advised the committee that the offer of the site could not remain open indefinitely, and that if other applications for the site were received, an auction would have to be held. This was an unexpected ultimatum. A legation consisting of Father, J.R. Jones, M.W. Lo and G. L. Wilson called on the Colonial Secretary, R.J. Nicoll, and an agreement was reached to reserve the site until January 1952. Thereafter, J.R. Jones would report orally to the government every six months. In the meantime, everything was on hold.

Up to the end of the 1950s, the plans for the Hong Kong Country Club remained unchanged. By May 1958, the acting Colonial Secretary, E.B. Teesdale, again warned that the site would not be reserved indefinitely. The government wanted a concrete proposal as evidence of a firm commitment from the sponsors to build the club. Unfortunately, at this time, the reaction from the sponsors was discouraging, and it looked as though the club would not be established.

In January 1959, the government gave the committee a deadline of April 1 for the receipt of a concrete proposal. This called for definite action, so Father and J.R. Jones called on two old friends, Sidney Gordon, an accountant with Lowe, Bingham and Matthews, and Y.K. Kan, a lawyer with Lo and Lo, to discuss whether the building of the club was viable. At this meeting, it was agreed that renewed effort should be put into building a club, particularly since so many refugees had arrived from China, and there was a great need for club facilities. J. R. Jones promptly called together as many former members as possible, and a new committee of ten members was formed. Since Jones was fully occupied with the Government Salaries Commission, Hugh Barton agreed to be the convenor, with Third Uncle as secretary.

In May 1959, a General Organizing Committee was formed consisting of five Chinese representatives, three Britons, two Americans, and one representative each from the Portuguese, Dutch, French, Scandinavian, Swiss and Italian communities. A legation consisting of Hugh Barton, J.R. Jones and Father called on the governor to seek his support. The government confirmed its willingness to lease about 5.25 acres at the Brick Hill site to the club at an annual ground rent of $10 per acre, with a building covenant of $1 million. Having secured the land, the committee decided to raise the necessary financing by issuing debentures at $5,000 each. By February 1960, sufficient funds were pledged. By December, when the club was incorporated, 420 interest-free debentures had been issued, and the subscribers were accepted as the first members of the club. From then on, good progress was made under the supervision of architect Eric Cumine, a friend of the Lee family.

In 1962, Father's dream of a multi-racial club for Hong Kong was a reality. Even though the construction was not quite completed, January 29 was picked for the official opening, since it was thought that the Year of the Ox would be a more propitious year for the club opening than the Year of the Tiger. The Hong Kong

Country Club was opened by Chief Justice, Sir Michael Hogan. He said that it was to be:

> a place where all nationalities and communities can meet and relax in the pleasant, easy, companionable atmosphere that one is accustomed to find in a club ... Ideas can be interchanged, views expressed and arguments deployed in an atmosphere conducive to goodwill ... I am sure that it will contribute to the future strength and stability of Hong Kong.[2]

Construction was completed in February, and the club opened its doors to members. In September, Jerry O'Donnell, a member of the first General Committee, proposed a fashion show for the members to view twenty of the latest fashions from eight cities from around the world. Mother and Mrs. Hugh Barton were invited to organize a Ladies' Committee to promote the show, and this became the first Entertainments Committee of the Hong Kong Country Club.[3]

Towards Racial Harmony

Father always believed that there should be harmony among all races. The Hong Kong Country Club was unique because of the membership structure which was an integral part of the club's philosophy, written into its Articles of Association. Admission to both ordinary and junior members would be according to a national quota system in order to maintain the truly international character of the Club: 10 per cent American, 20 per cent English, 50 per cent Chinese, and 20 per cent all other nationalities. However, due to anti-Japanese feelings which still existed in Hong Kong at that time, a special quota had to be created within the last group in order to maintain a truly multi-national character.[4] The chairman of the Club was elected yearly. The first chairman was the Hon. Hugh Barton, and Father followed for the term of 1963–1964.

In 1965, J.R. Jones, Hugh Barton and Father were nominated as honorary life members. The membership was extended to Mother after Father died. The then chairman, Q.W. Lee (Uncle Quo Wai), in bestowing the honour on J.R. Jones, cited:

> the invaluable work that Dr. J.R. Jones had done for the Club ... It can be said that, without Dr. Jones' pervasive and persuasive enthusiasm, it is very doubtful that we would have an international club at all.

J.R. Jones, in turn, said of Father that he had:

> worked in close co-operation with myself and was on the original Building Committee of the Club. Richard also worked very hard to get the Club on a sound footing and bring the venture to the successful conclusion that we see today.[5]

Since its opening, the Hong Kong Country Club has become a big part of social life for families in Hong Kong. The club was Father's pride and joy, despite the fact that during its first fifteen years, it struggled to be financially profitable. We had many wonderful lunches and dinners there (the dining rooms serve both Chinese and Western foods). Our children have spent many happy hours at the club during our visits to Hong Kong. We love the congenial and unostentatious atmosphere and it has become a second home for us as well as for many others in Hong Kong.

One Christmas, when we were in Hong Kong, our son Ashley, at the age of three, asked why there was a Santa Claus in Toronto and one in the Hong Kong Country Club, and why the latter had a female voice! Another year, the March break of our children's school happened to coincide with Easter. Our boys will never forget the fun they had at the Easter party with the magic show and egg hunt at the Club.

In the 1970s, when corporate nominee memberships were introduced, the Club became financially profitable, and it earned enough to embark on a complete renovation and beautification program. The understated and congenial atmosphere, the sports facilities, the swimming pools, the children's playground and the children's programs, the restaurants for casual and formal dining and the adult social programs made it popular, even though new clubs were being started in Hong Kong at the time. With the help of professional management, the Club blossomed. By the 1980s, companies were lining up to pay $1 million for a corporate nominee membership. Father was a happy man.

Swimming at the Club

Father was well known for his early morning swim at the Hong Kong Country Club. He would usually arrive around five o'clock, and the pool would be opened especially for him. Whenever we were home visiting, he would return after his swim in time to have breakfast with us. Even with that kind of schedule, he was still the first person to arrive at the office in the morning.

One morning, on his way to swim, Father was stopped by a policeman for a routine check. He was asked to show his I.D. card, which everyone in Hong Kong was supposed to have. Father had never bothered to get one because most people knew Father by sight. I'm sure if he had been chauffeured in an expensive car instead of driving himself in a Volkswagen Golf, he'd never have been stopped. When he returned to the office that morning, he told his secretary about the incident, and asked her to get him a card right away. Although I.D. cards had to be obtained personally, an exception was made for Father.

During the years when he drove to go swimming at the Country Club, he used to pick up poor schoolchildren from the area who had to walk to school along his route. He got to know a number of them, and their parents as well. One morning, one of the children he usually drove was not there. The child's father was waiting for him instead and he begged Father to help his sick wife. Father took them to the hospital, and saw that she was cared for.

In 1972, when Hong Kong Land wished to take over Dairy Farm, Father was asked to help. Dairy Farm's chairman and major shareholder was Sir S.N. Chau, a good friend of Father's. Hong Kong Land chairman Henry Keswick, nephew of Father's old friend, John Keswick, former head of the Jardine Group, came looking for Father. Since it was very difficult to get an appointment to see Father in his office, Henry Keswick decided to go early in the morning to the Country Club to catch Father while he was swimming. He followed Father along the edge of the pool as he swam back and forth, and tried to convince him to assist. His persistence paid off, and the takeover was successful. Hong Kong Land Company Ltd. and Dairy Farm, Ice & Cold Storage Company Limited merged in December 1972.[6] After that, everyone teased Henry Keswick about how nice it was of his Uncle Dick to help him take over Dairy Farm.[7]

8

The Lee Family: Business Projects

Rebuilding the family business after the war was a slow process. To start with, many of our property records had been lost. Father's first secretary after the war, Violet Kong (who later married one of Father's cousins and became Aunt Violet), used to follow Father to the Land Registry Office to look for the original records. Father's Eighth Uncle (a cousin of Grandfather's) worked there and was able to help. However, the work was complicated by the fact that the properties had been registered under different names by Grandfather when he purchased them. Some were under Grandmother's name, others under the names of Lee Hysan Estate Company or Lee Cheuk Yu Tong, the latter is the collective name representing all of Grandfather's descendants.[1]

Many of our properties were in bad condition because of the war. Some of the older buildings were so out-dated that they did not even have flush toilets. After the war, landlords were not allowed to raise rents above prewar levels, so most landlords could not afford to repair or upgrade their buildings; some could barely cover their taxes. Some of our old apartments had rented for as little as twenty dollars a month before the war. Moreover, during the Japanese occupation, some old tenants had gone to China, and others had moved into the empty apartments. There was a prevalence of multiple occupancy and multi-layered subletting that further complicated matters. It was difficult to establish who the legal tenants were.[2]

Those who profited from this situation were tenants who paid prewar rents and sublet their apartments at current rates. Businesses that occupied older premises benefited from the 10 to 12 per cent rise in prices of products which, unlike rents, were not controlled.

The problem of what to do with the prewar buildings was not solved until the mid 1950s. On March 19, 1956, Father was elected Chairman of the Hong Kong Association of Property Owners. Since the Lee family owned a lot of prewar properties, he was able to speak out for landlords in the same predicament. Father appealed to the government to allow rent increases that would be fair to both tenants and landlords.[3]

Our family company, Lee Hysan Estate Company, moved into an old building, Alexander House, in 1946. It was put under the management of Tsui Gang Bo, who later became Uncle Tsui to us. I particularly remember the creaky floors in the building. Throughout their lives, the Lee brothers had their offices together. Sometimes after school, I would go there to wait for Father to go home, and one of my favourite pastimes was to play with the typewriter. Cousin Hon Chiu remembers how impressed he was that Third Uncle had a window unit air-conditioner in his own office, which was considered very progressive right after the war.

There were two rental offices. One office, Lee Cheuk Yu Tong, collected rent from properties belonging to Grandmother. The other, Lee Doong, collected rent for Lee Hysan Estate Company.[4] As cousin Peter Lee told me, everything in the family company was done in the old-fashioned way for years after the war, agreements and decisions were by word of mouth or recorded on bits of paper that have since been lost. Peter, a lawyer and a director, has been general manager of the family company since the early 1980s. He has tried very hard to look for past company documents, such as land title deeds or company meeting minutes or contracts for our buildings, but with little success.[5]

At the beginning of the 1970s, the Lee brothers decided to abandon their conservative approach to business.[6] Through his friend the Hon.

J.D. Clague, Father was introduced to Chan Tak Tai, a developer who had been very successful in the development of the Chungking (Chongqing) Mansion in Kowloon. Chan suggested to Father that the family form joint ventures in developing two buildings in the Causeway Bay area, One Hysan Avenue and Leighton Centre, with Lee Hysan Estate putting up the land, and investors putting up the capital. Chan himself invested a small percentage.[7] In 1970, a private company, Hennessy Development Co. Ltd., was incorporated.

Up to that point, all our postwar buildings had been wholly owned by the family company and built by Lam Woo Construction because of the friendship between the two families. From the beginning of the 1970s on, building plans were sent out for tender. The new approach also demanded fresh blood in the family business. The first person the Lee brothers turned to was the eldest grandson, Hon Chiu. In 1976, while Hon Chiu was working for the Radio Corporation of America (RCA) in the United States, Fourth Uncle asked him to return to Hong Kong to help. Hon Chiu was in his forties with a growing family. He agreed to return to Hong Kong, but his wife, Doris, stayed on in the States so that their children could continue their education without interruption.

The Lee Theatre

The Lee Theatre was back in operation by 1946. International Entertainment was again under general manager Yuen Yaohong and manager Dong Zi Jun. At the end of the war, C.T. Wu was still working with the Overseas Union Bank of Singapore and was about to be sent to the branch in Shanghai, but Father convinced him that he would have a better future with us. So he came back to Hong Kong and became the house manager of the Lee Theatre. The theatre was renovated and a high quality screen, good lighting and comfortable seats were installed.[8]

There was no television in those days, and it was a treat for all the Lee children to go on Sunday mornings to the Lee Theatre to see cartoons and the Three Stooges. Box B, the best box in the theatre, was reserved for the family. We seldom went to other theatres because the

Lee Theatre showed some of the best movies in town. I sometimes went to see American feature films with other family members, but until I was able to understand enough English, they were not very meaningful, except for Tarzan and cowboy movies. Cantonese movies gradually gained popularity, but they were all sad. Most of them were about suffering in the last war. I stopped going to those because I didn't believe in crying when I wanted to be entertained. By then, I had noticed that Father never went to movies. He was much more interested in working.

In 1948, International Entertainment was asked to be the distributor in China for the London Film Company. Armed with four blockbusters which had been shown at the Lee Theatre with overwhelming success — *The Thief of Bagdad, Lady Hamilton, The Four Feathers* and *Elephant Boy* — general manager Yuen Yaohong and house manager C.T. Wu went to Shanghai, but the response was very disappointing. The theatres in Shanghai did not seem to know how popular these movies were in the rest of the world. The two men didn't even make enough money on that trip to cover their expenses.[9] However, while they were there, they made some important contacts with producer Xia Yunhu and director Cai Chusheng, who wanted to establish good relations with the Lee family, and subsequently sent the films *Yi Jiang Chun Shui Xiang Dong Liu (A River of Spring Water Flowing to the East)* and *Ba Qian Li Lu Yun He Yue (Eight Thousand Miles of Cloud and Moon)* to be shown in the Lee Theatre. These very sad movies, which depicted the life of the Chinese during the war and were critical of the actions of the Nationalist government in China, became great hits in Hong Kong. Despite their sympathy towards the Communists, both producer and director were later killed during the Cultural Revolution.[10]

Not long after Yuen and Wu left, Shanghai was liberated by the Communists.

The performance of Chinese operas in the Lee Theatre was on the decline, despite the fact that, from the mid-1950s to the mid-1960s, the most celebrated performances in Cantonese opera from the innovative Sin Fung Ming Company, which was very highly regarded by both the community and local government, were held there. At the same time, the Lee Theatre became a favourite venue for stage performances from different parts of the world. I especially loved Xavier Cougat and Abby Lane and their troop of Latin American dancers. The theatre also presented magic shows, and later, international beauty contests. In the early 1970s, after the Lee Gardens Hotel was built, the beauty contestants were always housed there. Mother's sisters used to love to go to The Lee Gardens to see the beauty contestants. At the end of the 1980s, Fourth Uncle and I were passing the Lee Theatre one day, and he told me about the International Chinese Beauty Contest that had taken place in the theatre that year. He said, "One of the contestants was from Scarborough, Ontario," and I told him that I had been one of the judges in the competition held by the Scarborough Chinese Business Association which chose that particular contestant.

The accountant for International Entertainment was Grandfather Wong who worked until he was over eighty years old. Father kept him in that position just so that he would have something to do. He was pampered whenever he was in the office. He remained very bright into his late eighties and he died at the age of ninety-two.[11]

Property Development

The perennial problem facing building developers in Hong Kong was the lack of flat land. It was the same with the Lee family. If we wanted to erect more buildings, we had to level the Lee Gardens hill and obtain dumping rights from the government. Before the Second World War, a small part of the Lee Gardens hill had been levelled and the soil moved to North Point for landfill. We then purchased that piece of land from the government and built two factories, a nail factory and a paint factory called Duro Paint. The nail factory was subsequently sold to another Chinese manufacturer. Duro Paint was sold to Swire[12] in 1948, and Duro Paint Holding Co.[13] was formed. The Lee Hysan Estate Company was given shares in lieu of payment, resulting in the family being one of the largest shareholders of Swire. This was the beginning of a long and meaningful relationship between the family and the Swire Group. Fourth Uncle was a director of Swire Industries, and Third Uncle became a director of Cathay Pacific (owned by Swire Pacific).[14]

The first postwar real-estate development by Lee Hysan Estate Company was the further levelling of the Lee Gardens hill. The Hong Kong government gave permission for dumping in Chai Wan and Aberdeen. Opening up the area also meant building roads. Hysan Avenue, named after Grandfather, became the main avenue; Lan Fong Road, named after Grandmother, was the one behind it. Other streets were named Sunning, Sunwui, Hoiping and Yunping, after the Szeyup counties in China which formed the nucleus of our ancestral and neighbouring villages. Pak Sar Road was named after Chan Pak Sar (Chen Buosha), a famous scholar in the Ming Dynasty from Sunwui, our ancestral village, and Kai Chiu Road was named after Liang Kai Chiu (Liang Qichao), another famous scholar at the beginning of this century from Sunwui. And of course, there had to be a Lee Gardens Road. These were all private roads that were subsequently turned over to the government.

One day in the 1950s, after we moved from the Lee Building to Embassy Court on Hysan Avenue, Father was driving me to school. As he was making a turn from Hoiping Road to Hysan Avenue, a man was taking his time crossing the road. Father, being very impatient, said to him, "Hurry up!" The man said, "I can take as long as I want. It's not your road." To which Father replied, "It *is* my road!"

In order to finance new buildings, the family sold some of our very old row-houses and apartments. The first postwar apartment building put up by the family company was Sunning Court, on the south side of Hysan Avenue. Sunning Court was the first building in Hong Kong that sold apartments outright.[15] It was built in a U-shape, with the bottom of the U facing Hysan Avenue. The part of the building with the frontage on Hysan Avenue was sold to Kwong Lee Enterprises, a company owned jointly by Lee Hysan Estate Co. and Shanghai Commercial Bank. It ran a small hotel called Sunning House, with fifty-two rooms. Father was the chairman of Kwong Lee, and its directors were Third Uncle, Tsui Gang Bo, Zhu Rutang and Wang Changlin of the Shanghai Commercial Bank.[16]

Sunning House opened for business in 1949 with C.T. Wu as manager. The Communist takeover of China had made it into an instant success. The connection with the Shanghai Commercial Bank helped bring many of the important Shanghai industrialists who came down to Hong Kong to stay there.[17] It became a landmark and its Champagne Room was the hottest spot in Hong Kong throughout the 1950s. There, guests could dine elegantly and dance to the beautiful music of the Three Bubbles, which was carried on Rediffusion[18] every Wednesday night. Guests had to be well dressed to be admitted into the Champagne Room, and gentlemen had to wear ties. I remember a humorous write-up in the newspaper in the mid 1950s about a minister of the church wearing a Roman collar, who was not allowed in because he was not wearing a tie. The Champagne Room was patronized by visiting movie stars, such as Hedy Lamarr, Clark Gable, Ava Gardner, William Holden and Rita Hayworth. A popular night spot for locals and for visitors, it was said that if you had not been to the Champagne Room, you had not been to Hong Kong.[19]

The next major project of the Lee family was Embassy Court on Hysan Avenue. It was the first high-rise owned by the family. When it was completed, my family, Fifth Uncle and his family and Third Grandmother moved into the building. Following that was the building of Caroline Mansion, at the intersection of Hysan Avenue and Yunping Road. When that was completed, the rest of the Lees who had been living in the Lee Building moved in.

The Lee Building was rented to outsiders, as it had been in Grandfather's day. It was an unwritten tradition in the Lee family that every member of Grandfather's family — wife, concubines and children — had free accommodation in family-owned buildings, and everyone got to choose where they wanted to live. Because of this tradition, family members tended to live very close to one another. This tradition does not extend to my generation.

In 1954, the Lee family built two more high-rise buildings, Tower Court and Caroline Mansion, just a few steps away from Embassy Court. On the weekends, whenever we were not on our launch, Father would go to check the new buildings. He would walk all the way to the top to see that the workers were doing their jobs properly.

My favourite haunts in the 1950s were the Lee Theatre, the Champagne Room in Sunning House and the soft drinks factory of Spa Foods Company Limited, also owned by the Lee family after the war. As children, we used to visit Spa and watch the bottling process with fascination. We could naturally drink whatever we wanted. The best seller at the time was the grape drink,[20] but my favourite was the red drink which I thought was cherry, but was really only coloured sugar water.

In 1953, Seventh Uncle came back to Hong Kong after graduating from Boston University. Together with Third Uncle, he bought the majority shares from Spa and formed the General Bottling Company. From then on, the Lee Hysan Estate Company only had a nominal share in Spa. In 1955, General Bottling secured the franchise for Schweppes, and a year later, the franchise for 7-Up, and subsequently a Japanese beer. The children in the family continued to be welcome to visit the factory, and any soft drink that we wanted would be delivered to our homes. Seventh Uncle became very successful. He used to ride in the delivery trucks (in American style) to the chagrin of the locals.[21] I still remember trucks driving up to St. Paul's Co-educational College during recess and handing out free 7-Up. A brilliant marketing ploy. Seventh Uncle named 7-Up as Seven Happinesses in Chinese. Because of its lucky name, 7-Up was served at all Chinese celebrations.

The Lee Gardens Hotel

By the late 1950s, the Lee Gardens hill was completely flattened. One of the people from our village in China, who was using part of the land for keeping honeybees, was worried that once the land was built on, he would have nowhere to keep his bees, and he went to the Lee brothers to express his concern. He was allowed to carry on his business on a piece of land in Sha Tin which was in the name of Lee Shiu Yuen, Grandfather's young cousin.[22]

The development of the first phase of what was later known as the Lee Gardens Hotel began in 1964. The original plan was to build a residential complex with an office podium. The office portion, consisting of the first six floors, was built and rented mainly to the Medical and Education Departments of the Hong Kong government. The ground floor was let to commercial establishments. However, construction of the residential component was stopped, because of the Cultural Revolution in China and the subsequent 1967 riots in Hong Kong. At the end of the 1960s, with the completion of the Cross Harbour tunnel whose exit was nearby, and because of the shortage of hotel rooms in Hong Kong at the time, the family decided that a hotel should be built. A nine-hundred-room hotel above the podium was completed at the end of 1971.[23]

The Lee Gardens Hotel was a private company, with Lee Hysan Estate Company as the major shareholder. Some of the other shareholders were Swire Pacific, Hong Kong Bank, Hong Kong Land, Tai Cheung Development and A.P. Møller. Swire chairman H.J.C. Browne was invited to be the first chairman of the Lee Gardens Hotel Company.[24] He was followed by Third Uncle. After the sudden death of Third Uncle, Father became chairman. Father was involved in the hotel right from the beginning as a director. Through his personal connections with China the original carpets for the hotel lobby were custom-ordered from Tianjin. Because of Father's connection with the Japanese community, tour groups from Japan always stayed at our hotel.

At the time, the Lee Gardens Hotel was one of the few locally managed hotels of international standard. It was initially associated with Forum Hotels, a division of Intercontinental.[25] Over the years, the hotel became the favourite of Asian tourists due to its location in Causeway Bay. The hotel once again put the name Lee Gardens on the map of Hong Kong.

As Mother was getting on in years, it became too much work for her to entertain at home, so when the hotel opened, my parents entertained almost exclusively there.

There were different restaurants in the Lee Gardens Hotel, but my parents' favourite was the Chinese restaurant, the Rainbow Room. When they had parties, they would usually reserve a private room (with a round table seating twenty-four guests), or take over the entire restaurant. My parents were very proud of the standard of the cuisine there, and Father always said that the Peking Duck was number one in Hong Kong, and better than in Beijing. He liked to point out to guests any special dishes introduced from mainland China. Friends from all over the world were invited to the Lee Gardens Rainbow Room.

With the completion of the Lee Gardens Hotel, the entire area of what was the Lee Gardens was developed. Along Hysan Avenue was planted a row of Bauhinia, which is now the symbol of the Hong Kong Special Administrative Region. Trees with yellow flowers were planted on the side roads, which were named after ancestral villages. Father showed them to me with pride, not only because they were usually in bloom when we visited in the winter, but also because he had them specially brought in from south China.

Father and Hon Chiu

When Hon Chiu returned to Hong Kong, the family company had just moved into its premises in the newly completed office building, One Hysan Avenue. Hon Chiu was able to learn how to manage an office building. Although Third Uncle wanted Hon Chiu to keep an eye on the staff on the twenty-second floor, Father gave him an office on the twenty-first floor with all the uncles, a corner office overlooking the construction of Leighton Centre.[26] Father gave him the responsibility of overseeing the actual construction of the building, taking over the responsibility Father used to impose on himself during the construction of our former buildings.

Hon Chiu had coffee with Father every day and gave his report, which "must not be longer than fifteen minutes." Father was an impatient man. He needed to know about progress, and if Hon Chiu ran into any difficulty, Father could usually solve it for him within half an hour because of his extensive connections.[27] Father also suggested that Hon Chiu join the Hong Kong Country Club. It had a long waiting list, but since Father was a founding member, there was no problem for his nephew to join. Father also introduced him to many of his good friends, such as Geoffrey M.T. Yeh and Yao Kang,[28] who turned out to be extremely helpful to him for years to come, and for which he was very thankful.

Every Sunday throughout the year, Father and Hon Chiu would spend the day on our launch. By the late 1970s, Mother had lost interest in the launch, and seldom went out with them, but if any of us were in Hong Kong, we loved to go along. Father no longer liked staying out late, so his habit was always to return to Queen's Pier around four in the afternoon. Father was grooming Hon Chiu for future leadership of the Lee family's many enterprises.

In 1978, a directive (not an order) was received by Lee Hysan Estate Company from the Hong Kong government to build on our empty land along Hennessy Road. There had never been any rush among the Lee brothers to build on this site.[29] In 1976, Third Uncle had held discussions with the Citibank about a joint venture to build an apartment building on the land, but the talks fell through. Now the area around it had been built up, but our land remained empty. People in Hong Kong were wondering why the Lee brothers didn't develop the land since it was so valuable. The truth was that nobody had the time, so no one bothered. Now that nephew Hon Chiu was back in Hong Kong, it became his responsibility to supervise the development of this project, known as Hennessy Centre, on Yee Wo Street, under the company name of Hennessy Development. It was again a joint venture between Lee Hysan Estate Company and investors.

When the foundation of Hennessy Centre was first excavated, Hon Chiu would go to the site every weekday, as well as after the launch picnic on Sunday. Sometimes Father would go along with him. The excavation dragged on, because the construction crew was having trouble reaching bedrock. It was very puzzling for both the foundation builder and for Professor S. Mackey, a retired engineering professor from Hong Kong University, who was hired as the consultant. In the meantime, Father was extremely impatient and was getting after everyone, including Hon Chiu. So, every weekday, after morning coffee with Father, Hon Chiu would call Professor Mackey to see if there was any progress that day. As Hon Chiu laughingly told me, "If you haven't reached bedrock, you haven't reached it. Getting after people wouldn't make it any faster!"

Finally, one day, Professor Mackey decided to go to the bottom of the hole to check the situation with the structural engineer Stanley Weber from Eric Cumine's architectural firm. He assessed the situation and gave his "O.K." for the foundation to be built. And that was good enough for everyone. Hon Chiu said, "When Professor Mackey said 'O.K.', it's O.K.!"

The Lee brothers disagreed over the plans for the top and the bottom floors. Fourth Uncle wanted the lower floors built as a theatre for Chinese opera and performances of Chinese music, but this was considered an unprofitable proposition by the rest of the brothers. Finally nephew Hon Chiu had the plans redrawn to the satisfaction of all the uncles. Hon Chiu moved the original carpark from the basement to the lower floors, and the basement became retail space. After many discussions, it was finally agreed that the top two floors would be retained for rental to a private club, and it was taken up by the Japanese Club. It was not unusual for the Lee brothers to disagree over family business, but matters were always settled within the family, and they always presented a united front to the community.[30] The Hennessy Centre was completed in 1981.

The next project was the redevelopment of Sunning Plaza. The property consisted of Sunning House, the small hotel with its main entrance on Hysan Avenue, and Sunning Court behind, which contained more than sixty apartments. Every apartment owner was a shareholder of Associated Property. Presentations were made to the shareholders, and after many questions and various disagreements, votes were taken. Hon Chiu noted that that was the only time in the seventy-four-year history of Lee Hysan Estate Co. Ltd. (the company founded by Grandfather in January 1924) that votes had to be counted, because of the involvement of so many outside shareholders. In 1980, the Sunning Plaza project, with I.M. Pei as architect, was begun.

The Public Company

Because the ownership of Leighton Centre, One Hysan Avenue, Hennessy Centre and Sunning Plaza and Sunning Court was split between investors and Lee Hysan Estate Co. Ltd., in many different shareholding structures, the Lee brothers decided to consolidate and create a public development company. The original Hennessy Development Co. Ltd., which was incorporated in 1970, became Hysan Development Company Ltd. in 1981,[31] and obtained listing on the Hong Kong Stock Exchange in August, issuing 500 million ordinary shares. Father was the chairman of the company. Hon Chiu and

Fourth Uncle formed a committee to take care of details, and every day, Hon Chiu gave Father his progress report over coffee.[32]

Wardley Limited, our merchant banker, advised the family that it would be more attractive to investors of Hysan Development if, in addition to rent collecting, there were other activities, such as buying and selling properties for further developments. Wardley suggested the injection of the property known as the Big House and the Lee Building, our ancestral homes with its surrounding gardens (74-86 Kennedy Road)[33] wholly owned by Lee Hysan Estate Co., into Hysan Development Co. Evaluations were done by Jones Lang Wootton. Since Hysan Development did not have the cash to buy the property, the property was exchanged for deferred shares in the company for the family in the amount of $875 million. When Hysan Development took over the property, it was developed in 1985 into a luxury residential complex known as Bamboo Grove, which consisted of 345 apartments. Again, many family members moved into this new complex, including Mother after Father passed away.

When Hysan Development first went on the market in 1981, its shares were valued at one dollar. From then on, the Hong Kong market started to slump and the shares gradually went down to as low as thirty-nine cents. One reason was the death of Chen Tak Tai, one of the big shareholders. His son David, who held his shares, decided to sell all of them, thus bringing down the value. Both Father, as chairman, and Hon Chiu, as the managing director, had a lot of responsibilities and worries. Father appealed publicly to the shareholders not to sell, reassuring them that the value would go up again. Time proved him right.

One day in the early 1980s, while out on our launch, Father told Hon Chiu that "if nobody says anything bad about you, you are already doing very well. Don't expect anyone to praise you for what you do." Hon Chiu said that these were some of Father's words of wisdom that he would always remember. After Father passed away in 1983, the chairmanship of Hysan Development went for a few years to Fourth Uncle, who then passed it on to Hon Chiu,[34] who remains chairman today.

At the beginning of the 1980s, Hong Kong faced a major economic downturn. I remember seeing pessimism everywhere, except in my own family. Father, of course, had never-ending faith in the future of Hong Kong. These were the years when Britain and China started talks for the return of Hong Kong to China. From the mid-1980s on, Hysan Development continued to buy more and more properties for development, not only in Hong Kong, but also in China, Singapore and San Francisco. The stock market gradually turned around, but Father never lived to see the great prosperity gained by Hong Kong in the early 1990s.

With the development of Caroline Centre, a joint venture between Hang Seng Bank and Hysan Development, the company shares went up to thirty-two dollars in 1994. Hysan Development, controlled by Lee Hysan Estate Co., the oldest Chinese property company in Hong Kong, is highly respected in the business world and is regarded as one of the top ten property companies in Southeast Asia. With its conservative policy and the high-end tenants it attracts, Hysan Development is regarded as a "boutique" property company.[35] Father would have been very proud of its achievements.

At the end of 1997, the Hong Kong stock market had another downturn because of the economic crisis in Asia. Although share prices of Hysan Development Company dropped, the profits of the company continued to increase and its future remains bright.

9

A Daughter Grows Up

By 1954, my parents were planning to move from Embassy Court to Tower Court, a new high-rise the Lee family was building on Hysan Avenue. Again we were going to occupy the penthouse, which took up the entire top floor and half of the floor below. We moved in 1955.

Grandmother's Funeral

At the beginning of 1956, Grandmother became very ill. When she died in early summer at the age of seventy-six, the Lee family held a traditional Buddhist funeral for her. Her body was kept on ice for forty-nine days in the pagoda by the fountain of Guanyin, the Goddess of Mercy, in the garden of the Big House. Matsheds built of bamboo and straw matting were erected in the bamboo garden next to it. The right side was reserved for the men in the family and the left side for the women. Robes of black or white were worn by the descendants who took turns keeping watch over the body. As a granddaughter, I wore white when I went every day after school. We had very plain rice and vegetables for dinner, and we all ate together in the matshed, sitting on the raised floor covered with woven straw.

Near the end of the forty-nine days, groups of monks and nuns were hired to burn incense, and chant and pray for her. I believe they were from different Buddhist denominations because they wore different types of robes. On the day of the funeral, the procession lasted for hours. Afterwards, we all went back to the Big House. I was told that the soul would leave the body in the form of a bird or a butterfly. As I was standing in the main hall and looking at Grandmother's picture hanging in the centre of the end wall, I suddenly saw a butterfly flutter towards it, stop on the photograph and then fly out to the terrace, and then it was gone.

That night, before we all gathered for dinner, paper objects were burnt in the terrace to send to Grandmother in the other world. The most important was a paper bridge, without which she couldn't reach the other side. Other paper objects were in the shape of servants, a big house, gold and silver money and a car. I was watching with fascination while these objects were being burnt, when Fifth Aunt's husband, Uncle Y.H. Kan, came up to me and said, "I guess Grandmother is going to the United States. The car has a left-hand drive!"

Then, we had a family dinner in the Big House. I remember Mother and all the aunts had to wear special dull-coloured costumes for that particular event, because the body had been buried and the family had entered another stage of mourning.

A few days later, all the sons returned to the Big House after dinner because the spirit would be coming home. They walked around the house and the garden, making sure the spirit knew that they were there. And while they were in the garden, they said to one another jokingly that they had better not relieve themselves since they couldn't see where the spirit was.

I remember that Hon Chiu was about to marry an American, Doris, in the United States when Grandmother died. Once they were married, he would be allowed to remain in the States to work. By Chinese tradition, descendants of the deceased were not allowed to marry during the period of mourning. With his usual good sense, Father put a stop to any objection from the family by saying that whoever objected to the wedding would have to offer Hon Chiu an equally good job in Hong Kong. So Hon Chiu got married and remained in the United States for the next twenty years.

Father and My British Education

Father had benefited a great deal from his studies and experiences in England, and he believed that what was good for him would be equally good for his children. At the beginning of the 1950s, he had sent my older brother and sister to England, but because of my different temperament, Father kept me at home. When I was fifteen years old, it was decided that I, too, would go to school in England.

In August 1956, my parents saw me off at Kai Tak airport. That was when Hong Kong was still in the process of building a much-needed new runway, which had been under discussion since the end of the 1940s. The airport at that time was very small and quite primitive. There was only one doorway for arrivals and departures.[1]

I flew to England with my sister and a friend, David K.P. Li.[2] My sister and David were returning to England after the summer holidays. It was my first time away from home.

I had heard of London fog, but never quite knew what to expect until our plane touched down in London. It was in the evening, and I couldn't see anything. Not only could I not see, I was choking on yellow smog. We were met by Uncle Ley On, Father's old friend, with his Bentley, driven by his Burmese chauffeur, Ah Ong. We stayed for a few days with him and his wife, Aunt Betsy, in their lovely house with a beautiful garden in Surrey, outside London. It was in Uncle Ley On's restaurant that I first came across the Chinese dish called "Chop Suey." I wanted to know what it was, so I ordered it, but the waiter wouldn't give it to me. He said that it was not for the Chinese; it was just a name for left-overs.

Between 1956 and 1958, I attended Upper Chine School in Shanklin, on the Isle of Wight, in southern England. I was sent there to join my sister. The total number of students in this exclusive private girls' school was just over two hundred, from Grade One to Upper Six (Grade Thirteen). Most of the teachers were excellent, and the more advanced students were put into special classes. The smallest class I was in was the mathematics class of two students, myself and a girl from Thailand.

The school was situated on the upper part of the Chine River, which was more a brook than a river. The school grounds, maintained by ten full-time gardeners, were very beautiful. During the summer holidays, the grounds were open to the public. In the spring, daffodils adorned the river-banks. During the summer term if it was warm enough, we would sometimes have our classes out of doors. Roses bloomed throughout the summer and fall. But in the winter, everything was grey, cold and miserable.

When I went to Upper Chine, I skipped a year from Form Three (Grade Nine) to Form Five (Grade Eleven). Since I was expected to go to Oxford, I had to take six "O" (Ordinary) level examinations at one time. I wrote the examinations in my first year, as well as the "A" (Advanced) level Chinese examination. In the following year, I took many more. My parents were very pleased with my academic progress because I came first in my class, but I was not happy.

What bothered me was not so much the school but the British public-school system. For a person like me who already had self-discipline and an artistic flair, the system just didn't work. I hated to be told what to do at what time and on what day. I needed time and space of my own and that was not possible when six to eight girls shared a room. Lights had to be out at a prescribed time at night. We were told when to eat, when to sleep, when to write our parents, when to bathe (three times a week; the weekend was free, so I managed to bathe five times a week instead of daily as I was used to at home), and almost when to breathe — that was when we were supposed to go outside for recess no matter how cold it was. In the afternoon, we were supposed to do sports. Since I hated sports, I always went for walks with some of the girls from the Middle Eastern countries who hated sports too.

I was always hungry and cold because there was no heating. We had to sleep with the windows open even in the winter with snow flying in. I slept with layers of clothing, and nine blankets on top and a hot-water bottle at my feet. Fearing that I didn't have enough fresh fruit in my diet, Father arranged for me to have two apples every day which I picked up in the kitchen during recess. And knowing that I was always hungry, he arranged to have Cadbury send me boxes of chocolate biscuits every term. But any food sent to the students could be eaten only on Saturday afternoons and Sundays. Those were the only years in my life when I became heavy, and I had chilblains on my fingers and toes.

I also didn't believe in a school for girls only. I felt it a very artificial environment with a lot of silliness that wouldn't exist in a co-educational school. No matter how well I did academically, or how much I liked my teachers, I didn't feel that I belonged there.

Mother came to visit us in England in spring 1957. She first went to see my older brother, Richard, who was in school in Nottingham. When she saw him, she felt something was not right. He was showing signs of mental illness that no one in the school seemed to have noticed. She asked to have him seen by a psychiatrist, and from then on, my parents' lives were never the same.

Since mental illness was something my parents couldn't cope with, they seldom talked about it. As a result, I knew little about my brother's condition. During my second year at Upper Chine, Richard was hospitalized outside London. That year, I made a Christmas cake in my Domestic Science class, the only Christmas cake I've made in my life. During the holidays, I went with an aunt living in England at the time to take Richard the cake. I felt that our childhood closeness was starting to come apart. His condition sometimes improved, and he had some good years, but his illness often caused him to stay away from family members. Only a number of years later did I learn that his condition was schizophrenia, which strikes about one child in a hundred, and which usually manifests itself in the late teens or early twenties.

During my second year at Upper Chine, I wrote my parents to say that I was leaving at the end of that year, and that I would finish my last year of high school at St. Paul's Co-educational College. I didn't list the reasons why, because I didn't want my parents to try to dissuade me. I was a wilful child.

Father was very disappointed because he believed in the English public-school system. To most people it was almost an admission of failure. However, that year, I came first again in my class. Besides adding many more "O" levels to my credit, I also passed the "O-A" level in Mathematics with high marks.

I went home to Hong Kong in the summer of 1958 and did my last year of school at St. Paul's. Father had very little to say to me at first, because he was still upset by my leaving England. I guess he also knew that I didn't intend to return to England for university as he had originally hoped. The direction in my life had also changed. I decided that I didn't want to study mathematics as my teachers at Upper Chine had recommended. (Mother thought I was such a good student that I should study law, but Father did not express an opinion.) Instead I wanted to study arts subjects, and take history at university. Because of my change of direction, and also the change of school system, I had to do two years' work in one in order to write my Matriculation examinations. I borrowed notes from my old school friends to catch up, but the results were not as good as before.

In 1958, my sister entered Oxford to study medicine, and Sixth Uncle returned from the United States after getting his Ph.D. at Princeton. He suggested that since I didn't want to return to England, I should apply to colleges in the United States. Father put a stop to that. He said that no child of his would be educated in the United States. I did not know why he was so anti-American. I applied to two Canadian universities, McGill University in Montreal and University of Toronto. It was Father who decided that I was to go to McGill.

That year, I was working so hard that I was hardly aware of what was happening in Hong Kong. I used to study in our roof garden, besides going out on the launch, which by now was the *Atalanta*, smaller than the *Fortuna*. The only other child left at home was my younger brother, Christopher. Our last coxswain, Ho Ning, came to work for us then and remained with us for over twenty years. My parents no longer wanted large groups of guests on our launch picnics, especially when I wasn't there to do the inviting. For relaxation from studying, I again turned to painting water-colours. It was then that I started drawing faces.

This was also the year that I asked my parents not to call me "May" any more, and to call me by my given first name, Vivienne, the name I always used in school. Mother said, "It is a little late for us to make the change now, but when you go to Canada, no one knows that we call you May, and people will only know you as Vivienne."

I was growing up, and would make many more decisions for myself.

McGill, Marriage and Family

In August 1959, Mother and I flew to Canada. As usual, Father made all the travel arrangements. We went first to the west coast, then to the Rockies. Mother's cousin Ethel and her husband, Bill Poy, invited us to stay with them in Ottawa and Bill and his son, Neville, came to meet us at the Toronto airport. We stayed in Toronto and visited Niagara Falls, then drove to Ottawa for a few days. From there, Mother and I flew to Montreal. Once I was settled in residence at McGill University, Mother left for New York, and went home via England, where she visited my older brother and sister.

I entered McGill as a sophomore, and Neville was in his final year of medicine there. The years at McGill were wonderful, but I spent so much time with Neville that I did not do as well as I should have academically. My priorities were different then. Mother wasn't happy because she had other plans for me, but Father was not opposed to my going out with Neville because he always appreciated able people.

In 1961, Neville wrote to Father to ask for my hand in marriage. Father thought it was rather premature since I was still in university. Later that year, I wrote to my parents to tell them that I was getting married the following year when I graduated and turned twenty-one. My parents had always known me to be headstrong but sensible. Father approved of Neville, but Mother was so upset that she didn't speak to me for years. She wondered why I had chosen a "poor boy." Knowing that love or happiness cannot be bought, I disagreed with Mother. In the short twenty years of my life, I had met many miserable, wealthy people, and I wanted to be sure that I was not going to join their number. As Neville himself said, he had no assets except for his training and abilities, and that was good enough for me. Besides, I was going to marry the man I loved, and Father understood that.

Since Mother was having nothing to do with my wedding, I had to look after all the arrangements myself, while studying for my final examinations. Neville and I also had to find a place to live. I wanted the graduation and wedding to be timed close together to make it easy for Father to be present for both occasions. In the space of two weeks, I had my twenty-first birthday, my graduation and our wedding. Right after the Convocation, Father asked me why I had only honours and not first-class honours. He didn't realize what stress I had been under in the last few months. However, I appreciated the fact that he believed I was capable of doing better.

Neville was working in burns research at McGill University, teaching anatomy, and getting his master's degree in surgery. The year after our wedding, he went into the plastic surgery training program at McGill. In 1964, he received a Molson Fellowship to spend a year in England, training in the Mount Vernon Hospital in Middlesex, a major plastic surgery centre. During that year, I took courses at the Institute of Archaeology, University of London. It was a wonderful year for both of us. We drove all over central Europe on twenty-five dollars a day, before Neville started at Mount Vernon on July 1.

During our year in England, we were able to see my brother Richard quite frequently. He was in London, married, and had a son. In the spring of 1965, we took a cruise in the Mediterranean, travelling steerage, and drove around Scotland and Wales at Easter. My parents were visiting England and I went to see them, and took Mother a bunch of red roses. She spoke little to me, though Father talked quite a bit. Mother's antagonism made it very awkward for him, and I appreciated his kindness.

That summer Neville and I returned to Montreal, where he continued his training at the Montreal General Hospital. In September, our first son, Ashley, was born. The following year, we began to hear about the separatist movement in Quebec, while the city of Montreal was busy getting ready for Expo 67.

The year 1967 was an important one for us. Neville wrote his fellowship examinations while bombs were going off in public places and mail boxes in Montreal. It was the beginning of the Front for the

Liberation of Quebec (FLQ) crisis in the province. Because of the political unrest, when Neville was offered a staff position in the plastic surgery department at the Scarborough General Hospital, we moved to Ontario, even though Neville had already been offered a junior staff position at McGill.

In February 1968, Mother suffered a minor heart attack. Subsequently, her doctor advised her to take a cruise abroad, so she took her cousin's daughter, Chi Chao, to study in the United States. Mother planned to visit her relatives there as well as in Vancouver. Her heart attack prompted her to get in touch with me and she asked me to go to see her when she arrived in Vancouver. That summer, I took Ashley to Vancouver to see her. Mother's change in attitude towards me made life a great deal easier for Father, and from then on, my parents came to see us every year.

Whenever they visited us, Father always noticed how wonderful Toronto was with all its parks and its residential areas lined with trees. Father loved nature, and often said there weren't enough trees in the populated areas of Hong Kong. Knowing me to be an avid gardener, he often told me about his friend Sir Evelyn de Rothschild, who also loved gardening.

We were living in a rented town-house complex in Toronto when my parents visited in 1970. Neville was the only staff surgeon at the Scarborough General Hospital who didn't own his own house. Father thought it inadequate for a growing family, as we already had two children by then — Ashley and Justin, who was born in 1969. He said we should be in a house with a garden. But I had very particular ideas about the type of house I wanted — I wanted one with an art room connected to the kitchen, and we hadn't been able to find one. A house like that just didn't exist, so we decided to build our own, and we were saving up for it. It had always been important to me to bring up our children with artistic training. I hadn't dreamt of asking my parents for help, but Father generously offered so that we could proceed to build our house on the land we had already purchased.

In the spring of 1972 we moved into our new house. When Father saw our unusually large living room, he offered to have a special carpet made for it through his connections in Tianjin, who had made the carpets for the lobby of the Lee Gardens Hotel. He told me that a custom-made carpet would take up to a year, but if I wanted it right away, I could have two carpets laid side by side. I chose to have something really special. I was sent books from which to select the style I wanted, and I clipped colour samples from pictures of flowers in a magazine to match the bricks of the living-room wall. Father also asked me to choose a standard-sized carpet for our blue dining room. It did take a year for the large carpet to arrive, but it was worth the wait. It was most kind of Father, not only to have given us the carpets, but also to have gone to all that trouble.

In 1972, Father arranged for my brother Christopher, who had graduated from The Chinese University of Hong Kong, to have international financial training. He was to go to Geneva, then Wall Street. The last stop was Tokyo, where he would work at Yamaichi Securities, and Fuji Bank, whose president, Yoshizane Yuasa, was a friend of Father's.[3] This was to be Christopher's golden opportunity.

Christopher was married and had a son. When he and his family were on their way to New York, they visited us in Toronto and we had a great time together. The strange thing was that he told me during that visit, "Second Sister, I don't think I have long to live. Maybe a maximum of fifteen years. But, I want to make it big before then!" He was overweight, but he had had a check-up just before he left Hong Kong, and had been given a clean bill of health.

One day, not long after Christopher and his family arrived in New York, I got a call from Father saying that Christopher had died. He was only twenty-five years old. Neville and I quickly left for New York. Father was on his way from Hong Kong, but Mother didn't come.

Apparently, Christopher had been walking with a friend during lunch hour, when he suddenly collapsed and died. All the Lee family members in New York were called, and they were there for us, helping Father make funeral arrangements. Sixth Uncle, who was teaching at the University of Kansas, also flew in. I was close to Christopher, but I couldn't even begin to feel the pain Father must have felt, or what Monica, my sister-in-law, must have gone through. Fortunately, the baby, Marcus, was too young to be traumatized by the event.

Father took Marcus and Monica back to Hong Kong with him after the funeral. He now had the added responsibility of Marcus's well-being. From then on, he became a father as well as a grandfather to Marcus. When Marcus was a little older, they spent every Saturday morning together. Marcus would go to Father's office to learn Chinese calligraphy, watched over by Father, and taught by Miss Leung, a staff member well known for her calligraphy.

In the early 1970s, I was made aware of the eventual change of sovereignty of Hong Kong. During one of my parents' visits, Father told me that he had been assured by the Chinese government that Hong Kong would remain the same for fifty years after 1997, so he was to feel free to invest and carry on with his business.

At Christmas 1976, as part of our annual visit to Hong Kong, Father treated us to a cruise on the *Rasasayang*, from Singapore to Bali. Our children— Ashley, Justin and Carter, who was born in 1973 — were so excited because it was their first cruise, and they thought they were going on the *Love Boat*, which they had seen on television. When the hotel reservations were made in Singapore, Father would not book the Mandarin Hotel despite the fact that it is regarded as the best, because his friend owned it, and would not charge if he knew Father was the one making the booking.

February 1978 was my parents' golden wedding anniversary. Father wasn't one to celebrate because he did not even celebrate his own birthday. He never wanted anyone to make a fuss. But Mother was very happy when Fourth Uncle insisted that such an important occasion should be marked, and the entire Lee family would do it for them.

As the celebration was in February, only Carter and I could attend. Our other sons had to stay in school and Neville stayed behind with them.

The party, held at the Lee Gardens Hotel, was attended by mainly family members and some very close friends. My parents had a really good time. They had a beautiful anniversary cake covered in golden Oncidium orchids. When Father spoke, he pointed out that fifty years ago, he and Mother had been married on exactly the same spot in The Lee Gardens. The only difference was, in 1928, they had stood on top of the hill. Father also mentioned that the recipe for a long-lasting marriage was "arguing a little from time to time!"

With Father in China

In the fall of 1978, I mentioned to Father that I wanted to take Neville and our sons to China. At that time, there was no tourism in China, only groups arranged by the Chinese government. We had to go to the Embassy in Ottawa for visas, and we could only get them because Father had made arrangements through Beijing.

Father planned a wonderful trip for us. We first went to Hong Kong for Christmas; we then went into China by train. Those were the days when you could tell immediately when you crossed the border, because the scenery changed from high-rises and motor cars to vegetable fields and bicycles. At the train station in Guangzhou, we were met by officials, who helped us through border checking and customs. Then we were met by our guide, who stayed with us throughout our trip.

We flew from Guangzhou to Beijing and then worked our way south, visiting all the major sights, as well as areas that tourists were not normally allowed to enter. We met Mother's cousin and his wife, Professors Eugene Chan and Winnifred Mao,[4] who were able to make special arrangements for us to visit the Plastic Surgery Hospital outside of Beijing, which was normally out of bounds. Neville marvelled at the work that was carried out under very primitive conditions. In the Central Hospital in Beijing, we watched surgery performed while acupuncture was used as anaesthetic. It was my first experience in an operating room, and was I amazed that the patient was talking to the nurse while undergoing a thyroidectomy. We were also shown various other traditional Chinese treatments.

We visited the Great Walls and the Forbidden City, then we went on to Hangzhou and Guilin. Everything we saw made a deep impression on us. At that time, people dressed in Mao suits, and referred to one another as comrades. There were no modern hotels, and we ate in dining halls. There was no water early in the morning. But I noticed that under the Chinese Communist regime, there were free markets on Sundays where the population could exercise their entre- preneurial skills.[5]

When we arrived in Guilin, our son Justin became ill. Neville diag- nosed it as scarlet fever, and put him on antibiotics right away. The last day we were there, Justin felt much better and came on the tour with us. We then flew to Guangzhou on New Year's Eve, where we were met by Father.

While in Guangzhou, we were guests of the government, because of Father, and we stayed in the guest house reserved for visiting heads of state. Our boys wanted to buy firecrackers, so Father took us in a minibus to look for some. We ended up having a city tour, but we never did find any firecrackers. However, Father showed me a bridge of European design which he had helped to build at the beginning of the 1930s while working for the city of Guangzhou.

That evening, we were the guests of the deputy governor of Guang- dong, since the governor was away. The dinner, held in the dining room of the guest house, was splendid. Food for officials, even in a poor Communist country, is the same anywhere in the world.

Father had planned for us to leave early the next morning to drive to our ancestral village, so the only time he could show me the garden in the complex was after dinner. We were all going to take a walk, but Justin said he couldn't walk because of swelling in his knees. Neville carried him to the bedroom while I took a walk with Father.

When I returned, Justin had a fever. Obviously, the antibiotic was not working. A doctor was called immediately, and she suggested that we take Justin to the hospital for a blood test. When we walked into the hospital, with Justin in Neville's arms, Justin said, after one look at the condition of the emergency department, "Don't leave me here!" We had no intention of doing that. Since it was New Year's Eve and all laboratories would be closed for two days, I decided that Justin should be taken back to Hong Kong right away.

When we returned to the guest house, I went into Father's bed- room and woke him up. I said, "Daddy, I have to take Justin back to

Hong Kong right away. Can you get us plane tickets for the earliest flight out?" He didn't have to ask me why and what happened at the hospital, because he knew there was a reason for my decision. "Tomorrow is New Year's Day. It may be very difficult," he said. "In that case," I said, "get me a car, and we will start driving to Hong Kong right away." He answered, "That would be even more difficult. The roads are bad, and it would take me longer to arrange for smooth passage through the border check points. I'll see what I can do. I'm expected at the ancestral village, Ashley and Carter can come with me." Unfortunately, Carter's name was on my passport, so he had to return to Hong Kong with us.

Neville and I started packing immediately while Father went downstairs to make arrangements. We were told by one of the officials that he would take us to the airport by five in the morning. He couldn't guarantee us four seats on the first flight to Hong Kong, but he would try his best. In the meantime, Father phoned Mother to say that she was to call Seventh Uncle to make arrangements for a paediatrician friend of his to see Justin when we arrived. On New Year's Day it would be impossible to find a private doctor willing to work. Father phoned the Hong Kong airport to arrange for us to be met with a wheelchair, and for a car to take us to the Lee Gardens Hotel. (We always stayed at the hotel unless I was in Hong Kong alone or with just one of the children in order not to inconvenience my parents and the household staff.) The hotel was right across the street from my parents' home. After making all the arrangements, Father then went back to sleep.

The next morning we were awakened very early. The kitchen had prepared us a sumptuous breakfast which we could hardly swallow because we were so anxious. We said goodbye to Father and Ashley and left. We were very fortunate to be on that first flight to Hong Kong, which took only twenty-five minutes. We were met as Father had arranged. As soon as we arrived in our suite at the Lee Gardens Hotel, Mother called to say that Seventh Uncle had made the medical arrangements. Then Seventh Uncle himself called to say that he was sending his chauffeur to pick us up and he would meet us at the Emergency Department of the Hong Kong Sanatorium.

At the Hong Kong Sanatorium, Seventh Uncle introduced us to a paediatrician friend who was trained in the United States. The doctor confirmed that Justin had scarlet fever and prescribed a higher dose of antibiotic for him to take for a few more days. Everyone in Hong Kong knew how expensive the Hong Kong Sanatorium was and still is, and we were overwhelmed when Seventh Uncle said it was "on the house," as he had already taken care of our medical bills. I've always had a very special relationship with him — he was more of a good friend than an uncle. After all, he was only ten years older than Neville. By that afternoon, Justin was already beginning to feel better. The next day, we all went to a movie at the Lee Theatre.

These events made me realize how very much I'm like Father. We understood each other without having to say a word, and I know that if I had been in his shoes, I would have made arrangements exactly as he did.

In the meantime, Ashley was having the time of his life being a VIP guest with Father in Sunwui city, our ancestral home in China. In anticipation of our visit, Father had also planned to take us all back to Neville's ancestral village of Sunning, which is close to ours, being one of the Szeyup villages. Although Neville wasn't there, Father took Ashley to Sunning anyway, because he felt it important that Ashley know where his ancestors from both sides of the family came from. To Ashley's surprise, villagers from Sunning brought gifts to them, including a live chicken.

Back in Hong Kong, Ashley told us about his adventures. He said, "Gung Gung (maternal Grandfather) took me to a firecracker factory where one of the people there brought me outside to light firecrackers. I was allowed to light as many as I wanted. We went to see a hydro dam, and a large banyan tree by a river that was inhabited by thousands of white cranes. We sat in a hot spring where Gung Gung and I put eggs into the water to cook. But sharing a room with him is a problem, he snores so loudly!"

Father was really glad to see that Justin had recovered his health. Knowing how much Ashley had enjoyed the experience, he said to Justin, "The next time will be your turn. I'll take you into the village."

Father was always happy when he was in China.

10

From Turbulence To Reform: A Vision For Higher Education

Hong Kong society in the 1950s was divided into a number of factions — pro-Communist, pro-Nationalist, Pro-British and others. Since politics were never mentioned in my home, I was not sure what faction my parents favoured. At that time, the Chinese government's attitude towards Hong Kong became more relaxed, and in 1956, due to strong local demand, the border between China and Hong Kong was reopened. Visitors from China were admitted freely into Hong Kong provided they possessed re-entry permits to China. From February to September, 60,000 came into Hong Kong and disappeared into the general population.[1] This became an added burden on the existing water supply, so the government moved to close the border again. That year, violence erupted soon after I left for school in England. A dispute over the Nationalists' National Day (October 10) celebrations led to rioting between Nationalist and Communist supporters and against the colonial authority. The riot lasted for several days until British troops were called out. Dozens were killed, and thousands were arrested, imprisoned or deported.

The Hong Kong government passed a series of laws to tighten control of the population, giving it the power to close newspapers and imprison its publishers for political offences. When any society was formed, it had to register with the commissioner of police and it was a criminal offence for any nine unrelated persons to assemble on the street. Even under these regulations, there was a certain amount of freedom as long as one did not advocate the overthrow of the colonial government. I was old enough to understand the restrictions, and they affected my attitude towards the colonial government of Hong Kong.

Then came the 1960s which witnessed the terrible Cultural Revolution in China (1966–1976). The upheavals spilled over to Hong Kong as social and political turbulence and riots. At the time, people were shocked. But there were some positive consequences, as social protests eventually led to social reforms.

The Riots of 1967

In China, in September 1965, Chairman Mao began to attack his opponents in earnest, and this led to the Cultural Revolution. The youths in China were given a free hand to attack culture, learning, and, worst of all, educated people whom China needed most. In the summer of 1966, there were eight parades by the Red Guards, a total of 15 million youths, in Tiananmen Square. On August 22, 1966, mobs of Red Guards, inflamed by reports of atrocities perpetrated in Hong Kong by the British, invaded the British embassy in Beijing. The gates were broken and petrol cans were thrown at the buildings which were set on fire. Zhou Enlai had to send the police and the People's Liberation Army to rescue the diplomats.

The Cultural Revolution in China did not prevent my parents from travelling there in the 1960s. On one trip, He Mingsi, the Secretary of Xinhua News Agency, accompanied them. They went to Chongqing, where we used to live during the war. While Father was reminiscing to He Mingsi about the old days, they were surrounded by crowds of Red Guards. He Mingsi was really afraid, but fortunately, nothing happened.[2] The Red Guards were apparently just curious, since my parents, who tried to dress like the locals, didn't really look like the rest of them.

In 1966, a peaceful protest in Hong Kong by a small group of young people over an increase in ferry fares led to days of rioting by frustrated working-class young men against what they saw as the inequalities of society from which they had no way out. The police stopped the riots by force. One young man was killed and many arrests were made, and one demonstrator committed suicide afterwards. On top of that, the unrest in China spread to Hong Kong.

In 1967, a factory labour dispute led to rioting in the working-class districts, which touched off continuous demonstrations by students from Communist schools against the Colonial government. This soon developed into sporadic acts of violence by students and workers. Some Hong Kong Communists or self-styled "Red Guards" manufactured homemade bombs which killed several people. Bombs, commonly known as "pineapples," were left in public places in order to cause maximum disturbance.[3] Some of them were real and some were not. C.T. Wu, Deputy General Manager of the Mandarin Hotel in Hong Kong at the time, said that the hotel remained open, but there was hardly any business at all. The police started taking the offensive that summer, making raids on Communist stores, unions and schools.[4] There were a few deaths and many people were arrested. During these times of unrest, hundreds of community organizations publicly declared their support for the government and against the Communists.

In one of the letters Canadian Ruth Hayhoe[5] sent to her mother from Hong Kong that year, she wrote that the bombs were "small and innocuous," and that she saw a Communist blown up by his own bomb in the summer. She also wrote that there was trouble in the Heep Yun Middle School where she was teaching. A fourth-form student put up a poster on the bulletin board denouncing the "slavery education" of the school (Heep Yun is a Christian missionary school), and hung a red flag outside the school. When reproached, the student was very defiant and brought her father to the school. He was so angry that he slapped the head teacher across the face. Such was the atmosphere in Hong Kong in 1967.[6]

Rioters threw stones at buses, and drivers were beaten up. The London Insurance Association ordered Hong Kong insurance companies to cancel all riot insurance. The managing director of the Kowloon Bus Company went to see Yao Kang, a junior manager of Swire Insurance, to appeal to the company not to cancel their riot insurance, in order to give their drivers some measure of reassurance.[7] Rumours even spread that the Red Guards were marching against Hong Kong. With growing panic throughout the colony, the population hoarded food supplies and store shelves were empty. While my parents were on a trip to Europe that summer, rumours spread that Dick and Esther Lee had left Hong Kong, so conditions must be irretrievable. On hearing that, my parents returned to Hong Kong immediately.

Father felt a deep sense of responsibility to the people of Hong Kong. He believed that he could make a difference by appealing to the Chinese government not to incite the crowd. Father's friend Jack Cater, who was Defence Secretary of the Hong Kong government at the time, came to Father's office every day during the worst period, asking for help.[8] Father appealed to Lian Weilin, Director of Xinhua News Agency and Fei Yiming of *Ta Kung Pao*, to ask Zhou Enlai not to allow the riots to spread into Hong Kong.[9] Actually, what happened in Hong Kong had very little to do with China, for Premier Zhou Enlai had instructed the Xinhua News Agency that there would be no change in the status of Hong Kong.

Memories of the fall of Hong Kong in 1941 came back to Mother, and she was frightened. Father, on the other hand, would never consider abandoning Hong Kong; he would defend it with his life. Father took the lead, speaking publicly to calm the populace. He was outspoken against the Communists for their actions, and for the disturbance caused in Hong Kong.[10]

Conditions in China went from bad to worse. Anyone could be subject to attack. Mother's cousins, Professor Eugene Chen and his wife, Professor Winnifred Mao, both opthamologists, were denounced, beaten and driven out of their home. Their crime was that they were educated, especially since Professor Chen had been trained at Johns Hopkins in the United States. They survived and moved away and lived in obscurity until my parents found them at the beginning of the 1970s. At the end of 1978, when we met them during our visit to Beijing, Professor Chen showed us the French beret and a pair of Western-style leather shoes he managed to hide from the Red Guards. He said that if these had been found, they would both have been killed.

As the Red Guards went through China like locusts, dead bodies were dumped into the rivers. Some of these floated into Hong Kong waters[11] and stirred up feelings of sadness and fear, since everyone in Hong Kong had relatives and friends in China.

However, conditions gradually improved in Hong Kong. By the beginning of 1969, everything was back to normal.

Social Reforms

The riots that started in 1966 prompted the Hong Kong government to triple public spending on education to provide more opportunities for young people, and to improve housing, health care and social welfare. In 1967 the government realized that its legitimacy was no longer based on the Sino-British Treaties of the nineteenth century, but had to be earned by its performance and by some sense of community involvement.

By the beginning of the 1970s, the children of the refugees had grown up. The census of 1971 showed for the first time a locally born majority. As the older generation among the refugees died and were buried in Hong Kong, their offspring gained a sense of belonging to the Colony. Those who had made possible the economic and industrial take-off in the 1950s and 1960s could now enjoy the fruits of their labour.

Improvements in government assistance in education meant that more children of illiterate parents now had the opportunity to finish high school. A grant and loan scheme introduced in 1969 guaranteed funding for needy students to complete courses at local universities. The availability of opportunities for those with merit helped to further economic growth and encouraged a sense of belonging. When the people of Hong Kong realized that they had not only been born and bred in the Colony, but had also made great contributions to its success, they started to demand improvements. The demands were not political, but social and economic.

There were successive strikes and protests spearheaded by university students, teachers, social workers, church leaders, nurses and trade unionists. These strikes were basically peaceful and orderly, and were characterized by a sense of purposefulness and self-discipline, even though they broke the law against illegal association and illegal assembly. The limited amount of violence that took place was often provoked by the police.[12]

University students led the Chinese-language movement which demanded that Chinese be made an official language along with English. After numerous sit-ins and public forums that were widely supported in the community, the government conceded official status for Chinese (Cantonese) for most public, administrative and political uses.

Corruption has always been endemic in Hong Kong. Not much was done until the 1970s, when demonstrations were organized by university students and church groups involving tens of thousands of citizens. The anti-corruption movement targeted the Hong Kong police and other public agencies. In 1973, High Court Judge Sir Alastair Blair Kerr was appointed by Governor Maclehose to sit on a one-man commission to investigate the conduct of the Chief Superintendent of the Royal[13] Hong Kong Police Force, Peter Godber, who sneaked out of Hong Kong while on suspension from duty during an investigation of his suspected corrupt activities. The two Blair Kerr reports and the ensuing public outcry led to the establishment of the Independent Commission Against Corruption (ICAC) in February 1974, with Jack Cater as Commissioner. Peter Godber was extradited from Britain and brought back to Hong Kong to face trial.[14] Many police officers were charged, many more resigned, and the force was reorganized. Eventually, the Independent Commission Against Corruption Ordinance outlawed gift-taking by public officials.

Throughout the 1970s, the Christian Industrial Committee and other church-related groups organized labour protests, and encouraged the development of a movement independent of the Communist or Nationalist parties, resulting in a number of improvements to the Labour Ordinance. A successful primary-school teachers' strike led to the formation of the Professional Teachers' Union. This was followed by a nurses' strike. Both white- and blue-collar unions raised the spectre of a rightful challenge to arbitrary authority. Areas such as Chater Garden, Victoria Park, the square outside Central Government Offices and the side gate of Government House became well recognized sites for public gatherings. While the ordinances against illegal associations and assembly remained in the statute books, their application became rarer. Demonstrators were met by police escorts who directed traffic, and by government officials who received the petitions.[15]

In many cases, significant concessions were made to the protesters. Through this process, both Hong Kong society and government became strengthened. Hong Kong changed from the colonial style of government to one that was more responsive to the needs of the population in education and language. The civil service was upgraded and social justice improved. The government, while retaining ultimate political power, exercised it in a radically different manner by the early 1970s.

It was my parents' view that since the 1970s, the governors of Hong Kong were diplomats who no longer dictated to the people of Hong Kong.

Father and Education

Father had always been a great supporter of education. Until 1969, there were no scholarships for higher education in Hong Kong, and students who were accepted into university but couldn't afford to pay for their tuition had to approach private individuals for financial help. Father was often approached with such requests. He kept letters from students in his pocket so he wouldn't forget to look into matters for them. He would check into the entrance records of these students, and if the requests came from a worthy student, he or she would be given financial support, consisting of money for tuition, lodging and expenses. In fact, in his later years, he gave financial support to worthy students a year in advance, just in case something should happen to him.[16]

We were told by some students that he was the only wealthy person in Hong Kong who bothered to answer their letters. Many of these students have gone on to great careers, and even though Father did not want any thanks, they never forgot him. Father's concern for the education of the young didn't end at the personal level. Despite being a Christian, he officiated at the opening ceremony of the Confucius Hall Middle School in 1964. In striving to help a greater number through the establishment of educational institutions, he helped in activities such as raising funds for the Mong Kok Workers Children's School, a school for the children of blue-collar workers.[17]

During the Cultural Revolution, Chi Chao, one of the daughters of Chen and Mao, Mother's cousins, escaped to Hong Kong. She and a classmate in her graduating class at Zhongshan Medical College in China came in a boat with other refugees. Mother got a call from her after she arrived in Hong Kong. My parents took it upon themselves to take care of her education and sent her to the United States to learn English. She later entered the school of medicine at Johns Hopkins University. In spite of having to start her studies all over again in another language, Chi Chao, to her great credit, completed her training in opthamology at Johns Hopkins, as her father had. She is now the head of the immunopathology section of the National Eye Institute in Bethesda, Maryland.[18]

When Father's secretary, Mabel Wu, retired in the early 1970s, he asked Anna Li, a secretary at Western Trading, one of our subsidiaries, to work for him. Anna told me that she was asked because she was not like other secretaries who would read popular magazines in their free time. On occasions when Father was at Western Trading, he always saw Anna studying, but he didn't know that she was studying for the TOEFL (Test of English as a Foreign Language) examination. She was then nineteen years old. She was reluctant to work for Father because she said she was too young and inexperienced. However, he convinced her that she could learn a great deal from him.

It was just like Father to send his secretary to evening school at the University of Hong Kong to learn English. Anna said she never missed a class even when she didn't feel well, because, with Father's connections at Hong Kong University, he would know if she missed one. When Anna first worked for Father, she said she didn't sleep for three months because she was so nervous. During the years she worked for him she spent many hours crying, because he was very direct, but she knew he always meant well. Anna was unsure of speaking English on the phone, and since this was very necessary in Father's office, he sent her to Oxford the following year for a six-week summer course, again arranged through Hong Kong University. The course was not to start until July, but Father paid for everything in January. Anna's sister took her place as Father's secretary during the time that she was away.

Father continued to help many students. One of them, Gloria Tam, wrote to Father during her two-year scholarship stay in England. She wanted to go to medical school at Hong Kong University, but her family couldn't afford it. When Father found out that she was a scholarship student, and that her parents worked as reporters at *Ta Kung Pao*, she was told that if she could get in, he would put her through. Gloria became a gynaecologist. After Father died, Anna's husband was helped by Gloria in finding employment, thanks to the relationship that Father had established.

Gloria is at present Assistant Director of the Department of Health in Hong Kong. During the H5N1 epidemic (chicken flu) in Hong Kong in 1997–1998, it was her responsibility to negotiate with China for the importation of healthy chickens to Hong Kong.

Anna was the one who knew how Father treated others, not only because she saw him every day during the week, but because she prepared the cheques for him to sign. Anna said, "I made out a cheque for eight hundred dollars monthly for one of the watchmen for his children's schooling because he had contracted tuberculosis. And when it came to help for university students, your father always gave them their allowance a year in advance."

Anna married the son of Father's old friend Tsui Gang Bo. In the late 1970s, when Anna had a family, Father would often let her use our launch with her husband and children when he wasn't using it himself.

Higher Education

After the end of the Second World War, and the civil war in China that followed, the great influx of population[19] from China into Hong Kong put heavy demands on the education system of the Colony, particularly higher education.

Up to the mid-1960s, there was only one officially recognized and government-funded university in Hong Kong, the University of Hong Kong. It was established in 1911 to serve as a centre for Sino-British contact in the sphere of learning, and for the maintenance of good relations with China. In other words, it was not intended to serve the Hong Kong public. Before the Pacific War, the university served mainly as an outpost of Western culture, admitting students from Southeast Asia and China, as well as Hong Kong. In 1946, it was felt that the greatly damaged university should be re-established because of the need to maintain the British position and prestige in the Far East. In 1948, when Father's friend Lindsay Ride became vice-chancellor, Father became a member of the Court of the University.

By 1950, the government was becoming aware that the University of Hong Kong should reflect the needs of local society, instead of being an institution to uphold British prestige.

With the continual political turbulence in China, foreign academic organizations withdrew from the mainland, and international cultural activities were interrupted. Hong Kong was now in a position to play an important role in Chinese and Western cultural contacts.

The demands of industrialization had created a need for higher education in the Colony. Among the refugee population was a large number of students from the Chinese middle schools who could no longer return to China and wanted to continue their higher education in Hong Kong. However, not only was the number of places available at the University of Hong Kong inadequate, there was little chance that any student from the Chinese middle schools could gain admission, since English was the language of instruction.

Governor Alexander Grantham appointed a special committee to look into the problem, and the result was the *Keswick Report*. It was the first public document to propose that higher education in Hong Kong should be geared to the needs of the people. It also recommended that the university remain the only institution to award degrees. The government immediately allocated funding to the university for the introduction of Chinese-language courses, beginning with the 1952–1953 academic year. This move was widely supported by the Senate of the university, but turned down by the Council. There was an underlying fear that the introduction of Chinese-language courses would eventually transform the university. The Council said that in the postwar period, what the university needed most was time for consolidation rather than a new direction in its development.

In 1953, Ivor Jennings and Douglas Logan, experts in British university administration, were invited to advise on the development of the university. The *Jennings-Logan Report* asserted that the University of Hong Kong should remain an English-speaking university. As far as they were concerned, it was the government's job to fill the gap between the university and the Chinese middle schools. In order to prepare these graduates for admission into university, a special two-year program was designed at Clementi Middle School. However, this program did not solve the problem, because it could accommodate only a very limited number of students.

The education system in Hong Kong has always been divided into Chinese and English. The students in the English system had access to a complete education from primary to university levels, whereas the students in the Chinese system could not go farther than middle school. Before 1949, these students were able to continue their education in mainland China. The Chinese system in Hong Kong followed the curriculum prescribed by the Nationalist government in China, and used textbooks produced in Shanghai. Many Chinese schools in Hong Kong were associated with schools in Guangzhou. However, after the establishment of the People's Republic of China, Hong Kong students could no longer go to the mainland to complete their studies. This placed an added burden on the education system, and the situation was exacerbated by the large influx of refugee students from China.

A number of dedicated and experienced refugee scholars from China took up the challenge. Driven by educational ideals, the mission of propagating Chinese culture and educating the young, as well as the need to earn a living, scholars and professionals in various fields used crude facilities and rented classrooms to establish so-called "refugee colleges." According to a government survey in 1952, there were more than thirty colleges of this kind, varying in standards and the length of their programs. Nine of these were of higher standard, offering four-year programs in arts and commerce. Among them were New Asia College,[20] Chung Chi College, and the forerunners of United College. These three were to emerge later as the Foundation Colleges of The Chinese University of Hong Kong. The survival of these colleges depended greatly on international support, and in the case of Chung Chi, the support of the Protestant church. The government granted the site of Ma Liu Shui Valley to Chung Chi College, thanks to the persistence of Rev. R.O. Hall, Bishop of the Hong Kong Anglican Church. It proved to be an important asset to the future Chinese university.

By 1956, the degrees awarded by the colleges gained recognition from many universities in America and Europe, some of which even granted scholarships to the more outstanding students. Yet in Hong Kong, the degrees were not recognized by the government for employment or for further training. The private colleges received no financial support, but were still subject to the control of the Education Department and the Education Ordinance of 1952. So in 1956, the three colleges banded together to strive for government recognition and support.

After consultation with the representatives of the three colleges, Charles Long, Yale-in-Asia representative at New Asia and a trustee of the College, sent a memorandum to D.J.S. Crozier, Director of Education, on August 16, 1956. The memorandum began by pointing out that the private colleges should not be governed by the Education

Ordinance of 1952, which was intended to apply to primary and secondary education in Hong Kong, and that special regulations should be drawn up for colleges that were aspiring to university standards. It went on to state that, as part of the Hong Kong education system, the colleges could not depend entirely on the financial assistance of foreign missions, foundations and private donations. The government should take responsibility for providing support for basic facilities and recurrent expenses. The memorandum also said that under the existing government policy, thousands of intelligent young people were leaving the Colony in search of higher education overseas or in Taiwan, thereby creating a potential loss in leadership. The memorandum concluded that it would be difficult for the private colleges to provide the best contribution to tertiary education unless the government offered support for them to develop university status for awarding degrees. This became the first document in the government file on the founding of The Chinese University of Hong Kong.

In January 1956, L.G. Morgan, Deputy Director of Education, observed that the Chinese middle school could not but feel grievance at a situation whereby the government provided $8 million annually to the University of Hong Kong for the students from the Anglo-Chinese schools, and made little or no provision for those from the Chinese middle schools. In another memorandum by Morgan in October the same year, five possible measures were proposed to meet the overall needs of the Chinese secondary-school students. The most significant proposal was "the establishment of a Chinese university with its own charter and degree granting powers."[21] However, Morgan's own recommendation still suggested that the University of Hong Kong broaden its function and accept a greater responsibility in meeting the needs of the community. In October 1956, there were bloody riots caused by confrontations between pro-Nationalist and pro-Communist political groups. This persuaded the government that it could no longer ignore the demand for more post-secondary education for its population.[22] In January 1957, representatives of Chung Chi, New Asia and United, the "refugee colleges," met with the Education Department. Bishop Hall and Charles Long also attended the meeting, which ended without any decision. In February, the Chinese Colleges Joint Council was established. After numerous meetings and discussions, in August 1958, it was finally decided that another university would be established in Hong Kong.

A New University

On June 2, 1959, the Hong Kong government officially announced that it was prepared to establish a new university with Chinese as the main language of instruction. Sir John Fulton, Professor of History and a tutor at Oxford for many years (and incidentally, a former teacher of Father's, as well as of Governor Sir Robert Black and Governor Sir Murray Maclehose), was appointed as advisor to Governor Sir Robert Black. In his 1959 report, *The Development of Post-Secondary Colleges in Hong Kong*, submitted to the Governor in March 1960, he stated that academic freedom, university autonomy, and research and bi-cultural mission were especially important in shaping the basic character of the future university.[23]

According to Professor Ma Lin, vice-chancellor of The Chinese University from 1978 to 1987, Sir John Fulton, now Lord Fulton, was the midwife of The Chinese University, and the good results of the delivery were in many ways due to the close friendship between Sir John and Father. On several occasions, Father flew to Yorkshire, where Sir John lived in his retirement, to speak to him regarding The Chinese University, and Father could be very persuasive.[24]

Up to this point, the colleges had their roots in China and an early association with American educational foundations and universities, but they lacked British experience and connections. Sir John Fulton brought with him the experience of three different British universities, Oxford, Wales and Sussex. The introduction of new ideas was facilitated by the British Council and the University of Hong Kong in a series of open forums and conferences held in 1960 and 1961. Following the *Fulton Report*, a Provisional Council was formed composed of twenty members: two government officials, the three presidents of the Colleges, the vice-chancellor of the University of Hong Kong, Lindsay Ride, and prominent members from the community. The Council was chaired by C.Y. Kwan, with Father as the vice-chairman. The Council promptly adopted the name The Chinese University of Hong Kong. Father had the added responsibility of being the chairman of the Campus Planing Committee as well as the chairman of the Tender Board. From then on, until the end of his life, Father spent a great deal of his time and energy promoting the establishment and growth of The Chinese University of Hong Kong. He considered it to be one of his "children." Prof. Ma Lin told me that without Father's dedication, The Chinese University wouldn't be the way it is today.[25]

It was to the credit of the Council that the magnificent site of three hundred acres adjacent to Chung Chi College at Ma Liu Shui[26] was secured from the government. The area was able not only to accommodate the university, but also provided ample space for future expansion. The Chinese University of Hong Kong Ordinance, together with its Statutes, was passed in the Legislative Council and came into effect in September 1963. On October 17, 1963, the governor, in his capacity as chancellor, officiated at the inauguration ceremony.

On October 9, 1964, the first meeting of the Campus Planning Committee was held in Father's office in Edinburgh House. These meetings continued to be held in Father's office at different locations until 1977, when the venue changed to the Lee Gardens Hotel. Father served on this committee and on the Council until he passed away in 1983.

Being a civil engineer, Father was in the perfect position to oversee the buildings to be erected on campus. The work was monumental. The project was similar to building a mini-city on hills that had to be terraced, and the mud and rocks were transported to the opposite side of Tolo Harbour for the construction of the Plover Cove reservoir.[27] Moreover, except for the campus of Chung Chi College, the Committee was working with raw land, most of which was without infrastructure, such as roads, water and sewer connections. In the minutes of the meeting of 1966, it was mentioned that sea water had to be used for flushing because it was not clear whether the government would be piping water from the Sha Tin Treatment Works within the next two years. In the minutes of 1967, it was noted that planting on steep hilly sections had to be done immediately because the slopes were too steep to be turfed.

The fact that Father had so many friends in the government was a great advantage for the university. Father's friend Szeto Wai was hired as the architect and Plover Cove Engineers were the engineers for the university. In the initial stage, Father asked Szeto to travel to the best universities in the world to learn from them. In the mid-1960s, Szeto visited fifteen of the best and most beautiful campuses in the world before he designed the campus for The Chinese University of Hong Kong.[28]

As the vice-chairman of the Council, Father would chair the meetings once or twice a year. Father had a reputation of chairing meetings that were short and efficient. They always started on time, and were seldom longer than forty-five minutes. Once, a Council member arrived ten minutes late, and by the time he sat down, his part of the meeting was over.[29]

On my parents' visits to Toronto, I often heard Father mention the importance of establishing a Chinese university in Hong Kong for the Chinese. Father not only worked very hard for the university in dealing with the government and getting the new buildings built, he also donated a great deal of money to its foundation. His greatest show of faith was when my brother Christopher attended the university and graduated from it. When Christopher lived in residence, he told Father that the mattress in the residence was uncomfortable. So, Father bought new mattresses for the entire residence!

At the beginning of 1983, Father wanted to experiment with the reproduction of purified yeast used in the production of Chinese rice wine, which many Chinese use for medicinal purpose. He asked Professor Ma Lin to see if it could be reproduced in the laboratory at the university. The experiment was successful, and Father planned to experiment with fermentation at home. Father was always interested in different medicines.

Father was so concerned about the well-being of The Chinese University of Hong Kong that he treated it as one of his "children" in his will. Mother not only continued to be a great supporter of the university after Father died, but she also considered it as one of her "children." And because of Father's influence, different members of the Lee family continue to be very generous to the university.

My favourite artifact from Grandfather's time, an ivory mammoth tusk carved with the story of the Three Kingdoms, is proudly displayed in the museum at the university.

Shortly after Father's death, Mother established the R.C. Lee Memorial Gold Medal in Surgery, to be awarded to the best student in the final year in the Faculty of Medicine, Department of Surgery.

In September 1987, the Council at the university decided to name the Science Centre Lecture Hall Complex the "R.C. Lee Lecture Hall" as a perpetual memorial to Father. In October 1988, The Chinese University of Hong Kong awarded Mother an honorary degree for her role as a public figure in Hong Kong, and for her continuous support of the university.

11

The Japanese Connection

For obvious reasons, after the Second World War, it was very difficult for Japanese businesses to get established in Hong Kong. Although Father had been in the resistance during the war, when peace came, he felt that everyone should put the past aside. He believed that Japan would prosper, and he wanted to build long-term relationships in order to bring prosperity to the people of Hong Kong.

As a progressive thinker, Father was always invited to the Sauntering meetings, started by a Chinese scholar who had attended Waseda University in Tokyo. It was a study group, a monthly dinner gathering of about twelve top Japanese businessmen in Hong Kong.[1] Father would always invite the group back. He was held in such high esteem that Japanese businessmen, and even the Consul-General of Japan,[2] would pay him a courtesy visit whenever they were in Hong Kong.

When the Japanese Club was established in 1955, Father was one of the first to offer assistance.[3] The Club was originally located in the Victoria Hotel, with 106 corporate and private members. By November 1996, the membership had increased to more than 25,000. Aside from dining facilities, the activities available included language instructions in Chinese and English, doll-making, Chinese painting and calligraphy.[4] And throughout the history of the Club, it has been located mostly in buildings owned by the Lee family.[5] Starting in the 1970s, my parents hosted a dinner at the Lee Gardens Hotel for all the Japanese executives in Hong Kong, once a year, in order for them to make friends with members of the Chinese business community.

By the late 1960s, it became absolutely necessary for the survival of Japanese financial institutions to establish Hong Kong subsidiaries in conjunction with leading Hong Kong business people. Father had been invited to be a partner by different Japanese enterprises but he made it his policy not to get involved.[6] However, he viewed his involvement in education quite differently.

The Japanese School

Father played an important role in the establishment of a Japanese school for Japanese children whose parents lived in Hong Kong. He helped the school acquire government permits to operate as a foreign school, and negotiated and sought approvals from the Departments of Education, Public Works, Health and Fire. According to a report sent to the Japanese government from the Consulate-General of Japan, without Father's help, the process would have been difficult and lengthy.

When Father first heard of the plans to establish a Japanese school, he suggested that it be located in the space in Tower Court, on Hysan Avenue, one of the buildings owned by the Lee family, which was about to be vacated by the Hong Kong Education Department.[7] However, the preparatory committee for the establishment of the school had not yet been formed,[8] and no action could be taken.

Fifth Uncle, who looked after rentals in the Lee Hysan Estate Company, had many inquiries about the space, but Father stubbornly insisted that it be held for the opening of the Japanese school, without any rent or deposit. It stood vacant for half a year. In January 1966, the Japanese government allocated a subsidiary budget for the Hong Kong Japanese School, and only then was the school able to pay rent. An official tenancy agreement was then signed. On May 10, 1966, the Japanese school,[9] located on the second and the third floors of Tower Court,[10] opened with seventy students. The following day, Fifth Uncle showed up at the school to see Ichiro Fujita, the principal, to return the cheque. Father had ordered that the rent from

January to March was not to be accepted. Everyone at the school was overwhelmed by his generous spirit.[11]

Father continued to take great interest in the Japanese School and gave advice to Ichiro Fujita. The school opened extension class-rooms in the Ling Ying Building,[12] and on January 24, 1976, a primary school opened on Blue Pool Road. The school kept expanding, and the junior high school opened on Braemar Hill Road on October 23, 1982. Father was their special guest at each of the opening ceremonies. At the opening ceremony of the Braemar Hill Road school, Ichiro Fujita made a speech in front of all the students and guests, referring to the cherished friendship between himself and Father, expressing his heartfelt and sincere gratitude, and introducing Father as the "true benefactor and patron of the Hong Kong Japanese School."[13]

On March 12, 1969, Father was decorated with the Order of the Sacred Treasure, Gold Rays with Neck Ribbon, by the Japanese Emperor. The third-highest Order in Japan, it was established in 1888.[14] The ceremony was held at the official residence of the Con-sul-General of Japan, Akira Okada, at 24 Po Shan Road in Hong Kong. Father was proud of this award, despite the fact that it took several years to get permission from the Queen of England to wear and use the name of the Order. One of the conditions imposed was that its name must always be given in full, to prevent confusion with British Orders.[15]

Japan and China

By the 1960s, the Japanese government wished to re-establish relations with the government of China. Since direct contact was not possible at the time, the responsibility was given to the Consul-Gen-eral of Japan in Hong Kong, Akira Okada, a close friend of Father's. In his book *Mizutori Gaiko Hiwa (The Secret Story of Mizutori's Diplomacy)* Okada mentioned that when he and his wife were guests of my parents on our launch on August 17, 1969, he and Father discussed the possibility of working towards the resumption of relations between Japan and China. At that time, Father offered help through his friends Zhou Enlai and Liao Chengzhi in Beijing.

On September 10, 1971, Consul-General Okada met with Japanese Prime Minister Sato to discuss the relationship with China. The prime minister told Okada that Japan was willing to accept the Chinese view that Taiwan was a province of China, and that Japan would not object to China's entry into the United Nations. However, he said, China must stop interfering with the internal politics of Japan. Also, although Taiwan's membership in the United Nations was considered temporary, Japan would not ask for its resignation in the immediate future. The Japanese government needed advice on how to proceed towards the normalization of relations with China, since at this time, the Chinese government would not receive anyone sent by the Japanese government. Prime Minister Sato asked Okada to seek help from his friends in Hong Kong to reach the right contacts in Beijing. Okada was given permission to go to Beijing if necessary to carry out his mission. This was so important in the agenda of the Japanese government that he was asked to report to the prime minister directly, bypassing the Department of Foreign Affairs.

Consul-General Okada returned to Hong Kong on September 14 to proceed with this mission. One of the friends he might have turned to for help was P.Y. Tang, who had been a classmate of Zhou Enlai's at Nankai University, but unfortunately, Tang had died on June 17. Father was on his priority list, not only because of his contacts in China, but also because of the friendship between him and Okada. However, Father was away from Hong Kong for a few weeks, so Okada turned to Father's cousin, Uncle Quo Wai of Hang Seng Bank. Uncle Quo Wai knew Consul-General Okada through the bank, but he had connections with China only through Father.[16] The two men met the following day. Uncle Quo Wai immediately contacted Father's good friend Fei Yiming of *Ta Kung Pao*, who relayed the message to Beijing.

On September 16, Zhou Enlai met with Hide Kawasaki, a member of the Diet, who was visiting China, and told him that Japan had to recognize the People's Republic as the rightful government of China, and accept the fact that Taiwan was part of China. If those conditions were met, he would welcome an official visit from Japan. Consul-General Okada wondered whether this reaction had been due to the contact Uncle Quo Wai had made, but he doubted that China would have responded so quickly. When he and Uncle Quo Wai spoke again on September 17, the latter said that it would not be difficult to arrange a meeting between a Chinese official and the Consul-General in Hong Kong, but an official meeting with the Japanese Foreign Office would depend on Beijing. He suggested that Prime Minister Sato personally write a proposal and have it passed on to Premier Zhou through unofficial channels by one of the many Japanese visitors to Beijing. On September 20, Consul-General Okada telephoned the prime minister's office, and learnt that the prime minister was not planning to write a personal letter to Premier Zhou as yet.

The following day, it was rumoured in Hong Kong that Chairman Mao had died, and the October 1 National Celebration would be cancelled. It was already in the news that Japan would bring up the question of China's representation in the United Nations. With all the recent events, Consul-General Okada wondered whether an answer from the Chinese government would be forthcoming by September 23.

On the evening of September 22, 1971, Consul-General Okada received an urgent call from Uncle Quo Wai, apologizing that due to an urgent matter, Beijing would not be able to meet with a representative of the Japanese government to discuss normalization of relations. As it turned out, the urgent matter was the Lin Biao incident.

Lin Biao was the originator of the "Little Red Book" of Mao's sayings, *Quotations from Chairman Mao*. In 1965, he produced a pamphlet, "Long Live the Victory of the People's War," suggesting that China could win over the world by mobilizing the people of backward countries just as Mao had mobilized the poor peasants of China. In the Ninth Party Congress in April 1969, he was named sole vice-chairman and Mao's official heir. However, by April 1970, Lin Biao and his wife, Ye Qun, detected Mao's changed attitude towards them and they plotted against Mao.[17]

On September 14, 1971, the Chinese ambassador to Ulan Bator was summoned to the Mongol Foreign Office early in the morning, and was told that a Chinese aircraft (transporting Lin Biao, Ye Qun and Lin Liguo) had violated Mongol airspace and had crashed at 2:00 a.m. the day before.

The news of this case was suppressed for months in China, and it took a year before it was disclosed to the foreign press. Even up till spring 1972, no one knew of this incident, and the Japanese press continued to mention Lin Biao as if he were still alive.[18]

On October 8, 1971, Uncle Quo Wai asked Consul-General Okada if he would like to meet Fei Yiming of *Ta Kung Pao* at the Australian National Day reception on October 25. The two were introduced on an unofficial basis. Fei Yiming confirmed everything that had been said and done by Uncle Quo Wai, and requested patience from the Japanese government in awaiting the next step from Beijing. On the same day, the United Nations admitted China as a member, and Japan's support of Taiwan's membership failed. Unfortunately, due to the Lin Biao incident, Okada was not able to complete his assignment of mending relations between China and Japan during his term of office. Uncle Quo Wai was sure that if he had been able to complete his assignment, Okada would have been named the first Japanese ambassador to China since the Second World War.[19]

Yamaichi Securities

In the early 1960s, Father re-established a friendship with his boxing friend from his Oxford days, Konosuke Koike, and they visited each other in Hong Kong and Tokyo. Koike was the eldest son of the founder of Yamaichi Securities,[20] and the chairman of the company. In 1964, Yamaichi encountered financial difficulties and asked for help from major Japanese banks headed by the Industrial Bank of Japan (IBJ). Koike resigned and Teru Hidaka from the Industrial Bank of Japan came to Yamaichi as president. By May 1965, the company's financial position had deteriorated further, and it sought more help from the Bank of Japan and the Central Bank.

At the beginning of 1970, when the situation had improved and Yamaichi Securities wanted to open a company in Hong Kong,

Yamaichi took advantage of the friendship between Father and the former chairman, Konosuke Koike. Officers from Yamaichi paid Father a visit with a letter from his old friend Koike requesting help in the setting up of the Hong Kong company. On hearing that his friend had taken the responsibility for mismanagement in the company and had resigned from the chairmanship, Father was sympathetic. He remembered his own experiences as the eldest son, and the financial difficulties our family had experienced when Grandfather was murdered. Father said that if by agreeing to join the board of Yamaichi (Hong Kong), he could help his friend, he would do so gladly. He immediately gave suggestions for possible contacts as directors and shareholders.[21]

Yamaichi International (H.K.) Ltd. opened its office in Hong Kong in July 1971. Teru Hidaka was named chairman and Father was the deputy chairman.[22] Konosuke Koike became an honorary advisor. Father brought many influential people into the company as directors, and introduced many important clients.

August 16, 1971, was the date set for the cocktail reception at the Mandarin Hotel, celebrating the opening of the Hong Kong company. The weather was dreadful and the typhoon signal was up. By evening, the cross-harbour ferry had stopped running. However, in spite of the weather, many distinguished guests attended, and Yamaichi credited Father's influence for the fact that so many people made the effort.[23]

Shinichi Shiraishi,[24] the sales manager of Yamaichi International (H.K.) Ltd.[25] came to know Father because it was his responsibility to increase business in Hong Kong. He met Father from time to time to explain the situation of the Tokyo stock market and to report the business results of the Hong Kong company. Father was pleased to see the business growing steadily, and was always very happy to see his old friend Koike at the shareholders' meetings which took place every July in Hong Kong. Shiraishi noticed how Father always paid a great deal of attention to Koike and his wife, even though Teru Hidaka was the "big boss."[26]

By 1982, Yamaichi Securities wanted to become a wholly owned company. Officers from the company consulted Father as to the possibilities of buying back the shares in the Yamaichi International

(H.K.) Ltd. With his usual wish to help others, Father asked them to leave the matter with him. He proceeded to contact the Hong Kong directors and shareholders and made arrangements for the company to buy back the shares. Yamaichi International (H.K.) Ltd. became a wholly owned company, and the board and shareholders felt greatly indebted to Father.[27]

Mother told me that the Causeway Bay area became very prosperous because of Father's Japanese friends. Causeway Bay is in the area where Grandfather bought East Point Hill, which his descendants have subsequently developed. It is also where many members of the Lee family lived from the beginning of the 1950s to the mid-1980s, including my own family. There are many Japanese businesses located in the area. When the first Japanese department store, Daimaru, opened in Causeway Bay in November 1960, a Chinese managing director was needed in addition to his Japanese counterpart, so Father introduced his friend Liu Huo Yan from Taiwan, who spoke Japanese, to the post.[28] Sogo Department Store opened its first store in Causeway Bay in May 1985 and has since opened many branches all over Hong Kong. The well-known up-scale department store Mitsukoshi, the Japanese Club and the Japanese Chamber of Commerce are all located in Causeway Bay.

Father often lent a hand to these businesses when they opened in Hong Kong. At the Mitsukoshi (Hong Kong) opening, he took part in the ribbon-cutting ceremony. In his letter of thanks, Shigeru Okada, President of Mitsukoshi Limited, wrote:

> ... I firmly believe that it was indeed in virtue of your personality and through your courtesy that we could have the notables and the potentates of all spheres of social activities in Hong Kong and varied V.I.P.'s at those occasions, and herein I express my sincere gratitude for it.[29]

By the 1980s, Japanese investments became one of the major economic forces in the colony. Father's gift for making friends and building relationships had helped to bring prosperity to Hong Kong.

During the Asian economic crisis at the end of 1997, Yamaichi Securities, the fourth-largest securities company in Japan, went bankrupt.

The Hong Kong operations, Yamaichi International (H.K.) Ltd., was sold to Core Pacific Group,[30] a Taiwanese conglomerate, at just under $88 million, which was the net value of the business. The offer was considered a good deal by Yamaichi advisors, given the tough Asian market conditions. The company was valuable because Core Pacific wanted to capitalize on Yamaichi International's strong business presence in mainland China. The company would be renamed Core Pacific Yamaichi.

In a letter to me, S. Shiraishi, former vice-president of Yamaichi wrote:

> Since YIH (Yamaichi International Hong Kong) started business in 1971 with great help of your father and your family members, YIH has established its name not only in Hong Kong but also in Asia in general during last 27 years. The co. has favorable financial conditions and many capable and dedicating local staff.
>
> YIH is very active in handling China related stocks in the last few years.[31]

Given the circumstances, Father would have been pleased to know that the purchase agreement with Core Pacific included keeping all 121 employees of the Hong Kong operation.[32]

12
The
Chinese Patriot

The leaders of China called Father a patriot, meaning he was loyal to the Chinese government. But I believe that patriotism meant something different to Father. He was patriotic to the Chinese people, irrespective of the governments they live under.

The letter Father wrote in his youth to his school in Hong Kong shows that he had always been proud of being Chinese, and at the same time concerned with the state of affairs in China. I became aware of this by the end of the 1940s, for by then I was old enough to observe how he conducted his life. He tried very hard to alleviate human suffering both in Hong Kong and in China. He was only one man, but he believed that one man could make a difference.

Mother told me one day that when she first met Father, he spoke English with an Oxford accent, but later (by the time I understood English), he spoke it with a Chinese accent. She was sure this was intentional. Most people would have flaunted their Oxford accent for the rest of their lives, but not Father. Because of his pride in Hong Kong, for a number of years Father arranged, at his own expense, for a number of students from Oxford to broaden their experience by practical studies in Hong Kong.[1]

Father had no interest in politics, and so was effective in helping many. There were times in his life, because of his friendship with the leaders of China, he was asked if he was a Communist. His answer

163

was, "No, I am not. Even if I were to want to join the party, I don't qualify, as I'm a capitalist."

After the Second World War, the civil war between the Nationalists under Chiang Kaishek and the Communists under Mao Zedong began in earnest in China. In a way, Father retreated to Hong Kong. He looked upon Hong Kong as a Chinese colony under a period of British management, and believed he could be just as useful in working towards the improvement of the life of the population there. From then on, he concentrated on Hong Kong, but he never forgot his roots in China, and waited until he could be of help to China again. At the same time, he always acted as a responsible citizen of the world.

Every year, on October 1, the People's Republic of China celebrated National Day. In the 1950s, Father was the first and only person (non-Communist) in Hong Kong to receive an invitation to attend the celebration.[2] As far as he was concerned, not only were his friendships important to him, but also his special and unique closeness to the leaders of China, which could bring about a better life for the people of Hong Kong. He realized how dependent Hong Kong was on China, not only as an entrepôt, but for its food and water supply.

Solving the Water Shortage

As the refugee population in Hong Kong increased, the water supply became insufficient. Hong Kong depended on rainwater collected in reservoirs during the rainy season and although the number of reservoirs was increased, supply could not keep up with demand. Rationing of water began in the 1950s, but that was only a temporary solution to the problem. Water was supplied a few hours per day, then every other day, and then once every three days. The decrease in rainfall in the early 1960s turned the water shortage into a crisis.

As always, when Hong Kong had a problem, Father regarded it as his own responsibility. His concerns and public appeals to save water were constantly reported in the newspapers. While Father appealed to the public to save water, he also explained to the population the reasons for the shortage and that the government was doing its best to solve the problem.[3] In fact, the only major long-term solution to the problem was to obtain water from China. Due to the fact that Beijing did not recognize the legitimacy of British presence in Hong Kong, they would not negotiate with London over Hong Kong issues. This meant that the Chinese in Hong Kong had to negotiate with the Chinese government. The job of negotiating fell on Father, who was the only person in Hong Kong who had access to the leaders in China.

Xinhua News Agency, also known as the New China News Agency, had established a branch in Hong Kong in 1947 and was the unofficial Chinese consulate. In the early 1950s, the director was Lian Weilin, a good friend of Father's. The issue of obtaining water from China was discussed and Lian was the go-between, with Father and Sir Tsun Nin Chau negotiating for Hong Kong, and Tao Zhou, the First Secretary, and Chen Yu, the Governor of Guangdong province, for China.[4]

In May 1963, Premier Zhou Enlai allowed tankers to go up the Pearl River daily to supply water to Hong Kong. At the same time, the Chinese government ordered a feasibility study for transporting water to Hong Kong from the East River in Guangdong province, in order to solve future problems of water shortage in Hong Kong.

While Father was in the midst of discussions, there was fear that Hong Kong would run out of water completely. On May 31, 1963, Father made a public appeal to save water, while he explained that transporting water from China was only a temporary measure and could not solve the problem completely. He also mentioned that talks with China were under way to bring about a permanent solution.[5]

The shortage became so severe that it was announced, starting June 1, 1963, that water could only be supplied for four hours every four days in the heavily populated areas, and three hours every four days in the less populated areas.[6]

On April 23, 1964, agreements were signed between the Hong Kong government and the Water Works Department of Guangdong, and work began on the building of conduits from the East River to reservoirs in Shenzhen.[7] From there water could be piped to Hong Kong.

In January 1965, Father was interviewed by *Wah Kiu Yat Po* about his hopes for the new year. Besides wishing for the prosperity of the citizens of Hong Kong, he looked forward to the completion of the water project, scheduled for March 1 of that year.[8]

The project was finished in January 1965 and by March it started to supply water to Hong Kong, 60 million cubic metres[9] per year. By summer, two-thirds of the water consumed in Hong Kong was from the East River.[10] My parents were the only people from Hong Kong who attended the opening of the facilities in Shenzhen. Sir Tsun Nin Chau had wanted to attend but was not allowed by the British Government.[11] No one could have stopped Father.

However, the water supply to Hong Kong was interrupted during the riots of 1967. That summer, the rainfall was below normal. The agreement with China was for 15,000 million gallons plus an additional 1,800 million gallons requested by the Water Authority, to be used between October 1 and June 30. By the beginning of June, this amount had already been drawn from the system in Hong Kong. By June 28, a request for an additional 2,000 million gallons for the month of July had still not been answered by China. Until the request was accepted, Mr. Michael Wright, Director of Public Works, announced that the supply of water would have to be reduced from eight hours each day at the beginning of June to four hours on alternate days, starting on June 29.[12] Under the existing agreement with China, the new water supply would not begin until October 1.

By July 1967, the water shortage was so severe that supply to the population was further reduced to four hours every four days, starting July 13.[13] No one really knows why the request for more water from China was not answered. One can only guess that, because of the turmoil caused by the Cultural Revolution, the Chinese government was in no condition to look after the needs of the population of Hong Kong.

By the end of the 1960s, life had returned to normal. There were two subsequent phases of redevelopment of the water supply from the East River. The first one started in 1976 and finished in 1978, and a second phase started in 1981, increasing the supply to 660 million cubic metres[14] of water to Hong Kong annually, which solved the water supply problem for Hong Kong once and for all.

Between Hong Kong and China

During the 1960s, Father's relationship with China was viewed by some with jealousy and suspicion. Although he helped solve the water crisis,[15] some people accused Father of negotiating for the benefit of China.[16] The colonial government needed him when it was necessary, but they also wanted him to stay away from China. That caused a great deal of conflict between Governor David Trench (1964–1971) and Father. Father had built long-term relationships with people in China and he was loyal to his friends. In the case of the water crisis, if it hadn't been for China's help, Hong Kong would have ceased to be a viable place in which to live.

Father believed that as a Chinese, he had a right to visit friends and relatives in China as long as he was allowed into the country. After all, he was a free man. When the Hong Kong government demanded that he stop his visits to China and that Mother stop visiting her relatives, I can imagine the fireworks. Father had no respect for Governor Trench, whom he believed was not qualified for the position of governor.[17] He believed that Trench used the Chinese and at the same time treated them badly. David K.P. Li, who used to see Father at least once a week, told me that Father, while pro-British, was fed up with the abuses of the colonial government towards the Chinese. Arguments ensued, and Father decided to resign from all his voluntary positions with the Hong Kong government.[18]

Up to that point, Father had been expected by everyone to be the next in line to be knighted by the Queen. Mother had bought a beautiful blue vase which was decorated with a deer, a pine tree, and a monkey holding a peach, signifying officialdom, wealth and long life, in preparation for the celebration of the event. Then Father gave her the news that he had resigned.

When my parents returned from a trip to Madagascar on June 13, 1965, they were met at the airport by a number of unofficial members of the Legislative Council. A letter accepting Father's resignation was handed to him by Y.K. Kan.[19] By 1966, Father had resigned all his voluntary positions with the Hong Kong government. His resignations meant that he was no longer given any official recognition for anything he did, but it didn't change his desire to help the people of Hong Kong. From then on, he represented himself instead of the Hong Kong government.

When David K.P. Li went to London subsequently to inquire why Father hadn't received a knighthood after all that he had done for Hong Kong, he was told that Father had been blacklisted by certain members of the colonial government.[20]

Father built good relations with the People's Republic of China, not only because he had many old friends in the government, but also because he knew very well that Hong Kong had to return to China one day, and he wanted to pave the road for a smooth transition. As he told me many times, "There must not be any fighting. The transition must be peaceful and beneficial to everyone." The leaders in Beijing knew of Father's sincerity and had great respect for him. Father believed that the people of Hong Kong had to rule Hong Kong one day, and that final decisions about their future could not be left to London or Beijing.[21] Unfortunately, he didn't live to see the peaceful change of sovereignty of Hong Kong.

Father and Uncle Quo Wai were the first people from Hong Kong to know about Deng Xiaoping's policy of "one country, two systems" and his fifty-year plan for Hong Kong. On one of Father's trips to China with Uncle Quo Wai in the early 1970s, Father was called into a room to be given special information. He said, "Quo-Wai, you come in too. I want you to hear what's being said."[22] Father was given the assurance that business would continue as usual after the change of sovereignty of Hong Kong.

When my parents visited us in Toronto at the beginning of the 1970s, Father and I had a discussion about China. It was his view that China had had its share of bad times for the last two centuries, but that the twenty-first century belonged to China and I would live to see China strong again. I realized how very concerned he had always been about China and the Chinese people.

Father had always maintained that there was a great difference between the relationship of the governments of Hong Kong and China, and that of the population of Hong Kong with China. In a speech Father gave in June 1982, in Frankfurt, Germany, at the International Conference on the Economic Opportunities in Hong Kong, he said:

> There was no doubt that the strained relationship between the Hong Kong Government and the Government of China, more apparent than real, was largely due to the short-sightedness of the former Colonial Cadet Officers and to the policy of the then Colonial Office in London, but not so between the Chinese of Hong Kong and the Chinese Government.

He was referring to the 1960s. He noted improvements under governor Sir Murray Maclehose in the 1970s:

> The relationship between China and Hong Kong started to improve steadily during his term of office. This improvement is due, in large measure, to his foresight and great administrative ability.[23]

The Chinese Connections

The 1970s were the years Father helped to build a bridge between Hong Kong and China. Having made the break with the colonial government, he could no longer be criticized by the Hong Kong government for his actions. Those were the years when business people in Hong Kong did not invest in or travel to China. In fact, mainland China was a place to be avoided.

Because of Father's wish for a smooth transition, dialogue was necessary. In order to help bring the two sides (Hong Kong and China) together, Father held a spring feast every Chinese New Year, inviting all the prominent members of the business community in Hong Kong, members of the Hong Kong government, as well as his foreign friends who might wish to make friends with China, to meet representatives of China. Because of Father's prestige, everyone came. By so doing, he was able to build friendships that continue to bring prosperity to all.

Xinhua News Agency would have liked to contact those in the business circles as well as the Legislative and Executive Councillors, but as the director of Xinhua in the 1970s, Lian Weilin, told me, "If I had sent out invitations, no one would turn up. But when your father did, everyone came."[24] Father's spring feast at the Lee Gardens Hotel was like a Who's Who in the colony. It became one of the most important annual events in Hong Kong.

At Father's spring feast, spouses were not included. It was generally known to be a party for men only, although women councillors were invited. Anna, Father's secretary, was required to help, but she had to leave before dinner started. There was a story in a celebrity magazine about how a foreign friend of Father's arrived in Hong Kong for the party with his wife, only to be told at the Lee Gardens Hotel that spouses were not invited. He had to take his wife back to the hotel and return to the party.[25]

One year we happened to be in Hong Kong when Father held his spring feast. Neville was invited, but I was not. Father asked me to take our boys to see the magic show at the Lee Theatre. Even though Father always thought of this as an event for men only, after he died, Mother, who had never taken part in the spring feast, continued to hold it for him for a few more years. If Father only knew!

Like all Chinese, Father frequently went back to our ancestral village, which was also the first area in China he helped after the war. The first thing he did in Garlieu village was to give money for the building of a new bridge over the river on which he had travelled as a child, when he and Grandfather brought Great-grandfather's body in a boat for burial. When I went back to the village with my family in the early 1990s, that was the first thing the villagers were proud to show us.

During our visit, we were also shown the school buildings and the playground that Father and Second Uncle had donated money to build. We were taken to a small hat factory which Father had helped the villagers to start. It was a very large room, clean, well lit and well organized. By the time we visited the village the second time, the hats they were making included well-known labels from overseas. The villagers were proud of their achievements.

Over the years, Father and his brothers helped build hospitals and schools in the city of Sunwui. By so doing, they were acting like generations of Chinese in the past by not forgetting where they came from, and offering help to those in their ancestral home town. In honour of Father, Mother was presented with a gold key in 1992 to the city of Sunwui, making her an honorary citizen. In 1993, Mother was also presented with a gold key to the city of Hoiping, where Great-grandfather had originally come from.

Because of my parents' frequent travels in China, Father was able to talk knowledgeably about the country. He Mingsi of the Xinhua News Agency, who often accompanied my parents to China, was impressed by how inquisitive a traveller Father was. He was interested not only in the development of the cities, but also in the outlying areas of the vast country.

In 1977, my parents went on an extensive trip through western China, visiting sights in Gansu province and Xinjiang Autonomous Region. The following January, Father gave a talk to the Chinese Bankers' Association. He showed, complete with slides, not only the sights, including the hydro-electric plants, but he also brought pieces of rocks from the area.[26] Father always had a special interest in the beauty of rocks. His enthusiasm in everything he did was infectious.

When my parents visited us in 1978, they told us about their trip to western China and gave us photographs of their visit. The one I liked best was a picture of Father on a dromedary. My parents had been invited to dine with the local chieftains in Ürümqi, Xinjiang Autonomous Region, who had served them their best. It was the first time they had ever eaten fresh *fat choy*, generally known as hair vegetable because it looks like hair. It is always used in dishes for Chinese New Year for good luck, because *fat choy* sounds the same as prosperity in Cantonese. The majority of Chinese don't know where it comes from, and generally presume that it is a seaweed. *Fat choy* is actually a desert plant. Being special guests, my parents were also served the local delicacy — sheep's eyes. Mother said, "When I saw the head on my plate with those eyes staring at me, I immediately felt sick!"

Father also promoted cultural exchanges. In 1968, during an excavation in the Man Chen District in Hebei province, the Tomb belonging to Prince Ching (Jing) of Chung Shan (Zhongshan) (personal name Liu Sheng) of the Western-Han dynasty (206 B.C. – A.D. 24) was discovered.[27] Inside was the body of a princess dressed in a garment of jade threaded together by gold filaments. This spectacular garment, 188 cm long, had never been shown outside of China. In 1978, Fei Yiming of *Ta Kung Pao* wanted to put on an exhibition in Hong Kong of this jade garment, together with other funerary objects, such as a gold-plated bronze Zhang Hsin Palace lamp from the same tomb, and bronze horses and chariots from a tomb from the East Han dynasty excavated in 1969.[28] Fei was not able to organize the exhibition and asked Father for help. Father asked Henry Fok to hold the exhibition in Star House and organized the insurance, security and ticket sales. It was a large collection which occupied three floors. It was the first time such an exhibition had ever been mounted in Hong Kong, and the attendance was overwhelming. At the same time, it gave China an archaeological presence in the colony.[29]

It was not uncommon for Chinese government officials to send special gifts, such as fruit, from a particular area of China, to Father through Xinhua News Agency. What they sent was often not available commercially in Hong Kong, and Father was always proud of these presents. During Chinese New Year, it would be peonies and kumquat plants and small tangerines. This show of respect continued towards Mother after Father died.

One day in the 1970s, a call came from Xinhua News Agency to say that they had a gift of "*yut lup leichee*," meaning a basket of leichee, which had been specially sent from China for Father. They asked the office to send a large car to pick it up. Anna, Father's secretary, wondered why a large car had to be sent for "*yut nup leichee*," which meant one leichee. She thought the person from Xinhua was speaking in slang by changing the "n" sound in the word "*nup*" to an "l" which was a common habit among young Cantonese.[30] However, she did send a large car as requested, and when the car came back, it held a huge basket of leichee. The term "*lup*," which meant "basket," was no longer commonly used by the younger generation, and Anna had been confused. She said that was an incident she would never forget. Anyway, there was a distribution in the office of leichee for everyone that day.

Father helped a great number of people in his life, and he often received gifts from them, but there were one or two people who were jealous of Father, and who would send him clocks. Anna found this most objectionable because, according to Cantonese folklore, giving a clock means that you want that person to die. But Father was not superstitious. He said, "If they want to give it to me, that's fine."[31]

As Father was very well known, and was the first prominent person from Hong Kong to travel extensively in China after the war, over the years, some young men from the mainland claimed to be his sons. What was not reported in the newspapers was the fact that Mother usually accompanied him and that he was always escorted by officials from the Chinese government. So, he ignored this nuisance. (In a similar way, young women in Hong Kong claimed to be Mother's goddaughters, since they could not very well claim to be her biological children.) It became a joke in the office whenever the staff heard about another claimant. Because of the way Father conducted his life, Grand-uncle Lee Shu Yuen and the office staff agreed that if it had been anybody else, the claims might be credible, but not Father. The claimants should have done their homework first.[32]

During the 1970s, Father became good friends with Yao Kang[33] of John Swire & Sons (H.K.) Ltd. Even though the Lee family had had a good business relationship with the company since 1948, and Father was the head of the family, the two men became close friends only when Yao became a Master in the Masonic Lodge in 1972. They often sat together at the Masonic meetings, and Father came to trust him. Yao often went with Father to the Masonic Lodges in Japan in January, and Father often called Yao to deal with both personal and business matters.

Yao, who had worked for many years in China, had established good relationships there, and spoke many Chinese dialects. Father often invited him to participate whenever there were visitors from China in Hong Kong, be it for breakfast, lunch or dinner. In this manner, Yao got to know people like the governor of Guangdong and vice-premiers and ministers from China while they were visiting Hong Kong unofficially.[34] Yao was impressed by Father's willingness to help others and by his extensive connections with top Chinese government officials.

In 1978, China opened up for business. The Chinese government invited the Swire Group to visit Beijing, since Swire was an old established foreign company that had operated in China since the 1800s. When the name of the representative from the company was submitted, Father said no, Yao should to be the one to represent Swire. Yao went, even though he was getting on in years, and thought a younger person should represent the company. Father trusted Yao, and believed he would do justice to both China and Swire.

One day in 1981, Father phoned Yao Kang and asked him to keep the following Wednesday clear because he needed him to look after a minister from China for the whole day. He asked Yao to plan a program for this man who was an engineer by training. At 8:30 in the morning on that day, with Hon Chiu at the Lee Gardens Hotel, Yao was introduced to Jiang Zemin who was then Minister of Electronic Industries. Father said to him, "Y.K., you better take good care of this man. He has great potential." Yao showed Jiang the airport, and in particular, the maintenance department, the facilities of Cathay Pacific (owned by Swire) and public housing in Kowloon, in all of which Jiang showed great interest. Yao also took him to lunch, and spoke to him about finance and commerce in general. Father thought Yao was the perfect person to take Jiang around since they were both from Shanghai, and would have a lot in common. As it turned out, Jiang's vice-minister Wei Mingyi had been Yao's roommate at Beijing University, and it was Wei who had originally advised Yao in 1948 to take the job with Swire in England. After that visit, Jiang became Mayor of Shanghai, and Yao visited him and they became good friends. After the June 4, 1989 incident at Tiananmen Square, Jiang became Party Secretary, and Wei Mingyi became the president of China International Trust and Investment Corporation (CITIC).[35] To this day, Yao Kang thinks that Father had vision, and like many others, always gives him credit for being able to see potential in others.

In 1979, Sir Murray Maclehose was the first governor of Hong Kong to be invited to visit Beijing and tour western China. At the end of his visit, he attended the Guangzhou-Kowloon Through Train[36] ceremony in Guangzhou. My parents, who were visiting Hainan Island, accompanied by the Director of Xinhua News Agency, Wang Kuang,[37] were invited to attend the ceremony. A special plane was sent to Hainan to take them to Guangzhou, but they almost didn't make it because of high winds. The plane had to take off due west instead of north, but finally landed in Zhaoqing, and from there they made it to Guangzhou.[38] The event was very important to Father because it signalled the beginning of communication in earnest between Britain and China.[39]

Not only did Father build a relationship between Hong Kong and China, but his international network also extended to Europe and Japan. He worked with N.M. Rothschild and Sons of London, A.P. Møller of Denmark, Yamaichi Securities of Japan and many others. Foreign investments poured into the colony and eventually into China. His prestige rose while he kept busy looking after his many businesses and starting new ones. Once there was friendship, dialogue and business followed. And when China opened up for business in the late 1970s, Father took the lead in the first joint venture.

By the 1970s, Father had attained the respect and trust of different segments of society in Hong Kong, members of the government as well as by the leaders in China. He was regarded internationally as one of the "decision makers" in Hong Kong.[40] He was satisfied that the Hong Kong government was working on behalf of the population. These were important years, when he helped to lay the foundation for a peaceful transfer of sovereignty, both in business links between Hong Kong and China, and in the structure of the future government of Hong Kong.

He was regarded by many in Hong Kong as the ideal person to be the Chief Executive when Hong Kong returned to China on July 1, 1997. Whenever I heard that mentioned, I always pointed out that by 1997, Father would be ninety-two years old.

I'm sure that Father was able to work at the age of seventy-eight like a young man of thirty-five because he was full of ideas, and was always starting new projects. By the beginning of the 1980s, he had planned two new projects in China: to improve the international telephone system in Guangzhou, and to build a double railway line between Shenzhen and Guangzhou. These unfortunately could not be realized before his death.[41]

By January 1982, China was the largest supplier of goods to Hong Kong, overtaking Japan for the first time in recent history. Father believed that the increase in trade between Hong Kong and China called for improvements in China's transportation system:

> To meet the ever-increasing volume of trade, the means of transportation between Hong Kong and Guangdong must be improved. In order to reduce delays in the transit of goods and to reduce the cost of transportation and handling, the Guangzhou-Shenzhen railway must be double-tracked to link up with Kowloon as an order of first priority. Hong Kong is the only deep-sea port with all modern facilities on the South China coast and an increasing number of containers will flow in both directions between Hong Kong and Guangzhou. This traffic must, in the near future, be carried by rail....The double tracking of the railway could be carried out with comparative ease and completed quickly at reasonable cost — to the benefit of Hong Kong, China and the world.[42]

When our family attended the grand opening of the Garden Hotel in Guangzhou in 1985, and one of our sons could not be with us, I was able to call direct from our hotel room to Toronto without any problem. I was very impressed.

The Garden Hotel

When China was opened for joint ventures with foreign capital, Father immediately responded. In taking the lead, he wanted to give the Chinese government credibility. Since he knew that the hotels in China were all substandard, he planned to build the largest and most beautiful hotel in China.

In the late 1970s, the Chinese Communist Party was inexperienced in dealing with joint ventures, and Father's was the first. It became extremely trying for him because of endless negotiations, red tape, delays, and the resulting escalation in cost.

Father had originally wanted to build a hotel in Beijing, but was asked to build one on Hainan Island instead. He realized then that those in the Chinese government involved in this project had no concept of business. Hainan Island in the 1970s did not have the infrastructure to support a project of that magnitude.

Instead, Father chose a prime location in Guangzhou, close to the train station which would be convenient for business people coming to the Guangzhou Trade Fair. The site was near Beiyunshan, which had an important airfield, and was a high-security defence location for Guangzhou. Father was asked to build a hotel with anti-aircraft guns on the roof and a bomb shelter underneath. It again took time and patience while he and Yang Shangkun, who was then the vice-chairman of the Military Commission, talked to those who had made the request in Beijing, and the demands were dropped. The hotel, however, was built with its own emergency generator, which was and still is very necessary.

So the Garden Hotels Holdings (Hong Kong) Limited was formed and a joint venture agreement[43] was signed between it and the Guangzhou Lingnan Enterprises Company on March 28, 1980.[44] The development site, covering 52,600 square metres, was located south of Guangzhou Baiyun Guest House, on what had been vegetable farmland. The Garden Hotel[45] was to be built by Guangzhou Pearl River Foreign Investment Construction Company in two phases — 1,300 rooms to be completed in the first phase and 940 rooms in the second — at an estimated cost of about US$50,000 per room.[46] The project was comprised of a hotel, a conference centre and an apartment tower.

Father raised the capital among his friends and from the banks, with himself as the major shareholder. Many of his friends rallied behind him. Swire was asked to participate, and even though it was totally against Swire's principles to take part in this type of investment, Yao Kang persuaded the company to become a minor shareholder. A.P. Møller, the Danish company which continues to this day to have a close relationship with the various businesses of the Lee family, invested in the company because of Father. The total amount raised was HK$700 million.[47]

I remember the enthusiasm with which Father talked about the project. It was to be not only a five-star hotel, the largest in China, but one of the largest and most beautiful in the world, and it was to be his gift to China. On December 27, 1980, Yang Shangkun laid the foundation stone for the Garden Hotel. Father expressed the hope that this would contribute in a small way to the modernization of China.[48]

The architect for the Garden Hotel was Szeto Wai, Father's friend who had designed The Chinese University of Hong Kong. The Chinese parties in the joint venture[49] requested that all the rooms be almost identical. C.T. Wu and his son were drawn into the planning, because Father had wanted them to help with the future management of the hotel. They objected to making all the rooms the same and insisted that there should be many different configurations of rooms in a modern hotel. They also objected to the design of a revolving restaurant because they felt that it was not suitable for the location. All this caused delays in the construction. Corrections were made to construct the rooms in different sizes, and suites were added to make the hotel more marketable. But the revolving restaurant remained. Unfortunately, this led to bad feelings between C.T. Wu and his son on one side, and the hotel group on the other.[50]

By early 1983, because of bad financial management, there were huge cost overruns. The problems of the construction became obvious and it was very stressful for Father.[51] When he passed away in July, Beijing requested that Mother take over the chairmanship of Garden Hotels Holdings (Hong Kong) Limited.[52] Xu Jiatun, the newly appointed director of Xinhua News Agency, organized a dinner for the representatives from China, and Mother agreed to become the chairman. Now it was up to her to solve the financial crisis. Despite the fact that Swire was only a minor shareholder, Yao Kang took the lead in helping to solve the problem. He told the representative from the Chinese side of the hotel company that Swire would raise sufficient additional capital, on condition that the company could send auditors into China to check the books. But when the auditors went in, they couldn't get the information they needed. There were no books to show how the US$100 million had been spent. In order for the project to carry on, all the original investors were asked to put in additional capital, not only because of China's appeal for foreign investment but also out of respect for Father's memory. Swire took the lead in putting in additional capital, and also made up the difference when an investor failed to put in their share. The accountant for the company was set aside, and the hotel proceeded to completion.[53]

On October 28, 1984, the hotel opened for business. Among the major tenants were offices of the American Consulate and the Japanese Consulate,[54] and their residences were in the twin tower.[55] My parents' old friend Reiko Ogata became the liaison in the Garden Hotel for the Japanese government and businesses. She later worked in promotion for the hotel in Tokyo until 1988.

The grand opening of the hotel was planned for August 28, 1985, and guests were invited to stay for three days. We flew to Hong Kong to join the group for the celebration. Many cars of the through train from Hong Kong to Guangzhou were booked for guests, and the party really started at the train station in Hong Kong.

We arrived to a red-carpet welcome. Just as I expected, the hotel was not only grand, it was absolutely beautiful. When I saw Mother making her speech in Mandarin, I felt very proud, and wished that Father could have been there too.

In 1989, after the June 4 incident in Tiananmen Square, all businesses in China suffered. The Garden Hotel had no income, yet it still had interest payments to make to the syndicated loan.[56] It faced foreclosure by the banks. Mother decided to go to Beijing to seek help. An official visit was planned to see President Yang Shangkun, who was a pragmatic person and had great respect for my parents.

In early 1990, accompanied by a senior official from Xinhua News Agency, Mother paid a visit to President Yang, who invited her to dinner at Diaoyutai.[57] Mother told the president that the investors had come to the end of the road, so the choice was for the Chinese government to take over the hotel, or else it would have to be closed. President Yang said to her, "The Garden Hotel will never close, Mrs. Lee, don't worry."

A month after Mother's visit, the Bank of China called to say that the Garden Hotels Holdings (Hong Kong) Ltd. had an unsecured line of credit of US$25 million. Mother's "rescue" mission was successful. Fortunately, the line of credit didn't have to be used, because business gradually returned to normal, and within a few years, the entire loan was paid off.[58]

In Father's later years, he was sometimes asked why he put money in the Bank of China. The bank's interest rate was only 4 per cent, whereas he could get a much higher return at other financial institutions. His answer was, "I don't intend to take the money out. China is my country."[59]

13

The Businessman

"Victory in war and profit in business,"[1] was what Father once said the name Lee stands for, and he certainly had a winner's mentality. However, he never could be a "successful" businessman in the true sense of someone who is completely profit-oriented. People often said that Father could have been a lot wealthier than he was, but he had a different agenda. He was a socially responsible businessman for whom people came first and profit second. He believed that money ought to be used to benefit people and not to pamper oneself. When he was interviewed in 1975 by Berta Manson for a series called "The Empire Builders" in the *South China Morning Post*, he lamented that the rich industries were doing "too little for the lot of Hong Kong's underprivileged youth."[2]

Many people in Hong Kong had become overnight billionaires through speculation.[3] It was a practice Father abhorred, because it upset economic stability and drove prices up, making life difficult for ordinary people. He considered speculators the scourge of mankind. Although the Lee family owned many properties in Hong Kong, he cringed whenever property prices were driven sky high, because it meant that many people would not be able to afford a place to live.[4] He spoke very publicly on this issue on many occasions, and certainly practised what he preached.

Investment and not speculation was, to Father, the key to responsible and good business. Father believed "a company must have a solid foundation and expand over the years....The best improvement is long, gradual and steady."[5] In a speech in 1982, he said:

> Such business activities [speculation], which may enrich a few individuals, bring no real wealth to the community and provide little employment to the local population. Activities of a highly speculative nature cannot be of benefit in a new "Hong Kong Order."[6]

It was something I have learnt from him. With speculation, one can make a great deal of money overnight, but one can also lose everything, and many people are destroyed along the way. Investment to him also meant investment in people, providing jobs and improving people's standard of living. Many young people nowadays might think this philosophy belongs to the dinosaur age, but I still believe it is the basis of a sound and stable society.

Father tried to instill his belief in others. Anna, his secretary, told me about an incident in the 1970s that concerned the purchase of condominiums. The procedure for purchasing condos in Hong Kong was and still is quite different from that in other parts of the world. People have to line up for numbers just to obtain the right to purchase. Many people go without sleep just to get to the front of the line. One day, Father told all the office staff that if they were interested in purchasing a condo in one of the new developments owned by someone he knew, he could get them low numbers (meaning they would have priority), but they had to promise him that they were purchasing a condo to live in and not for speculation. Anna said, "I missed a chance to make some money, but I didn't dare disobey your father!"

Father did not believe in bargaining because he felt that everyone had a right to make a living. If the price is not right, you don't buy. I remember being with him and some of my parents' friends at a Chinese New Year bazaar. A friend of Mother's wanted to buy a budding peach tree[7] for her home and bargained for a lower price, but was stopped by Father. He believed that people should be able to make a bit more money around Chinese New Year.

Father was known as a thorough person. Whatever he took on, he gave it a great deal of his time and effort. As company chairman — and he was chairman of many companies — he would check the annual reports carefully and make corrections before they went to print, which was normally not his responsibility.[8] And yet, as an entrepreneur with a lot of ideas and great connections, he was not interested in the details of operations. He was more excited in making deals than in the bottom line, so at times he trusted the wrong people in management, and certain businesses didn't do well for him.[9] Because he was an honourable man, he expected others to be the same. Once he trusted someone, he would continue to trust, despite warnings from others that the person was working against him. At times like these, it was very upsetting for Mother, who could see what was going on, but was powerless to do anything about it.

This was true of his experience with Kowloon Taxi, which he started soon after the war. Father was probably one of the first people to buy diesel-fuelled Mercedes-Benz cars as taxis. But Kowloon Taxi eventually went downhill because of bad management, and was finally sold when the Cross Harbour tunnel was built.[10]

I often heard Father say that he wasn't interested in being the wealthiest man in Hong Kong, even if with his connections, he could have been. This doesn't sound like a statement by a businessman. He was a thrifty person, and money didn't have great significance to him personally. Like most members of the Lee family, Father never wore flashy clothes or drove fancy cars. I remember him telling me when Rolls-Royce first came to Hong Kong, that he was approached to buy one, and his answer was, "I can't afford the ostentation." He would rather drive around in a Volkswagen Golf. And yet, at the same time, nothing would stop him from buying Mother precious jewels. Those probably were the only times he ever splurged.

In March 1960, Father led the Hong Kong Trade Mission to West Africa. On his return, he made suggestions to Hong Kong manufacturers about packaging, pricing, sizing and marketing. He recommended that shoeboxes be improved because rats ate the Chinese glue made from rice flour that was used to make the boxes, that chinaware be shipped in wooden crates to prevent breakage, and that clothing sizes be standardized. He lamented that manufacturers had lost orders because of poor quality. He believed that Hong Kong products could command the same prices as Japanese products if they were well made, because there was a demand for them. He also suggested that all Hong Kong manufacturers get together to print a catalogue to make ordering easier for buyers.[11]

In 1963, Father was asked by the Hong Kong government to lead a delegation to the Frankfurt International Trade Fair in August. Since he had already been invited by the German government to tour Germany as their guest, he made arrangements to do both around the same time. Upon his first stop in London, he was handed a letter from St. James's Palace, inviting him to attend an Investiture at Buckingham Palace on that Wednesday, July 24, to receive a CBE from the Queen. Since Mother was not with him on that trip, he invited two friends, Colonel Jack and Major General Tom Churchill, to accompany him to the palace. Everything happened so suddenly that he had to rent a morning coat for the occasion.

It was Father's habit to make frequent trips to Europe. That summer, Father flew from London to Denmark to visit friends, the Jebsens, in Aabenraa and at their cottage on Romo Island. When Mother, who was not with him on that trip, heard about Father swimming in the frigid water of Als Fjord, her comment was that Father still thought himself a young man. Father was driven by another friend, Martin Schroter, from Romo Island to Hamburg, Germany, where he was taken to major centres, guided by officials of the German government, Helmut Kluge and Verner Walbroel. From there, Father flew to Vienna to meet Uncle Quo Wai and they toured factories and hydro-electric stations in Austria. At the end of August, he led the trade delegation to Frankfurt. Father was a tireless learner.

In the 1960s, as many small factories sprouted up in Hong Kong, land became a problem. In March 1963, Father spoke in the Legislative Council, on behalf of the new and small factory owners, against the government's policy of forcing them off the land in order to sell it to developers. He said that the industries had obtained their licences to operate from the government, and should be protected. If the government wanted them to move, alternative locations ought to be provided at a reasonable rent. They should also be notified when the land they occupied was to be auctioned, as they had a right to put in a bid. He rejected the suggestion that small industries should be absorbed by the large ones, and stressed the importance of protecting hard-working small-industry owners who were the backbone of society.[12]

There were concerns during those years that Hong Kong was losing investments to other areas of the world. It was a problem that Father had often mentioned. In 1963, Father suggested at the Legislative Council meeting that the inheritance tax be abolished. The tax collected that year only came to $20 million, which was a fraction of the amount of investment lost to other jurisdictions because of it.[13] Unfortunately, his advice was not taken.

Besides helping other industrialists, Father was involved in industries himself. In 1964, he started the Hong Kong Tube and Metal Products Ltd. in Peng Chau, one of the islands off Hong Kong. The product from this factory was new to the colony. In the opening ceremony on December 21, Father was proud to announce the establishment of a new industry for Hong Kong. The Hon. D.R. Holmes officiated at the opening, and in commemoration of the event, the board promised to make an annual donation to provide for ten free places in two local schools for the children of Peng Chau.[14] Hong Kong Tube and Metal Products used only the best supplies. For example, they purchased their steel from Nippon Steel Corporation, and hot rolled steel coils from Yawata Iron and Steel Co. Ltd., both Japanese companies. The Hong Kong Tube and Metal Products continued in operation until Father's death, at which time it was sold.

Although he was involved in many businesses, Father never lost his interest in engineering problems. Soon after the war, Father suggested that the government build a tunnel through the mountain from Happy Valley to Aberdeen. At that time, he estimated that it would cost only a little over $1 million. However, the government was not interested. A tunnel was finally built at a much later date and at much greater cost.[15]

In 1964, the Legislative Council was planning to erect additional buildings for the British armed forces stationed in Hong Kong in areas such as Shek Kong in the New Territories. Father recommended that all buildings be designed so that they could be converted to libraries, schools or offices with minor alterations. Thus, when the time came for them to be handed back by the British to the government of Hong Kong (Hong Kong people ruling Hong Kong), they would remain valuable properties.[16] Father was already preparing Hong Kong for the change of sovereignty in 1997, and he did not want to see resources wasted.

Also in 1964, he experimented with solar heating for hot water by building a contraption on the roof of Tower Court where we lived. The structure was of canvas and inside were six black tubes each six inches wide. The black tubes would absorb the heat of the sun and warm the water in the structure. It was the first solar heating system ever built in Hong Kong and cost only a hundred dollars. Although it was successful, and his efforts were reported in the media, it was never built for commercial use.[17]

A New Tunnel

Ever since 1955, there had been public discussions in Hong Kong of improving harbour crossings between the island and Kowloon by building either a bridge or a tunnel. A bridge would be exposed to the weather, and it might not be safe during the typhoon season. However, a tunnel would be a much more complicated engineering undertaking and would cost much more than a bridge. Public discussions on the subject continued for a number of years. It was not until May 1963 that the Hong Kong government made the decision not to build a bridge. After that, discussions were concentrated on the tunnel.[18]

A tunnel between Hong Kong and Kowloon would put an end to the long line-ups at the Yaumatai Car Ferry. In those days, no one took a car across the harbour unless it was absolutely necessary, because it was a full-day excursion. Our family would take the car across only for special family gatherings and Chinese New Year. Most people crossed the harbour by ferry and then hired a taxi on the other side.

In 1963, Father, J.L. Marden of Wheelock Marden, the Hon. J.D. Clague and Lawrence Kadoorie formed the Victoria City Development Co. Ltd., whose main objective was the building of a cross-harbour tunnel between the island and Kowloon. The name was later changed to Cross-Harbour Tunnel Company Limited, Hong Kong. The original plan was to build a tunnel for both cars and pedestrians.[19] It was to be a two-lane tunnel and the plan and the layout were sent to the Colonial Secretary and the Crown Lands and Survey Office in January 1964.[20] But by August 11, 1965, when approval for the construction of the tunnel was finally passed by the Hong Kong government, the plan had changed. The tunnel would be for cars only. It would be open twenty-four hours a day even during typhoon season, and it would cost an estimated $210 million. The Hong Kong government would be the owner of one quarter of the project.[21] Construction was to start the following fall.

When the right to build the tunnel was granted, Father worked very hard to find investors for the project. Most of the financing came from a British merchant investment banker.[22] During the 1960s, the economy was poor in Hong Kong and it was difficult to persuade people to invest. Father and Lee Hysan Estate Co. were some of the original investors, together with Marden and the Kadoorie family. Father tried to convince the owner of the Yaumatai Car Ferry, Lau Ding Kuok, to invest in the company, especially when the business of his ferry service would be affected by the building of a tunnel, but Lau declined, and to this day, he regrets it.[23]

During the formation of the company, Father went to visit Fei Yiming of *Ta Kung Pao* to ask if he thought the timing was right to build the cross-harbour tunnel. I believe he meant the political timing. Fei's answer was that it would be absolutely necessary for the convenience of the citizens of Hong Kong, and assured Father that Hong Kong's political stability would be maintained for a long time.[24]

During my parents' visit to us in Toronto in the early 1970s, Father told me how difficult it was to get the cross-harbour tunnel under way. In the beginning, it was difficult to get the Hong Kong government to provide financial support. However, when the government of France showed interest in injecting capital into the project, the Hong Kong government immediately became interested.

Father oversaw the engineering of the tunnel. Building a tunnel under the harbour in the 1960s was a difficult feat, although Hon Chiu told me, "Today, it is as easy as making duck soup."[25] Being a civil engineer, Father always liked to get involved in the construction. When the first section of the tunnel was completed, Father invited Fei Yiming to inspect it. The night before the tunnel was due to be opened for traffic, Father invited Fei to drive with him from Hong Kong to Kowloon. He explained the technical aspects of the construction to his friend, about air circulation and the prevention of water seepage.[26] Fei was most impressed by Father's complete involvement. Father was very proud of this project.

When the tunnel was opened on August 2, 1972, traffic between Hong Kong and Kowloon was revolutionized.[27] It was no longer a big undertaking to cross between Hong Kong and Kowloon by car, and line-ups at the Yaumatai Car Ferry were a thing of the past. Business was not brisk at the beginning, because it cost five dollars for the crossing, but people soon appreciated the convenience and there was no turning back. Subsequently, when the exchange rate of the HK dollar became very favourable against the pound sterling, the loan was quickly paid back and the company went on to make great profits.[28]

During one of our visits after the tunnel was first opened, we were in a car with cousins driving across from Kowloon to Hong Kong. One cousin said to me, "Every time we pay five dollars to cross, two out of that goes into your father's pocket!" I was sure she was exaggerating.

The Telephone Company

In January 1962, Father was appointed to the board of directors of the Hong Kong Telephone Company Limited by the chairman, H.R.M. Cleland. In 1965, he himself became the chairman.[29]

The Hong Kong telephone system was rather backward in the 1960s. In 1966, there were only 300,000 telephones lines in Hong Kong, which came to eight for every one hundred persons. At the same time, sixty thousand people were waiting in line for telephone service. That year, Father decided to expand the operations of the company by building more stations in different parts of Hong Kong, to make it possible to increase the number of telephones lines to 1.8 million. Cables were laid under the ocean in Southeast Asia to improve communications, and technical and management level personnel were hired to manage the increased demand. The profit that year went up to $29 million.[30]

Because of his admiration for German engineering, Father decided to purchase German equipment to improve the performance of the telephone system. He was advised by Jardine Fleming[31] to use Swiss francs to fund the purchase. Unfortunately, the rate of exchange on the Swiss francs appreciated many times against the Hong Kong dollar, which made the purchase very expensive. Yet Father did not want to raise the telephone rate. This produced great controversy and Father had to shoulder the blame. David K.P. Li, whose father, Fook Su Li, was on the board, believed that Father was badly advised.[32]

In 1969, despite the public outcry, the number of telephone lines had increased to five hundred thousand, which was 12.45 per one hundred persons, the second highest per capita in Asia after Japan. When satellite communications were established in Hong Kong that year, communications with other parts of the world were greatly improved. The most important work for the company in 1970 was the building of computerized connectors in the Lai Chi Kok station. When it was completed, it was the most advanced independent system in the world, able to service the New Territories as well as Hong Kong. In the technical department, almost two thousand employees were trained. Four Chinese engineers were sent to England for advanced training, and six were sent to Munich in Germany for technical training. A school in Kwun Tong to train employees was scheduled to be finished by April 1971.[33]

During Father's term as chairman, it was discovered there were a great many problems in the management of the company. Rumour had it that there were people within the company who were taking bribes, and that this problem went all the way up to the general manager, Charles Male.[34] Lydia Dunn, the present Baroness Dunn, was one of the people sent by the government to investigate the mismanagement.

Unfortunately, the investigation could not proceed because Charles Male left for South Africa. Since there was no extradition treaty between South Africa and Hong Kong, he could not be brought back to answer questions.[35]

At that time, Father's office was on the twenty-fifth floor of the Prince's Building, and the Telephone Company was on the fourth floor. He was very much aware of the constant flurry of investigative activities between the two offices and this caused a great strain on him.

Father asked his friend Jack Cater[36] to be the general manager of the Telephone Company, but since Governor Sir Murray Maclehose needed Cater to head the Independent Commission Against Corruption (ICAC), which was established in 1974, Father decided that the public needed his friend more, and the general manager's position went to F. L. Walker.

Father waited until the controversy was over and the company was back on its feet, then he resigned. He expressed to Fei Yiming that, in time, people in Hong Kong would appreciate what he had done to improve the telephone system.[37]

The Gas Company

In 1964, Father became the first Chinese chairman of the Hong Kong and China Gas Co., which was established in 1862 to provide gas lighting to the colony. In 1975, Hong Kong Electric, which was controlled by Jardine, attempted to take over Hong Kong and China Gas. Father resisted. It became a high-profile takeover attempt that Father referred to as "a big fish swallowing a small fish."[38] He was constantly on the news explaining to the shareholders why they shouldn't sell their shares to Hong Kong Electric, and exposing the financial position of the latter which he believed would be detrimental to the shareholders of China Gas. Even though the Hong Kong and China Gas Company was a much smaller company, he managed to show his shareholders how economically stable and profitable it was.[39]

In all this, Father spent a great deal of time with two of his board members, the Hon. J.D. Claque, a taipan of the Hutchison Group, and Noel Croucher, a leading stockbroker, who helped prevent the hostile takeover by advising his clients not to sell their shares to Hong Kong Electric.[40] By August 20, 1975, Father and the board of directors succeeded in preventing the takeover.

The Gas Company was originally registered in the United Kingdom. In 1982, Father, as chairman, made the decision to move the registration to Hong Kong. At the time of the transfer, only 2 of the 2,238 shareholders were registered on the London Register. Father explained to the shareholders that while the company had always been at a disadvantage because it had to comply with British legislation, Britain's entry to the European Economic Community in 1973 had resulted in an even greater degree of legislative control, most of which was inappropriate to a company operating in Hong Kong. At a cost of $1.2 million, the company severed its ties with Britain. The ceremony was held in Hon Chiu's office in Sunning Plaza, and Hong Kong and China Gas became a Hong Kong company. To commemorate the event, all employees were presented with a one-ounce gold coin, and grants of $250,000 each were made to the University of Hong Kong, The Chinese University of Hong Kong and the Polytechnic.[41]

The Hong Kong and China Gas Company's profits rose from $39 million in 1980 to $235 million within six years, and it achieved the status of a major utility company after 125 years of operations. Gas was no longer the fuel of the wealthy, but an everyday necessity for the people of Hong Kong.

Ever since the 1970s, Father had worked towards obtaining natural gas from China, building pipelines under the ocean to Hong Kong. This would not only bring in foreign exchange for China, but would benefit the people of Hong Kong. Unfortunately, due to safety problems and engineering difficulties, his dream was not realized during his lifetime.[42]

After Father died, the Hong Kong and China Gas company signed a joint memorandum with Qin Wencai, president of the China National Offshore Oil Corporation in 1985, to bring natural gas to Hong Kong, at a date to be determined.[43] When this finally happens, it will usher in an era of cheaper gas for Hong Kong.

The Rothschild Bank

The Rothschild Bank wanted to establish a bank in Hong Kong and approached Father to be a founding director. In March 1973, N.M. Rothschild & Sons (Hong Kong) Limited was formed, and in January 1974, Father was appointed deputy chairman. Everyone wondered why he was approached by a Jewish bank, and the rumour in Hong Kong was that he must have been circumcised. The fact of the matter was that the bank needed someone with an impeccable reputation to head it. Sir Evelyn de Rothschild was the chairman, but since he was not based in Hong Kong, Father chaired many of the meetings. In the meantime, the two became very good friends. Sir Evelyn referred to Father as the first chairman of the bank in Hong Kong.

During Father's term as deputy chairman, 1974-1978, he introduced potential business opportunities to the bank and assisted in the recruitment of local executives. Sir Evelyn wrote to me that Father was very keen on putting the following motto in Chinese in front of the bank office:

> Devotion with zeal in Finance,
> Wealth is developed by the golden mean;
> Enterprise is all-embracing,
> Exchanges pervade the four seas;
> Assets abound in resources,
> Making fortunes by fair and honest dealing;
> Steering a course in economic growth,
> For the benefit of commerce and industry;
> With united and popular support,
> The outlook for prosperity is bright![44]

Having an international outlook made it easy for Father to make friends and have business associations with people from all over the world, as with the Rothschild Bank. In a 1979 letter to Father,

Sir Evelyn wrote:

> ... I was also very pleased to see that N.M.R. Hong Kong is doing so well and I know much of the success is due to your guiding hand, which is greatly appreciated.
>
> ... Again my grateful thanks to you for all the help and kindness you showed me ...[45]

The Danish Connection

Father's association with Messrs. A.P. Møller of Denmark began in the 1960s. The relationship grew stronger as time went on, and the company invested in many of Father's projects. The owner, Mæsrk Mc-Kinney Møller and Father became good friends.

Messrs. A.P. Møller was started in 1904 by Arnold Peter Møller with his father, Captain Peter Mæsrk Møller, in Svendborg, Denmark, as a shipping company. In 1965, on the death of his father, Mærsk Mc-Kinney Møller assumed the leadership of the A.P. Møller Group and the company developed into a major international enterprise. The Group consisted of Mærsk Line, Mærsk Tankers, Mærsk Drilling in the Danish part of the North Sea, Odense Steel Shipyard, Mærsk Container Industries, Mærsk Air, A/S Roulunds Fabriker for the production of fan belts and brake linings for European cars, Pharma-Plast for the production and sale of medical supplies, Mærsk Data for the supply and sale of data processing, Dansk Supermarked, the second largest supermarket chain in Denmark, and many more.

When Per Jorgensen, managing director of Messrs. A.P. Møller, arrived in Hong Kong in August 1977, he and Father immediately became good friends. By that time, the company already had three joint ventures with the Lee family: the Lee Gardens Hotel and the office towers One Hysan Avenue and Leighton Centre. Jorgensen said, at the time, his international corporate experience was limited, and Father took him under his wings and introduced him to the sophisticated corporate life and its procedures in Hong Kong. Father offered friendship, guidance and goodwill, and Jorgensen appreciated Father's openness, dynamism and his modern and efficient way of handling matters.[46]

My parents visited Denmark in July 1982. Per Jorgensen and his wife spent a lot of time with them and Mr. Jorgensen told me that Father was a good tourist because he was inquisitive, interested and tireless. Apparently, he visited many castles and constantly asked questions. At the end of 1982, the chairman and CEO of A.P. Møller, Mr. Mærsk Mc-Kinney Møller, accompanied by his daughter Ane Uggla, visited my family in Hong Kong.[47] Neville and I were in Hong Kong at the time and had the pleasure of having dinner with them.

A.P. Møller continued to be a great supporter of all Father's business undertakings as in the Hysan Development Company and the Garden Hotel Holdings (Hong Kong) Ltd. Per Jorgensen became one of the first directors of Hysan Development Company.

A Shipping Company

Father had an indirect interest in Japan in connection with Grand Marine Holdings Ltd., a Hong Kong shipping company that built many of their cargo ships in Japan. The names of most of their ships started with the word "Grand," such as *Grand Eagle* and *Grand Jade*, the latter being named after Mother, whose Chinese name means jade.

Grand Marine was owned by Li Ping San, the father-in-law of my mother's niece Greta Li. Because of the family connection, Li asked Father to become the chairman of his company and Father helped the family to take the company public in the 1970s.

My parents went to the launching of many of their ships in Japan, and for a number of years, the company's profits soared. Unfortunately, Li became very ill. Just before he died, he asked to see Father and made him promise to look after his two sons who would be inheriting the company. Unfortunately, after Li died, the sons sold the company to Carrion, an investment group headed by Malaysian-born businessman George S.G. Tan, for what they believed to be a large amount of money. Actually most of it was in the form of shares in the Carrion Group.

Since Father was not consulted, he decided to sever his ties with Grand Marine and sell all his shares in the company. This was fortunate, because the sale of Grand Marine eventually bankrupted the Li family. The original personal guarantees that the father, Li Ping San, had given to the banks were passed on to the sons even though the company had been sold.[48] In 1983, the collapse of the Carrion group became the biggest corporate scandal ever in Hong Kong, when Malaysian banker Lorrain Osman and Tan were found guilty of defrauding Bumiputra Malaysia Finance Ltd. (BMFL) of $6 billion (US$769 million). BMFL was a subsidiary of Bank Bumiputra, the second largest bank in Malaysia.[49]

The Canadian Connection

In Father's speech in Frankfurt in June 1982, he said:

> There is no doubt at all, in my mind, that Hong Kong can assist China in her oil exploration programme in many ways. The importance of Hong Kong to China is undeniable, but of course we all realize too that Hong Kong depends on China for her survival. Could the China offshore oil and gas tilt the balance of the industrial world one day?[50]

In the late 1970s, Ranger Oil of Calgary, Canada, approached Father to form a company for oil exploration in China. Father turned down the offer. The company then turned to the Hambros Bank of London, a merchant bank in England. Through Hambros' connection with Yao Kang, they tried to reach Father. The proposal was to set up an oil company that would have the rights to drill in the South China Sea, recognized to be rich with oil reserves. Yao thought it was a sound idea and called Father. The two men decided that this would be good for China.

Father called a meeting between the Hon. Victor Lampson, a partner of Cazenove & Co.[51] of London, accompanied by David Lewis, a director of Hambros Bank, at the Lee Hysan Estate Company boardroom at One Hysan Avenue. Father agreed to the proposal, and invested US$1 million in the company. He became the chairman of Canada & Oriental Oil Limited (COOL) in 1981, and Yao Kang became one of the directors. There were many other investors, including some of Father's friends in Hong Kong.

Father believed that China had a rich oil reserve that had never been tapped. The drilling started in the South China Sea at the end of 1981 or the beginning of 1982. At that time, there were seven foreign oil companies drilling in the Yellow Sea, the South China Sea and near Hainan Island. Father described these developments as "one of the most important steps in the Four Modernisations of China."[52]

Between 1981 and 1984, thirty-five wells were drilled in the China Sea without success. Then the world oil prices collapsed. Between 1986 and 1987, Ranger Oil bought back the shares and sold all the rigs. In the end, the company was liquidated. As of June 1997, there has not been any successful drilling by any oil company in the South China Sea. The prospect of COOL was based on the original survey from Ranger Oil.[53]

By 1981, Hong Kong was already importing 20 per cent of its petroleum products from China. Father believed that when China's reserves came on stream, they would have a tremendous economic impact on the world.[54] Despite the lack of success of COOL up to the time of his death, Father continued to have faith in China's offshore oil reserves.

14

The Freemason:
A Lifetime
Commitment

For as long as I lived at home, I always heard about Father going to Masonic meetings. These meetings were a mystery to me because freemasonry was a close-knit society for men, although, in later years, it became more open.

Freemasonry is a system of morality based on the principles of brotherly love and charity — not only of money but also of the mind — truth and personal integrity. It is entirely non-political; political discussions are forbidden in its premises.[1] It is a bond of fellowship that unites its members all over the world. Despite the general misconception in Hong Kong that only the rich and powerful are members, it is actually open to every honest, free man, over twenty-one years of age. A new mason is taught to be "exemplary in the discharge of his duties as a citizen of the world."[2] Masons refer to one another as brothers, and freemasonry is proud of its philosophy of making good men better.

With its basic teaching of charity, Masonic philanthropy helps a great number of people worldwide. Masons run hospitals and look after the handicapped, the blind, the mentally ill and the crippled. They manage homes for seniors, provide scholarships and funds for research work, and perform public service for their communities.

Some scholars trace the origin of freemasonry as far back as the Garden of Eden, others to the Emperors of China and others still, to the Emperor of Japan. In the Far East, two aspects of the Oriental origin have been developed: the secret societies of China have many practices in common with masonry, and Confucian rituals performed by the Emperor of China to ensure continuance of the mandate of Heaven also bear a close relationship to its ceremonials.[3]

Present-day freemasonry originated with the stonemasons who built the great churches of Europe. They developed a society of masons, which took simple medieval legends based on the art of building, as well as stories from the Bible, and folklore, and developed them into complex rituals capable of universal appeal. The process was formalized by the creation of Grand Lodges, which spread rapidly throughout Europe and North America, and in just over forty years, reached the Far East. Freemasonry started in Hong Kong in the early 1800s. The Royal Sussex Lodge was established in 1845, and its daughter lodge, Zetland Lodge, was established eighteen months later.

Father's connection with the freemasons started during his years in England when he was introduced to it by his guardian, Mr. Churchill. The concept of brotherly love, charity and truth appealed to him. It was highly probable that he would have been initiated in Apollo University Lodge No. 357 if Grandfather had not suddenly passed away.[4]

In January 1929, Father was initiated into the University Lodge of Hong Kong Chapter No. 3666. Masonry has a system of so-called "higher" degrees, for which ordinary lodge members are qualified by experience. Father eventually became a member of every one of these that existed in Hong Kong before the Pacific War. His enthusiasm also led to a life-long commitment, culminating in his becoming the District Grand Master for Hong Kong and the Far East.

During the war, when we lived in Chongqing, Father was such an enthusiastic mason that he took part in the revival of the Lodge Star of Southern China No. 2013, which originally met in Guangzhou. He was also a visitor of Fortitude Lodge, which the Grand Lodge of California had temporarily set up in Chongqing. Although these two lodges were located in the same city and were only a couple of miles apart, they were separated by the swift-flowing, bridgeless Yangtse River which could rise forty feet within a couple of hours. Attending a meeting could mean spending a day to get back home.[5]

After the war, Father continued to be active with the freemasons in Hong Kong. In 1950, he assumed the chairs of both the Lodge Star of Southern China (by then moved from Chongqing) and Concordia Mark Lodge. In 1951, he took the First Principal's chair of the University Lodge. Around the same time, Zetland Hall, at 1 Kennedy Road, was under construction. As the District Grand Superintendent of Works, a nominal office, Father took it seriously as he did everything else, and put his civil engineering training to work by making daily visits to the site.[6] The new Zetland Hall was located right across from the steps that lead to the lower entrance of my school, St. Paul's Co-educational College. I used to go there for lunch, and around noontime, there was always someone playing the bagpipes, a sound which I came to love.

In April 1961, Father was made the District Grand Master of Hong Kong and the Far East by the Grand Master of England, the Right Honorable the Earl of Scarborough. The district was formerly known as the District of Hong Kong and South China. The geographical jurisdiction was expanded to absorb the Masonic District of Japan, which had been reduced to one lodge, and which had been working as an unattached lodge answering directly to United Grand Lodge in London. (Masonic lodges were first established in Japan in the 1870s, and by the 1960s, the only one left was the Rising Sun Lodge.)

The moment Japan was under Father's district, he went to their installation in Kobe every January. Father was known to be at his mellowest at the festive boards that followed the Kobe installations, and his enthusiasm was so catching that his Masonic brothers started to join him for the trip from Hong Kong, despite the chilly January weather in Japan. After a few years, the wives were invited to join the trip. The number had increased to almost twenty by the time Father passed away, and the trip to Kobe had become a major annual event for the Hong Kong masons.[7] He also made the journey with the Scottish District Grand Master to consecrate beautiful Kirby Hall where the Kobe lodges meet.

In his new position, Father also inherited the difficult problem of the disposal of the Masonic hall and its grounds in Yokohama, Japan, a dilemma which would take the next twenty years to resolve. The land had been owned by six English constitution bodies which operated in Yokohama before the Pacific War, but had not been revived afterwards. Members of the Scottish lodge and new Masonic bodies, which had been started by the occupation forces in Japan, had used the hall and were deeply concerned at being left without a meeting place. However, they had no financial resources to purchase the property, even at a specially reduced price.

The matter was finally settled harmoniously in 1982. The site was sold to the City of Yokohama for a public park, and most of the funds were used to provide new premises, headed by the Scottish Lodge, Star in the East No. 640. The balance of the funds was to be administered by the English District for the Endowment of Freemasons' Research Fellowships at the University of Hong Kong and The Chinese University of Hong Kong.[8] With Father's interest in education, and his specially close relationship with the two universities, this solution was of great personal satisfaction to him.

Even though Father was a member of the English Craft, he was a regular visitor to other jurisdictions with lodges in Hong Kong. The Grand Master of Ireland conferred honorary past mastership of the constitution upon him, and the Grand Lodge of Scotland made him an Honorary Deputy District Grand Master.

As the District Grand Master for twenty-one years, Father served the freemasons with great dedication. There were fourteen lodges and four associated Chapters in Hong Kong, each one with an installation once a year and an annual general meeting. He attended all the installations and chaired all the annual general meetings without fail. These were usually scheduled between October and April, and the dates were picked either when he was in Hong Kong or when he could fly back from wherever he might be in the world.

George Todkill, who was Father's Director of Ceremonies for many years, told me that Father was easy to work with because he always knew what he wanted. Being a prompt person, Father always entered the hall at exactly twenty minutes past six in the evening, and at six-thirty, he was in his chair giving orders and running the meeting. At exactly ten-twenty, Todkill was instructed to end the meeting, no matter who was speaking at the time. A farewell toast was made, and while all were standing, he would conduct Father out of the hall to his car, although members who wished to stay to talk could do so. Father was one for early evenings because he was an early riser.

Father may have hoped for the revival of freemasonry in mainland China. On several occasions, when he had friends and acquaintances visiting Hong Kong from China, he would invite them to private lunches at Zetland Hall. When asked, he would explain the non-political nature of the order and showed his guests the inside of the meeting rooms. In his travels in China, he visited four Masonic halls of former lodges in South China, being careful to avoid any suggestion that he was trying to claim them back. He also made sure that books on freemasonry which gave the correct view and history of the Craft were available to officials in Beijing.[9] Giving the correct view was very important, for in 1974 an alleged exposé of freemasonry was published for Chinese readers. The books described the Hong Kong lodges as foreigners' triad societies, and compared freemasonry to the Chinese secret triad societies. It attributed to freemasonry many of the failings of the triads, and called it the "white men's international triad society."[10]

After Father passed away, people wondered whether the Chinese government would allow freemasonry to continue in Hong Kong after the transfer of sovereignty in 1997. Yao Kang went to speak to the leaders in Beijing, stressing the fact that Father had been a mason all his life. He came away with confirmation from the Hong Kong-Macao Office that freemasonry would be allowed to continue after 1997, as long as it abided by the Basic Law. The meetings would continue to be conducted in English. However, the society would have to be more open, since it was perceived as a secret society. This openness would also apply to its social and charitable work. Since masons always swear allegiance to the existing government, as of July 1, 1997 the Chinese government is toasted instead of the British Crown.[11]

15

A Look
Into The Future

The early 1980s were years when the Sino-British discussions about the handover were under way. The economy was on a downswing and there was constant talk of emigration from Hong Kong because of a lack of confidence in the future of the colony. Many people left for countries such as Canada, the United States, Australia and New Zealand. The talk of the town was, "We've been refugees once, we don't want to be refugees again." Emigration became such a hot topic that there were even special magazines catering to potential emigrants.[1]

Statistically, the picture looked brighter for both China and Hong Kong. Between 1977 and 1982, the import of Chinese products into Hong Kong increased by almost 32 per cent, at a value of $29,510 million, and the export of products from Hong Kong to China increased by 187 per cent. The large increase in the latter was due to the electricity provided by China Light & Power Company to Guang-dong province. The modest modernization program in China was already helping Hong Kong to re-emerge as an entrêpot.[2]

In 1981, the Hong Kong government introduced district board elections which became the first phase of a move to a more representative style of government. Because the British government was preparing to negotiate the future of Hong Kong with the Chinese government, they felt a need for the people of Hong Kong to have a greater say in their own domestic affairs.

In my family, life went on as usual, and Father maintained his everlasting faith in Hong Kong and in China. His view on the idea of "one country, two systems" was:

> ... the event will signal a new approach to international relationship. The foundation of this relationship will be based on the mutual respect of the two governments with the interest of all parties, including that of the local population in mind.

His vision for the future, beyond July 1, 1997, was that:

> Hong Kong, as far as China is concerned, has a role to play in her modernization for many more years to come, far beyond 1997, provided that free enterprise tempered with social justice remains and that we will not be crippled by the introduction of slothful work ethics.[3]

Father maintained that people in Hong Kong still made their living in the old-fashioned way — by working hard. He pointed out that even though people said China depended on Hong Kong for large amounts of foreign exchange, where would Hong Kong be without China?[4] Since Hong Kong depended on China for food and water, and a cheap labour force, he wondered why most people seemed oblivious to the fact that Hong Kong relied on China for its existence.

The biggest concern of the business community in Hong Kong after the change of sovereignty to China in 1997 was whether it would be overtaken by Shanghai as the leading business centre and the gateway to China. There has always been competition between Shanghai and Hong Kong as commercial ports, and historically, Shanghai was the most important centre in China for foreign trade until the establishment of the People's Republic of China in 1949. Father's view was that:

> With the absence of foreign exchange control and very low taxation, Hong Kong is also one of the important centres for capital formation.... In order to retain our advantage permanently over other localities, such as Shanghai, we

must devote all our resources to constantly upgrading our financial infrastructure and industrial technology.[5]

Father thought it preposterous that the delegation of British Members of Parliament led by Edward Du Cann, who visited Beijing at the invitation of the Chinese government in 1982, should even suggest that the Chinese government begin "negotiations" with London.[6] He thought it was totally unrealistic to expect China to renew treaties that were obviously unequal. And since the People's Republic of China had never recognized the Treaty of Nanking of 1842, and the Conventions of Peking of 1860 and 1898, China had already claimed sovereignty over Kowloon and Hong Kong. This claim had never been formally rejected by the British. It was Father's belief that both sides regarded Hong Kong as part of China under British management until July 1, 1997.[7]

Father believed that the future of Hong Kong would depend, in part, on the population. If they remained productive and could serve a unique economic function for China and the world, he believed that a practical and sensible solution could be reached through dialogue before 1997. The solution had to be formulated more on the basis of mutual economic interest rather than military power, political ideology or even international law. The most important factor was to perpetuate Hong Kong's independent economic status so that it could serve as one of the financial centres of the world where modern technology and know-how could be transferred into China. In order to do so, laws and commercial practices in their existing forms needed to continue and the Hong Kong dollar had to remain freely convertible.[8]

Father ventured a few suggestions for the future government of Hong Kong:

> ... the Government of Hong Kong could perhaps be a modified form of the present system with a Governing Committee. Hong Kong would be an "Independent Special Zone" within China under the Chinese flag. The Headship of the Governing Committee to be taken in turn by a Chinese and a Briton, say, every three or four years. The modification should be introduced gradually before 1997 to prevent any shocks due to abrupt changes.... The Legislative

Council would continue with some appointed members as an interim measure for a few years, after which the entire Council could perhaps be elected.... The Civil Service could, with careful planning, remain much the same as at present.[9]

In legal matters, Father recommended that the existing laws of Hong Kong, recognized worldwide, should continue to be enforced after 1997 with the consent of China. The final appeal for court cases would not go to Beijing or to London, but to the final court of appeal created in Hong Kong, and special arrangements would be made for English judges who were members of the Privy Council to continue to assist Hong Kong with their services in a new capacity acceptable to China, United Kingdom and Hong Kong.[10]

In financial matters, Father believed that Hong Kong had learnt a lesson from the disaster caused by the Exchange Fund and General Reserves being tied to sterling under Colonial Regulations. Since the diversification of the fund in 1972, Hong Kong had become the world's third largest financial centre. He said in 1982 that:

> This advantage should be maintained with full vigour. I think that is one of the points the Chinese leaders had in mind when they spoke about preserving Hong Kong's present status. When the year of 1997 arrives, the Exchange Fund must not be transferred to London or to Beijing but should be kept locally at all times or at any other place which Hong Kong itself may determine. This will perpetuate the independence of the Hong Kong dollar and continue to strengthen the confidence in Hong Kong by the international commercial community.[11]

At Peace with Himself

In a letter written to Father on July 14, 1981, Lord Lawrence Kadoorie said:

> When I look back to immediate post-war Hong Kong and see it today, I cannot fail to appreciate that it is due to the confidence and enterprise of people such as yourself and your family who have made this possible.

We hope you both enjoy good health, long life and every happiness and that our friendship may continue for many more years to come.

In 1982, Father decided that he no longer wanted to go out on the *Atalanta*. He gave the launch to our long-time coxswain, Ho Ning, so that he could sell it and use the money to retire.[12] Ho had been with our family for a very long time, and had watched us and all the grandchildren grow up.[13] On our visit to my parents that year, I couldn't believe that Father would ever give up his launch, which had been so dear to his heart for as long as I can remember. What I didn't know was that the doctor had told him that he was suffering from hardening of the arteries, and should no longer swim. It was just like Father to want to see Ho Ning happily retired during his own lifetime.

Father had always been proud of the fact that he had good genes from his own mother, Second Grandmother. I often heard him talking proudly of his mother's alertness at a great old age, and I do believe that he thought he would also live a very long time. In a letter to Horace Kadoorie on February 1, 1983, Father wrote:

It is most kind of you to have sent us the tangerines from your farm each year for the past many years.

My mother, who very soon will be 98, always looks forward in receiving your tangerines for her altar. She is a Buddhist and is in very good health. She plays 4 rounds of mahjong every day as exercise...

Mother saw Father smiling to himself early one morning in 1983. When she asked him why, he said that he had dreamt of Grandmother, and she was calling him to her.

In the early summer of 1983, Father's old friend Liao Chengzhi died. Father was the only person from Hong Kong invited to attend the funeral, which was held in Beijing. Since Liao was not only a good friend but someone Father had a great deal of respect for, he would not have missed the opportunity to pay his last respects.

On June 26, 1983, Fei Yiming saw Father on the top floor of the Beijing Hotel. Fei needed to write something down but did not have a pen. He borrowed Father's and happened to mention how well the pen wrote. When they said goodbye, Fei had no idea that it was to be the last time they would see each other.[14]

Beijing was very hot that summer, the temperature was over 100°F. On the way back to Hong Kong, the plane was delayed for a few hours and there was no air-conditioning at the airport. Father was finding it difficult to breathe.

When Father returned from Beijing, he didn't feel well. He consulted his doctor who immediately sent him to St. Paul's Hospital. When he arrived at the admitting office, he was asked for an advance payment of $2,000 as a deposit. Since Father didn't carry cash, he had to phone his secretary, Anna, to get the money from Mother, with the strictest order that no one was to be told, not even his brothers.[15] That day, all the Lee brothers at the Lee Hysan Estate office were wondering where Father was, because he had never missed a day of work in his life. Anna could say only that he was not coming in. However, when the head supervisor at the hospital, Sir Albert Rodrigues, made his rounds, he saw Father, and he told the Lee brothers. The following day, they scolded Anna for not telling them.

The doctor ordered Father to rest, an impossible task. Mother hired a private nurse for him, but he sent her away. He gave the order that very few people should be told, since he expected to be home soon. Mother wasn't even allowed to tell us, because he hated anyone making a fuss. Besides, he never took illness seriously. None of us knew that he had even been in hospital until after his death.

Of the very few visitors he had were Xinhua News Agency Director Xu Jiatun and his deputy, Li Chuwen, who went to see him on July 2. In the meantime, Father kept threatening to leave the hospital. Mother thought that Director Xu might have some influence and asked him to persuade Father to stay a few more days. Xu and Li found Father waiting in a chair to receive them when they entered his hospital room. Father said he was feeling fine, and that everyone worried too much.[16] After three days in hospital, he felt restless and wanted to leave. He gave his doctor an ultimatum: either he was to be discharged or he would check himself out of hospital, despite the fact that he was still being given oxygen. It was the morning of July 5.

A luncheon in honour of Director Tucker of the Water Department, who was retiring, was scheduled for that day at the Lee Gardens Hotel, and Father insisted on hosting it, even though arrangements had already been made for the secretary of the China Gas Company to take his place. Before the luncheon, he asked Anna to get ready all the cheques that needed to be signed and take them to the hotel. When Anna saw him, she thought he didn't look well, and noted that he was speaking more slowly than usual. When she told Aunt Violet, who was still working in the Lee Hysan Estate office, Aunt Violet said, "If he wanted to leave hospital, no one could stop him!"

Early on the morning of July 6, Father had his usual breakfast in the pantry. He got up from the table to get dressed for the office, and as he walked out of the pantry, he collapsed. An ambulance was called, but he was pronounced dead on arrival at the hospital.

When Anna went to work that morning, she walked past Tower Court as usual because she lived opposite us. Our watchman/chauffeur, Ah Lay, said to Anna, "Mr. Lee is gone." Anna said, "Where did he go?" not realizing what Ah Lay meant. His eyes became red as he started to cry. Anna found it difficult to believe and was walking around in a daze when she bumped into Hon Chiu who had just come out of Caroline Mansion, diagonally opposite to Tower Court. She asked him what she should do, and he said, "Just go back to the office." Even months after, Anna could not accept Father's death, and still had the feeling that he would be back. She would look out the window expecting to see him coming back to the office after having his customary lunch at home.[17]

A friend got into a taxi the morning of July 6, and the taxi driver told her that Hong Kong had lost a very fine man that morning. She asked who it was and realized that it was Father who had passed away.

At seven o'clock in the evening, of July 6, Yao Kang arrived at the airport from Los Angeles. He was in shock when his driver told him that Father had passed away. He said, "What am I going to do now? All my China connections are gone."[18]

After dinner on the evening of July 5, in Toronto,[19] I received a call from Seventh Uncle telling me that Father had passed away. I was completely dumbfounded. We hadn't known that Father had been in hospital, and besides, everyone expected him to be around forever.

Telegrams poured in from all over the world. The ones from President Li Xiannian, Yang Shangkun, Xi Zhongxun, Gu Mu, Yu Qiuli, Ji Pengfei, Jing Puchun and Liao Mengxing were reported in the Chinese newspapers.

One day in July, three pens like the one Fei Yiming borrowed from Father at the Beijing Hotel arrived at Fei's office at *Ta Kung Pao*. He was very moved that Father, even though he was ill, had instructed his secretary to send them to him before his death.[20]

In honour of Father's position as District Grand Master of Hong Kong and the Far East, a memorial service was to be held by the masons for him on July 18 at St. John's Cathedral. Neville had to return to Toronto to attend to his patients, so our eldest son, Ashley, flew to Hong Kong in his father's place. For that particular service, Mother decided that all female family members had to be in black cheongsams, and all the grandsons in black suits. I don't know where our relatives found tailors to make them, but these garments were made to order within forty-eight hours.

The day of the memorial service was a very hot, sunny day, and the Cathedral was filled. The eulogy was given by the Honorable Mr. Justice Cons. In relating Father's life, he said that, charity, which was the distinguishing virtue of a freemason, was prominent in Father's life. One of his first acts as District Grand Master had been to reassess the existing practices for the collection and distribution of charity in the District, and place the responsibility in the hands of the District Board of Benevolence, an organization in which he took the keenest interest. Father, he said, was more than a very successful businessman and a man of many talents; he was, first and foremost, a philanthropist of great generosity who inspired others to contribute. Father's favourite scripture reading in Masonic ceremonies was St. Paul's paean to charity.[21] Father was described as a man of infinite charm who never failed to arouse an affectionate response in those with whom he came into contact. His leadership and quiet authority inspired confidence and enthusiasm in others. He was quick to praise, but he did not hesitate to criticize whenever he felt a proper effort had not been made. However, he never lost his compassion for his fellow men.[22]

On October 8, another memorial service was held by the freemasons in Kobe, Japan, at St. Andrew's Chapel, the Flying Angel. A telegram of condolence from the mayor of Kobe, Tatsuo Miyazaki, was read. When Deputy District Grand Master Christopher Haffner gave the eulogy, he mentioned that Father had always looked upon Rising Sun Lodge in Kobe with special favour, for this was the lodge that first responded to his plea to endow medical research fellowships in celebration of the 250th anniversary of the Grand Lodge of England. Haffner mentioned Father's relationship to the leaders of China, and noted that he had been the first Hong Kong resident to be received by the new Chinese President, Li Xiannian. He said that Father's common sense approach to the practicalities of Hong Kong's 1997 problem would be sorely missed.[23]

Father's secretary, Anna, had a number of offers of well-paid positions because she had worked for Father for more than twelve years and presumably knew a great deal and had a lot of contacts, but she turned them all down. To her, Father was irreplaceable. She kept a small photograph of him smiling, which she said was his best, as well as some of his papers, a few of which were copies of the Chinese letters she had written on his behalf. She said these were souvenirs, and she very kindly handed them over to me to use as references for this book. Anna described Father as a man not without faults, but kind, honest, upright, and always a gentleman.

Father's death was covered widely in both Chinese and English newspapers, on television and on the radio. Father's sisters immediately disconnected Second Grandmother's television set, which she watched frequently, in order to keep the news from her, and told her that it was out of order. Since she was illiterate, she didn't read newspapers. She seldom went out in her later years, and the family and servants were instructed not to mention Father's death to her. For a number of years afterwards, whenever she asked why her eldest son didn't come to see her, Mother made some kind of excuse, and after a while, she stopped asking. We believe she knew, but didn't want to have her fears confirmed.

It was Father's wish that his ashes be scattered in the Hong Kong harbour, where he felt he belonged. Mother, in her old-fashioned way, refused to follow his wishes because she wanted to be buried next to him.

Father, always referred to by everyone respectfully in Chinese as "big brother," is greatly missed. During the writing of this book, I received great help and co-operation because there is still so much love and respect for him. He was referred to as a "great man," a "good friend" and even a "legend." Many remember him with gratitude and appreciation. Others lamented that his death was a blow to the Sino-British talks over the sovereignty of Hong Kong.

Even in death, as demonstrated by his funeral, Father built bridges for China and for Hong Kong, bringing peace and prosperity.

EPILOGUE

In honour of Father, the widow of Premier Zhou Enlai, Deng Yingchao, nominated Mother as a member of the Chinese People's Political Consultative Conference, a representative from Hong Kong to China.

Mother often said, "Even though your father was such an impatient man, and so rigid in his ways, I really can't complain about him, because he treated me so well." She had always been regarded with great respect and importance in Father's life. In his tradition of great generosity, whenever he made an investment, he automatically put half in Mother's name. Since he was so honest and straightforward, she came to rely on him completely, and depended on him for all decisions, solutions to all problems, even looking after household bills and her travel arrangements. She had always assumed that she would die first, and was not only saddened, and completely lost when he died, but insulted that she was left behind. It took her months to be taken off sedatives, but at the age of seventy-four, she did her best to carry on.

As for me, I wish I had been able to spend more time with Father. I wish I had asked many more questions than I did, but then I too expected him to be around for a very long time. I learnt from the examples he set, and try to live up to his standard. The fact that he always made it known that he cared will be with me forever. I thank him for the good name he left me with, and I am very proud to be his daughter.

Richard Charles Lee:
A Career Summary

Graduated from Oxford University, B.A. 1927, M.A. 1932
Appointed Justice of the Peace, 1946
Rice Controller, 1946–48
Order of the British Empire, 1949
Delegate of Hong Kong at the 4th & 5th Sessions, Economic Commission for Asia and the Far East, 1948, 1949
Leader of the Hong Kong Trade Mission to West Africa, 1960
Leader of the Hong Kong Trade Mission to Frankfurt, Germany, 1963
Commander of the British Empire, 1963
LL.D. University of Hong Kong, 1964
LL.D. Chinese University of Hong Kong, 1964
Order of the Sacred Treasure, Japan, 1969

Member Of Hong Kong Government Councils And Committees:

Panel of Inland Revenue Board of Review, beginning in 1949
Urban Council, 1953–60
Salary Commission, beginning in 1953
Hong Kong Housing Authority, 1954–60
Public Service Commission, 1952–59
Building Regulation Committee, 1953–59
Air Transport Licensing Authority, beginning in 1955
Legislative Council, 1959–65
Executive Council, 1961–66
Advisory Commission on Corruption, 1962–65
Fisheries Development Loan Fund Committee, 1960–65
Board of Education, 1961–66

Masonic Involvement:

President of the Board of Trustees, Hong Kong and South China Masonic Fund Corporation, 1961–83
District Grand Master of Hong Kong and the Far East, 1961–83

The University Of Hong Kong:

Member of the Court, beginning in 1948
Member of the Council, beginning in 1954

The Chinese University Of Hong Kong:

Vice-chairman of the Council, 1963–83
Chairman of the Campus Planning Committee, 1963–83
Chairman of the Tender Board, 1963–83
Member of the Nominating Committee for Honorary Degrees, 1963–83

Chairman Of The Board Of Directors:

Associated Properties Ltd.
Canadian and Oriental Oil Ltd.
Duro Holdings Ltd.
Garden Hotels Holdings (Hong Kong) Ltd.
Gande Price Investment Co. Ltd.
Grand Marine Holdings Ltd.
Hong Kong & China Gas Co., Ltd.
Hong Kong Telephone Co. Ltd.
Hong Kong Tube & Metal Products Ltd.
Hysan Development Co. Ltd.
International Entertainment Enterprises Ltd.
Kowloon Taxicab & Transport Co. Ltd.
Kwong Lee Enterprises
Lee Gardens Hotel Ltd.
Lee Hysan Estate Co. Ltd.
RCL Semiconductor Ltd.
Western Trading Co. Ltd.

Deputy Chairman:

N.M. Rothschild & Sons Hong Kong Ltd.
Yamaichi International (Hong Kong) Ltd.

Director:

Associated Bankers Insurance Co. Ltd.
Bank of East Asia Ltd.
Eastern Asia Navigation Co. Ltd.
Hong Kong Building & Loan Agency Ltd.
Hong Kong Land Investment & Agency Co. Ltd.
Hong Kong Realty & Trust Co. Ltd.
The Textile Corporation of Hong Kong
Wheelock Marden & Co. Ltd.
& other companies

Other:

Chairman of the Hong Kong Association of Property Owners
Chairman of the Hong Kong Country Club, 1963–1964
Chairman of the South China Athletic Association
Director and Honorary Lifetime Director of the Szeyup Business
  Association
Director of the Wan Chai (Kaifong) Benevolent Association
Honorary Member, Chinese Business Association
Honorary Lifetime Member, College of Chinese Engineers
Honorary Lifetime Member, Hong Kong Country Club
Honorary Lifetime Member, Hong Kong Japanese Club
Lifetime Director, Sunwui Business Association
Member of the Hong Kong General Chamber of Commerce,
  1960–1968
Member of Permanent Board of Directors, Po Leung Kuk, 1959–1960
Vice-president, Po Leung Kuk, 1960–1966

List Of Richard Charles Lee's Siblings

Second Uncle - Ming Hop

Third Uncle - Harold, Hau Wo (Wing Gun)

Fourth Uncle - Jung Sen (J.S.)

Fifth Uncle - Wing Kit

Sixth Uncle - Jung Kang (J.K.)

Seventh Uncle - Wing Tat

Second Aunt - Doris, Shun Wah

Third Aunt - Ansie, Shun Ying

Fourth Aunt - Joyce, Shun Kum

Fifth Aunt - Dione, Shun Yin

Sixth Aunt - Amy, Shun Ho

Seventh Aunt - Diana, Shun Yee

Eighth Aunt - Vivien, Shun Ngor

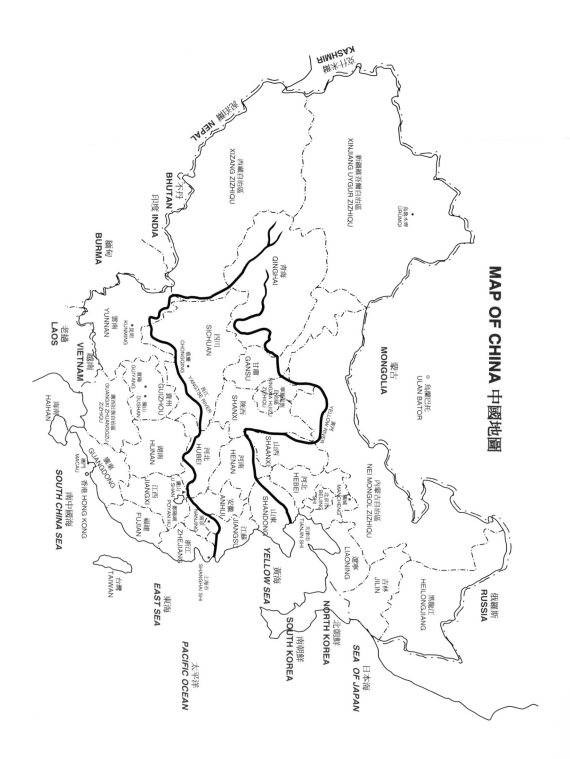

MAP OF CHINA 中國地圖

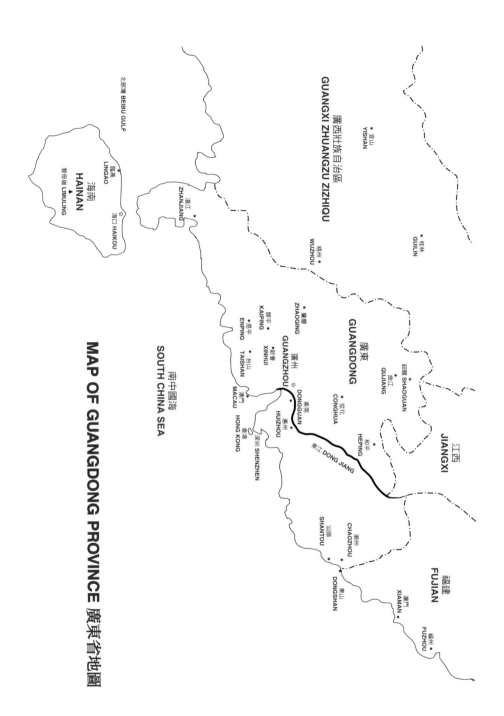

MAP OF GUANGDONG PROVINCE 廣東省地圖

219

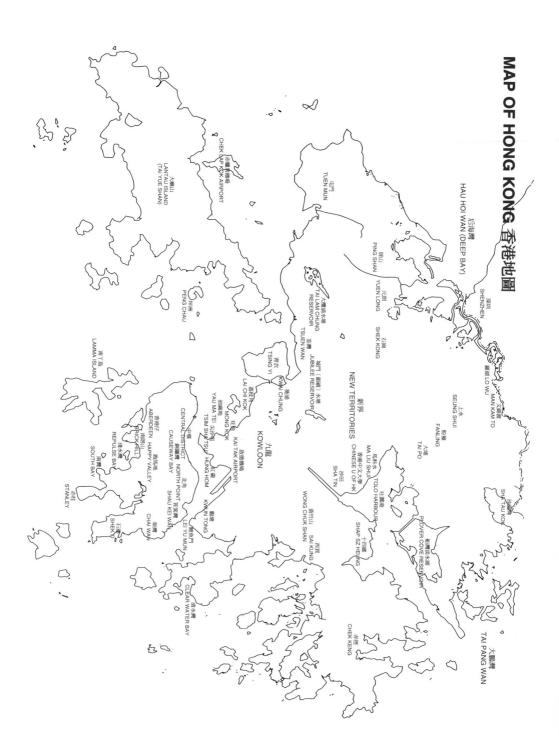

MAP OF HONG KONG 香港地圖

后海灣
HAU HOI WAN (DEEP BAY)

深圳
SHENZHEN

羅湖關
MAN KAM TO LO WU

沙頭角
SHA TAU KOK

大鵬灣
TAI PANG WAN

所頭機場邨
CHEK LAP KOK AIRPORT

大嶼山
LANTAU ISLAND
(TAI YUE SHAN)

屯門
TUEN MUN

屏山
PING SHAN

元朗
YUEN LONG

石崗
SHEK KONG

上水
SEUNG SHUI

粉嶺
FANLING

大埔
TAI PO

赤門
CHEK KENG

八洲洲
PENG CHAU

大欖涌水塘
TAI LAM CHUNG
RESERVOIR

荃灣
TSUEN WAN

城門（銀禧）水塘
JUBILEE RESERVOIR

NEW TERRITORIES
新界

馬料水
MA LIU SHUI

香港中文大學
CHINESE U OF HK

吐露港
TOLO HARBOUR

十四鄉
SHAP SZ HEUNG

企嶺澳水塘
PLOVER COVE RESERVOIR

南丫島
LAMMA ISLAND

青衣
TSING YI

葵涌
KWAI CHUNG

荔枝角
LAI CHI KOK

深水埗
SHAM SHUI PO

旺角
MONG KOK

油麻地
YAU MA TEI

尖沙咀
TSIM SHA TSUI

紅磡
HUNG HOM

啟德機場
KAI TAK AIRPORT

九龍
KOWLOON

觀塘
KWUN TONG

黃竹山
WONG CHUK SHAN

沙田
SHA TIN

西貢
SAI KUNG

香港仔
ABERDEEN

鴨脷洲
BRICK HILL

跑馬地
HAPPY VALLEY

中環
CENTRAL DISTRICT

北角
NORTH POINT

銅鑼灣
CAUSEWAY BAY

筲箕灣
SHAU KEI WAN

鯉魚門
LEI YU MUN

柴灣
CHAI WAN

清水灣
CLEAR WATER BAY

淺水灣
REPULSE BAY

南灣
SOUTH BAY

赤柱
STANLEY

石澳
SHEK O

220

ENDNOTES

A Farewell

1 *Hong Kong Standard*, July 7, 1983.
2 *South China Morning Post*, July 7, July 12, 1983.

Chapter 1

1 All Uncles and Aunts preceded by a number are siblings of Father.
2 A village in south China, it is also the Lee family's original ancestral village. Chinese tend to be very clannish, and I am sure Father was very proud that these two men were from the same area as our family.
3 *Zibao Xuexiao Nianbao* (*Zibao School Magazine*), July 31, 1921, 5-7.
4 Letter from Percy O'Brien, Oxford, October 17, 1997.
5 V.H.H. Green, *A History of Oxford* (London, 1974), 188-189.
6 Letter from Percy O'Brien, Oxford, October 17, 1997.
7 Letter from Percy O'Brien, Oxford, October 30, 1997.
8 Letter from Percy O'Brien, Oxford, October 30, 1997.
9 Letter from Percy O'Brien, Oxford, October 17, 1997.
10 Konosuke Koike, article in *Yamabiko*, a bi-monthly newspaper published by Yamaichi Securities Co. Ltd., circulated only among the Yamaichi Group, Sept. 7, 1971, translated by Shinichi Shiraishi, Deputy President of Yamaichi Securities Co. Ltd.

Chapter 2

1 Interview with Josephine Chiu and Jenny Hoo, Vancouver, April 1997.
2 Interview with Jenny Hoo, Vancouver, April 1997.
3 Zhang Lianjue (Lady Clara Hotung), *Mingshan Youji* (*Memories on Famous Mountains*) (Hong Kong, 1934), 105.
4 A photograph of Father supervising the workers was taken in 1931. Interview with George Todkill, who used to work for Whampoa Dockyard, Hong Kong, June 1997.
5 Interview with Hon Chiu Lee, Hong Kong, January 1996.
6 Interview with Josephine Chiu and Jenny Hoo, Vancouver, April 1997.
7 Chungshee H. Liu, *Hainan, The Island and the People* (Shanghai, 1939).
8 Wang Shaoping, *Feidao Qiongya Yinxiang Ji* (*Philipines and Hainan Impressions*) (Hong Kong, 1939), 81. Wang was one of the investors in Father's company.
9 Wang Shaoping, *Feidao*, 66-7.
10 Wang Shaoping, *Feidao*, 69.
11 Wang Shaoping, *Feidao*, 81.

12 Wang Shaoping, *Feidao*, 89-90.

13 Interview with He Mingsi, former secretary of the Xinhua News Agency who often accompanied my parents during their travels in China, Hong Kong, January 1996.

14 Names such as Shen Yi, who was Chairman of the Technology Department of Chinese Resources Committee (CRC) and Minister of Communications Bureau; Qian Changzhou, Vice-Chairman of the (CRC) and Jiang Pingbo, Purchasing Manager of the CRC. Interview with C.T.Wu, Toronto, Spring 1995.

15 He was well known for establishing precision for train schedules by using Omega equipment and was highly respected by Chiang Kaishek.

16 Interview with C.T. Wu, Toronto, Spring 1995.

17 Interview with C.T. Wu, Toronto, Spring 1995.

18 Phone interview with Sir Jack Cater in Hong Kong, June, 1997.

19 Interview with C.T. Wu, Toronto, Spring 1995.

20 Interview with C.T. Wu, Toronto, Summer 1995.

Chapter 3

1 Xie Yongguang, *Xianggang Kangri Fengyun Lu* (Hong Kong, 1995), 72-73.

2 Tim Carew, *The Fall of Hong Kong* (London, 1960), 26-27.

3 Xie Yongguang, *Xianggang Kangri Fengyun Lu*, 96.

4 Ted Ferguson, *Desperate Siege: The Battle of Hong Kong* (Toronto, 1980), 5.

5 Ferguson, *Desperate Siege*, 6-7.

6 Sir Selwyn Selwyn-Clarke, *Footprints: The Memoirs of Sir Selwyn Selwyn-Clarke* (Hong Kong, 1975), 58.

7 Interview with Jeanne Tam, who was then known as Tsui Ling Fai. She was one of the air-raid wardens. Toronto, January 1996.

8 Interview with Bill Poy, Toronto, November 1996.

9 Ferguson, *Desperate Siege*, 7.

10 Son of Liao Zhongkai, leader of the left-wing Nationalist party.

11 Interview with Lian Weilin, former Director of the Xinhua News Agency (New China News Agency, or NCNA), Hong Kong branch, Guangzhou, November 1996.

12 Interview with He Mingsi, former Secretary of the Xinhua News Agency, Hong Kong Branch, Hong Kong, January 1996.

13 Selwyn-Clarke, *Footprints*, 64.

14 She was single and working under her maiden name, Elizabeth Teng.

15 Interview with Joseph Tam, Toronto, January 1996.

16 Interview with Joseph Tam, Toronto, January 1996.

17 David Faure, co-ordinator, and the members of the Oral History Project Team, Centre for East Asian Studies, The Chinese University of Hong Kong, "Saikung, The Making of the District and its Experience During World War II," *Journal of the Hong Kong Branch of the Asiatic Society*, vol. 22, 1982, 184-185.

18 Interview with Bill Poy, Toronto, November 1996.

19 Selwyn-Clarke, *Footprints*, 65.

20 The entire story of the Poy family experience during the attack and surrender of Hong Kong was told by Bill Poy, Toronto, November 1996.

21 Interview with Joseph Tam, Toronto, January 1996.

22 He wanted to remain in Hong Kong to take care of the medical needs of the population. He was accused by some of being a collaborator and was later interned by the Japanese.

23 Interview with Joseph Tam, Toronto, January 1996.

24 Jiang Shui, "Husong He Xiangning, Liao Chengzhi Muziliang De Jingguo," *Huoyao Zai Xiang Jiang: Gangjiu Dadui Xigong Diqu Kangri Shi Lu (Anti-Japanese Activities of the Hong Kong-Kowloon Brigade in Saikung)*, ed. by Xu Yueqing (Hong Kong, 1993), 22-26.

25 Jiang Shiu, *Huoyao Zai Xiang Jiang*, 20-21.

26 Edwin Ride, *B.A.A.G., Hong Kong Resistance, 1942–1945* (Hong Kong, 1981), p. 27, footnote 2; p. 17; p.29, footnote 17.

27 Wang set up the puppet regime in Nanjing as an alternative to Chiang's in Chongqing.

28 Ride, *B.A.A.G.*, 31-44.

29 Col. L.T. Ride, *Report on the Activities of a M.I.9/19 Organization in South China by Colonel L.T. Ride, lately Commandant B.A.A.G.*, written at Whitehall for the War Office, 1946, Public Record No. WO 208/3260, Section B.

30 Interview with C.T. Wu, Toronto, Spring 1995.

31 Interview with Lian Weilin, Guangzhou, November 1996.

32 Interview with He Mingsi, Hong Kong, January 1996.

Chapter 4

1 Selwyn-Clarke, Sir Selwyn, *Footprints: The Memoirs of Sir Selwyn Selwyn-Clarke* (Hong Kong, 1975), 69.

2 Interview with Joseph Tam, Toronto, January 1996.

3 Interview with Raymand Lee, Vancouver, February 1997.

4 Interview with Hon Chiu Lee, October 1996.

5 Interview with Hon Chiu Lee, October 1996.

6 Interview with Bill Poy, Toronto, November 1996.

7 Interview with Hon Chiu Lee, Hong Kong, January 1996.

8   Interview with Bill Poy, Toronto, November 1996.

9   Interview with Hon Chiu Lee, October 1996.

10 They are filled with silk fibres instead of eiderdown and are very light and warm.

11 From Guizhou to Guilin.

12 Ling Hongxun, Shi Zhiren, Hou Jiayuan, Yuan Menghong.

13 Father never joined any political party.

14 The position was given to him by Cheng Goonshing who was married to Second Aunt. Yong Guang Coal Company was very profitable because of the need for coal for the railways and their sales were guaranteed. Tan Nailiang, Cheng's nephew, was the accountant. Tan and C.T. Wu lived in a bamboo-mud house right by the office of the Company.

15 Interview with C.T. Wu, Toronto, Spring 1995.

16 C.T. Wu participated in the supervision of this building.

17 Interview with C.T. Wu, Toronto, Spring 1995.

18 C.T. Wu was very happy to have a free economy railway pass. He was always welcomed by the railway staff because of his love of ping-pong. He said there really weren't too many forms of entertainment available during the war, and ping-pong was one of them. The games usually lasted much longer than the work supervision. Interview with C.T. Wu, Toronto, Spring 1995.

19 General Manager of Guo Hua Bank, and an influential person in financial circles, both in China and among overseas Chinese.

20 Chairman of the Overseas Union Bank of Singapore.

21 General Manager of the Overseas Union Bank of Singapore.

22 Interview with C.T. Wu, Toronto, Spring 1995.

23 Interview with Hon Chiu Lee, Hong Kong, January 1996.

24 Interview with Hon Chiu Lee, Hong Kong, January 1996.

25 Third Uncle was a director.

26 Letter from Sing Sheng, Hong Kong, October 1997.

27 Interview with C.T. Wu, Toronto, Spring 1995.

28 Interview with Josephine Chiu, Vancouver, April 1997.

29 Interview with Hon Chiu Lee, Hong Kong, January 1996.

Chapter 5

1   Every five days, each person was allowed one catty and four taels of rice, one catty of flour and half a catty of green peas. 1 catty = 1.32 pounds; 1 tael = 1.33 ounces.

2   Reported in *Wah Kiu Yat Po* between 1946-48.

3   C.T. Wu expressed the opinion that if it had been anybody else who had that post, he would have made a fortune, but Father would not even think of a profit for himself. Interview with C.T. Wu, Toronto, Spring 1995.

4   Interview with Violet Lee, Hong Kong, January 1996.

5 Doctors with non-Commonwealth training were not allowed to practise in Hong Kong.

6 In 1963 Sing Sheng renewed his relationship with my family when he was offered a position as Director of Sales and Marketing for the Mandarin Hotel in Hong Kong. He married Dorothy's sister Grace.

7 Letter from Sing Sheng from Hong Kong, October 14, 1997.

8 *Wah Kiu Yat Po*, July 2, 7, 12, 23, 1951; August 9, 1951; November 5, 1951; February 23, 1952; April 1, 15, 27, 1952; June 16, 1952; July 12, 15, 16, 19, 20, 29, 1952; January 10, 16, 1953; March 15, 31, 1953; May 10, 17, 31, 1953.

9 *Wah Kiu Yat Po*, June 2, 1953.

10 *Wah Kiu Yat Po*, March 23, 1961.

11 In 1941 one-quarter of the workforce in Hong Kong was already engaged in industrial manufacturing.

12 At the time of the Japanese surrender, the population was at 500 thousand. In 1949, it reached 2 million.

13 A Communist college which recruited for the Party in China and Southeast Asia was closed in 1949. Very few schools were closed by the Hong Kong government until 1967, but schools were inspected regularly for "subversive" activities.

14 Alexander Grantham, *Via Port* (Hong Kong, 1965), 115.

Chapter 6

1 Interview with Anna Li, Father's last secretary, Los Angeles, April 1995.

2 Interview with Anna Li, Los Angeles, April 1995.

Chapter 7

1 Sue Heady, *The Hong Kong Country Club* (Hong Kong, 1992), 2.

2 Heady, *Hong Kong Country Club*, 13-14.

3 Heady, *Hong Kong Country Club*, 79.

4 Heady, *Hong Kong Country Club*, 16-17.

5 Heady, *Hong Kong Country Club*, 20.

6 *Hong Kong Standard*, December 14, 1972.

7 Interview with Hon Chiu Lee, Hong Kong, January 1996.

Chapter 8

1 Interview with Violet Lee, Hong Kong, January 1996.

2 Interview with Violet Lee, Hong Kong, January 1996.

3 *Wah Kiu Yat Po*, July 31, 1956.

4 Interview with J.S. Lee, Hong Kong, January 1996.

5 Interview with Peter Lee, Hong Kong, January 1996.

6 Interview with Hon Chiu Lee, Hong Kong, November 1996.

7   Between 5 to 10 percent. Interview with Hon Chiu Lee, November 1996.

8   Interview with C.T. Wu, Toronto, February 1997.

9   Interview with C.T. Wu, Toronto, February 1997.

10 Interview with C.T. Wu, Toronto, February 1997.

11 Interview with Violet Lee, Hong Kong, January 1996.

12 John Swire & Sons Limited was established in the United Kingdom in 1816. The company established Butterfield & Swire Co. in Shanghai on January 1, 1867, importing cotton and woolen fabrics and exporting tea and silk from China. In 1872, Swire established China Navigation Company (C.N.Co.). After the Second World War, the company's centre of business moved to Hong Kong. In July 1946, Swire and Maclaine Ltd. was established for import/export business. The company established Taikoo Wharf and Godown Company in June 1947. In 1948, it acquired a majority share of Cathay Pacific Airways Ltd. The company is also involved in manufacturing and engineering industries, beverages, properties, insurance, agriculture and retailing.

13 Registered in Hong Kong on October 19, 1948.

14 The company was founded in 1948.

15 Interview with C.T. Wu, Toronto, February 1997. It was a major innovation in business practice and land law; the basis of much of Hong Kong's economic growth in subsequent decades.

16 Interview with C.T. Wu, Toronto, Spring 1995.

17 I am sure its connection with the Shanghai Commercial Bank helped.

18 It was a wire (cable) commercial service in Hong Kong.

19 Interview with C.T. Wu, Toronto, Spring 1995.

20 Interview with Raymand Lee, Vancouver February 1997.

21 In Hong Kong, bosses do not ride in delivery trucks. Interview with Hon Chiu Lee, Hong Kong, November 1996.

22 This was subsequently sold by the family in the 1990s.

23 Note from Chien Lee, Hong Kong, January 1998.

24 Interview with Hon Chiu Lee, Hong Kong, January 1996.

25 Note from Chien Lee, Hong Kong, January 1998.

26 Interview with Hon Chiu Lee, Hong Kong, November 1996.

27 Interview with Hon Chiu Lee, Hong Kong, January 1996.

28 Interview with Hon Chiu Lee, Hong Kong, January 1996.

29 The Hong Kong stock market crashed in 1973, followed by a worldwide oil crisis, which brought economic recession until 1976.

30 Interview with Hon Chiu Lee, Hong Kong, November 1996.

31 The company was originally incorporated in October 1970 as a private limited company under the name of Hennessy Development Company

Limited, and was a wholly owned subsidiary of Lee Hysan Estate which was incorporated in 1924.

32 The original board consisted of Father as the chairman, and directors David P. Chan, F.K. Hu, Michael Jebsen, Per Jorgensen, T.S. Kwok, Hon Chiu Lee, J.S. Lee, Quo Wai Lee, Ian Robert Anderson and Geoffrey M.T. Yeh.

33 Total area of 80,881 sq. ft. Grandfather had originally bought this property in the names of Grandmother and his first four sons – Father, Second Uncle, Third Uncle and Fourth Uncle. To the credit of the Lee family, the property was given back to the family company, Lee Hysan Estate Co., for the benefit of all family members. In fact, it was also to the credit of Grandmother who turned over all the properties in her name to all the children during her life time.

34 At the end of 1997, besides many other positions, Hon Chiu Lee was elected chairman of the Hong Kong Stock Exchange.

35 Interview with Hon Chiu Lee, Hong Kong, January 1996.

Chapter 9

1 A new airport was originally planned for Ping Shan in the New Territories. However, the colonial government realized that planes taking off and landing would have to circle over Chinese territories, and could be shot down. In fact, in the 1950s some civilian aircraft were shot down. The new runway in Kai Tak airport, which was capable of accommodating the largest jets, ran out into the sea at Kowloon Bay. It was completed at the end of the 1950s.

2 At present the chairman and CEO of the Bank of East Asia.

3 Notes from S. Shiraishi, Osaka, March 1997.

4 Since the 1970s, they were the opthamologists who looked after the eyes of the top leaders of China, including Deng Xiaoping.

5 Apparently this practice was only allowed to revive in 1978, after having been banned for twenty years.

Chapter 10

1 Alexander Grantham, *Via Ports* (Hong Kong, 1965), 188-189.

2 Interview with He Mingsi, Hong Kong, January 1996.

3 Interview with C.T. Wu, Toronto, Spring 1995.

4 Letter from Ruth Hayhoe to her mother, July 17, 1967.

5 Appointed Director of the Institute of Education in Hong Kong in 1997, and simultaneously is Professor of Comparative Education at the Ontario Institute of Education, University of Toronto.

6 Letter from Ruth Hayhoe to her mother, October 28, 1967.

7 Interview with Yao Kang, Hong Kong, June 1997. The chairman, Sir Adrian Swire, was in Hong Kong at the time. Yao, as a junior manager, told Sir Adrian that since these were political riots, the chances were that the material damage would not be large, and besides, the company should not let their clients down just when they needed help most. With the powers delegated to the Hong Kong company, it had the right to make its own decisions. As a result, Swire maintained riot insurance for its clients, and in the end, not a cent was lost by the company, and Swire gained a lot of public confidence.

8 Interview with Violet Lee, Hong Kong, January 1996.

9 Interview with Lian Weilin, Guangzhou, November 1996; article by Fei Yiming, "Mian Huai Li Ming Ze" ("Remembering R.C. Lee"), *Ta Kung Pao*, July 16, 1983.

10 Interview with David K.P. Li, Hong Kong, November 1996.

11 Letter from Ruth Hayhoe to her mother, July 3, 1968.

12 Bernard Luk, "The Rise of a Civil Society in Hong Kong," presented at the Human Rights and Democracy in Asia Conference, Joint Centre for Asia Pacific Studies, 16-17 May, 1997.

13 The word "Royal" was added to the Hong Kong Police Force only after the disturbances of 1967. Sir Jack Cater, Hong Kong, June 1997.

14 Notes from Sir Jack Cater provided by Lady Cater, Hong Kong, August 1997.

15 Luk, "The Rise of a Civil Society in Hong Kong."

16 Interview with Anna Li, Los Angeles, April 1995.

17 *Ta Kung Pao*, January 29, 1977.

18 Interview with Dr. Chi Chao Chan, Baltimore, October 1997.

19 The population increased four fold between 1945 and 1949.

20 It became associated with Yale University.

21 Alice N.H. Lun Ng, editor, *The Quest for Excellence* (Hong Kong, 1994), 18.

22 Ng, *Quest for Excellence*, 20-21.

23 Ng, *Quest for Excellence*, 25.

24 Interview with Prof. Ma Lin, Hong Kong, June 1997.

25 Interview with Prof. Ma Lin, Hong Kong, June 1997.

26 Established in October 1951 by representatives of Protestant churches.

27 Minutes of the Campus Committee meetings from 1964 to 1983. Provided by Vincent W.S. Chen of the Campus Committee of The Chinese University of Hong Kong.

28 Interview with Prof. Ma Lin, Hong Kong, June 1997.

29 Interview with Prof. Ma Lin, Hong Kong, June 1997.

Chapter 11

1 Interview with Reiko Ogata, Hong Kong, June 1997.

2 Interview with Reiko Ogata, Hong Kong, June 1997.

3 Achievement Report from the Consulate-General of Japan sent to the Japanese government, 1968.

4 In 1969 a Japanese Chamber of Commerce was established, separate from the Club.

5 Interview with Y. Yoshioka, Secretary General of the Hong Kong Japanese Club, Hong Kong, June 1997.

6 Notes from S. Shiraishi of Yamaichi Securities, Osaka, Japan, March 1997.

7 The latter was to move into the Lee Gardens Hotel podium upon its completion across the street.

8 Established on October 2, 1965.

9 In 1975, the Japanese School moved into its own building at 157 Blue Pool Road.

10 Special guests were Father, Consul-General of Japan Mr. Endo, Deputy Director of the Department of Education Sir Y.K.Kan as Chinese representative, and Sir Kenneth Fung Ping Fun who successfully persuaded the Hong Kong government to allow the Japanese School to teach pupils in accordance with the formal school curriculums laid down by the Japanese government.

11 Ichiro Fujita, *The Twentieth Anniversary Special Issue of the Hong Kong Japanese School*, May 10, 1986, 39, translated by Y. Yoshioka, Secretary General of the Hong Kong Japanese Club. The original article appeared in Phoenix Publication no. 13.

12 In 1994, it was demolished and rebuilt as part of Caroline Centre.

13 Fujita, *The Twentieth Anniversary Special Issue of the Hong Kong Japanese School*, 39.

14 It is associated with the sacred mirror and the string of gems with gold rays, which is only used for higher grades of decorations. Notes from Y. Yoshioka, Hong Kong, August 1997.

15 Christopher Haffner, *The Craft in the East* (Hong Kong, 1988), dedicated to Father, 424.

16 Interview with Sir Quo Wai Lee, October 1996.

17 That was when Project 704 (April 1970) in Hangzhou started construction. It was an underground military complex, built to withstand nuclear attack, covering fifty acres, with two beautiful above-ground buildings, one for Lin and the other for Mao. The project might not have been built with a plot in mind (to hold Mao hostage), but it could be used for that purpose.

  In August 1970 in Lushan, Mao shot down Lin's effort to declare him the "genius of the world" in another of Lin's repeated attempts to make him into a figurehead. Lin knew that it was time to act and commenced Project 571, a homonym for "armed uprising."

It is likely that the plot against Mao began in the spring of 1971 in Suzhou, when Lin Biao, his wife, Ye Qun, and their twenty-six-year-old son, Lin Liguo, were vacationing. The conspiracy was to be under the command of Lin Liguo. According to the official government version, the original plot was to feign an attack on Mao, and Lin Liguo would "rescue" him. Zhou Enlai, Jiang Qing, Kang Sheng and some other key military leaders would be neutralized. The plan was abandoned because Lin did not have enough manpower to carry it out.

They then planned to assassinate Mao on his special train during his tour of south and central China. Lin depended on the military where he had been gathering supporters ever since he replaced Peng Dehuai in 1959 as defence minister. The airforce was to be the main component of this coup. Mao got wind of the plot, changed his schedule and sped through Shanghai, arriving in Beijing on the morning of September 12.

On September 11, Lin Biao and Ye Qun were at the seaside resort of Beidaihe, approximately 130 miles east of Beijing, awaiting word. Late that evening, the telephone rang with the news. Ye Qun immediately packed her bag, taking with her two dictionaries: English-Chinese and Russian-Chinese. Around five o'clock the same day, their son, Lin Liguo, had flown in from Beijing in a Trident three-engine plane, number 256. The plane had been assigned for Lin Biao's personal use. A crew of three had been assigned to it on September 6, and was told to be ready to take off at seven the next morning.

On the evening of September 12, after postponing a meeting with a delegation from Japan, Zhou Enlai received a call from Security Unit 8341 that Lin Biao, Ye Qun and Lin Liguo appeared to be leaving the country. Within the next half hour, Zhou ordered all planes grounded in China, and specifically the Trident assigned to Lin. According to one account, Zhou telephoned the Lins at Beidaihe to inquire about their health. They realized that Mao and Zhou were too close on the trail. Around midnight, the three airmen were awakened to prepare for immediate take-off. Aside from the Lins, there were three others who boarded the plane.

Mao was at the Swimming Pool House at Zhongnanhai when Zhou burst in to tell him that the Trident had taken off. Zhou suggested shooting it down, since it would still be in China's air space. Mao is reported to have said, "Let nature take its course."

Harrison E. Salisbury, *The New Emperors* (New York, 1993), 284-303.

18 Akira Okada, *Mizutori Gaiko Hiwa (The Secret Story of Mizutori's Diplomacy)* (Tokyo, 1983), 149-161. Translated into Chinese by the staff of the Hang Seng Bank, Hong Kong.

19 Interview with Sir Quo Wai Lee, October 1996.

20 Founded in 1897.

21 Notes from S. Shiraishi, March 1997. Shiraishi was the sales manager in Hong Kong under Shigeki Morishita when Yamaichi International (H.K.) opened.

22 Until September 1982, when Yamaichi International (H.K.) became wholly owned by Yamaichi.

23 Notes from S. Shiraishi, February 1997.

24 At the time of the writing of this book, he is deputy president of Yamaichi Securities Co. Ltd., one of the four largest securities companies in Japan.

25 Between 1971-73.

26 Notes from S. Shiraishi, Osaka, March 1997.

27 Notes from S. Shiraishi, Osaka, March 1997.

28 Interview with Reiko Ogata, Hong Kong, June 1997.

29 Letter to Father from Shigeru Okada, president of Mitsukoshi Limited, September 3, 1981. Mitsukoshi was established in 1673 and incorporated in 1904.

30 *Asian Economic News*, December 22, 1997. Core Pacific is a group of engineering and securities companies led by Taiwanese businessman Tony Shen.

31 Letter from S. Shiraishi, January 11, 1998.

32 *Asian Economic News*, December 22, 1997.

Chapter 12

1   Christopher Haffner, *The Craft in the East* (Hong Kong, 1988), 422.

2   Interview with Yao Kang, Hong Kong, June 1997.

3   At the same time, world-class reservoirs continued to be built, and desalinization of sea water was being carried out.

4   Interview with Lian Weilin, Guangzhou, November 1996.

5   *Ta Kung Pao*, May through June 1963.

6   *Ta Kung Pao*, May 31, 1963.

7   *Ta Kung Pao*, April 23, 1964.

8   *Wah Kiu Yat Po*, January 3, 1965.

9   1 cubic metre equals approximately 220 gallons.

10 *Ta Kung Pao*, April 21, 1965.

11 Interview with Lian Weilin, Guangzhou, November 1996.

12 *Hong Kong Standard*, June 28, 1967.

13 *Hong Kong Standard*, July 13, 1967.

14 1 cubic metre equals approx. 220 gallons.

15 *The Times*, July 8, 1983.

16 Interview with David K.P. Li, Hong Kong, November 1996.

17 Interview with Violet Lee, Hong Kong, January 1996. She remained a secretary in the family company, Lee Hysan Estate, until her retirement at

the age of sixty-five. Father used to give her a ride home every day after work, and he would tell her about confidential matters which he would not repeat in his office.

18 Member of the Legislative Council, member of the Executive Council, member of the Advisory Committee on Corruption and member of the Fisheries Development Loan Fund Committee.

19 *Wah Kiu Yat Po*, June 14, 1965.

20 Interview with David K.P. Li, Hong Kong, November 1996.

21 Fei Yiming, "Mian Huai Li Ming Ze" ("Remembering R.C. Lee"), *Ta Kung Pao*, July 16, 1983.

22 Interview with Sir Quo Wai Lee, Hong Kong, January 1996. The person who divulged this information cannot be named because he is still living.

23 Address given by Richard Charles Lee, "The Importance of Hong Kong to China" at the International Conference on the Economic Opportunities in Hong Kong, held at the Gravenbruch-Kempinski Hotel, Frankfurt, June 14-15, 1982.

24 Interview with Lian Weilin, Guangzhou, November 1996.

25 *Celebrity Monthly*, January 1979, 24.

26 *Ta Kung Pao*, January 11, 1978.

27 Letter from Prof. Ma Lin, November 27, 1997.

28 *Ta Kung Pao*, March 24, 1978.

29 Interview with Prof. Ma Lin, Hong Kong, June 1997.

30 Young Chinese tend to slur the distinction between the "n" and "l" sounds, and thus cause great confusion.

31 Interview with Anna Li, Los Angeles, April 1995.

32 Interview with Anna Li, Los Angeles, April 1995.

33 Yao Kang joined the Shanghai office of Swire in 1948, straight out of university. He was sent to England to train in the cadet program. He was the first local to be picked for this program which was usually reserved for Oxbridge graduates. In 1951, when the Korean War started, Swire was no longer willing to send its specialists to China. Yao was asked if he would like to go back. In his early twenties, he became the manager for Swire's China insurance operations, based in Shanghai, with branch offices in Tianjin, Qingdao, Hankou, Xiamen and Shantou. In 1953 he recommended that Swire get out of China, because he felt there was no future. The company followed his advice and withdrew from China. Yao arrived in Hong Kong at Christmas 1953. By the time Yao retired, he was chairman of six Swire subsidiary companies.

34 Interview with Yao Kang, Hong Kong, June 1997.

35 CITIC is the best-regarded and the most international company owned by Beijing, with twenty subsidiaries in China and abroad and a total of 26,000 employees. Its assets total US$5 billion. Abroad, the company

concentrates on development of natural resources and communications. An example is Citifor in Seattle, Washington, one of the major suppliers of timber in the northwest United States. Other business interests include China Light & Power, Dragon Air, Hong Kong Telecom, trading, distribution and property, mainly in Hong Kong, Macau and mainland China. It is a publicly traded company listed on the Hong Kong stock exchange. The friendship between Yao and Wei is, "The reason why Swire Pacific is so close to CITIC. They have many joint ventures." Yao Kang, Hong Kong, June 1997.

36 Passengers could get on the train in Hong Kong and go through immigration in Guangzhou when they arrived, without being stopped at border check-points.

37 Director from 1978-82.

38 Interview with Wang Kuang, Guangzhou, November 1996.

39 Lee, "The Importance of Hong Kong to China."

40 Letter to Father from H.A. Washcheck, Senior Vice-President of the Bank of America, September 4, 1980.

41 Fei Yiming, "Mian Huai Li Ming Ze" ("Remembering R.C. Lee"), *Ta Kung Pao*, July 16, 1983.

42 Lee, "The Importance of Hong Kong to China."

43 The agreement stipulated that the ownership of the hotel revert to China after fifteen years. This was later extended to twenty years.

44 A Supplemental Agreement was signed on May 3, 1983.

45 Referred to as Garden Guest House in the Joint Venture Agreement.

46 Joint Venture Agreement on the Construction and Operation of Garden Guest House in Guangzhou between Guangzhou Lingnan Enterprises Company and Garden Hotels (Holdings) Limited, March 28, 1980.

47 Supplemental Agreement between Guangzhou Lingnan Enterprises Company and Garden Hotels (Holdings) Limited in respect of the joint venture for the construction and operation of the Garden Hotel, May 3, 1983.

48 *Ta Kung Pao*, December 27, 1980.

49 This apparently was insisted on by the Chinese side of the joint venture. Interview with C.T. Wu, Toronto, Spring 1995.

50 Interview with C.T. Wu, Toronto, Spring 1995.

51 By its completion, there was a cost overrun of 80 per cent. At its completion, the cost was $1.5 billion. Interview with Yao Kang, Hong Kong, June 1997.

52 She was therefore Vice-Chairman of the Board of the Garden Hotel, Guangzhou.

53 Interview with Yao Kang, Hong Kong, June 1997.

54 It was Father's plan to establish a liaison office in Tokyo which would be run by Reiko Ogata.

55 In 1997, the Japanese Consulate was still there, and even though the American Consulate has moved out, their Cultural Centre is still in the Garden Hotel complex. Interview with Reiko Ogata, Hong Kong, June 1997.

56 $700 million.

57 Chinese Government guest house in Beijing where senior government officials entertain V.I.P. guests. The name in Chinese depicts a platform where the Emperor did his fishing inside the inner palace.

58 Interview with Yao Kang, Hong Kong, June 1997.

59 Interview with Anna Li, Los Angeles, Spring 1995.

Chapter 13

1   Berta Manson in the "Empire Builders," a series that appeared in the *South China Morning Post*, October 26, 1975.

2   *South China Morning Post*, October 26, 1975.

3   This was a new phenomenon in the early 1970s in Hong Kong, which culminated in the crash of 1973.

4   *Ta Kung Pao*, January 1, 1972.

5   *South China Morning Post*, October 26, 1975.

6   Address given by R.C. Lee, "The Importance of Hong Kong to China" at the International Conference on the Economic Opportunities in Hong Kong, held at Gravenbruch-Kempinski Hotel, Frankfurt, June 14-15, 1982.

7   For Chinese New Year, homes are decorated with budding peach or plum trees, in the same way Christmas trees decorate the homes of Westerners. If the flowers open on New Year's Day, it is considered a sign of prosperity for that year.

8   Interview with Anna Li, Los Angeles, Spring 1995.

9   Interview with Hon Chiu Lee, Hong Kong, October 1996.

10 Interview with Hon Chiu Lee, Hong Kong, October 1996.

11 *Wah Kiu Yat Po*, April 1, 1960.

12 *Wah Kiu Yat Po*, March 19, 1963.

13 *Wah Kiu Yat Po*, March 19, 1963.

14 Opening speech of the Hong Kong Tube & Metal Products, Ltd.

15 Interview with Violet Lee, Hong Kong, January 1996.

16 *Ta Kung Pao*, August 20, 1964.

17 *Celebrity Monthly*, August 1979, 24.

18 *Ta Kung Pao*, 1955, 1956, 1959, 1960, 1961, 1962, 1963.

19 *Ta Kung Pao*, January, February and April 1963.

20 Letter to Father from the secretary of Victoria City Development Co. Ltd., January 6, 1964.

21 *Ta Kung Pao*, June 24, 1965.

22 Interview with Hon Chiu Lee, Hong Kong, January 1996.

23 Interview with Hon Chiu Lee, Hong Kong, January 1996.

24 The Chinese government was not planning to let political unrest spill over from China to Hong Kong.

25 By 1997, the third cross-harbour tunnel was completed. Hon Chiu Lee, Hong Kong, January 1996.

26 Fei Yiming, "Mian Huai Li Ming Ze" ("Remembering R.C. Lee"), *Ta Kung Pao*, July 16, 1983.

27 This was also the turning point in the urban history of Hong Kong, the change from two cities into one.

28 Interview with Hon Chiu Lee, Hong Kong, January 1996.

29 He was chairman until December 1975, when G.R. Ross took over.

30 *Wah Kiu Yat Po*, March 31, 1967.

31 Jardine Fleming & Company Limited is a restricted licence bank, owned jointly by Jardine Matheson Holdings Limited and Robert Fleming Holdings Limited. Established in 1970, it was the first merchant bank in Hong Kong.

32 Interview with David K. P. Lee, Hong Kong, November 1996.

33 *Wah Kiu Yat Po*, March 31, 1970.

34 During the 1950s and 1960s when telephone lines were in chronically short supply, bribery was rampant, probably even institutionalized.

35 Phone interview with Sir Jack Cater, Hong Kong, June 1997.

36 Jack Cater went to Hong Kong right after the war as part of the postwar military administration. He met Father at that time and they became good friends. His term as Commissioner of ICAC actually started in October 1973 and lasted until October 1978, when he became Chief Secretary. He was subsequently knighted.

37 Fei, "Mian Huai Li Ming Ze."

38 *Ta Kung Pao*, July 29, 1975.

39 *Ta Kung Pao*, July and August 1975.

40 Note from Hon Chiu Lee, Hong Kong, August 1997.

41 Robin Hutcheon, *The Blue Flame*, Hong Kong, 1987.

42 Fei "Mian Huai Li Ming Ze."

43 Hutcheon, *Blue Flame*, 128.

44 Letter from Sir Evelyn de Rothschild, London, June 11, 1997.

45 Letter to Father from Sir Evelyn de Rothschild, London, December 4, 1979.

46 Notes from Per Jorgensen, Copenhagen, June 1997.

47 Notes from Per Jorgensen, Copenhagen, June 1997.

48 Interview with Greta Li, Vancouver, April 1997.

49 *Far Eastern Economic Review*, July 8, 1993.

50 Lee, "The Importance of Hong Kong to China."

51 The company is based in London and is the only major securities business in the United Kingdom to have remained an independent partnership. In the past thirty years, the company has opened offices in eleven other financial centres. The one in Hong Kong was opened in 1974. Worldwide, the company has more than one thousand employees in three areas of business: corporate finance, institutional brokering and fund management. Yao Kang, Hong Kong, February 1998.

52 *Ta Kung Pao*, August 4, 1981.

53 Interview with Professor Paul Lin, who was the former Vice-chancellor of the University of East Asia in Macao during the 1980s, Vancouver, April 1997; interview with Yao Kang, Hong Kong, June 1997. Both Prof. Lin and Yao Kang were directors of COOL.

54 Lee, "The Importance of Hong Kong to China."

Chapter 14

1   Christopher Haffner, *The Craft in the East,* rev. ed. (Hong Kong, 1988), 252.

2   Haffner, *Craft in the East*, Preface.

3   Haffner, *Craft in the East*, Preface.

4   Haffner, *Craft in the East*, 422.

5   Haffner, *Craft in the East*, 422.

6   Haffner, *Craft in the East*, 422.

7   Haffner, *Craft in the East*, 425.

8   Haffner, *Craft in the East*, 422.

9   Haffner, *Craft in the East*, 424.

10 Haffner, *Craft in the East*, 362-364.

11 District Grand Lodge of Hong Kong & the Far East, Spring Newsletter 1997, from the Deputy District Grand Master, W. Bro. Yao Kang.

Chapter 15

1   The economic recession in North America in the early 1980s deterred potential emigrants. However, after 1986, with Xu Jiatun's opposition to elections in Hong Kong, and with economic upturn in North America, emigration became massive.

2   Address given by R.C. Lee, "The Importance of Hong Kong to China," at the International Conference on the Economic Opportunities in Hong Kong, held at the Gravenbruch-Kempinski Hotel, Frankfurt, June 14-15, 1982.

3   Lee, "The Importance of Hong Kong to China."

4   Lee, "The Importance of Hong Kong to China."

5   Lee, "The Importance of Hong Kong to China."

6 The United Kingdom and People's Republic of China delegations agreed at the United Nations in 1971 to remove Hong Kong from United Nations' list of colonies. Talks on Hong Kong were to be carried out bilaterally.

7 Lee, "The Importance of Hong Kong to China."

8 Lee, "The Importance of Hong Kong to China."

9 Lee, "The Importance of Hong Kong to China."

10 Lee, "The Importance of Hong Kong to China."

11 Lee, "The Importance of Hong Kong to China."

12 I met the brother of the person who bought the *Atalanta* in June 1997, in Hong Kong. His name is Ah Ming and he is the coxswain of R. G. Ross, Chairman of Deacon & Co. I learnt that for a number of years, the *Atalanta* was available for hire for launch picnics. I also learnt that Ho Ning, in his later years, became the big brother for all the young men who wanted to work towards being coxswains for the wealthy.

13 By the time he came to work for us my older brother, Richard, and sister, Deanna, had already gone to England to study.

14 Fei Yiming, "Mian Huai Li Ming Ze" ("Remembering R.C. Lee"), *Ta Kung Pao*, July 16, 1983.

15 Interview with Anna Li, Los Angeles, Spring 1995.

16 Xu Jiatun, *Xu Jiatun Xianggang Huiyi Lu* (*Xu Jiatun's Hong Kong Memoirs*), (Hong Kong, 1993), 43.

17 Interview with Anna Li, Los Angeles, Spring 1995.

18 Interview with Yao Kang, Hong Kong, June 1997.

19 Hong Kong is twelve hours ahead of Toronto in the summer because of daylight saving time.

20 Fei, "Mian Huai Li Ming Ze."

21 Christopher Haffner, *The Craft in the East*, (Hong Kong, 1988) 424-5.

22 Haffner, *Craft in the East*, 424.

23 Haffner, *Craft in the East*, 424.

Photos

1 The translation of the letter on pages 280-281:
    Dear Mr. Lee,
      Thank you so much for your hospitality and for the thoughtful arrangements you made during my visit to Hong Kong.
      We returned to Beijing on February 5. I regret the delay in writing this thank you, but I have been very busy because of Lunar New Year.
      I trust you had a very happy New Year.
      Wishing you good health and long life.
      Jiang Zemin, February 22
    (The tone in the original Chinese indicated the esteem held by Jiang for Father. Jiang was then the Minister of Electronic Industries in Beijing.)

BIBLIOGRAPHY

Anonymous BAAG officer, "Notes on organization of the Red Guerrillas," private collection of Col. L.T. Ride.

Asian Economic News, December 22, 1997.

Birch, Alan, and Cole, Martin. *Captive Christmas, The Battle of Hong Kong, December 1941.* Hong Kong, 1979.

Brown, Wenzell. *Hong Kong Aftermath.* New York, 1943.

Cameron, Nigel. *Hong Kong, the Cultural Pearl.* Hong Kong, 1978.

Cameron, Nigel. *Power.* Hong Kong, 1982.

Carew, Tim. *The Fall of Hong Kong.* London, 1960.

Celebrity Monthly, 名流月刊. Hong Kong, January 1979, August 1979.

Clark, Ann B., and Donald W. Klein. *Biographic Dictionary of Chinese Communism, 1921–1965.* Cambridge, Massachusetts, 1971.

Courtauld, Caroline, and May Holdsworth. *The Hong Kong Story.* Hong Kong, 1997.

Endacott, G.B. *Government and the People in Hong Kong 1841–1962, a Constitutional History.* Hong Kong, 1964.

Endacott, G.B. *Hong Kong Eclipse.* Hong Kong, 1978.

Far Eastern Economic Review, July 8, 1993.

Faure, David, co-ordinator, and members of the Oral History Project Team, Centre for East Asian Studies, The Chinese University of Hong Kong, "Saikung, The Making of the District and its Experience During World War II," *Journal of the Hong Kong Branch of the Asiatic Society*, Vol. 22, 1982.

Ferguson, Ted. *Desperate Siege: The Battle of Hong Kong.* Toronto, 1980.

Gao Tianqiang and Tang Zhuomin, editors. 高添強，唐卓敏, *Xianggang Ri Zhan Shiqi*, 香港日佔時期 (*Hong Kong Under Japanese Occupation*). Hong Kong, 1995.

Gittens, Jean. *Behind Barbed Wires.* Hong Kong, 1982.

Grantham, Alexander. *Via Ports.* Hong Kong, 1965.

Green, V.H.H. A History of Oxford. London, 1974.

Guan Lixiong, 關禮雄, *Ri Zhan Shiqi De Xianggang*, 日佔時期的香港 (*Hong Kong During Japanese Occupation*). Hong Kong, 1993.

Haffner, Christopher. *The Craft in the East.* Hong Kong, 1977.

Hahn, Emily. *China to Me.* Philadelphia, 1944.

Han Suyin. *The Eldest Son.* London, 1994.

Hayhoe, Ruth. Letters to her mother from Hong Kong, 1967–68.

Heady, Sue. *The Hong Kong Country Club: The First 30 Years*. Hong Kong, 1992.

Hong Kong Standard, June through July 1967; December 14, 1972; July 7, 1983, July 12, 1983.

Hong Kong Urban Council. *Official Report of Proceedings*. Hong Kong Government Press. 1955–60.

Hong Kong Legislative Council. *Official Report of Proceedings*. Hong Kong Government Press. 1959–65.

Hutcheon, Robin. *The Blue Flame: 125 Years of Towngas in Hong Kong*. Hong Kong, 1987.

Hysan Development Company Annual Reports.

Jiang Shui, 江水 ."Husong He Xiangning, Liao Chengzhi Muziliang De Jingguo," 護送何香凝、廖承志母子倆的經過. In *Huoyao Zai Xiangjiang: Gangjiu Dadui Xigong Diqu Kangri Shi Lu*, 活躍在香江：港九大隊西貢地區抗日實錄 (*Anti-Japanese Activities of the Hong Kong–Kowloon Brigade in Saikung*), ed. by Xu Yueqing, 徐月清. Hong Kong, 1993.

Joint Venture Agreement on the Construction and Operation of Garden Guest House in Guangzhou, between Guangzhou Lingnan Enterprises Company 廣州市嶺南置業公司 and Garden Hotels (Holdings) Limited 花園酒店〔香港〕有限公司. March 28, 1980. And the Supplemental Agreement between Guangzhou Lingnan Enterprises Company and Garden Hotels (Holdings) Limited in respect of the joint venture for the construction and operation of the Garden Hotel 花園酒店. May 3, 1983.

Koike, Konosuke, 小池厚之助."Notes on Hong Kong" 香港雜感. *Yamabiko*, bi-monthly newspaper published by Yamaichi Securities Co. Ltd., September 1971.

Lee Hysan Estate Company, Limited. *Memorandum and Articles of Association*. Hong Kong, November 20, 1956.

Lee, R.C. "The Importance of Hong Kong to China." Speech given at the International Conference on the Economic Opportunities in Hong Kong at the Gravenbruch-Kempinski Hotel, Frankfurt, June 14–15, 1982.

Lee, R.C. Correspondence.

Li Shufen, 李樹芬. *Xianggang Waike Yisheng*, 香港外科醫生 (*Hong Kong Surgeon*). Hong Kong, 1965.

Lin Yutang. *The Vigil of a Nation*. New York, 1944.

Lindsay, Oliver. *At the Going Down of the Sun, Hong Kong and South East Asia*. London, 1981.

Lindsay, Oliver. *The Lasting Honour*. London, 1978.

Liu, Chungshee H. *Hainan, the Island and the People*. Shanghai, 1939.

Louis, William Roger. *British Strategy in the Far East*, 1919–1939. London, 1971.

Luk, Bernard. "The Rise of a Civil Society in Hong Kong." Presented at the Human Rights and Democracy in Asia Conference, University of Toronto-York University, Joint Centre for Asia Pacific Studies, May 16–17, 1997. In *Human Rights and Democracy in Asia*, ed. by A. Acharya and B.M. Frolic. Forthcoming.

Marsman, J.H. *I Escaped from Hong Kong*. New York, 1942.

Ng, Alice N.H. Lun, editor. *The Quest for Excellence, A History of The Chinese University of Hong Kong from 1963–1993*. Hong Kong, 1994.

Okada, Akira, 岡田晃. *Mizutori Gaiko Hiwa*, 水鳥外交秘話 (*The Secret Story of Mizutori's Diplomacy*). Tokyo, 1983.

Ride, Edwin. *B.A.A.G. Hong Kong Resistance, 1942–45*. Hong Kong, 1981.

Ride, Colonel L.T. Diary, Private Collection, 1942.

Ride, Colonel L.T. *Report on the Activities of a M.I.9/19 Organization in South China by Colonel L.T. Ride, lately Commandant B.A.A.G.*, written at Whitehall for the War Office, 1946, Public Record No. WO 208/3260, Section B.

Salisbury, Harrison. *The New Emperors*. New York, 1992.

Scott, Ian. *Political Change and the Crisis of Legitimacy in Hong Kong*. London, 1989.

Segal, Gerald. *The Fate of Hong Kong*. London, 1993.

Selwyn-Clarke, Sir Selwyn. *Foot Prints: The Memoirs of Sir Selwyn Selwyn-Clarke*. Hong Kong, 1975.

South China Morning Post, 1945–1983.

Stokes, Gwenneth, and John Stokes. *Queen's College, Its History, 1862–1987*. Hong Kong, 1987.

Ta Kung Pao, 大公報. 1945–1983.

The Chinese University of Hong Kong. *Minutes of the Campus Planning Committee*. Hong Kong, 1964–1983.

The Garden Hotel Guangzhou, 1985–1995. The 10th anniversary publication. Guangzhou, 1995.

The Times. July 8, 1983.

The Twentieth Anniversary Special Issue of the Hong Kong Japanese School. Hong Kong, May, 1986.

The Yellow Dragon, 黃龍報 (Queens College publications). Hong Kong, 1923–27.

Wah Kiu Yat Po, 華僑日報. Hong Kong, 1945–1983

Wang Shaoping, 王少平. *Feidao Qiongya Yinxiang Ji,* 菲島瓊崖印象記 (*Philippines and Hainan Impressions*). Hong Kong, 1939.

Welsh, Frank. *A History of Hong Kong.* London, 1993.

Who's Who in Communist China. The Union Research Institute, Kowloon, Hong Kong, 1969.

Wright, George-Nooth, and Nark Adkin. *Prisoner of the Turnip Heads.* London, 1994.

Xie Yongguang, 謝永光. *San Nian Ling Ba Ge Yue De Ku Nan,* 三年零八 個月的苦難 (*The Suffering of Three Years and Eight Months*). Hong Kong, 1994.

Xie Yongguang, 謝永光. *Zhanshi Ri Jian Zai Xianggang Baoxing,* 戰時日 軍在香港暴行 (*Atrocities Under the Japanese Occupation of Hong Kong*). Hong Kong, 1991.

Xie Yongguang, 謝永光. *Xianggang Kangri Fengyun Lu,* 香港抗日風雲錄 (*Major Events of the Battle of Hong Kong*). Hong Kong, 1995.

Xin Dong Ya, 新東亞 (*New Asia*). A collection of articles by different authors, edited by the *Xin Dong Ya* editing department. Published in Hong Kong during the Japanese occupation, 1942.

Xu Jiatun, 許家屯. *Xu Jiatun Xianggang Huiyilu,* 許家屯香港回憶錄 (*Xu Jiatun's Hong Kong Memoirs*). Hong Kong, 1993.

Yang Guoxiong, 楊國雄 (Peter Yeung). "Huang Long Bao Yu Zibao Xuex-iao Nianbao," 黃龍報與子褒學校年報, In *Xianggang Zhang Gu,* 香港掌故 (*Hong Kong Stories*), Book 7, ed. by Lu Yan, 魯言. Hong Kong, 1989.

Zhang Lianjue, 張蓮覺 (Lady Clara Hotung). *Mingshan Youji,* 名山遊記 (*Memories on Famous Mountains*). Hong Kong, 1934.

Zibao Xuexiao Nianbao, 子褒學校年報 (*Zibao School Year Book*). Hong Kong, 1921.

PHOTOS 相片

G. E. R.

EXTRACT OF AN ENTRY

IN A REGISTER KEPT IN THE COLONY OF HONGKONG.

IN TERMS OF ORDINANCE NO. 7 OF 1896.

Audit No. 787

No.	When and where born.	Name if any.	Sex	Name and Surname of Father.	Name and Maiden Surname of Mother.	Rank or profession of Father.	Signature Description and Residence of Informant	When Registered.	Baptismal Name, if added after Registration of Birth
128	7th March 1915 St. Paul. Hongkong 生于五棧二十九月喜澤	Lai Ming Chak Chak 利銘澤	男 Male	La. W. Kau 利紀臣	Cheung Nau Li 張門喜	Merchant 商業	La. W. Kau, 74 Bonham April 1915 Merchant Resid of ... 五棧二十九月...	5th April 1905	Ricard Charles (See)

True Copy

Extract from the Register of Births in the Colony of Hongkong this ___ 3rd ___ day of ___ 1919.

Per, Head of Sanitary Department.

Registrar General. 29-11-48.

Fee, $1.

Father's birth certificate.
父親的出生紙

Father and Grandfather, circa 1909.
父親與祖父，約於一九〇九年。

Father as a student at Oxford, 1923–27.
1923年至1927年，牛津大學學生時期的父親。

England, 1923–27
英國，1923年至1927年

Father driving his friends.
父親駕車接載朋友

Father riding.
父親騎馬

The Big House, 1920.
大屋，1920年

The Wong clan, 1921.
黃氏家族攝於1921年

My parents' wedding, February 28, 1928, at St. John's Cathedral.
父母親於1928年2月28日在香港聖約翰大教堂結婚

Friends and family at home in Conghua, 1935. Mother and Father on left.
1935年父母親〔左一、左二〕和親友攝於從化寓所

In Conghua with Mother's family, 1935. Mother and Father on left.
1935年父母親〔左一、左二〕和母親家人攝於從化

Hainan Island, 1935–37
海南島，1935年至1937年

Father at plantation.
父親於牧場

Father on a tractor.
父親駕駛農耕機

Li aborigines in Hainan Island, 1935–37

海南島原住民黎人，1935年至1937年

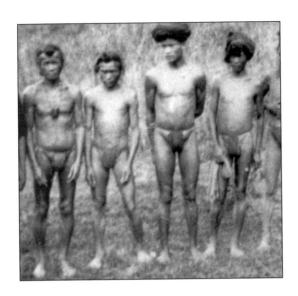

Hainan Island, 1935–37
海南島，1935年至1937年

Father with friends.
父親與友人

Primitive transportation.
原始的交通工具

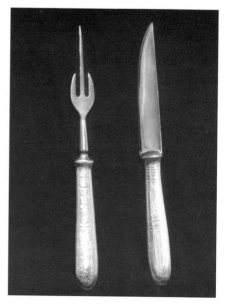

Mango fork and knife designed
and crafted by Father.
父親設計製造的芒果刀叉

Family in Yishan, 1943. Left to right: Richard, Father, Deanna, Mother, and me.

1943年全家在宜山，左起：哥哥、父親、姐姐、母親及我。

Family in Chongqing, 1945. Left to right: Mother, Deanna, Richard, me and Father.

1945年全家在重慶，左起：母親、姐姐、哥哥、我及父親。

The Lee Building, 1945.
利行，1945年

Admiral Sir Cecil Harcourt, governor of postwar military government of Hong Kong, with Mother (immediate right) and Fourth Aunt (immediate left), April 11, 1946.

1946年4月11日母親〔右二〕、四姑姐〔左二〕與
戰後香港軍政府總督Sir Cecil Harcourt 合影。

Sir Alexander and Lady Grantham with my parents (on right), Hong Kong, 1950.

1950年父母親〔右〕和香港總督葛量洪夫婦攝於香港

On our first launch, 1947. Left to right: Mother, Deanna, Richard, me
and Father.

1947年全家首次出海，左起：母親、姐姐、哥哥、我及父親。

Family picture, 1949. Left to right in front row: Deanna, Richard,
Christopher and me. Second Row: my parents.

1949年的全家福，前排左起：姐姐、哥哥、弟弟及我，
後排為父母親。

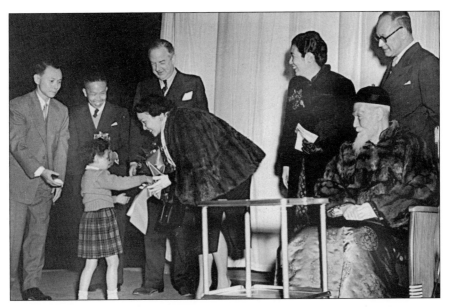

Mother at the opening of Sir Robert Hotung's Princess Theatre. Father (second from left) and Sir Robert Hotung (seated) look on, December 1952.
1952年12月母親為何東爵士〔坐者〕的樂宮戲院開幕剪綵，
左二為父親

Launch picnic, 1955.
1955年出海野餐

Father, 1952.
父親，1952年

Mother, 1952.
母親，1952年

Father presenting ancient Chinese wine cup to President Kwame Nkrumah
of Ghana, 1960.
1960年父親致贈中國古酒杯給加納總理

Father, leader of the Hong Kong Trade Mission to West Africa, 1960.
1960年父親率領貿易訪問團赴西非考察

Father at Michael Jebsen's Farm in Elsholm, near Aabenraa, Denmark, 1963.
1963年父親攝於丹麥友人農莊

Father swimming with Michael Jebsen in Als Fjord, 1963.
1963年父親與友人在丹麥內海海峽游泳

Father with Her Royal Highness Princess Alexandra.
父親與英國亞歷山大公主

Father with Her Royal Highness Princess Margaret.
父親與英國瑪嘉烈公主

Proposed layout and alignment of the two-lane tunnel, January 1964.
1964年1月雙車道海底隧道計劃圖及預定路線

Chinese dinner party after signing of the Cross Harbour Tunnel contract,
Father (second from left), June 26, 1969.
1969年6月26日海底隧道合約簽署後的中式慶祝晚宴，
左二為父親。

I posed with my parents just before Mother and I left for Canada,
August 1959.
1959年8月母親送我赴加拿大讀書，行前與父母親攝於機場。

Neville and me on either side of my parents and Ashley,
Hong Kong, 1968.
1968年我與衛權同長子偉雄回港時與父母親合照

The Freemason. Father as the Grand Master of Hong Kong and the
Far East, circa 1964.
父親佩掛共濟會香港及遠東區區總監的配飾，約於1964年。

My parents, 1968.
父母親，1968年

The Order of the Sacred Treasure, Gold Rays with Neck Ribbon.
日本瑞寶勳章

Father (on far right) awarded The Order of the Sacred Treasure,
March 12, 1969.
1969年3月12日父親〔後排右一〕攝於瑞寶勳章授勳典禮

The establishment of Yamaichi International (Hong Kong) Ltd.,
Hong Kong, July 5, 1972. Father on the far left.

1972年7月5日山一國際〔香港〕有限公司成立，左一為父親。

Father (far left) with Konosuke Koike next to him, circa 1980.

父親〔左一〕和小池厚之助〔左二〕，約於1980年。

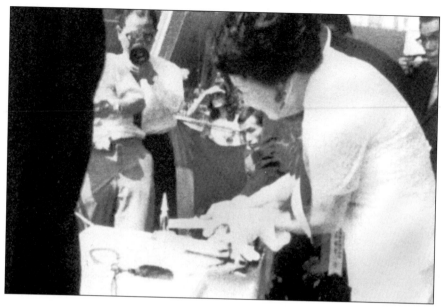

Mother at the launching.
大玉號下水典禮中的母親

Launching of M.V. Grand Jade, (named after Mother, whose Chinese name means "Jade'), a 30,000 DWT Bulker, at Koyo Dockyard on June 30, 1973.
1973年6月30日以母親命名〔璧為玉的通稱〕的三萬噸大玉號
新貨輪在日本正式下水

Launching of M.V. Grand Jade, 1973.
1973年新船大玉號下水慶典

Mother dancing.　　　　　　Father.
母親跳舞　　　　　　　父親

Father and me in Toronto, 1974.
1974年父親和我攝於加拿大多倫多市

Father swimming at the Hong Kong Country Club, October 1975.
1975年10月父親在香港鄉村俱樂部晨泳

Visit to Xinjiang Autonomous Region, 1977.
1977年訪問新疆維吾爾自治區

With village leaders.
父親與自治區領袖

Father and village head.
父親與自治區領袖

My parents.
父母親

From left to right: I.M. Pei, Father, W. Szeto, Hon Chiu. Architects Pei and Szeto show Sunning Plaza model, 1977.

1977年（由左至右）貝事銘、父親、司徒惠及利漢釗與新寧大廈模型合影，新寧大廈為貝事銘和司徒惠合作設計。

Second Grandmother (in centre), on her 90th birthday, 1976.

1976年二祖母〔正中〕九十大慶

My parents' Golden Wedding Anniversary, February 28, 1978,
at the Lee Gardens Hotel.

1978年2月28日父母親金婚紀念日攝於香港利園酒店

Father with our son Ashley at ancestral graveyard in Sunwui, January 1979.

1979年1月父親和作者長子偉雄攝於廣東省新會縣祖墳

Guangzhou-Kowloon Through Train ceremony, 1979. Centre: Governor Sir Murray Maclehose. Front row: fourth from right, Father; second from right, Mother; fifth from left, Lian Weilin.

麥理浩〔正中〕、父親〔右四〕、母親〔右二〕及梁威林〔左五〕攝於1979年廣州至九龍直通車通車典禮。

理事聘書

茲敬請 利銘澤先生　　　為

紀念宋慶齡國家名譽主席基金會理事

特此敦聘

名譽主席　鄧小平

顧　　問　廖承志

主　　席　康克清

聘証字第 0000031 號　　　一九八二年十月八日

Formal letter inviting Father to be administrator of the Song Qingling
Foundation from the honourary chairman Deng Xiaoping, 1982.

1982年父親的聘書

Letter from Jiang Zemin to Father, 1981.[1] See endnotes (p. 237)

江澤民在1981年給父親的信函

中华人民共和国电子工业部

诺泽先生大鉴：

此次应邀访港，承蒙
圆刊安排和热情接待，
不胜感谢之至。我们已于二月
三日安返北京。由于临近春节，
未克及时修正向候，殊以
为歉。遥想阁下春节愉

中华人民共和国电子工业部

快，诸事顺遂。谨祝

健康长寿！

江泽民
二月廿二日

Father with President Li Xiannian, circa 1982.
父親與中國國家主席李先念，約於1982年。

Father with leaders of China, circa 1982. Far left: Yang Shangkun next to Father, Third from right: Jiang Zemin.

父親〔左二〕與中國政要，楊尚昆〔左一〕、江澤民〔右三〕，約於1982年。

Father with Gu Mu, Vice-Premier, circa 1982.

父親與中國國務院副總理谷牧，約於1982年。

Father welcomes the most Worshipful The Grand Master His Royal
Highness The Duke of Kent, October 28, 1982. Courtesy of Zetland Hall.

1982年10月28日父親以共濟會香港及遠東區區總監身份，歡迎
最高總監根德公爵來訪。相片由香港共濟會泄蘭分會提供

Mother with Cai Chang, Chairwoman of the All China Women's Federation.
母親與中國婦聯會主席蔡暢

Mother with Deng Yingchao, widow of Zhou Enlai.
母親與周恩來遺孀鄧穎超

Mother with President Yang Shangkun, 1989.
1989年母親和中國國家主席楊尚昆

I revisited Chongqing, 1996. Photo taken by the Yangtse River.
1996年我回重慶攝於長江江畔

My parents, 1981.
父母親，1981 年

築橋

利銘澤的生平與時代

香港：一九零五年至一九八三年

利銘澤，1964年

築橋

利銘澤的生平與時代
香港：一九零五年至一九八三年

CALYAN
PUBLISHING LTD.

利德蕙著

目錄

与先父交往过
谨就路
的人

謝言

這本有關先父生平的傳記，是匯集了各方熱心人士的幫助才能完稿付梓。我首先要向希慎興業有限公司主席利漢釗先生，謹致最深的謝忱，沒有他的支持和鼓勵，不可能有這本書的誕生。同時要多謝香港太古集團公司及分公司董事長姚剛先生、恒生銀行董事長利國偉爵士、父親生前秘書李樂君女士、東亞銀行董事長李國寶先生、香港中文大學逸夫書院校董會主席馬臨教授、日本山一證券前任副主席白石信一先生、父親和利氏家族的好朋友吳慶塘先生、多倫多大學、約克大學聯合亞太研究所的加港文獻館館長楊國雄先生、和香港日本人俱樂部事務局局長吉岡義之先生，他們不厭其煩的回覆我的問題及為我提供許多珍貴的資料。

另外要向Barbara Bennett女士、Sir Jack and Lady Peggy Cater、陳之昭醫生、陳紀萱先生、加藤智惠子女士、招黃瑤芬女士、Ruth Hayhoe教授、何銘思先生、何建立先生、胡黃瑤芝女士、黃茂蘭先生、Per Jorgensen先生、關榮昌先生、利乾先生、利榮森先生、利定昌先生、利漢輝先生、利江蕙蘭女士、李國章教授、李國星先生、利廓靈愛女士、梁威林先生、林達光教授、廖烈文先生、Percy O'Brien先生、緒方鈴子女士、伍英才先生、Lady May Ride、Elizabeth Ride女士、Dr. Ray Rook、Ronald Ross先生、Sir Evelyn de Rothschild、盛樹珩先生、譚葆和先生、譚徐靈輝女士、George Todkill先生和王匡先生為此書所作的貢獻致謝。

在為此書作研究工作時，我非常感激香港中文大學的大學投標管理委員會委員兼秘書陳尹璇先生、中華人民共和國駐多倫多總領事館文化領事陳榮生先生、遠東經濟評論高級編輯秦家驄先生、香港大學孔安道紀念圖書館主任尹耀全先生、加港文獻館李有名先生、多倫多大學鄭裕彤東亞圖書館李三千女士、香港大學畢業生陳家慧小姐、香港大學圖書館員朱進榮先生、希慎興業有限公司主席的秘書黃徐秀蘭女士、多倫多大學聖麥可書院中古歷史研究院秘書Karen Diensdale女士所給我的協助。

我特別要多謝多倫多大學特等教授秦家懿，對我耐心指導，幫助我規劃出此書的格局，及整理大量的資料。多倫多大學、約克大學聯合亞太研究所，加港研究計劃主任陸鴻基教授給我的意見和指正，我由衷的感謝。同時要對學者顧漢昭先生及前香港政府退休公務員簡仲元先生，為我所做的中文校對和建議，表示謝意。

此外，我的助手陳小芳女士，對我不斷的協助並將此書譯為中文，及她所複製的地圖，我也非常感激。最後要向我丈夫衛權為我攝製的新、舊相片，次子俊雄所做的封面設計，及為出版此書所付出的心力，致上我最深的謝忱。

序

利銘澤博士的一生，從任何標準看，都有卓越不凡的成就。他經歷過現代中國歷史上眾多的動亂事件，而在發展香港成為今天我們所見繁榮蓬勃的國際大都市中，扮演了舉足輕重的角式。

他出生於香港富貴家庭，在牛津大學受教育，見聞廣博，年紀輕輕即主掌家族企業王朝。他高瞻遠矚，認為現代中國需要國際間的聯繫及友誼，並肯定香港所起的作用，這些見解在他的時代以至將來都一樣適用。從他致力改進市民住屋、教育、福利問題，及其幼女德蕙在此書所述的其他重大貢獻，可看出他對香港民眾的關懷愛護。作者在書中與我們分享了一位才智之士的生平，其中不乏個人悲劇，包括青年喪父和中年喪子的悲痛。利博士慈善為懷但不感情用事，雖然家境富裕但自奉甚儉。

利博士為人果斷堅守原則，極少人能像他一般會辭去香港政府的行政議員席位。他為人公平正義，揉合了中國儒家精神與西方思想的優點。

正如德蕙在書中以玩笑口吻，提及當年利博士被港人推測為一九九七年香港回歸中國後，首任的特區首長人選，他們卻不曾想到他屆時已是九十二歲高齡了！雖然這只是當時的一種推想，但其中不無出於香港市民對利博士的期盼和景仰，渴望有像他這等地位和成就的人物來帶領香港。也許，利銘澤博士正是香港無緣擁有的最佳總督或首長。

香港中文大學校長
李國章
一九九八年三月

前言

我的父親利銘澤是個怎樣的人?

他作風嚴謹,主見頗強,律己甚嚴,自我要求極高。他是個典型的中國父親,對子女的疼愛很少形於外,從無摟抱親暱動作,但對子女關懷備至。不知他為人者初見他時都會敬畏三分,因為父親不笑的時候看來非常嚴肅,事實上他為人和藹可親平易近人,也常面帶笑容,但在照像機前,他認為應有莊嚴的形像,所以從無笑容。他誠實聰穎,工作勤奮,樂善好施,待人慷慨大度,但自己則甚為儉樸。他又是一個極有原則能為奉行理念獻身的人,而且熱心公益,關懷社會與民眾。由前來父親喪禮弔唁的賓客中,可反映出父親的一生。

父親生前是土木工程師,他在有生之年建造了兩種橋樑;一種是鋼筋水泥有形的橋樑,另一種是用愛聯繫的精神橋樑。兩種橋樑中,以他為香港及中國所建的人際橋樑最為重要。

我自一九五六年即離家出外求學,其間僅有一年時間在香港,所以失去許多與父親相處,及耳聞目睹父親為人的機會。父親去世後我才明瞭,他不僅是屬於我們的,他也屬於香港、香港社會和香港市民的,他也是香港歷史的一部份。我對他的生平一直充滿好奇,現在我終於可以將它公諸於世。

這本有關父親生平的記事,是根據我對父母親的回憶,和他們的往來信件,及探訪接近父親的人士,加上我自己個人的觀察及與父親的關係所匯集而成。父母親共育有子女四人,二子二女,性格各異,與父親的親情關係也各有不同。本書所述全基於個人的觀點,並為尊重家人隱私起見,家族成員將會不時提及,但並非本書重點。

利德蕙

一九九七年於多倫多

永別

一九八三年夏日炎炎的七月十一日，香港正值盛暑，這是父親出殯的日子，母親一早便帶領哥哥、姐姐、我和孫輩，與其他家眷穿好黑色孝服，準備去香港殯儀館。

喪禮之前幾日家屬在殯儀館守靈期間，已有三千多人前往靈堂致哀。依據中國習俗，弔唁者在靈前對父親遺像鞠躬三次，然後由全體穿著殯儀館孝服的家屬起立，一致鞠躬致謝。其中一日我們必須極早到達靈堂，因為一些香港政府立法局議員及行政局議員，安排在飛往北京與中國會談之前，先來殯儀館致哀。七月十一日早上八時便陸續有各界人士前來弔唁，許多人一直留到十時以便參加安息禮拜。

由靈堂陳設，任何人都會一眼看出父親生前絕非一個普通人。遺像一旁最大的花圈是由剛上任的中國國家主席李先念所送，另一旁則是港督尤德送來的花圈。此外中央軍事委員會副主席楊尚昆、國務院副總理谷牧、中共中央顧問委員會常務委員姬鵬飛、中央政治委員習仲勛、廣東省委員會第一書記任仲夷、人民解放軍政委余秋里、廣東省省長梁靈光、香港政府布政司夏鼎基爵士及其他多位社會知名人士均有致送花圈以表哀悼。

當天除親友之外，尚有香港及中國的各界知名人士前來參加父親的喪禮。包括香港上海匯豐銀行主席Michael Sandberg、置地有限公司行政董事Trevor Bedford、財政司彭勵治、市政局主席張有興、行政局議員方心讓及羅德丞、立法局議員田元灝及黃麗松，另有鄧肇堅爵士及電影界巨子邵逸夫爵士等人。兩位前任香港新華社社長王匡及梁威林分別由北京及廣州前來參加喪禮。但其中令我印象最為深刻的是一般市民，我只認得一些我們公司以前的員工，今天這些市民來到這裡，只因為在他們的人生歷程中曾經與父親接觸過。

十位扶靈人士為：《大公報》社長費彝民、日本駐港總領事山田中正、行政局議員簡悅強爵士、香

xix

港中文大學校長馬臨、友人胡百全和李福樹、共濟會愛爾蘭總會駐遠東最高代表Arthur Gomes、香港大學資深總務長N. J. Gillanders、《華僑日報》社長岑維休，及特別得到北京准許為父親扶靈的香港新華社社長許家屯。

喪禮採基督教儀式，約有一千五百人參加，在父親生前所屬二十多年位於銅鑼灣的聖瑪利亞教堂舉行，由林汝升法政牧師主持安息禮拜。禮拜之前並由我們家族的老朋友胡百全律師略述父親生平；父親一生不僅各方面成就卓越，表現非凡，更可貴的是生命中充滿了慈愛。

香港總督尤德爵士因於七月十一日赴北京會談，署理港督夏鼎基爵士聞悉父親逝世後說：「本港失去了一位戰後以來主要的公眾人物」[1]。父親生前與香港中文大學成立前後的關係深遠，一直將此大學視為自己「兒女」之一，校長馬臨博士說父親的逝世是大學極大的損失。工商界友人形容父親是個「有遠見」及「深具影響力的大好人」，更是利氏家族的「棟樑」。中國的領導人則稱父親為「老朋友」及「愛國者」[2]。

香港市民皆惋惜他們失去了一位關心、體恤他們的好人。而我則痛失了一位摯愛我的慈父。

築橋

利銘澤的生平與時代

香港：一九零五年至一九八三年

第一章

青年期：香港到牛津

十

九世紀末的香港，有皇宮似的華廈，是一個比義大利熱那亞海港還更美麗的地方，在維多利亞市區懸浮雲端的山頂，是富有英國人居住的地方。以上是美國作者Eliza Ruhamah Scidmore，在她一九〇〇年出版的《中國—長存帝國》一書中，對香港的描寫。這時香港山頂為歐洲人而設的新醫院剛落成，《南華早報》正初創刊。當時華人除何東爵士家族外，只有歐洲人可以居住山頂地區。

太平山下又是另一番景像，一九〇四年開始有單層電車，全天候開放。舊式交通工具漸由街上消失，華廈的廠房也暫空置。那時香港尚未有汽車，人們外出坐黃包車〔人力車〕或乘轎，貨車多用黃牛或水牛拖行。街上隨時可見苦力肩挑重擔，喘著大氣。

當時島上人口已有三十二萬五千人，多為華人。一九〇一年遭受旱災，須由新界運送食水至維多利亞，政府為解決日趨嚴重的水荒問題，開始計劃興建全新和較大的水塘。

由九龍海傍排列的大貨倉，及比十年前增加六成入港的船隻看來，香港這個港口是開始興旺了。香港置地公司開始在中環〔維多利亞商業區〕進行開發後，中環滿佈新的四、五層樓建築物，煉糖廠、麵粉廠、棉紗廠、及水泥廠皆相繼創立，分別由渣甸及太古集團這類商行控制其營運，匯豐銀行主導金融，太古獨佔煉糖業。

儘管英國國內強烈反對販賣鴉片，但香港政府每年由競投鴉片專利權上獲利超過二百萬元，此時多家商行亦開始將販賣鴉片所獲利潤投資於正當事業。當年國人吸食鴉片之風頗盛，約有一成男子皆抽大

煙。雖然政府由一九一〇年開始不再發售新的煙館〔中國男人聚集抽大煙的場所〕牌照，但至一九四五年由澳門葡萄牙政府持牌所出售之鴉片皆為合法。

那時香港華人及非華人居民分為兩個不同的社區，除工作外各不相涉，華人日常起居與歐人完全隔離。華人男子大多留滿洲式的長辮或馬尾，很少著西服，多數穿唐衫褲或長袍馬褂及軟黑布鞋，極少參與與西方運動或游泳，他們與洋人幾乎全無交往。老先生喜歡在白天拎著鳥籠去戶外溜鳥，孩子們便踢毽子或放風箏，入夜則可聽到此起彼落的麻將辟啪聲，麻將是當時華人最喜歡的休閒娛樂。

至於中國婦女，除了街頭小販、蛋家婦女、掃街婦及補衣婦外，從不出門。有錢人家纏小腳的婦女足不出戶，穿著華麗，裙褂繡滿花紋，窮苦女子只能穿粗布衫褲。

儘管當時有人將香港形容為皇宮一般，但香港華人居住環境卻非常不衛生，鼠疫及瘧疾等傳染病甚為流行。根據一九〇七年調查，政府衛生隊在對違反衛生條例的屋主及建築包商的物業，做滅鼠行動及在蚊蟲滋生地方噴灑殺蟲藥時，發了一筆小財。衛生問題後來演變成種族偏見，遂有華、洋分區而居之要求。繼在山頂區為歐人設保留區之後，在一九〇二年基於衛生理由，更將九龍的一個地段劃為歐人居住區，因政府不信華人之衛生習慣能改善蚊蟲繁衍問題。但日後外務大臣Joseph Chamberlain對此規定加以修正，而將此區開放給「清潔習慣良好之人士」居住，附註包括有良好水準的中國人在內。

香港在一八四一年淪為英國殖民地之後，經過很長一段時間華人地位之被肯定。逐漸出現的華人富商，因他們在生意上的成功及社團的領導地位，如慈善機構東華醫院，其董事局成員是華人的權位的表徵，被殖民地政府認為是華人社區的代表人物。雖然一般學校仍採種族隔離，皇仁書院仍鼓勵不同國籍男生入學。中國學生更有機會學到西方文化及西方人士經營商業的方法。

這就是父親出世時的香港。

童年

祖

父希慎公和二祖母張門喜，在一九○五年三月七日生下長子銘澤。祖母婚後雖產下一女，但不幸夭折，所以我父親當時不僅是長子，亦是家族中唯一的後代。祖父結婚七年仍未有後，所以以當二姨太有喜的消息傳出之後，家人都極為興奮，亦是家族中唯一的後代。祖父並特別安排歐洲助產士接生，認為歐洲助產士比中國接生婆衛生及較有見識，因在長女生下夭折之後，祖父不容許在生產過程中有任何差錯。

父親出世後福星高照，不僅是家族有了後嗣，而且祖父進出口事業亦開始一帆風順。祖父所購之南亨船務公司旗下貨船，頻密往來於中國、香港、新加坡、馬來亞與仰光之間，後來祖父漸成為南北行行商中頗受尊重的知名人物。南北行是一個由華人和東南亞商人所組成的商會組織。

按照中國舊時風俗，若妾室先於正室生子，此子須交由正室撫養，祈能借福生男育女。父親幼時亦是如此，他由祖母親自撫養，果然，在二祖母生下次子之後，祖母也陸續生下二子、二女。父親自小即與祖母感情融洽，一如親生母子，祖母對父親任何決策上的尊重，在祖父死後對家族裨益極大。

孩提時的父親健康壯碩且頗精靈，一如二祖母他面窄身形不高，雙手剛強有力，並有祖父黝黑的皮膚。中國男子在一九一一年革命後才剪去髮辮，所以我猜父親和祖父都曾留過辮子。

父親幼年住在香港，但也常拜訪住在廣東祖祠所在嘉寮村的曾祖父母。父親曾經告訴過我，照那時鄉下人的生活習慣，曾祖父母一天只吃兩餐飯，一餐早飯，另一餐則在下午四、五點鐘吃。對我來說非常奇怪，但想是當年糧食不足的原故。祖父財產日增後，謠傳土匪企圖綁架曾祖父母，祖父便將他們移至離嘉寮村不遠的新會城內，另建新屋奉養。

身為長子的父親，不僅在祖父心中非常重要，同時也極得祖父母的寵愛。當他們在一起的時候，曾祖父總是以餵食的方式，來表示對他的鍾愛，甚至在父親熟睡時，都要塞雞腿在他口中！曾祖父也常告訴父親在歐美淘金熱時，他坐小船橫渡太平洋去金山〔三藩市〕的艱苦旅程，與海外美

洲華人的生活情形。雖然祖父身為次子，但父親在家族的地位十分重要，曾祖父去世後，依我們鄉下風俗，遺體由嘉寮村沿河船運出殯時，由父親坐船頭，祖父坐船尾，中間則是曾祖父的棺木。

祖父後來在香港的生意及地產投資日漸成功，成為島上首富之一，便陸續收納三姨太及四姨太。他也非常了解在英國殖民地區的子女接受英國教育的重要，所以祖父便將父親由澳門送入香港最好的皇仁書院就讀，皇仁書院當時被視為遠東的 Harrow 和 Eton。

祖父幼年與曾祖父住舊金山時即開始學習英文，返國後曾祖父非常有遠見地將祖父送至皇仁書院就讀，以繼續他的英文教育，這不但對他日後在香港事業的發展助益極大，而且與皇仁校友奠立起未來良好的社會關係。所以祖父要他的子女也能得到同樣有利的條件。

當時男人均以妻妾成群，子孫滿堂來炫耀財富，祖父對家中日漸眾多的子女都非常鍾愛。他也非常了解在英國殖民地區的子女接受英國教育的重要，所以祖父便將父親由澳門送入香港最好的皇仁

下風俗，遺體由嘉寮村沿河船運出殯時，香港再度流行鼠疫，祖父便將家人移至澳門，自己留在香港工作，多數家人在澳門住到一九一八年為止。祖父本人受過良好教育，所以對子女教育問題極為重視，當家人住澳門期間，特聘名師陳子褒先生為子女授課。

父親五歲時，香港再度流行鼠疫，祖父便將家人移至澳門，自己留在香港工作，多數家人在澳門

牛津求學

祖

父對英國教育制度非常了解，認為最好的方法就是將子女送到英國，完全浸淫在異國環境，學習英國人的生活習慣，並有機會交到日後對他們有幫助的朋友。一九一七年父親十二歲時，與三弟在保姆陪同下赴英求學，住在塾師邱吉爾(Churchill)家中接受教導，準備申請入大學，此時他們才有英文名字，父親為 Richard Charles，三叔[1]名為 Harold。數年後父親的兩位妹妹也陸續赴英就讀，祖父希望一旦將子女們送往英國之後，他們皆能在當地完成學業。父親和叔叔們出國之前均被告誡若他們與異國女子成親的話，將會喪失家產繼承權。

父親非常喜歡邱吉爾先生，對我們稱他為「邱老」，直到邱吉爾先生去世，他們都保持書信往

來。邱吉爾先生晚年時視力漸失，我相信在他人幫助之下才能與父親仍保持通信，我還記得看過他潦草的字跡。

一九二〇年代時，較為先進及富有的華人家庭，非常盛行將大學年齡的子女送到英國、法國、德國或日本求學。香港華人學生多數選擇英國，當時只能坐船經蘇伊士運河前往英國，路程須費時數星期。

父親由英國寄給澳門舊日鄰居的書信，後轉載於香港母校《子襄學校年報》中，提到當地華人奮鬥經歷，及一些枉負父母苦心，無心向學的富家子女在國外的情形，原文如下：

敬稟者。生等到英已來。平安無事。至於水土。則凡華人無有不合者。生等現寄居前香港工程師處。地名惡斯佛。華人號之曰牛津。為世界最有名大學之地也。華人極少。連生等亦不足十人。其中二人者。使人聞之驚駭。及可振人人自立之精神。二人者。周陳其姓。開平人[2]。於十一年前彼等欲往北美洲加拿大謀生。豈知地球上不止一倫敦。英京亦名倫敦。當彼由鄉出港時。託人代購船位。彼等尚未知之。但其代購之票。是來英國之倫敦。不是往加拿大之倫敦。久無親戚前往接船。心知有異。於是上岸行遊。全未見有黃面黑髮之人於道上。後來查問。乃知此是英國。非彼二人所欲往之地。只識往倫敦其地耳。船到後。時旅費將空。二人以為發奮自立。尚可希望將來。於是設洗衣店於此焉。生意興隆。此處數十間之大學學生。多往交付。時欲哭不能。欲笑不可。如是數日。游蕩至牛津。為時不久。名馳遠近。至今十一年。凡人出外。苟能自立。則不愁度日無方矣。生等今忘記彼等之名。彼此不暇。故未能時往相見也。無有不知之者。潔淨而已。今之留學於此者。多是不知稼穡艱難之輩。往考大學試時。此科曰難。別科亦曰難。科科均以難字自騙。覺難懶惰非常。於是不考。若不考。則父母必有責罵。於是入一不用考試之大學矣。他無⋯⋯譯之曰無

病。大學。不論何人均可入者。於此掛號後。則寫信回家曰。我今已考入牛津大學矣。其在金橋者。則曰我今考入金橋大學矣。豈知金牛各有大學數十間之多。其家人則全不知其中之弊也。以為牛津金橋二大學而已耳。待至三年期屆。及刊於報紙上曰。某某牛津或金橋之畢業生也。則買一紙文憑回國。蓋極奢華。苟有知之者而問之曰。汝於牛津或金橋何校畢業。彼等必無以對。虛張聲勢。此等之人。今也中國如此之弱。苟無人材。將何以救國。因父兄無力供給。致不能往。欲出洋留學。其氣候使人極為疲倦。故當夏季將至。人多往近海之地。中國許多志士。今此輩尚不自猛醒也。而尚不努力。哀哉。生等今亦到心麻舌處居住六星期。當暑假將完。然後返牛津也。否則必發生疾病。[3]

由此信中可看出，父親早已立下他畢生獻身中國救國救民的志願。

一九二三年時父親進入牛津班堡克(Pembroke)書院攻讀土木工程，同學都稱他Dickie Lee。歐百恩(Percy O'Brien)比父親晚一年進班堡克書院讀化學，他記得父親在校時十分精明，面帶笑容非常開朗，總是疾步走極為守時，而且衣著整齊，常在背心口袋掛懷錶。父親是個勤學用功的學生，經常在Radcliffe理工圖書館研究功課，歐百恩記得好幾次父親演算一些工程方面的數學給他看，他看後一頭霧水不明所以[4]。

雖然那時他對英國生活已漸習慣，但大學生活卻是非常不同。牛津學生的風紀均以一六三六年所訂de Moribus Conformandis之現代版本為規範。其中規定：逾時返校之學生將課小額罰金；學生可購買香菸〔一六三六年時禁止購菸〕，但身穿校服則不許吸菸；又直到近年廢除學生不可有汽車之條例後，父親方可有車代步；並禁止在下午一點前及晚間十點後打桌球；學生不可在戲院後台入口處徘徊遊蕩；不得涉及賽馬或參加射擊及其他運動；對社交舞會餐飲均有嚴格規定；男學生不得進入女同學生之房間，但女學生經院長特別許可，有女伴陪同之下可進入男同學房間[5]。

班堡克書院有些沿習已久，但現在已不存在的校規，一是規定學生每天必須早上八點去學校的禮拜堂，否則即罰款二先令六便士。另一規定是學生不得在學校走廊談論私事，違規學生須一口氣由大啤酒量杯中喝下一品脫或更多的啤酒[6]。

父親在大學住宿時，在校園舊四方院擁有一般學生認為是特權的私人房間，他的房間在一樓，有臥房、小儲藏室及寬敞而附有壁爐的客廳、飯廳兼書房。冬日學生須舉步維艱地走過泥濘冰雪，才能去到位於舊四方院後方的公共房間。那時校方認為學生都應強健，所以沒有駐校醫生或護士。晚上九點舊鐘樓的鐘聲一響，就關閉宿舍大門，對遲到學生會科以罰金，但是學生還是有各種辦法可以神不知鬼不覺的爬回宿舍[7]。

住校時期非要有「校工」照顧寄宿學生不可，每位校工負責「一段樓梯」，就是照顧樓梯兩旁房間的學生。在某些方面來說，校工的工作像僕人，但很多地方他又像學生的「妻子和父母」，他照顧學生的生活起居，病痛時護理他們，又提供意見代為解決難題，酒醉時服侍他們上床等等工作。父親非常幸運有位很好的校工叫Fred照顧他，他會幫父親點燃壁爐、整理房間床舖、清洗衣物及預備早餐和午餐，並在父親請客時打點一切[8]。

父親在班堡克書院讀書時院長是Holmes Dudden博士，他博學多才富管理校務經驗，也是一位頗有名氣的作家。二〇年代班堡克書院餐廳以佳餚美酒著名，所以能被邀在書院用餐，是非常令校外人士人嚮往的[9]。

友誼

大學期間父親結識了一些後來成為莫逆之交的終生好友，其中多位回國後地位顯赫。據我所知的頗有；歐百恩後來是班堡克書院的導師及院士，一九七四年退休之前擔任牛津醫學院的臨床生化研究部主任。

還有一位是錢昌照，他成為國民政府委員長蔣介石手下的要員，父親與他畢生為謀求國人福祉努力不懈，日後二人分別在香港及中國各盡心力。在文化大革命期間受到迫害，種種限制而令他們友誼中斷，直到六〇年代初，二人才恢復聯絡。

另一位同學是劉佳，他是蔣介石在五〇年代派駐聯合國的代表。還有一位日本朋友是東京帝國大學畢業的小池厚之助，後來成為日本山一證券公司的主席，太平洋戰爭期間他們曾失去聯絡，到一九六〇年代才再有交往。

父親年輕時在英國所交朋友中，只有利安不是牛津的同學。利叔幼時被我們鄉下祖居嘉寮村的一個利姓無子人家收養，在十多歲時便將自己賣身至北美做苦力，契約期滿後便跳上一艘遠洋貨輪偷渡離美，事前全不知將開往何處，糊里糊塗的竟到了法國，一句法文也不懂的利叔，又再踏上另一艘開往說英語的國家，便偷渡到了英國倫敦，恰與父親及三叔同一時期在英國。利叔頗有生意頭腦，不久便在倫敦開了一間很小的中國餐館，顧客多為中國留學生。

父親與他的年輕朋友在倫敦時常去利安的餐館捧場。父親常對我說利叔有一次不知用什麼配料做豆腐，害得客人腹瀉！儘管如此後來他們也成了好友。我相信父親對利叔的勤奮創業精神十分欽佩，日後利叔在倫敦飲食業中非常成功，並擁有多匹賽馬。他的餐館經常有著名的電影明星光顧，利叔與他們皆成了朋友，也許因為他身高膚黑，又有高顴骨、單鳳眼典型的中國面孔，後來他還在荷里活電影中扮演過小角色。我第一次見到他是在一九五〇年代初，他來香港住在我們家的時候，那時他已開始酗酒，我記得父親曾對他說：「香港習慣日落之前不能喝酒！」

所有牛津學生均須在學校寄宿，在大堂與校長、教師一起用晚飯。學生有選擇聽課與否的自由，但卻「硬性規定」務必出席晚餐，參加晚餐次數不足者會失去期終考試資格。每張餐桌可坐十至十二位同年級同學，大家同檯共餐，雖然讀的科系不盡相同，但後來都成了好朋友。

小池厚之助在一九二三年時入牛津班堡克書院，與父親同年入學又同坐一桌用膳，後來便成了莫逆之交，經常一起運動。英國學生冬日多打橄欖球，父親同小池厚之助則去體育室打拳[10]，班堡克

祖父的企業

父親

親與弟妹留英期間，祖父事業仍在英國，祖父在堅尼地道山坡購入大幅土地，預備自建住宅。但因戰爭及勞工問題，一直拖至一九二○年才開始動工，由Palmer and Turner公司設計營造，此建築公司亦負責建造國內位於上海外灘的匯豐銀行總部大樓，是當時香港極為雄偉的住宅，父親在一九二七年回港後才見到此屋。

大屋有香港內港最佳的景觀，高牆內有美麗的花園、噴泉、寶塔、假山岩洞、竹林、及雞舍菜畦。大門由印度錫克族警衛佩槍看守，因錫克族人相貌兇狠，當時香港多僱用他們做警衛，家中的錫克警衛及其家人，均住在花園觀音池旁的房舍。

大屋共有三層，二、三樓為家人起居使用，各有大陽台及廚房。用餐時男人在二樓，婦孺則在三樓。一樓有寬大的宴客廳、書房、竹房、幾個小客廳及屋後的大廚房，由前廳走到花園陽台可瀏覽香港海港全景。大屋四處陳設來自世界各國的藝術品。

事業是發展地產為中產階級提供大批住屋，更企業化的投資於中華糖房、香港電燈公司、香港上海匯豐銀行，牛奶公司，並成為對南中國及香港供電的中華電力公司之顧問及主要股東。很不幸的，由一九二四年開始，祖父在葡屬澳門享有鴉片獨家專賣權的裕成公司也有投資，因而種下禍根。

第一次大戰期間父親仍在英國，祖父事業不斷成長，不僅是香港首富之一，社會地位亦漸提高。他的主要

書院也有許多學生喜歡打拳。雖然父親鼻樑曾被打斷，但年輕時拳擊一直是他喜歡的運動。

父親是個具有崇高理想的領導人物，在一九二五年時，他成為中國歐洲留學生總會會長，那時他已立定終生將盡其心力為民服務的大志。多年來父親一直珍藏著每份留學生總會聚餐的菜單，這些菜單上，有他們當年聚餐時草擬的新中國未來大計。

氣派雄偉的大屋，亦是所有嘉寮村鄉下親戚朋友來訪的臨時住所，一樓大廳後方有多間客房，隨時歡迎他們住宿用飯。一如大家長的祖父對所有遠近親戚均妥善照顧，極為慷慨大方。終其一生，祖父都使得他的兄弟姐妹經濟無虞，並讓所有姪甥均能受良好的教育，或獲得工作機會。祖父逝世後，他的兒子都繼承了這個傳統家風。

大屋完工之後四周仍有大片空地，稱為利行，利行中堂有開闊的樓梯，每個單位都有獨立的大陽台。祖父在世時利行全部出租，我想當時祖父已有遠見，他的子孫將來會住進利行，我們一家在一九五〇年代初期，一直住在大屋及利行。

英國港務專家在一九二〇年來港勘查海港及土地發展時指出，西環發展已達飽和，將來新發展勢必向東轉移至九龍灣，祖父便計劃在該區購地發展房地產。香港島地多山陵，建屋十分困難，須先夷平山坡以山泥填平土地，方能大量造屋。一九二四年一月祖父由渣甸(John William Buchanan Jardine)手中，以港幣3,850,960.35之價格購得銅鑼灣土地，成為他一生中最引人注目的交易。此幅銅鑼灣土地原為各渣甸大班的住宅、辦公室及貨倉所在，其中有頭號及二號大班的宅院，中間以一馬房相連。購地時祖父與香港政府協定，利用銅鑼灣土地山泥作為北角填海發展，但計劃因政府毀約而告擱置。祖父便以營利生意眼光將此山地闢為華人之遊樂場，稱為利園山，更將大班之住宅改為酒樓。由於當時政府極少興建華人遊樂場所，所以利園成為週年開放的娛樂場地後，業務非常興旺。

祖父預先在一九二五年為家族設立利希慎置業有限公司，將銅鑼灣土地及其他若干產業歸屬公司名下。祖父後來繼續發展利園山下原屬貧民區的土地，將街道拓寬，改建堅固的屋宇。

祖父非常富有企業家的精神，對開創新事業極為熱衷。他愛看大戲，覺得當時有必要興建一所較易轉換場景的劇院，便計劃建造一所有旋轉舞台的中國劇院，演員不必離開舞台即可變換場景。於

是在一九二六年建成利舞台，高高聳立於波斯富街上，劇院的華麗拱形圓頂繪有金龍圖形，並掛滿燈飾。當年港人最普遍的娛樂即為看粵劇，所以利舞台不但在票房上極為成功，亦造就了幾位出名的藝人，日後又為放映電影添置了大銀幕。

第二章

香港結婚到中國工作

父親一九二七年自牛津畢業，離家十年後在二十二歲時，終於回到思念已久的香港，並計劃假期結束後再赴英國做實習工程師。祖父非常高興見到長子回家，一心希望在他赴英之前完成婚姻大事。消息傳出後，媒人便帶了許多女孩給祖母過目。

父親回到香港後，發現香港已非他記憶中的社會。他在英國時受到同等的待遇，回到這片殖民地上，卻處處脫不開英國人在亞洲的民族優越感，島上幾乎各方面都有種族隔離現象。例如一九四〇年香港山頂的明德醫院曾拒收一名美國女子就醫，只因她丈夫是中國人。政府機構直到一九四二年才取消只准歐人參加僱員應試之規定，到最近一九九二年時香港政府高級職位皆為英人擔任。當年匯豐銀行明文規定不得有華人擔任董事，許多英國公司皆不許員工與非英籍女子成婚。

父親在英國求學時是個勤勉用功的學生，受到英國自由博雅的教育影響，思想上認為人人平等，所以當他回到香港這塊英國殖民地時，決不能接受二等公民的待遇。父親留英期間經常騎馬，返港後亦想加入香港馬會，豈知卻因身為華人被拒，祖父知悉後馬上說：「不需要他們，我們自己來搞一個華人馬會。」香港馬會聽到風聲後，便又立刻准許父親在俱樂部騎馬，因為馬會知道如此一來，必將失去其所倚靠華人投注賭馬所帶來的豐厚入息。

12

一位在上海及香港皆非常成功的商人嘉道理（Ely Kadoorie），將當時的國際大都會上海與英化的香港兩個城市相比較，形容香港殖民地式的勢利眼是一種「小家氣的心態」，但至少中國人在商場上倒沒有因種族差異而被拒門外。祖父在事業上的成就，令當時回港度假的父親，十分明瞭香港是個創業的好地方，但以父親深信人人平等、四海之內皆兄弟的個性，香港決非他喜歡居住的地方。

父母親初會

父

親年輕時十分好客，總是朋友成群。由英返港那年夏天，一日父親與友人在海邊時，有兩位女孩打完網球回家途中路過，父親立刻為其中一位少女所吸引，這位黃瑤珍介紹認識。瑤珍卻說：「別煩她，她是我的小妹妹！」但在父親堅持下，終於結識了母親，當日午後兩人便一起相處。

母親與父親開始這段旋風式戀愛時年方十七，仍在拔萃女書院就讀，她根本不急於結婚，只想先完成學業。祖父母知悉兒子已有心儀對象時非常欣慰，更急切的要促成這門親事，在父親向母親求婚之際，祖父也同時拜訪外祖父母，徵求他們的同意。但問題不在外祖父母，而是母親表示自己年紀還小，應該繼續學業，不想太早結婚。於是祖父便提出一個好辦法，就是婚後父親赴英完成工程師實習訓練時，母親亦可隨同赴英國牛津大學讀葡萄牙文，將來可對家族事業有所助益，並答應次年陪同她父母環遊世界赴英國探訪他們，總算這樣才打動母親同意嫁給父親。

由於一切發生得太快，父母親在婚前都不及認識對方，他們在婚後相處多年後，才逐漸培養出維繫一世婚姻的互信、互重和互相體諒的情感。

母親本姓黃，生於一個現代先進的家庭。外祖父當時是香港社會的中堅份子，與何東爵士及周壽臣爵士等知名人士都是好友。黃家住香港太子道時的生活非常優裕，母親與她的兄弟姐妹在成長的過程中，家中不祇有許多的僕人及園丁，還有四部汽車供孩子使用。

母親對外祖父在一九一二年時已擁有全港第一輛進口汽車，感到非常自豪，但當時華人形容汽車

駕駛執照。

是「嘩噗鬼叫又咳個不停的怪物」。外祖父黃茂霖公與外祖母麥玉珍共育有子女十一人，八女三子，母親排行第五。當年母親與兄弟姊妹生活十分優閒，經常開車四處游泳、打網球及跳舞。她也受過飛行駕駛訓練，但從未取得駕駛執照。母親有一次也許是在去買她最愛吃的朱古力途中，因超速被警察攔截，因超速被警察攔截。

母親對她自己的家庭非常熱愛並感光榮。曾外祖父黃有傳年輕時便遠赴西印度群島工作，三十多歲略有儲蓄後，便返回中國，曾外祖父因能說英文，便在香港政府擔任法庭傳譯員。後來便自己挑選與一位德國修女院的華人女子成親，她的父親和兄弟都是教會的牧師。曾外祖母不僅能說流利的中、英文，並能說德文，但只穿歐式服裝，在當時華人女子中是非常少見的。他們二人婚前未曾見面，曾外祖母後來常告訴她的兒孫，她在新婚之日覺得很奇怪，為什麼她這富裕丈夫竟會有對那麼粗糙的手。

曾外祖父在法庭擔任傳譯員薪俸不錯，所以黃家生活十分優越，住在九龍界限街附近的大宅院

〔後來土地被政府收回之後，便搬到現時的太子道〕。

母親時常提起童年時代，與她祖父母相處的種種趣事，兒孫輩最喜歡曾外祖母，她也喜歡孩子，常教兒孫唱德文歌，她信仰虔誠，並用獎金鼓勵兒孫唱聖詩。曾外祖母對慈善公益非常熱心，甚至坐著輪椅都要出份心力。其實她為曾外祖父納妾的真正原因，是要有人留在中國鄉下照顧她的公公和婆婆。因為曾外祖父母後來因疲於不停生育，便為曾外祖父納妾，兒孫都覺得她思想很開通。曾外祖父祖父是獨子，有了妾室之後，曾外祖母才可擺脫這份自己不願意做的差事。他們共有十六個子女，其中十一個是她所生。

當曾外祖父衣錦還鄉回到廣東省東莞縣時，在祖居河伯橋造了一棟附有炮樓的房子。黃家是客家人，非東莞本地人，所以住的地區比本地人較為貧瘠，經常為灌溉農田水源與鄰人發生爭執。黃家除了稻田和荔枝園之外，還有花生油廠，曾外祖父或兒子每次由香港回鄉下視查業務時，大家都先在火車站集合，然後在武裝團隊的保護下才一起回去〔一〕。由於國內法治不修，農村各組武備，地主僱請武裝保護毫不為奇，尤以在外地主為然。

傳統上客家和本地人互不通婚，父親是本地人，常取笑母親同鄉大腳客家女人。中國舊日審美觀念認為女人大腳極為不雅，事實上，客家婦女從不纏腳，因為她們平日須要在田野做活，加上發生糾紛需要幫忙時，有對大腳才跑得快。

曾外祖父在祖居大門口懸有一張「百鳥歸巢」的巨畫，希望有朝一日他的子孫都能落葉歸根回到祖居。但只有妾室所生長子，排行第八的兒子長住鄉下照顧田園和生意，其他子女都寧願留在香港。有幾年國內政治局勢不穩，香港的黃家家人甚至無法回去探親。唯有在二次大戰日本佔領香港時，香港糧食缺乏，黃家才回到有自家稻田不愁糧食匱乏的祖居避難。

曾外祖父在香港德高望重，逝世時有很多人前來太子道住宅致唁，有人甚至由大門口一路叩頭至靈前。曾外祖父喪禮備極哀榮，他的棺木置於馬車中，由四匹白馬拖載，當日香港花店的鮮花，都因他的喪禮而被訂購一空。[2]

外祖父黃茂霖公排行第二，是香港頗負聲望的特許會計師，並擔任首屆香港華人會計師公會主席。第一次大戰時外祖父曾任後備警察，當時因許多英人回國參戰，所以祖父因得填補空缺。瑤芬和瑤芝阿姨都記得她們的父親穿白色警察制服英姿挺拔的模樣。

每當法庭人手不夠時，外祖父便充任傳譯員，他一九二三年被委為太平紳士，又榮獲英王喬治六世及國父中山先生授予勳章。當第一任妻子病逝後，因未有生育，便再娶外號為「靚妹」的歐亞混血女子麥玉珍即外祖母為妻。曾外祖母常鼓勵兒子娶歐亞混血女子，這樣她才會有漂亮的孫輩，結果她真有不少俊美的兒孫。

外祖母是約翰‧麥克斯維爾(John Maxwell)和一中國女子所生的四個子女中的獨女，我們從不知她的姓名，因為自小母親及她兄弟姐妹均對我們稱她為外婆。麥克斯維爾在十九世紀時由蘇格蘭來香港之後就在當地成家立室。保良局是香港富紳在一八七八年專為收容無家可歸的婦孺而設的慈善機構，麥克斯維爾曾外祖父便在此機構選得一華人女子為妻，也唯有如此他才能在香港成家，因為當時極少有門當戶對的歐籍適齡女子，而正當華人家庭又不會將女兒嫁給洋人。麥克斯維爾曾外祖父一直在香港警隊服務，是個好父親。

當年歐亞混血兒在香港既不屬於中國社會也不屬於歐人社會，所以他們要非常努力的做到非此即彼。外祖母比中國人更中國化，她能說、讀英文，但中文只限能看。她又熟知中國民情風俗，是黃氏家人經常請教的對象。印象中我仍記得她身穿旗袍頭梳髮髻，一片慈祥端莊的模樣。

婚禮

一

一九二八年二月二十八日父母親在香港聖約翰大教堂舉行婚禮。少女時的母親常常希望她結婚時的潮流是長婚紗禮服，而不是短禮服，結果為了時尚，她還是穿了銀紗鑲珠的短禮服，手捧白玫瑰花球。母親是個美女，比一般中國女子身材修長高窕，骨骼較大。結婚之日她只能穿低跟鞋，以免看來高過父親，事實上，她婚後仍繼續長高，後來真的比父親高些。結婚皮膚白晰，不像父親膚色黝黑。她深褐色的髮上披著當時非常流行的頭紗，飾花低至眼眉，正如曾外祖母所願，這群美麗的少女都是她的孫輩。母親的婚禮非常隆重，她的姐妹及堂、表姐妹均穿著不同顏色綴滿小花的禮服，正如曾外祖母所願，這群美麗的少女都是她的孫輩。

結婚當日教堂內外中西賓客雲集，有些賀客因人太多無法進入教堂，只好站在外面。婚禮由香港主教 A.Swann 打破傳統，首次為華人證婚。當時香港的社會華、洋分隔，唯有在這樣的場合大家才能相處在一起。

因利園大班舊宅所改的酒樓不夠容納兩千賓客，故慶祝酒會須在利園內臨時搭造的竹棚舉行，酒席菜餚由祖父喜歡光顧的香港酒店燴製，又特別另搭一檯架放置六層的結婚大蛋糕。酒會中何東爵士代表賓客向新人敬酒，並由何東爵士、羅旭和博士分別致賀辭及父親致答辭。

婚禮後父母親即乘郵輪經蘇伊士運河赴歐洲渡蜜月，在埃及時一如一般遊客，亦騎駱駝及在獅身人面像前留影。到達歐洲第一站瑞士時，母親首次見到正在當地求學的三叔，到英國後再和寄宿女校就讀的二姑姐舜華及三姑姐舜英見面。

祖父遇害

父親返港探親時，適逢祖父為股東之一的裕成公司因鴉片牌照問題與澳門政府涉及官司訴訟。利氏家族擁有三分之一股份的裕成公司，自一九二四年即享有鴉片專賣權，祖父為公司總經理。

一九二七年三月間葡萄牙政府在政府公報宣佈；任何有關鴉片進口、加工及買賣的專利合約均告終止，故政府與裕成公司之間的合約將全部無效，改為政府專賣，由消費稅督察監管，並另設鴉片管理委員會，由羅保（Pedro Jose Lobo）出任行政管理官員。裕成公司總投資額為三百萬元，一九二七年時投資人已收回四分之一成本，並有心理準備與澳門政府訴訟後，他們其餘的投資本金可能化為烏有。

但後來祖父發現澳門政府將收回的鴉片專賣牌照，反以十二萬元的代價，轉讓給另一家名為又成的公司。又成公司在香港有利銀行開戶後，銀行買辦即知悉又成公司已獲澳門鴉片專賣權，公司並公開招股吸資，祖父一友人被招攬入股時曾向祖父徵詢意見。

祖父認為澳門政府既已終止裕成公司的所有合約在先，便不應由政府再發牌照給任何其他公司。因此祖父向澳門總督呈遞陳情書，請求政府對裕成公司給予公平待遇，及對此事件詳加調查。祖父亦將陳情書送交香港駐澳門總領事、立法委員及十六位律師，陳情書中有行政官員羅保名字在內。

一九二八年春天祖父正為我父母準備婚禮時，羅保向法院對祖父提出誹謗控告，並請求法庭禁止祖父繼續寄發對澳門總督之請願書。在官司纏訟期間，祖父曾收到威脅生命的恐嚇信，更聲稱將在父親婚禮中投擲炸彈，眾親友皆勸祖父應要加倍小心及改變日常生活作息習慣，但祖父對這類威脅全置之不理，結果父母親婚禮順利舉行即赴歐洲後，恐嚇一事也漸被淡忘。四月十七日香港高等法院首席法官Gollan宣判祖父得直，祖父認為此事應已告一段落。

四月三十日下午一時，祖父如常前往位於威靈頓街的裕記會所用餐，在廊外遇刺中槍，叫了幾聲救命，會所會員聽到槍聲和求救聲後，一名叫羅流的伙計首先衝到台階，見祖父身受重傷靠著牆

度祖父[3]。

事後何東爵士夫人張蓮覺建議為祖父建水陸法會，便特別在利園搭建竹棚，延聘眾僧誦經七日超

海灣的香港仔永遠墳場。五月二十五日，祖父下葬於風景優美、可遠眺航海行程費時甚久，他們無法趕上祖父的喪事，由於港、英之間經由蘇伊士運河惡耗傳到英國後，父母親及父親的弟妹立刻全體準備返港奔喪，

於極度驚恐，他遺下一妻、三妾、七子、六女及排行第八的遺腹女。案發後雖然家族懸賞一萬元，及警方掌握若干線索，但一直未能緝獲真兇。祖父的遽逝令全家陷所以無暇照料祖父。其他會員趕到現場時，祖父已氣絕身亡，享年四十七歲。壁，面色極為蒼白，因羅流瞥見一名穿短衫白褲的男子，正由會所奔向暗巷，他為追趕這名男子，

一家之主

年

僅二十三歲的父親，頓時成了一家之主，而十八歲的母親已不再求學，開始與父親共同挑起這個重任。由於祖母不識字，所以照顧這一大家庭生活的責任就全落在父親肩上。父親為了籌措足夠資金以支付祖父的遺產稅，須拋售許多祖父的股票套換現金。他永遠不會忘記在這不得已的情況下，曾經求助多位當年祖父所謂的「老朋友」時所受的委屈，多次甚至被拒門外。唯獨在父親非常難堪的向匯豐銀行會計主任Arthur Morse借貸時，他對父親的體諒與熱心支持，令父親永誌在心，二人日後成了終生好友。

祖父許多物業都有抵押，其中最大宗為由渣甸集團手中購下的銅鑼灣土地〔今利園〕，若我們無法繼續分期償還抵押，即可能失去物業產權，於是父親便向匯豐銀行安排貸款，清還抵押。當年有許多人慇懃祖母出售產業，幸好在父親鼓勵下，祖母堅不變賣任何產業。由此時開始為應付每月靠收租償還抵押，家人經歷了幾年手頭非常拮据的日子。

父親將祖父遺產稅清理完畢後，即開始留在香港，替柯倫治建築工程行工作，以完成他的實習工程師的在職訓練。其中一項工程是九龍黃埔船塢的第一號船塢加長工程[四]，現在這個地方已成了一個船形建築的購物中心。

父母親此時與祖母及其他家人同住大屋，家中月入償還抵押及貸款後所剩無幾，而父親又正在受訓階段毫無收入，所以祖母控制家用非常謹慎。年方十八的母親剛嫁入一個完全陌生的傳統大家庭，父親又無法經濟獨立，她頓時失去財務及精神上的自由，開始日漸消瘦及精神沮喪，於是外祖母決定要母親換個環境，便帶她去廬山靜養。

廬山位於江西省九江縣的鄱陽湖附近，空氣清新、風景優美，是休閒或養病的清靜地方。直到現在許多外國人及富有華人在山邊皆築有別墅，後來蔣介石、毛澤東在此亦有避暑山莊，母親稱它為中國的瑞士。

母親告訴我她剛到廬山時非常瘦弱，那時要上廬山只能步行或坐轎子，轎伕們都爭先恐後的要抬她上山，但等到她與外祖母下山時，卻胖得沒有轎伕願意抬她。母親從不說她在山上住了多久，她靜養期間吃得好、睡得好，直到父親上山接她回家。

廣州工作

父

親於一九三一年在柯倫治建築工程行受訓完畢後，成為檢定工程師，並想以此為專業。當時利家各項業務都有職員照顧，父親覺得只要他在附近即可隨時聯絡，不須一定長期留守香港。三〇年代時國內亟需各方協助建立新國家，正如許多其他愛國青年一樣，父親對未來充滿熱情與希望，便決定赴中國奉獻己力。

因父親是廣東人，很自然的便前往廣州工作，他在劉紀文任廣州市市長期間於廣州工作數年，曾任廣州市政府主任秘書、總工程師、自來水局委員及審計部稽核等職位。

父親於廣州工作時，母親曾獨留香港住大屋三樓一段時期。那時利家的孩子有：六叔榮康、七叔榮達、七姑姐舜儀、八姑姐舜娥及堂兄漢釗，漢釗哥為銘洽二叔之子，亦是家族第一個孫子，他常記起當年家中因現金短絀加上祖母又特別儉省，幾個孩子整日感到飢腸轆轆。父親經濟獨立後，這位時髦摩登的大嫂頗受父親弟妹的敬愛。幾位父親的妹妹因祖父早逝而無法赴英國求學，便要求母親為她們取了英文名字，分別是；四姑姐為Joyce，五姑姐為Dione，及六姑姐為Amy。

父親在廣州市政府工作日漸穩定後，母親也搬至廣州與父親團聚，住在廣州市郊東山一個很好的住宅區，與劉紀文市長全家成了好朋友。他們參加許多官場的應酬，官太太都希望母親能多與她們交往。有一天幾位官太太相約一起去看相，相士直言她們運道都不好，唯獨母親命相最佳。幾位太太聽後都不甚高興，令母親非常尷尬，因為她的丈夫在廣州市政府的職位最低。然而在那時又有誰能料到中國政局會有如此大的變化，這些國民黨官員在共產黨當政之後都成了難民。

父母親住在廣州期間，周末便乘火車返香港大屋探望祖母及其他家人，那時已有許多利氏成員住進山坡上大屋旁邊的利氏大廈即利行，父母親周末返港時則仍住大屋。

祖母是家中唯一有汽車的人，星期六中午放學後我們家的孩子都來大屋吃中飯，飯後母親、三叔〔剛由牛津畢業返港〕或是二姑姐開車帶大家去南灣別墅玩。孩子都非常期盼這個周末郊遊，他記得游完泳後，父親常帶領我們可在別墅附近游泳、野餐，漢釗哥那時才開始學游泳，多半在海灘玩，他記得游完泳後，父親常會去牛奶公司的攤位買雪糕請大家吃⑹。

那幾年父母親在每周往返香港與廣州火車途中，交了幾位朋友，常在車上打橋牌。父親當時與廣州市工務局局長袁夢鴻工作相當密切，他的姪子袁耀鴻是木工出身，常嘲諷父親是留洋學生只知書本理論，對建築毫無實際概念。但後來二人也成了好友，我們都稱他袁叔。

袁叔於三○年代中來到香港，加入利氏家族的民樂公司做總經理，利舞台即為民樂公司的附屬機構。成立民樂公司的原因是祖父的一位弟弟常去利舞台戲院銀櫃索錢花用，員工無法阻攔。因他是長輩，父親與叔叔等原因雖身為戲院老闆，但礙於輩份難以阻止，有了民樂公司後員工便可直言戲院已

海南島墾荒

父

父親在一九三四年辭去廣州市政府工作，計劃去海南島做些與眾不同的事。海南島位於南中國海及東京灣之間，面積與台灣不相上下。除西沙群島有中國、台灣和越南分別駐軍外，海南島是中國最南的疆土。

我從來沒有想到問父親，是什麼原因使一個牛津畢業生，帶著年輕的妻子到海南島這樣落後的地方？我想部份原因是他好奇，又富冒險精神，畢竟父親一生對新鮮事物一向有追根究底的個性。但

父母親生活較為穩定之後，便在離廣州不遠的從化溫泉區買了一幅地，父親在風景優美的山邊設計了一幢紅牆綠瓦的中式小屋，四周遍植各類果樹，並將溫泉引進屋頂水塔以供使用。廚房設於屋外，全屋除主臥室外，無其他房間，為開放式的空間，親友來訪時皆睡地上的榻榻米。

他們與親友在這裡度過許多快樂的時光，常去附近的小湖游水，湖下方是瀑布，有一次瑤芝阿姨游水時太近瀑布差點被淹死。從化溫泉水質以可醫治皮膚病聞名，瑤蓮阿姨有皮膚病的兒子也來洗過溫泉浴[6]。

後來劉紀文市長及其他許多廣州政要，皆彷效父親在此建築鄉村度假屋，日後國內許多黨國領導人在從化亦都有別墅，這個地方便成了富人的度假區。

第二次大戰後因國內政局不穩，父母親不再住從化後，我見過他，當時父親還特別詢問果樹成長的情形。一九四〇年代末時他來香港對父親報告屋況時，我才有機會看到這幢房子。只見往日庭園雜草叢生，不見果樹，屋宇年久失修，十分殘破，原本的紅牆綠瓦全部改為白色，鄰近又蓋了一間甚為醜陋的房屋，以前的停車場也為一公眾食堂所佔用，令母親非常傷心。

一九八〇年底，母親帶著我與衛權及友人李太太返從化時，我

屬其他公司，櫃檯銀錢不可隨便動用。日後他若需要零錢便須直接去利希慎置業公司，或利東即我們的租務辦事處索取。

我認為主要原因是父親想由較為僻遠落後的地區開始幫助中國，父親相信盡他自己一份綿力，一樣能造福有數千百萬人口的中國。

海南地區在三〇年代時，財政部長宋子文曾赴當地視察，並認為有開發價值，中國企業界及教育界人士才開始重視這個有「中國糧庫」之稱的熱帶天堂。島上稻米農作一年可收成三次，四季鮮花不斷、盛產水果，樹木林立，亦稱為「中國天堂」。有位古印度詩人形容海南島是「棕櫚島」，因為有六種不同的棕櫚樹在島上繁茂生長，為島民帶來可觀的收入。海南島是個熱帶氣候型的海島，白天烈日當空，島民出門非要打傘或戴帽不可，整年潮濕，夏天溫度可高達華氏九十八度，冬天則在華氏四十五度左右，但島中部的黎母嶺山區則氣溫較低。

中國在秦始皇時代〔公元前二四五年至公元前二一〇年〕即開始知道海南島，島上最初居民全為原住民黎人。西漢時代〔公元前二〇六年至公元二十四年〕大約有二萬三千人首次自中國移居至此，東漢時期〔公元二十五年至公元二一九年〕海南島被收入版圖，土著被迫遷至島中央，元朝時因此島在「大海之南」，故命名為海南島。

一九二一年正式將海南島劃為廣東省的一部份，一九二〇年代後期島上約有二百萬中國移民，大多定居於北部沿海一帶，與大陸保持密切聯繫。位於海南島最北端的主要城市海口，不僅是島上行政首長的官邸，亦是駐防司令總部所在[7]。

海南島亦稱瓊崖，中國政府在一九二〇年代初開始在海南島建築公路幫助開發。在人口較多的地方，除了有商店、餐廳、旅館及銀行之外，還有些中國人投資的橡膠園和甘蔗田，但部份公司後來因為盜匪猖獗而被棄置[8]。在三〇年代時全島被劃分為十三個縣，其中兩個縣全為華人居住，黎人與華人雖然住在同一地方，但屬完全不同的社區[9]。

島上最原始的居民即為黎人，他們的體形和文化與住在泰國、緬甸、中國雲南省及印度支那半島的泰族人頗為相似。黎人外形粗壯，中等身材，膚色褐黃，頭髮黑直，眼睛深褐，臉孔輪廓亦異於一般華人〔數百年來，中國學者稱黎人為不知文化的南方紋身蠻人〕。黎人稱紋身刺花為「灘灘」〔音譯〕，僅有婦女紋身，以不同花紋令後裔容易辨認。雖然黎人有他們自己的服裝，但在炎夏時，

成年男人只穿丁字褲和戴頭巾，在三○年代黎人皆靠狩獵耕種為生。

由於父親想盡盡心力，幫助中國開發這個荒蕪之地的農業及貿易，就帶著母親來到海南島做墾牧先鋒，有意養牛將牛隻推銷至歐洲，此地氣候和地形對畜牧業非常適合[10]。父親在海南島購買的土地，根據地契所述，面積之大是「極目所及」。然後父親便由歐洲進口最好的牛隻來海南島繁殖。

父親冒險性強，他在海南島時，曾橫跨越過黎人居住的黎母嶺山脈。當地中國政府事前警告父親切勿輕易入山，以免感染瘧疾及其他疾病。常有人說十人進山只有一人能活著出山，但父親對現代科學極有信心，認為只要他隨身帶有奎寧和其他藥物，他即可平安無事，結果倒也如此。

父親和陳顯彰及其他股東，在一九三六年買下由許承和李實熙創設的實成公司，開始務農種植黃麻和甘蔗。實成公司於一九二八年創立，擁有五千畝地，專種高價值的黃麻，當時每噸黃麻成本只有七英鎊，運到倫敦後的售價可高達三十英鎊，是利潤極高的生意。但因地方盜匪為禍，公司被迫在一九三○年至一九三一年之間結束營業[11]。

父親買下實成公司後，將公司改稱為利興種植公司，位於海南島北部海口以西的臨高縣內，共有一萬五千餘畝地，種植黃麻和甘蔗。一九三七年一月時又增添土地至兩萬畝，公司並備有壓麻機、貨倉機器房、四十五匹馬力的發動機、電油庫、車庫、辦事樓和員工宿舍等設備[12]。

父母親著銘洽二叔及另一年輕人梁光榮來到瓊崖，光榮由此時開始為利家工作，後來是大屋園丁之一，一直做到退休。父親同時也僱用了許多黎人幫助開發土地及看顧牛群。

黎母嶺深山黎人部落所在的溪流中產金，他們常用撿到的小金塊做裝飾，或與外人交換物品。父親告訴我他曾用玻璃珠、鏡子及肥皂與黎人交換金塊，這些黎人在鏡中看到自己的身影覺得非常奇妙，也喜歡在河中玩弄肥皂泡沫。況且對黎人來說五彩繽紛的玻璃珠確實比金塊好看得多。有一天，父親發現二叔用槍枝與黎人交換物品時非常不悅。

父親亦曾購置槍枝武器用來狩獵或自衛，但嚴禁黎人使用。有一天，父親發現二叔用槍枝與黎人交換物品時非常不悅。

父親說過海南島水域屬偏遠地區，常有不尋常的海洋生物游入港灣。有一天父母親正在海邊，見到漁船拖回一條長約十呎的暖洋鱸魚，令村民非常驚訝，因為他們從未見過這麼大的鱸魚，結果全

村居民與父母親和隨員，一起慶祝享用了這條大魚。我們都覺得這是個不可思議的故事。

父親在島上時常去打野豬，這是非常危險的，因為野豬受傷後會攻擊狩獵者。母親有時也會騎著小馬跟著去打獵，她騎術不佳，當小馬被槍聲所驚跳起時，都會令她害怕，但又不得不用這唯一的山區交通工具。

父母親在島上過了一段拓荒者的生活，他們打獵並自己種食物。島上無電力供應，父親便自己設置風力發電機發電[注]。他們在這裡也交了些朋友，多數是島上其他墾荒的人士及傳教士還有幾位部落族長。他們進城住入小旅館時，常與朋友會面，有時也帶來訪遊客到島上各地遊覽。父母親都非常喜歡住在這裡，那時父親被熱帶陽光曬得像黎人一樣黑，父親提到瓊崖時總是充滿懷念，那是一段他最珍貴而又無法再擁有的日子。父親由海南島帶回來最好的紀念品，是他自己特別設計製做專吃芒果用的刀叉，到今天我仍使用這些珍藏。

此時在海南島以外的地方卻發生了大事。一九三七年七月七日中、日軍隊在北京附近的蘆溝橋衝突，引發了不宣而戰的中日戰爭，父親明白該是回中國做事的時候了。母親日後告訴我：「就算中國不打仗，到一九三九年歐洲也爆發戰爭，根本不可能有船可運牛隻或農產品到歐洲去。」

返回香港

一九三七年底，父母親返回香港。父親返港後又繼續在中、港之間奔波，這次是為國民黨政府效力。母親則一直覺得身體不適，經醫生診斷後，才知道她結婚十年首次有喜，一九三八年我大哥志翀出世。

父親當時以為返港只是暫時性的，計劃戰後再返回海南島繼續他的農牧事業。行前他將牧場業務托人代管，卻未料到從此不能再回海南島，後來農場所有土地都被中國政府接收。記得母親提過她將海南島的地契，妥善保存在保險箱內，但她去世後我們卻無法找到。

一九三〇年代，蔣介石的中央政府，頗受許多受過良好教育、資歷優越的人士支持，他們都有建

設進步新中國的崇高理想[14]。一九三一年日軍侵佔東三省及一九三七年的蘆溝橋事變之後，國內許多問題亟待解決。在香港有一群傑出的工程師，經常聚集研討戰後重建新中國的問題，於是在一九三八年成立了中國工程師協會香港分會，規定須有至少七年以上經驗的工程師，方能申請加入成為會員。首屆會長為黃伯樵[15]，曾任京滬鐵路局局長，父親為副會長。當時非常年輕的吳慶塘受僱為香港分會秘書，這是他與父親相識的開始[16]，後來他們不但成了好友，吳也一直是父親的親信得力助手，同時亦為此書提供許多非常珍貴的資料。

一九三八年日軍侵佔中國南部，十月間廣州亦告失守。父親在香港淪陷前幾年經常往返香港與中國大陸之間，抗戰時期他不但以工程師身份更在許多其他方面參與抗戰。中國茶葉公司為直屬中央政府財政部的重要機構，父親曾在此公司任採購部經理及顧問，當時茶葉外銷所得為國家帶來大量庫收[17]。日後經母親解釋才明白父親加入中國茶葉公司的原因是：中茶公司用茶葉外銷所賺得的外匯在國外購買武器以供抗日之用。中茶公司總部設於重慶，所以那段時間父親經常由香港去重慶。後來中國政府又要求父親負責食鹽分銷[18]，當時中國內地許多居民因缺碘而普遍甲狀腺腫大，故亟須解決缺鹽地區的困難，記得戰時常聽大人討論這個問題，我們也在中國內陸地區見過甲狀腺腫大的病人。

一九三九年母親生下姐姐德蓉。

一九四〇年時父親因熱心公益聲望日隆，被推選為中國工程師協會香港分會會長。因他在香港社會的人際關係及為人，大家都信任他決不會洩漏任何商業機密，故得以參觀到許多工廠及不同的機構。天廚味精廠即為一例；當時香港所用味精皆為日本製造，本港僅有一家由吳薀初經營的天廚味精廠，在正常情況下他決不會讓任何人參觀他的工廠，但在父親安排下，天廚味精廠願意開放給工程師協會的晚宴多半在我們的大屋舉行，吳慶塘說那時他在父親身邊做事總是西裝革履，常有人誤會他也是會員之一。

吳慶塘任職工程師協會秘書時，月薪為港幣三十元，父親對吳頗為賞識，便允許為他留意一份薪俸較高的工作。中國茶葉公司在香港設有一研究機構，負責人為祝百英，一九四一年初父親請祝百

英將吳慶塘安插至此研究機構，雖然僅是文員，但月薪加上津貼已跳升三倍。吳母說他既然賺這麼多錢，應該可以結婚成家了[20]。

第三章

戰雲密佈：香港淪陷

自一九三七年日本侵華後，在一九三七年至一九四一年間，大批難民由大陸逃至香港，使得香港人口由七十萬突增至一百五十萬人，他們的話題總是不離他們目睹殘暴日軍對華人的屠殺、強姦及遍地的飢荒。但英軍既無對付日軍的軍事力量，又無法依賴美國支持，只好採取懷柔政策。英方認為他們只要與日方保持友好態度，香港便能免於受到侵犯，並為討好日本政府起見，香港英政府下令禁止所有反日宣傳[1]。再加上英國政府根本忽略了香港對日本戰略位置的重要性；香港不但是日本在戰爭中的運送戰略物資及軍力中心，亦是海防重地。駐港英軍情報人員亦忽略日軍在中國邊境的調度行動，對遍佈香港各階層的日本間諜毫無所悉。

在特務機關代表伊藤陸軍少將的指揮下，日本情報工作人員在香港無孔不入，他們在英軍常去的消費場所偽裝成酒保、理髮師、按摩師及侍應生做為掩護，對英軍提供各類賒欠容易的吃喝玩樂，如冰凍啤酒、新奇食物及女伴，伺機搜集情報。有一位香港最出名的理髮師，在香港七年期間，曾為歷任港督、將軍、警察局局長、情報組官員及匯豐銀行主席等高層人員理過髮。當一九四一年聖誕節香港對日本投降後，他搖身一變竟穿著日本皇軍海軍指揮官制服，出現在他的僱主面前[2]。

廣州在一九三八年十月淪陷後，日本便在香港邊界北方集中兵力，第三十八軍團每天都在廣州白雲山集訓，利用此地與新界西邊醉酒灣防線相似的地形，演習在夜間由邊界深圳進攻香港[3]。

27

捍衛香港

一九三九年第二次世界大戰在歐洲爆發，倫敦陸軍部深知香港兵力不足，但以其殖民地之地位，而且在軍事上亦無法防守，故未予重視。當邱吉爾首相的參謀長伊斯曼（Hastings Ismay）在陸軍部會議中提出對香港撤軍時，被譏為失敗主義者。港督羅富國（Sir Geoffrey Northcote）卻認為伊斯曼意見實際，便在一九四○年十月去信英國政府要求撤除駐港之防衛以「避免日軍襲港時平民受到生命及財產的損失」[4]，但卻無人理會，後來羅富國因健康欠佳退休在即，其職位則由楊慕琦（Sir Mark Young）接替。

當時一位多倫多出生的英國駐香港指揮官葛賽（Edward Grasett）少將認為日本決不敢對英國及美國宣戰，但仍主張英國對香港軍力應該增強，英國政府及許多香港居民都希望能採信此論調，但增兵要求為英國軍部所拒。一九四一年英駐遠東司令官Sir Robert Brooke-Popham空軍元帥認為香港遇侵時可抵擋六個月以上，對港增兵確有必要，但此請求再度遭受否決，因首相邱吉爾認為英國毫無機會守住香港。

葛賽少將雖然明知邱吉爾首相不願對香港增兵的決定，但仍續持己見。他在一九四一年七月自中國退休，返英途中，路經加拿大渥太華與舊日同窗加國參謀總長Harry Crerar會面，會中談及若香港能獲得一或兩個大隊的兵力支援，香港必能支撐抵抗日軍更久。他並未直接對加拿大求援，但對英國參謀長則有提到此項建議[5]。

英國對香港的防衛措施全不熱心，唯一的英國皇家飛行中隊已轉調馬來亞，僅留下五架舊式的戰鬥機作為香港的空防。至於海防只靠Prince of Wales號及Repulse號兩艘軍艦，需要時才由南中國海開過來支援香港。同時英方亦認為香港若有戰事發生，美軍在太平洋珍珠港的艦隊必會牽制日軍行動[6]。陸地方面則全靠1,387名的義勇軍和一萬一千名英國及印度部隊防守。香港島上近港灣入口處設有多處炮台，而在醉酒灣的防線則為第一防線。為防日本飛機轟炸，市區到處設有防空洞。

香港居民對躲避飛機轟炸都略有訓練，中學生皆有發放軍服，並受訓練成為民間防空隊員[7]，燈火管制隨著戰情緊張而日漸頻繁。香港義勇軍在民間徵兵時，母親表姐林美娥的丈夫伍英才，後來成了我的家公，他是以一種「與年輕朋友一起組摩托車隊覺得好玩」的心態，加入了香港義勇軍，當時貪圖可分配到摩托車，而加入義勇軍的亦大有人在[8]。伍英才是生於澳洲的華人，當時正在加拿大駐港貿易專員公署工作，他常將兒子衛權背在身後，騎著自己的摩托車，載他去利園山上的嶺英小學上課。

一般市民甚至在大批難民逃到香港之後，都不願相信香港會受日軍攻擊。許多國內的藝術家、文人、學者到香港避難，令香港在一夜之間成了世界華人的文化中心，又因人口突增三倍，製造業快速成長，經濟開始繁榮。更有人在日軍控制地區與中國內陸做走私生意，發了不少橫財。

在一九四一年五月這紛亂的時期，我剛好來到人世。

在英、美兩國相繼凍結境內日本財產後，一九四一年七月香港政府亦凍結日本所有在香港的產業，但英國仍堅信日本不會侵犯香港，留港日人仍可自由來去未受監視。甚至英國情報單位在獲知一位鈴木上校實為日方間諜身份後，礙於英、日兩國非敵對國家，外交部並未將他驅逐出境。此人在十一月底，即日軍攻打香港僅兩星期前自動離境，竟身懷全套詳盡的英軍防衛計劃。

一九四一年九月十九日倫敦自治領部致密電給加拿大政府，要求加國提供一個或兩個大隊軍力增援香港[9]。十一月十九日兩個大隊的加拿大兵到達香港，受到香港市民歡迎。豈知這些部隊不但全無戰鬥訓練，而且在部隊抵港前，有關方面竟將香港資料錯送至澳洲，使部隊對香港人文、地理環境一無所知。

由於國內受中、日戰爭影響情況較香港混亂，所以家中並無人打算離開香港還算太平的日子。父親與中日戰爭時任中共華南書記的廖承志[10]，由此時相識成為好友，廖承志原本在廣東及香港工作，直到一九三八年廣州淪陷後逃至香港組隊支援惠州及寶安，此即為東江縱隊之前身。他們二人曾與英國政府協商，請求英方對港九大隊游擊隊支援彈藥軍需品，以防禦香港，但為英政府所拒，因英方顧慮彈藥會落入親共游擊隊手中[11]。

父親和廖承志及另一英國友人，計劃在日軍佔領九龍之前破壞當地一發電廠，豈知日軍出人意料提早進攻，計劃未能實現[12]。

利家在戰時做過一件備戰的事，就是在大屋囤積米糧，那時利園山下灣仔居民皆知大屋藏米甚多，這也是戰時及戰後大屋常遭劫掠的原因之一。

港督楊慕琦於一九四一年十二月六日出席半島酒店慈善晚會的第二天，即星期日中午，無線電台即對義勇軍發佈緊急全體總動員集合令，伍英才說他應召報到後，發現許多義勇軍因怕戰爭危險而臨陣脫逃。伍英才和香港富紳余東旋之子余經鉞因隸屬野外工程部隊，故在九龍火車站集合報到，義勇軍動員工程部隊準備在日軍來襲之前，先破壞新界預定地區的橋樑及公路。同一天亦是母親的小妹瑤芝結婚前夕，他們計劃第二天先去香港大會堂註冊登記結婚之後，再去九龍舉行婚禮。

香港戰役

十

二月八日星期一早上八點半，我的未來夫婿，才小學一年班的衛權因不必上學，便跟著僕人在九龍郊區及啟德機場上空，已開始彈如雨下。

瑤芝阿姨及其丈夫夫剛在香港大會堂婚姻註冊處簽完字，就無法返回九龍繼續舉行他們的婚禮。婚後直到姨丈去世，瑤芝阿姨常開玩笑懷疑他們的婚姻是否合法，因為他們既無證人也無婚禮。因他們的房子位居戰略要點所以被英軍強佔，並限四小時之內搬遷。在不及收拾任何細軟的情況下，只好來我們家暫住。外祖父母此時住在香港仔的壽山村道，與好友周壽臣爵士是鄰居。

日軍將五架停在啟德機場的古老戰鬥機全部炸毀之後數小時，又傳來日軍摧毀美軍在珍珠港的艦隊，同時馬尼拉、新加坡均首次遭受轟炸，及香港僅有的Prince of Wales號和Repulse號海防艦隻也相繼被炸沉的消息[13]。

香港遭受轟炸後，我們家因地勢高目標顯著，所以大屋亦被散彈擊中，利行的牆壁也炸開一個大洞。家人立刻收拾細軟，由大屋躲到利舞台戲院的後台，我們非常感激祖父將戲院造的如此堅固，讓他的後代在戰爭中可有碉堡般的避難所。當時外祖父母也與我們一起住在戲院後台的房間，還有一個廚房，雖然住得擠些但很安全。由於日軍轟炸事發突然，家人走避不及，未能帶夠米糧所帶米糧需維持多久，所以只能吃粥度日，稍大的孩子肚餓時在兩餐之間就吃些米通〔爆米花〕充饑。我那時才七個月大，原本是個健康的嬰兒，但在避難期間，母親用隨身帶來的奶粉餵我，我吃後立刻生病，母親說是因為戰時利舞台沒有清潔食水，只好用井水調奶所致，從那開始到戰爭結束，我的健康一直不佳。

在戰時市民聽到空襲警報時就要立刻躲進防空洞，利舞台附近的防空洞在禮頓道上，有一次警報來時外祖父不及躲進防空洞，結果被散彈擊中肩膀。日軍佔領九龍之後，隨即在岸邊設起對準香港的大炮陣營。母親妹妹瑤芬在尖沙咀的住宅，就因此被日軍強行霸佔。

做實習男護士的譚葆和此時正在瑪麗醫院，輪值晨間六點早班。香港受轟炸後，他們立刻移開住院病人，將床位讓給炸傷的傷者，仍須留醫的病人，就送去改為臨時救傷醫院的聖士提反女子中學。又為安全理由，除了志願留下的女護士，其餘全部遣送回家，正在受訓的譚葆和，就一人負責照顧二十四位大多數是加拿大籍下午已有許多受傷士兵送來此地，看護工作全由男護士擔任。當日的傷兵。當時有許多醫生已赴中國，僅有部份醫生受徵召留港服務，與譚葆和一起工作的醫生有周錫年和韓素音[14]。愛爾蘭是中立國家，所以其中也有許多愛爾蘭醫生[15]。

日軍入侵後，瑪麗醫院的醫生辦事處，及護理學校改為宿舍後，很多政府官員都來此避難，其中包括港督楊慕琦、愛爾蘭駐香港總牧師T.F Ryan及一些香港大學的教授[16]。

一九四一年十二月十日清晨三時，新界黃竹山居民鍾本〔音譯〕被急促的拍門聲驚醒，為防劫匪，他手中持刀開門，發現幾支槍正對著他，原來此時新界的西貢已被日軍佔領，大埔、沙田在兩天前淪陷，另外城門在前一日亦告失守。英軍已自新界醉酒灣防線撤軍到香港，僅由印度部隊在魔鬼山掩護撤退。日軍從十四鄉往九龍途中，或許因迷途而誤入黃竹山，日軍入村後便逐戶騷擾，強

逼村民做日兵腳伕擔抬重物。十二月十一日，日軍輕裝甲部隊兵不血刃通過西貢市區，因當地警察在日軍進佔之前早已撤離，村民全都留在戶內[17]。

英軍在新界及九龍所設的防禦措施，目的是用來鞏固保衛香港本島，但日軍在四十八小時內就輕易攻破防線，佔領了銀禧〔城門〕水塘的城堡〔銀禧城堡位於醉酒灣防線城門水塘上方，九龍、新界分界群山以北〕。香港義勇軍全部撤退至香港本島總部集合，日軍只以榴彈著射擊，但無轟炸。十二月十二日，敵軍沿九龍碼頭排出炮陣，十三日早上九時，一名日本參謀官舉著免戰旗，渡海到維多利亞港碼頭，帶來一份交給港督楊慕琦的信函，命令香港對日本投降，否則將遭受嚴重陸、空攻擊轟炸。港督拒降後日軍對港開始大舉進攻。

十二月十八日晚到十九日，日軍登陸北角、寶馬山及筲箕灣三地，將香港分割為東、西兩半。北角日軍佔領發電廠後，將看守發電廠年紀稍大的平民義勇軍全部殺害[18]。日軍橫掃香港本島後，繼續向淺水灣及赤柱方向進攻，伍英才曾親眼目睹一名加拿大將領，在總部及部隊傳遞消息途中遇害，死於黃泥涌峽內的防護壕內。十二月二十一日英首相邱吉爾再度對港督下令「決無投降之意」[19]。

日軍進佔香港時父親正在重慶，聽到消息立刻搭乘中國茶葉公司飛機趕回香港，不料飛機在香港領空無法降落，只好折返惠州。豈知如此一來或許救了他一命，日後他常說，當時若被日軍捉到他這類抗日份子，非殺頭不可。

英軍與加拿大軍均以為日軍已佔領黃泥涌峽，在聖誕夜全部撤退至山頂區後，便派伍英才出去打探風聲，但伍未見任何動靜，部隊又再移返。在日軍佔領香港一半地區，但尚未進入維多利亞城，傳來雙方談判略有進展的消息。

日治時期

港

督楊慕琦於一九四一年聖誕節晚間六點半正式向日本投降，日軍將他先移至半島酒店，又轉送到日本統治的台灣，再去遼寧省的瀋陽。至於戰後生還的外籍香港義勇軍士兵，許多戰俘被迫運往日本或其他日本佔領地的勞動集中營做苦工。華籍香港義勇軍士兵脫去制服後即可回家。另外日軍視為敵人的平民俘虜全被關在赤柱戰俘營，因作業程序較慢，所以一直到戰爭結束才得釋放。日後我們聽到許多這段期間在集中營內發生的各種英勇事蹟，和受盡折磨忍辱求生的故事。

伍英才聽到英軍投降消息後，立刻詢問義勇軍部隊動向，長官回答須先觀望日軍動靜，伍說：「我不等了，家中還有妻小，我非走不可」，於是轉身對余經鉞說：「我們走吧！」兩人將武器及摩托車交至葡萄牙籍義勇軍單位後，脫下制服，換上隨身一直攜帶的唐衫褲，走向余經鉞父親余東璇的中藥舖余仁生中藥房，到了店中余便打電話給他母親詢問家中狀況，余家在香港有兩幢出名的古堡式豪華巨宅，當時余母正在般咸道人稱Euston的一幢，余母說家中一切安好，日軍准許家人繼續住在家中。當晚二人暫宿店中，可清晰聽到日軍進城並在市區架起崗哨的聲音。

伍、余兩人第二天一早起來，因急於去余府，但見到藥舖門口己設起日軍崗哨，便商議先保持鎮靜，然後裝成若無其事的樣子，口中吃著陳皮梅，由藥舖出來。豈知一出大門，伍英才的腦袋就莫名其妙的被日軍重重打了一記，原來他不懂見到日軍要鞠躬行禮的規矩，於是二人就一路鞠躬哈腰的來到余府。

此時伍家其他家人都住在跑馬地，因為糧荒問題，他們無法再繼續養一頭叫白雪的俄國狼狗，令衛權非常傷心，這頭狗大概一放出去就被人捉來吃了。此時香港街頭一片混亂，日軍當中有些士兵來自台灣，他們奉命可任意姦淫殺掠。日軍挨家挨戶的到處找所謂的「花姑娘」年輕女子及少婦，所以這些女子平日都盡量躲藏，並將自己弄得灰頭土臉衣衫襤褸，以避免遭受日軍凌辱。每逢戰亂

就必有苦難，只是每人遭遇不同而已。香港此時籠罩在一片恐怖的氣氛下。

次日余府廚子遲歸挨余母訓斥時，廚子告訴余母因在回家途中被日軍捉去當差，並拿出一張日軍給他的通行證，憑證可在市區自由行動。伍英才與廚子的年齡不相上下，所以第二天他就借了這張有廚子姓名及年齡的通行證，通過日軍崗哨去跑馬地藍塘道找他的家人。到了住處，發現日軍在他們所住的公寓大樓不但強姦婦女還殺死數人，九龍巴士公司的鄧肇堅，是香港知名人士，也被日軍剌了好幾刀，他誤信相士胡言，以為可以靠這座公寓的風水趨吉避凶，豈知反而受害。

衛權母親有一次在日軍搜查他們住處時，幸好她母親也在，便幫她帶著兩個外孫，她自己就躲在櫥櫃的被褥下面，一動也不敢動，她母親故意讓日軍知道家中只有老小，就這樣衛權母親逃過一劫，無法得逞的日軍只得悻悻離去。衛權母親在日軍離開他們住處後，就帶著她母親和孩子去投靠弟弟林安邦及弟婦楊懇，後來伍英才向住處的工人打聽，才知道妻子和孩子的下落。

伍英才找到家人後，告訴妻子他必須返回公寓一趟，取出藏在餐櫥櫃腳內的三粒鑽石。他再次用余府廚子的通行證返回公寓，途中被日軍哨兵盤問時，他就用那幾句早年在滿州中國東北學的日文告訴日兵，他必須回家為孩子取換洗衣物。快到家時，就看到家中的餐桌正在大街上拍賣。

當他與日軍進到家門時，雖一眼即見那餐櫥櫃，但礙於日軍在一旁監視，無法下手取出所藏的鑽石，公寓內只見衣物雜亂散佈四處，有些衣物甚至來用做廁紙。後來所幸隨身哨兵被叫開幾分鐘，他乘著這機會飛快的取出鑽石，剛好日兵進門就問：「你是不是二十六歲？」那正是通行證上廚子的年齡，若當時日兵改口問：「你多大年紀？」的話，那就麻煩大了，因為伍英才根本忘記查看通行證上的年齡。

鑽石到手後，伍英才就回去預備帶家人去余府避難，但因天色已晚又開始宵禁戒嚴，妻子美娥便說：「你先回去，明早再帶人來幫忙一起過去。」

第二天一早，伍英才依約帶著余府工人回到住處，卻發現公寓空無一人，牆上滿是子彈孔及血

漬，後來經由鄰居，他才找到躲在樓梯腳下的妻子及兒女，只見衛權抱個瓶子，美娥身背手中抓著餅乾的女兒。美娥的弟弟和弟婦已先離開住處，她只好自己一人帶著孩子在原地等丈夫回來。

原來前一天伍英才離開住處後，日軍又來強抓年輕婦女，美娥的母親便將美娥及媳婦楊懇藏在櫃中用被覆蓋，自己與兒子安邦帶著兩個外孫在櫃前打地舖，正當兩名日軍進屋用電筒〔當時已斷電〕找女人時，幸好憲兵及時命令日軍離開。

伍英才夫婦帶著衛權及背著女兒的工人，一行人由跑馬地走向灣仔時，在街上遇到騎著白馬的日軍，和士兵捧著陣亡戰友棺木的大遊行。此時剛好路經一家餐廳，便入內買些食物果腹，結果花了一百元買隻熟雞，大家邊吃邊等遊行隊伍通過。終於到了毫無戰亂氣息但卻有食物的余府，當晚衛權就寢前請求他可否在余府住一輩子不走了[20]。

日軍進佔瑪麗醫院後，將所有醫院醫療用品丟棄，以日貨取代。員工除了阿劉必須留下操作機房及鍋爐，其餘全部遣散，阿劉在幾個月後也被解僱[21]。

瑪麗醫院在戰時將許多員工調至聖士提反女子中學的臨時醫院服務，聖士提反中學改為臨時醫院已有五年之久，學校一間小課室被改為輕微手術室和醫療室，只收香港華人，醫生多為華人和愛爾蘭醫生，如G.E.Griffiths、林開弟和李有璇醫生。至於英國的修女護士和醫生，除了醫療服務團的總負責人克拉克(Selwyn-Clarke)[22]醫生之外，大多仍在實習階段。香港淪陷期間，克拉克醫生在任內，利用職權幫助了許多香港市民，譚葆和及其他醫務人員都得到他的信函，介紹他們日後逃到自由中國，可繼續為英政府服務[23]。

香港淪陷後中茶公司設於香港的研究部門也被迫關閉，經中國財政部指示，將中茶公司在香港所存的公款悉數發放全體員工，平均每人可得約四個月薪資。吳慶塘便自告奮勇去匯豐銀行提款，發放現金時，他很有先見之明的將面額十元的鈔票留給自己，因為他覺得戰時小鈔較為通行，果然後來日軍禁用十元以上大鈔。伍慶塘帶著這筆錢，便以難民身份離開香港逃到中國。

伍家在余府借住兩天後，伍英才出門前往畢打街，途中有一家懸掛法國維琪政府旗的法國珠寶店，他曾和余的父親余東旋去過幾次。伍英才頓時靈機一動，他知道很多日本兵都想要手錶，就進

去問店東華許（Walsh）先生是否信任他代售手錶給日軍，商量之下華許便給了他十隻銷路較差的手錶，和一些便宜的勞力士錶。伍拿了這些錶就直接去日本憲兵隊總部兜售，看到那軍曹便問伍英才想要香菸、威士忌酒和食米。主管日軍詢問勞力士錶價格時，伍說：「免費給你」，那軍曹不但將這些東西全送給他，還派人幫他送回余府。伍便要了一袋麵粉、一些香菸、洋酒及食米，拿回去的麵粉長滿了虫，他聽後便要求伍設法幫他賣掉部隊這批麵粉，伍就找到一位中國朋友，將這些麵粉又再賣給日本人，每賣一袋麵粉，他們二人就四、六分帳，軍曹得四十日元，伍得六十日元，當年一元日幣可兌換兩元港幣，而且身邊有日軍又方便許多。從此，日本人想要買任何東西，伍英才就四處為日軍搜購。

伍英才在憲兵隊總部混熟之後，不但常幫朋友弄到食米和麵粉，而且和幾位憲兵也成了朋友，並常去余府走動，有時日軍還會送些食米過去。自從日軍憲兵控制香港以後，伍家從未吃過苦頭。那時衛權六歲，妹妹才三歲，他記得日本軍官很喜愛他們兄妹倆，尤其衛權頗有音樂天份，日軍來余府作客時常要他表演，他父母就開始提心吊膽，因為衛權愛唱學校早會集合唱的革命歌曲「義勇軍進行曲」，及彈「鬼怪上校」鋼琴曲，所以每次有憲兵在衛權身邊，他要表演這些曲子的時候，他父母都要立刻制止他。衛權母親始終對日本人存有恐懼及厭惡的心理。

日本不僅需要香港戰略地理位置作為海軍基地，同時亦覬覦香港的財富和資源，因為香港可為日本帶來大量收入及物資。日軍任意搜掠他們所需的物資，將所有可用的貨物，如汽車、機械、建築材料沒收後全部運回日本。瑤芝阿姨家中的汽車，在當時算是幸運的被日軍以一袋白米徵用，日軍甚至將他們所養的猴子都搶走。當時香港港口滿是船艙貨品堆積如山的貨船等候出港開赴日本。但日本僅得到少量英軍留下的武器，因為中國游擊隊已搶先一步，將英軍留下物資偷運回中國。一九四一年十二月十日至三十一日之間，九龍城內的英軍剩餘物資買賣市場非常活躍，香港居民、西貢村民和游擊隊，都買了不少英軍留下的武器。

中國游擊隊

香

港投降後，利家許多人便由利舞台的避難所搬回住所，戰時大屋曾受搶掠，日軍見有搶匪便開槍射擊，所以大屋留有不少搶匪的屍體。對這母親來說這是一段非常艱苦的日子，一個年輕的母親，獨自帶著三個孩子，丈夫又不在身邊，但她全然不知自己受到父親派來的「情報員」暗中照顧。

所謂「情報員」是指中國游擊隊員或同情游擊隊的民眾，很少香港人知道他們在一九四一年初已滲透新界地區，準備在日本侵犯香港時能有所抵抗。當時官方的游擊隊，是由蔣介石國民政府支及供應武器，但香港在一九四一年聖誕節投降後，最為活躍的游擊隊是廖承志於廣州淪陷後，在香港組成的東江縱隊的港九大隊。港九大隊在一九四三年十二月正式納入共產黨旗下，易名為廣東人民抗日游擊隊。

中國游擊隊在香港設有情報交通網及破壞工作小組，日本佔領香港初期，不同政治背景的游擊隊曾積極活動，幫助國內要人和國際友人逃出香港，包括有最早在一九四二年一月五日脫逃的廖承志[24]。在最初七個月當中，共有三百多人獲救，其中知名人士有：何香凝、柳亞子、鄒韜奮、茅盾、喬冠華、薩空了、梁漱溟、著名影星胡蝶，及國民黨第七戰區司令官余漢謀夫人上官賢德[25]。陳策將軍是國民黨駐香港與英軍聯絡的情報單位最高負責人，則自行設法逃走。另外尚有戰俘從戰俘營逃出後，皆由游擊隊安排他們經水路坐舢板，或走山路進入自由中國。游擊隊員並與新界村民合作幫助戰俘躲避日軍搜捕，並提供食物，甚至孩子們也徵召成為「小鬼」的小游擊隊員，當時年紀最小的僅九歲，他們常為游擊隊跑腿或刺探消息。

戰俘營第一次逃亡計劃是在一九四二年一月，由香港義勇軍野戰醫院的賴廉士中校，及原屬香港義勇軍第三機槍隊的一位上等兵李堯標〔音譯〕，在深水埗戰俘營策劃。賴廉士是來自澳洲的醫生兼教授，一九二八年到香港大學生理系擔任講座教授，第一次世界大戰參戰時曾兩次在法國受傷。身

材瘦小的李某戴著眼鏡，個性內向，是香港大學生理系的職員，因景仰賴廉士為人，故要求調至野戰醫院與賴廉士同一單位。李其實不須關在深水埗戰俘營，因香港投降後，日軍准許華人香港義勇軍脫除制服即可解散回家，但他告訴賴廉士他想體驗戰俘生活，及萬一賴廉士需要逃亡時，他可隨時在旁幫助，此外他覺得在營內比在外面更能提供支援。果然在集體逃亡時，他就扮演了極重要的角色。

此次逃亡路線策劃全由李在營內暗中安排，與游擊隊員及同情游擊隊員的民眾，利用運送食物及其他日常用品的機會互相聯絡，許多人因此被日軍殺害。後來他們兩人會同一起在香港大學任教，同屬香港皇家後備海軍義勇軍的工程系講師Morley中校，及另一位物理系講師Davies中尉，四人一起在一九四二年一月九日成功的逃出戰俘營[26]。

他們四人乘舢板至青山道附近的海灘，再步行到新界，沿途一路躲避日軍搜索後抵達西貢邊緣。他們一行四人到達西貢的同一天，游擊隊已將西貢情況控制。他們逃出後，消息傳到了游擊隊及汪精衛手下控制〔汪原為國民黨要員，是蔣介石在黨內最主要對頭，後來背叛國民黨投靠日本〕[27]，加上土匪四處流竄，市面一片混亂，幸好在一月九日，就成了兩方爭先搶奪的對象。在李的安排下，他們在約定地方和港九大隊隊長蔡國樑見面。賴廉士在他的日記中，對這些素不相識的熱心村民所提供的幫助，有非常詳盡的描述。村民不但給他們食物，並提供住處，更將他四人扮成鄉民模樣以避日軍耳目，若沒有這些村民的協助，他們決不可能成功逃出日軍魔掌。四人終於在一九四二年一月十七日安全到達自由中國[28]。

到了中國，賴廉士被指派成立英軍服務團，負責運送醫療物品進入戰俘營，及安排逃亡計劃，並協助自行逃出的戰俘到達安全地方。英軍服務團直屬MI9英國情報單位，中國政府最初極不願意有外國情報單位在國內活動，但礙於戰時英國為同盟國，而勉強同意。英軍服務團在香港的活動，則全靠游擊隊協助而得以順利展開。賴廉士致英國陸軍部報告中稱中方游擊隊員為「我們的游擊隊」，或「紅色游擊隊」，因他們較親共產黨。對逃亡戰俘來說，這些中方游擊隊是他們的生命線，賴廉士認為這些游擊隊員是「抗日戰爭期間，中國所有組織中是最活躍、可靠又有效率」[29]。

香港在日治時期，中國游擊隊員就滲透到香港社會生活各方面。他們活躍在各個市區、鄉村角落。他們在日本銀行、印刷廠、甚至日軍高層指揮部都廣佈眼線，專門從事間諜、破壞及救援任務，成為日治時期香港與自由世界的重要聯繫。

事實上，日軍對佔領區的控制仍有隙可尋來往香港與中國大陸，同時也可利用如澳門及廣州灣的法租界中立區進入中國。戰爭初期游擊隊曾成功地救出許多戰俘逃離香港，直到後來不但因為任務愈見艱難，而且事成之後日軍對營中其他戰友的報復行動亦太過殘酷，才不得不放棄搶救工作。游擊隊員搜集到情報後，立即報告中國高層，有些情報亦轉達其他盟國。美國空軍就全靠這些珍貴的情報，在戰爭末期得以準確地向香港日軍基地投擲炸彈，美國飛行員被擊落時，也幸得這些游擊隊員協助逃生。

父親是抗日戰士

父

親由一九三七年就開始在中國以官方身份，及用私人關係積極加入抗日行列，他將家人安置妥當後，便全力幫助更多的人逃離香港。父親在國民黨游擊活動，及親共的廣東東江游擊隊均有參與。我們利家在戰時幸而受到這些游擊隊員的保護，不但毫髮無損，而且得以免受日軍和同樣殘酷兇狠的土匪迫害[30]。

父親不屬任何政治黨派，他的獨特作風令他與國民黨和共產黨之間的關係非常微妙，他記得有一次在無意中獲悉國民黨要捉拿當時身處在國民政府內的周恩來〔周得蔣介石保證安全，為共產黨駐國民黨的聯絡官〕，父親立刻警告周恩來，令他得以順利脫逃〕，周對此事一直銘感於心。戰後他知會中國駐香港非正式官方辦事處的香港新華社，父親可以自由出入中國任何地方[31]。

母親帶著我們兄妹三人進入中國時，父親已在廣東東江地區游擊隊的基地惠州活動。我想父親從未直接參與游擊隊，因為當時情況非常混亂，各種不同組織在抗日同時互相競爭。實際上，有兩種游擊隊：一是親共的「紅色」游擊隊，另一種是由余漢謀將軍指揮的官方游擊隊，在廣東地區活

戰後賴廉士成為香港大學校長，父親則是校董會的校董。

敦，一直工作到一九四七年。父親與賴廉士在這段期間，因工作而互相了解尊重成了好朋友。

賴廉士上校在英軍服務團總部一起工作。後來四叔非常幸運的，隨同服務的中國銀行調到英國倫

年時，去廣東北部曲江〔廣州被日軍佔領後，曲江成為廣東的臨時省會〕探望父親，當時父親正和

當年父親可能是以他中國紅十字會司庫的身份，為英軍服務團取得所需物資。四叔說他在一九四二

廉士在他的日記中經常提到，父親如何為在香港的戰俘和逃到中國的難民取得醫藥及毛毯等物資。

父親當時以人道主義者自居，是那些逃出香港的人士，游擊隊及中國政府三者之間的聯絡人。賴

諾每到香港辦事時，都會借用父親的辦公室[32]。

的遺孀宋慶齡女士，和毛澤東好友斯諾（Edgar Snow）及多位蔣介石國民黨政府的高層官員。戰後斯

動，此外還有汪精衛手下的奸細，和英軍服務團及其他不同組織。這段時間父親結識了孫中山先生

第四章

家族逃難

一九四一年至一九四五年，是我在兵荒馬亂年月中的孩提時期，跟著家人逃難至中國。雖然許多戰時的經歷是別人告訴我的，但在幾十年後，我自己對那個年代的某些事情仍是記憶猶新。

在日本統治之下流行一句「大東亞共榮圈」的口號，即指亞洲人應由日本人統治。此時香港市民人心惶惶，有錢人還可由黑市買到食米，無糧可吃的窮人只有活活餓死。

一九四二年初日軍宣佈計劃縮減香港人口，目標由當時的一百六十萬人，減至他們認為「可以控制」的五十萬人，經過各種手段，他們幾乎達成目標。其中最不幸的一批人當街被日軍捉上卡車，整車人運到海港後丟進帆船，然後拖到大海淹死，或放火活活燒死。僅在一九四二這一年內，根據正式紀錄顯示，共埋葬了83,435因戰爭恐怖行為、搶劫而死亡的人(1)。亦有很多人餓至骨瘦如柴，甚至吃人肉。所謂每人每日六兩四的配米，不但混有砂石，還要憑運氣才能得到。

那時香港街頭充滿恐怖景像，街邊常可見到垂死的餓莩，尚未斷氣已被切割分食，若有人見到日軍忘記鞠躬行禮，即冒斬首之險。每當我的朋友譚葆和去般咸道女友家時，常見到載滿死屍的卡車，將屍體丟棄在山頂警署附近的方形長坑內(2)〔現今佐治六世紀念公園地點〕，地點剛好在當時伍家借住的余府巨宅之下。此時中環市區的茶樓全被改為賭場，市區亦開始為日軍特闢紅燈區慰安所。

逃離香港

日本政府鼓勵香港華人返回中國，我們家族亦在遣返中國之列，許多利氏和黃氏家族成員就分別到了中國不同地方，但也有極少數親人願意留守香港。

利氏家族中，只有銘洽二叔夫婦帶著三個小的孩子，回到利氏祖居嘉寮村，因此他們戰時的經歷和其他家族有不同。他們坐船經珠江，再赴嘉寮村。兩個較大的男孩在戰爭初期才三歲及五歲，都在村裡學堂讀書。

祖母及二祖母〔父親生母〕分別與自己家人逃返中國，二叔大女兒慶雲亦跟隨二祖母避難。四祖母〔四姨太吳月，又名吳佩珊〕則回到自己廣西梧州老家，她的孩子皆已十幾歲，則跟著其他家人回國，孩子無論住在何處均在當地就學。唯有三祖母〔三姨太蘇嫻，又名蘇淑嫻〕決定與她兒子五叔留守香港，五叔在戰時一直於家族租務公司工作，負責收租[4]。當時家人經兩種不同路線由香港進入中國；一是陸路入沙頭角，或坐船至湛江即舊時所稱的廣州灣，此區當時屬法國維琪政府故為中立區，家人到國內之後再會面[5]。

只要聽到有日軍進村的風聲，全村人不是躲到田野的茅屋，就是逃到鄰近村莊避難。漢輝堂哥記得當時他才三歲，每逢逃難時，大人便將他與妹妹分別塞入兩個竹籮筐內，用扁擔挑著跑，五叔的漢楨哥就只得跟著大人自己走。戰時不但要躲避日軍騷擾，亦要提防當地土匪隨時入村搶掠。天真的漢輝哥聽到土匪要來就十分興奮，因為全村村民都聚集在我們的利氏祠堂內，等候二叔發槍給所有壯丁，防守各人的崗位，將祠堂變成了堡壘。漢輝哥未曾憶及在嘉寮村的數年中，土匪曾造成任何重大的傷害[3]。

因為父親無法親自返回香港照料我們，便託一地下工作人員，也許就是東江縱隊港九大隊的游擊隊員，帶信給母親，信中要母親帶著我們跟隨此人去中國，母親生恐其中有詐，不肯起程，直到父親捎來第二封信，母親才決定準備離開香港。

逃難時很多人都將值錢珠寶縫在衣服夾層，或藏在鞋底，以防日軍搜身及土匪搶劫，戰亂時這些珠寶可隨時賤賣換取現金急用，但除了現金之外，還是金幣最容易換取食物和其他用品。母親一定儘可能的藏了不少細軟在我們行李中，但她大部份的珠寶，都由她表姐美娥的丈夫伍英才，幫她埋藏在大屋後院。

一九四二年二月，我們一家跟著其他成千上萬的香港難民，踏上逃往中國的路程。母親帶著我們三個孩子：四歲的哥哥、兩歲的姐姐和才九個月大的我，加上兩個傭人，六大件行李。伍英才為防日軍阻擋或搜查我們，他告訴日本憲兵朋友，母親是他妹妹，並為我們弄到一張特別通行證，還利用關係在行前為母親換到些現金。戰後父親曾向伍英才詢問這名憲兵的姓名，以便去函致謝[6]，但是否打聽到他的下落就不得而知。

英才陪同，及游擊隊員暗中保護下，一行人坐船過海來到九龍火車站。伍英才為防日軍阻擋或搜查我們，他告訴日本憲兵朋友，母親是他妹妹，並為我們弄到一張特別通行證以免麻煩。我們由沙頭角船行一段路後，步行一日到了惠陽，然後再坐船去惠州與父親見面。

四叔在車站與我們道別後，由伍英才陪同我們坐火車進中國邊界粉嶺，車廂擁擠不堪，我們的行李幾乎無法上車。粉嶺下車後，母親就僱了幾部單車載行李，傭人背著哥哥和姐姐，母親抱著我，跟著大群的難民，步向中國與香港邊界的入口之一沙頭角，伍英才在此與我們分手返港，到中國就立刻撕毀日軍的特別通行證以免麻煩。我們由沙頭角船行一段路後，步行一日到了惠陽，然後再坐船去惠州與父親見面。

到惠州之後我們便坐卡車去廣東省北部的韶關，再轉乘火車到桂林。父親亦指示他的弟妹和漢釗姪兒走此相同路線，到桂林與我們相會[7]。大家深信我們是因為受到游擊隊員一路保護，才得順利通過敵人和土匪控制的地區。

我們家離港不久，伍英才接到他所服務的加拿大貿易專員公署通知，他們一家可能有機會去加拿大，因為他們的名字很幸運的在美、日政府互換境內外僑名單之內[8]。由於美、日雙方交換人數不平衡，當時談判地點正在香港，而所有加拿大士兵全關在香港戰俘營內，只好用部份在香港的加拿大公務員，彌補美方不足之人數。

伍英才懷疑這個消息是日軍設下的陷阱，就由他的家庭醫生亦是他姐夫處，取到一張他妻子肺部

有陰影結疤的舊X光片，然後去憲兵隊打探虛實。伍英才拿著這張片子給憲兵看，證實他妻子確實有病須要治療，憲兵就建議伍帶著家人去加拿大，根本不知伍給他的是張舊X光片。

伍英才帶著妻子美娥和兩個孩子一家四口，在一九四二年八月離開香港，直到今天，伍家仍不明白他們的名字如何會在交換名單之內。到加拿大時，移民局官員因為他們是華人而不許他們入境，但四人名字又確在交換名單之內，只得允許他們居留。伍家是加拿大史上第一批收容的華人難民，政府不但供住屋，伍英才還可繼續在渥太華政府貿易部工作。伍英才原本計劃戰後返回香港，但因一九四五年時香港居住環境太差，才決定全家在加拿大定居。後來他們全家在一九四九年四月於加拿大國會議會典禮中，宣誓成為加國公民。

桂林的日子

桂林途中，吳慶塘再度與我們一家在柳州會面，這是他第一次見到母親和其他家人，他與我們家的關係從此更加密切。

往

一九四二年在桂林時，我們在風景優美的旅遊勝地七星巖正對面，蓋了一幢房子，現在此屋已被夷平改為馬路，以輸送此區旅客。日軍向廣西省方向迫進時，飛機轟炸亦漸頻密，每當日機來襲，我們就躲進七星巖裡。

漢釗哥當時寄宿學校，戰時學校伙食僅供兩餐，孩子們總是吃不飽，所以他周末常來我們家吃飯。在桂林一直跟著我們的一個女傭順姐，告訴漢釗哥我們屋子有鬼，他聽後老覺得晚上睡覺有人壓著他，但又不敢對我父親開口，所以開始找藉口去離我們家只有五分鐘路程，在建幹路上的二姑姐家住宿⑨。漢釗哥說其實只要那一家吃的東西多，他就去那裡，漢釗哥在戰時與二祖母常和我們同住。

我們在桂林住了一年多，此時家中兩位女傭預備辭工，母親便決定在女傭未離開之前，她先單獨一人回港。因為母親相信女傭一定知道她在大屋後院埋藏珠寶的地方，她要盡快在她們回港之前，

先回去取出這些財物。戰時家人在必要時可變賣這些首飾以求生存，同時她也須要回港儘可能取出我們日常生活需用品。

母親將我們交由父親和傭人照顧之後，便和瑤蓮阿姨一起經湛江回香港，但瑤蓮阿姨無法取得通行證，只能在湛江等候母親。於是母親便獨自上路，還得加多一件為阿姨帶回所需衣物的責任。

母親回到大屋後由留守大屋工人協助，收拾我們的衣物。大屋一樓和二樓遍地都是被散彈炸死或日軍殺死的劫匪屍體，我們住的三樓似乎未受騷擾。日後母親對我們說，當時他們必須繞過死屍，然後在三樓收拾衣物，因為二樓地上滿是結成厚塊的血漬（戰後重整家園時，無法清理這些血漬，須重新更換地板）。我實在無法想像母親是如何經歷這段日子的。

母親回港期間住在灣仔較遠，未被劫匪騷擾。外祖父母和瑤芬阿姨都有來利行與母親見面，有一天母親和外祖母在街上，經過一個躺在地上奄奄一息的人，向他們叫著「求你救我！」當時外祖母和母親都自身難保，對他實在無能為力，信仰虔誠的外祖母就說：「你向耶穌禱告，祂會幫助你的。」

母親對我說過在她晚年，尤其父親去世後，遇有任何困難時，只要想到這場戰亂的經歷，她便無所畏懼。

母親在香港住了幾個星期之後，便坐船赴湛江與瑤蓮阿姨會合。大家都相信母親是受游擊隊的暗中保護才能安然無恙。母親將她的首飾，極為巧妙地藏在各個隱密的角落，另外加上二十大件我們家和瑤蓮阿姨的行李，一起帶到桂林，其中有我們最需要的厚外衣和絲棉被[10]。

戰時人們總是想盡辦法收藏貴重物品，我最喜歡聽的一個故事是，我在一九四九年見到的一位父母親的朋友陳律師的妙計。當年她毫不遮掩的，堂堂皇皇的將大鑽戒等所有首飾全戴在身上，讓日軍誤信她身上戴的都是假珠寶，得以過關。

吳慶塘非常感激母親送給他的絲棉被，因為逃難時他總是怕冷，而自己又買不起絲棉被。直到今日吳慶塘仍常讚美母親是個非常勇敢的女人。

戰時我們全靠變賣或典當母親首飾維生，父親為了私人原因拒絕為美國政府在中國做工程師，而

他對中央政府、東江游擊隊及英軍服務團的種種抗日活動，均為義務性質，全不取薪，此時父親毫無入息。父親生性儉樸，個人需要極為簡單，又為了衣物耐髒好洗，他將淺色衣褲全染為深色。經濟上我們僅能勉強維持，他安慰母親只要打完仗，一切情形都將好轉，並必會補償她所失去的個人財物及珠寶。的確，這些承諾他都一一兌現。

一九四二年日軍進逼，廣西情況告急，中央政府亟須整修黔桂〔貴州、廣西〕鐵路[11]以疏散難民，於是便成立一個共有四位工程師組成的委員會[12]，由國民黨黨員侯家源主持，但他們仍需一位有能力及可靠的人手監督工程進展，所以推選父親為此委員會的國民黨榮譽執行委員[13]。他雖此時吳慶塘在桂林的永光煤炭行任經理[14]，但父親認為吳跟著他較有前途，便說服吳成為他的秘書。因父親不會說國語，所以在代表中央政府參加會議時，須要吳在一旁代為傳譯及發言。他們雖然身為中央政府代表，但都不屬國民黨[15]。

吳跟隨著我們家到了廣西省宜山，鐵路局總部所在，局長侯家源便給父親一塊位在總部附近的土地，讓父親自己監工設計蓋了一幢兩層樓的房子給家人住。房屋外型完全依照當地風格，用竹片混和泥土建造，父親又特別改良將泥土混合部份水泥，令屋牆密不透風[16]，宜山房子完工後，二祖母也搬來與我們同住。

戰爭歲月中，父親積極抗日行動之一，是做中國紅十字會義務司庫，因著這層關係，他可取得一種中國無法找到的西藥，學名為對胺基苯磺醯胺，專治敗血病。在宜山時，吳慶塘手臂受傷感染發炎十分嚴重，幸有此藥治癒[17]。

有一次父親因得瘧疾病倒[18]，須由吳慶塘代表監督鐵路工程，父親晚年時常自誇身體硬朗從無病痛，他大概忘了這段打仗的日子。父親後來實在體力不支，須辭去國民黨榮譽執行委員監督黔桂鐵路工程的職位，便託盧衍明[19]、連瀛洲[20]及歐陽奇[21]，安插吳慶塘去柳州的新加坡華僑聯合商業銀行工作。這家銀行為汕頭華僑所有，在一般情況下他們只用汕頭籍的員工，但在父親的推荐下破例錄用吳慶塘，並信任他在銀行負責採購事務[22]。但柳州不久也告淪陷，銀行被逼遷至重慶。

再度逃難

一九四三年時，利家尚有五個大孩子留在桂林讀書，他們是六叔、七叔、七姑姐、八姑姐及漢釗哥，因桂林情況日漸危急，須將他們疏散較為安全的地方。由於當時火車票極難買到，幸好有一位前利舞台員工，袁耀鴻出面相助，他認識中央政府專員的黃茂蘭，黃的父親是位將軍，袁便說服他們，將這五個大孩子塞進將軍的私人火車車廂內。五個孩子終於到達柳州，得以暫時躲避日軍，然後他們再由柳州坐火車去宜山，此時我們一家已離開宜山赴貴州的獨山，五個孩子到達宜山時，與二祖母一起住在我們家中。漢釗哥記得我們在宜山房子後院種有蕃茄，也養雞隻，這時他學會殺雞，他說若不自己動手，晚飯大家就沒難可吃。他們在宜山沒住多久，也跟隨我們到了獨山。

交通運輸一直是中國的一大問題，尤其戰時更是困難，父親認識一位中國銀行交通部門的負責人王藹佳，憑他所提供的卡車，我們一家得以由宜山搬至獨山。貴州獨山是個丘陵小鎮，我們住在城郊，生活情況非常落後，又無自來水供應。幾位叔叔和姑姐到獨山後，就在當地入學，漢釗哥正讀高中，不論天氣多冷，父親每天都帶他去附近的一條小溪瀑布洗澡。那時我大哥還太小，無法跟他們去。這段時間叔姪之間建立起深厚的感情，父親常告訴漢釗哥他在牛津讀工程的點點滴滴[23]。母親說年紀小小的漢姪哥，已經立定志向長大要像父親。

我在獨山開始得病，骨瘦如柴，弱得連頭都抬不起來，母親形容我那時就像一頭快要餓死的小貓一樣瘦弱。當我病重住在獨山非常落後的醫院時，六叔來看我，正巧醫院的女傳教士醫生，向母親發出我的病危通知，要父親儘快來醫院看我最後一面。十幾歲的六叔正和我母親在一起，馬上跳上單車去找父親，父親接到消息，立刻帶了他身邊僅有的「仙丹」對胺基苯磺醯胺，來到醫院。醫生對此藥一無所知，但見我已無藥可救，也只有死馬當活馬醫的給我服下此藥，奇蹟般的，竟救了我一命。

戰時我一直體弱，走到那裡，病到那裡，最後總要住進醫院，成為家人的一大負擔。從香港對日投降，我七個月大開始，就一直多病，經常腸胃毛病弄得脫水，還有一次大腿淋巴腺受感染，好幾次父母親都以為要失去我。雖然戰時父母親和大哥也曾得過瘧疾，但是我身體最差，所幸我們都走過來了，今天我還能寫這個故事。

日軍漸近貴州時，我們又被逼離開獨山，這時我已開始懂事，日軍轟炸過後，當母親牽著我走回家時，她非常驚訝我居然能馬上認出我們屋頂已被炸毀，只剩下厚厚牆壁的房子。

離開獨山時，我們又再次使用王藹佳借來中國銀行的車輛，一路坐在行李上，來到貴州省省會貴陽。沿途山路彎曲顛簸，尤其下坡剎車失靈時，更是驚險萬狀。途中我們的車隊曾數度被流為土匪的國民黨散兵阻攔，幸好無人受傷[24]。當時我才兩歲，依稀記得坐在車上，要像爬粗繩樓梯一樣爬到行李上，上路後小手要抓緊繩索以保性命。每當我們走到國內落後地區，因衛生環境太差，父親絕不買任何熟食〔他形容零售的肉類因蒼蠅滿佈，看來是黑色的〕，只有靠水煮蛋充飢，記得我一路暈車，將胃中的蛋嘔吐的一塌糊塗。五十年之後，我才克服了對水煮蛋的恐懼。

經過漫長辛苦的旅程，終於在天黑時份到了貴陽，車隊在一間戲院前停下，見到前利舞台員工袁耀鴻由戲院出來，將手中的一包東西塞進父親手中，說：「澤哥，請收下，是給你的」，原來袋中全是現金。我們家在戰時沒有人身上帶錢，所以漢釗哥對剎時看到那麼多錢，所留下的深刻印像，至今記憶猶新。袁當時在貴陽戲院當經理，他將我們安排住在一間全不隔音的房屋。我們家住樓上，二祖母，年輕的叔叔、姑姐和漢釗哥、慶雲妹睡樓下，漢釗哥說我們在樓上的一舉一動，他全聽得清清楚楚。

重慶的日子

中國銀行的車輛又一次載我們由貴陽來到四川省的重慶，沿途情勢受國民黨控制較為穩定，所以一路還算安全。我們到達四川省後發現此地生活、飲食習慣和南方人不大相同，尤其我們不慣是很恐怖的習俗。

幼年時的戰亂，對我來說只有美好的回憶，煩惱憂慮都屬於大人，我不生病住院時，就是個旁觀者。天熱時我穿著木屐，跟著工人在鄉間到處亂跑，經歷了最精彩的探險，冬天就穿布鞋。戰時平民沒有皮鞋，因為皮革須留給士兵做軍靴。有時我們走到稻田間去看農人作活及撈田螺，雖然我們家不許吃田裡的田螺，怕有寄生蟲，但看人撈田螺也非常有趣。有一天我和傭人在外散步，忽然聽到一陣騷動，連忙趕去查看，原來是一條大鯰魚困在淺水泥塘中掙扎，有人晚餐可打牙祭了。又有一次聽說附近農村有頭母牛快要生產，傭人就帶我過去看熱鬧，正好見到剛生下的小牛，對孩子來說，真是經歷了一堂活生生的學習課程。我們也曾一起去買雞蛋，將部份雞蛋用來孵小雞。有一次不知是誰的主意想要喝羊奶，於是十幾歲的七叔便捉了隻羊想擠羊奶，當時景像真是好看煞人！

我們橫渡長江入重慶與祖母、三叔及五姑姐會面，他們很幸運的能搭乘上海商業銀行的運輸機[25]，由桂林直飛重慶，不必像我們飽受舟車勞頓之苦。十六歲的六叔因年紀還小從軍不成，便停學憑著優厚的英文底子，加入中國政府機構任傳譯員，以賺取收入，後來調至緬甸。

在重慶時我們住陶園社區，此社區是我父母朋友陶家的產業，由中國最大的承包商陶桂林建造，他曾負責中國一些最主要建築物的工程，尤其在南京及上海地區[26]。陶家住在社區入口左邊的大房子，我們則住在右邊最後一間。

三叔是上海商業銀行的董事，所以他和祖母及一些叔叔、姑姐，可以住在上海商業銀行在重慶所

擁有的天壇新村其中一個住宅單位。

當時我年約三歲，仍記得我們住在長江江畔陶園的一幢小平房。此屋是沿著河床地形斜坡而建，結構簡單，前面是客廳，後面為臥房，所以雖然房子大門臨街，但後面臥房已在河堤坡上，最有趣的是廚房與房子遠遠分開，另在坡下河邊。

我們兄妹三人常喜歡在晚飯後去捉螢火蟲，然後將螢火蟲放在瓶中看它發光。我們還將由河邊捉來的烏龜，綁在客廳沙發腳邊，讓那些烏龜吃蚊蟲。因為廚房在坡下河邊所以常遭水淹，每遇河水上漲，家中的大人就得趕下去，將廚房器皿食物移至屋內。水退後河床岸邊總會留下一些跟著河水沖上岸有趣的東西。有一次我們捉到一隻螃蟹，我想留下來玩，父親怕蟹箝傷我，但又不知如何細綁蟹箝，只好把那對箝子活生生的敲下，居然還給螃蟹傷口塗抹紅汞藥水，然後再用繩綁好螃蟹給我牽著走。雖然那個年代我們沒有玩具，但我在這方面卻一點都不匱乏。

從我當年經常往來的玩伴中，我學到一些童言稚語的普通話，至今仍有些記憶。在中國時因我排行最小，大家都叫我妹妹，所以戰後便慣用 May 為我的英文名字。因中國女孩常以「美」字為名，我嫌俗氣不喜歡這個名字。

一九四四年除夕，母親的弟弟錦彰及弟婦仲霞，帶著孩子來陶園看我們。晚飯後大人在客廳聊天，一群表兄妹的孩子們就在父母親的臥房玩，我哥哥突然覺得不適，便使用椅子爬到窗邊對外嘔吐，當時年紀最小的我起來，其他的孩子也跟著爬上去一探究竟。霎時間，鳳恩表姐由窗口跌了出去，當時年紀最小的我在一旁觀望，幾個大孩子都嚇傻了，只有我當機立斷的跑到客廳，告訴大人鳳恩表姐掉出窗下的意思。

中日戰爭日軍步步逼進時，重慶是戰時臨時首都，是當時最安全的地區，有些親戚來重慶探訪我們之後，也決定在此地留下。

當時混亂的情況真是可想而知，幸好鳳恩表姐跌出去時被後窗下的電線截住，沒有從兩層樓的高度跌到地面。戰亂時期的重慶，又逢除夕，要送醫治療實非易事，後來總算舅父和舅母找到一部黃外。

包車，將鳳恩表姐送到附近醫院。幸好她傷勢不重，只在下巴留下一道疤痕。父母親直到晚年時仍常談起，難得當年我才三歲半，就能如此鎮定機智。

日本投降

歐

洲戰事在一九四五年五月結束之後，對抗日本的策略開始轉變，太平洋地區只求在最低傷亡情況之下，能儘快結束戰事。終於在八月六日在廣島上空投下第一枚原子彈，三日後另一枚原子彈又在長崎上空投下。結果於東京時間一九四五年八月十四日夜晚十一時三十分，日本天皇正式宣佈向同盟國家最高統帥無條件投降。

同一天晚上，重慶的新加坡海外聯合商業銀行，正舉行晚宴款待外交部長陳慶雲，及前上海市市長吳鐵城。陳慶雲家人聽到日本投降消息後，馬上打電話通知銀行，銀行主席連瀛洲和總經理歐陽奇，立刻要吳慶塘上街買炮仗來燃放慶祝，他們二人都是廣東潮州人，不知四川人是報喪才放炮竹，所以街上市民聽到炮竹聲，還以為是銀行有人去世。晚上消息傳開後，無人再肯睡覺，市民都湧上街頭通宵達旦狂歡慶祝，個個都喝得酩酊大醉[27]。

日本投降的消息傳到香港之後，市民上街見到日軍就打[28]。蔣介石認為香港在中國戰區之內，故應由他本人代表香港接受日本投降，關於香港前途曾在戰時高峰會議中討論過，交回香港方案也得美國羅斯福總統支持，但英首相邱吉爾反對。日本投降後數日，香港情況仍混淆不清，不知應由何方政府從日本政府手中收回香港。八月二十三日代號為鳳凰的梁姓英軍服務團工作人員，帶信給赤柱營內的吉姆森(Franklin Gimson)，要他出面接掌香港政權。三日後吉姆森由赤柱營釋放，駐進法屬使館大廈。八月三十日英國皇家海軍Sir Cecil Harcourt上將抵港，成立戰後香港軍政府，由此政府接管香港至一九四六年五月一日止。

一九四五年八月父親、三叔及祖母，與邱吉爾首相駐派中國戰區的特別代表Sir Adrian Carten

de Wiarte中將同班飛機，由重慶飛回香港。自從一九四一年十二月香港被日本佔領後，金融制度已完全脫序，因為父親身為第一批返港人士，匯豐銀行便委託父親帶回大量現金[29]。

因父親須先趕回香港參加重建工作，母親便獨自帶著我們三個孩子及傭人，經一般的路線坐火車及船回香港。記得有一段路，我們須擠在一個小平底船上，一個個平排而睡，像其他難民，一點也不像桂林學校只有兩餐可吃，所以家中大人回港時，他們還不至於太難過。此時這些孩子若教育或生活費用有問題，漢釗哥記得那時多向三叔在匯豐銀行一位姓吳的朋友求助，漢釗哥去的時候，吳會請他一起喝咖啡，他對吳家華麗的巨宅，印像非常深刻。

一九四八年漢釗哥中學畢業後，計劃去上海三姑姐與她美籍丈夫Henry Sperry家，預備參加清華大學和交通大學在上海舉辦的入學考試，但此時共產黨已開始控制中國東北及北京，所以父親去電要漢釗哥立刻回港，參加廣州嶺南大學在香港的招生考試，同時等待機會赴美國求學。漢釗哥離開重慶時，吳還去機場送行，翌年中國解放，就再也沒有吳的消息。

漢釗哥和十多歲的叔叔姑姐仍留在重慶繼續學業，重慶學校伙食分量很夠，不像桂林學校只有兩訴我們戰爭結束，可以回家了。最後一段路我們須坐火車，但火車坐位非常有限，幸好家人認識的火車站站長告訴母親，要清早四點以前到車站才可能有坐位，於是我們便一早到了車站搶到坐位，踏上歸途。

第五章

戰後：社會變遷

戰後香港市面殘破蕭條，其時中國爆發內戰，大批難民湧入香港，令香港人口在一九四六年至一九五〇年之間，由原有的一百六十萬人，驟增至二百三十六萬人。僅在一九五〇年上半年即有七十萬人由大陸蜂擁至香港，同年五月政府在邊界成立的配額制度證明完全無效。多數難民皆為無特殊技能的勞工階級，有些人在來香港之前根本不知香港在何處，但他們都立定決心要在香港工作定居。

父母親偶爾會在晚上接到由大陸逃至香港親友的電話。香港到處可見人們露宿街頭，滿街都是乞丐，山坡上有很多人住在由撿來的鐵皮和木板搭成的木寮裡。

那段時期共產黨在羅湖及文錦渡邊境地區，架起擴音器對香港喊話，整天播放宣傳口號，侮蔑英國人，特別是港英政府。邊界雙方互設崗哨對峙，若有任何人企圖由中國偷渡來香港，邊境中國士兵奉命對他們格殺勿論，但仍有人冒死逃亡成功，這也是香港人口增加的原因。

幸好我們有家可歸，庭園、果樹、雞舍及網球場一切依舊。祖母和她自己的子女在戰後搬回大屋，和五姑姐與祖母一起住大屋二樓。祖母的另一個女兒即二姑姐在戰前已出嫁。

我們家此時搬至利行左翼的頂樓居住，利行共有六個公寓住宅單位，左、右各三個，中央共用寬闊樓梯。我們樓下的單位空置，一樓則租給父親游擊隊時期的老朋友蘇雲(Shulwan)少校，他在中國時或許和英軍服務團有關係。他是英國工程師，能說流利的國語，從未成家，只對汽車引擎有興趣。當時他新婚的三叔，如我們在戰前一樣住在三樓，四叔在一九四七年由英國返港後，和五姑姐與祖母一起住大

53

的玩偶。

是香港勞工處處長，下班回來總是見他換上工作套裝，一頭鑽進車底。他身材高大，穿著油污工作衣的模樣，令我看得非常入神，我們都稱他蘇雲叔。

二叔和他家人住在利行右翼頂樓，四祖母則住一樓，二叔的孩子常和我們玩在一起，所以我們玩伴很多。

住在利行時，我們兄妹三人共用一間大房間。晚上有個女傭會搭張床在我們房間，陪我們同睡，她常常一連幾晚的講大戲故事給我們聽。夏天睡覺時，我們的床上都要掛蚊帳，冬天就用大毛巾包好灌滿熱水的銅壺，然後用大扣針包牢，放在被褥中暖床。我生平第一次也是唯一的一次，穿母親為我們做的衣服，母親那時衣著簡單，只戴些假首飾。四歲半時我得到第一個玩具，是一九四五年我在香港首次過聖誕節時，父母親送給我的洋娃娃，童年時這個娃娃是我最喜愛

雖然父親可稱得上是個富人，住的環境不錯，但我們家銀根仍不很寬裕。

配糧及缺糧

戰

後香港軍政府所面對的最大難題是，戰俘和戰犯的處置及遣返問題，加上關閉戰俘營，遣散武裝部隊及輔助防衛服務隊伍等。政府亟需工作人手，首次加重本地華籍及葡萄牙籍員工的職責，也因此令未來的香港政府，不得忽視這些非英籍員工的工作能力及貢獻。

香港戰後第一年，市民生活還是非常艱難，糧食仍是主要問題，糧食配給由聯合國糧食局控制，糧食嚴重缺乏對建設日漸增長的健全社會是一大威脅。香港政府於一九四六年五月十四日，委任父親為香港穀米糧食統制處處長，父親上任一星期後於政府新聞處對記者解釋，聯合國糧食局只能配給香港二萬噸米，為本港所需半數，所以必須增加麵粉及青豆替代（二）。月底他並向聯合國糧食局抗議香港配米不足，由九月開始至一九四七年間，配米量再減而增配餅乾和麵粉，情況總算穩定。到一九四八年，米價及麵粉價格開始上漲，父親為平抑米價，便一面維持米、麵配給制度，一面應大眾

需要，推出由泰國和越南進口的廉價米。一九四八年父親向政府辭去這份義務工作，但政府仍請父親為顧問[2]。

父親在任期間，精明強幹、公正無私，沒有任何人，甚至親戚朋友，可循私多配糧票[3]。有一次我在學校遭受男同學戲弄，他說：「你爸爸是屎桶官」父親聽我告狀後，笑著說：「你去問問他吃什麼的。」

父親任穀米統制官時，與東南亞有「米王」之稱的泰國華僑馬祿臣成為好友。從那時開始馬祿臣每年必定送我們成袋的暹羅米，暹羅的白花芒果，泰國的柚和芒果，我想是世界上最好吃的，但因果實不宜長途運送，所以市面無法買到，父母每年必將這些禮物分贈給其他家人一起享用。這個習慣在馬祿臣去世後，一直由他的兒子沿襲至一九九六年我母親去世。

早年因物資缺乏，小型工業難以發展，父親曾盡力幫助這些「小工業」，像專做糖薑的余達之，和製糕餅的嘉頓等公司，他們都非常感激父親協助他們取得糖的供應[4]。以前在飯後常可吃到美味的糖薑，我記得裝薑的罐子特別好看。嘉頓在年節時常送糕餅給我們，而且在父親去世後仍繼續贈送。嘉頓還送了一個非常美麗的聖誕蛋糕給母親。

一九九五年母親去世前一年，嘉頓還送了一個非常美麗的聖誕蛋糕給母親。

大量難民湧入香港後，面臨最大的問題之一就是水荒，當年香港仍全靠積存在水庫的雨水供應用水，水庫水量不足時就開始限制用水。一年當中總有一段時間，一星期僅有兩天可供水數小時，高樓住戶常因水壓不夠經常無水。因為旅館不限水，有錢人至少還可去酒店旅館開房間洗澡，窮困地區市民須拿著盛水器皿，排隊在街頭公眾水喉取水，報章及電台經常報導有糾紛發生。這段時間我記得非常清楚，我們每個人的日常生活都受到水荒的影響，水來的時候父母親總是叮嚀我們要節約用水，每逢輪水時傭人們必將浴缸和各種盛水器皿都儲滿水備用。

政府此時發現新完工的新界大欖涌水塘的儲水量，根本無法應付日益增加人口的需求。

健康問題

香

香港戰後的另一主要施政重點，就是改善市民健康問題，我記得政府派公共衛生護士來學校，給學童注射傷寒和霍亂預防針，我打完針不是手臂痠痛，就是有發燒的反應。我們做完肺結核試驗及種過牛痘後，傷口還須用有鐵絲的護罩保護避免抓傷，總之每逢這些「公護日」，我就怕得要死。

我天生有追根究底的個性，有一天我放學回家後，發覺父親比平日早回家，探問之下，才發現原來父親經常去紅十字會輸血，戰後早幾年中國人少有輸血救人的觀念，但他自己從未對人提起。

只要一提起戰後幾年的日子，就不由得讓人聯想到我們「杜蟲」的經歷，父親非常注重健康，對戰時中國及戰後香港的衛生狀況非常注意。每年秋涼的一個周末，我們全家須禁食一日，只能喝些薄粥，晚上父親就要我們吞服杜蟲藥。理論上是，我們體內的寄生蟲，在一天沒有其他食物的情況下，就會吸收我們吃下去的杜蟲藥。第二天一早，我們喝下極其難飲的橙汁和蓖麻油的混和液後，體內的蟲和卵就應該會順利排出。不只是我們自己家人須禁食吃藥，若有其他親人在我們家時，也須一起參加。雖然堂兄妹很喜歡來我們家玩，但總希望能避開這件大事。可是父親從不事先宣佈，因為要他自己時間方便，那麼我們就長不大了。他說的一點不錯，我真的看見我體內有寄生蟲排泄出來。

父親非常注重健康，他要我們養成每天晚間定時如廁的習慣，所以每晚飯後，我們三個孩子就排隊上廁所，哥哥坐馬桶，姐姐坐高痰盂，我就用小痰盂，我們經常只是坐著嘰嘰咕咕聊天，根本沒有做過什麼。

我們家在一九四七年有了第一艘叫天鵝號的遊艇，阿根是看船工人之一，父親覺得他患有寄生蟲，就逼他服用杜蟲藥。他為我們工作多年後，真的長高些，健康得多。

難民家庭

一

一九四七年農曆新年，重慶陶家的親戚盛樹珩和朱翹仙突然來訪[6]，令我第一次感覺中國的動亂。他們二人在一月份時，搭機離開上海計劃來香港取赴美簽證，飛行途中因天候惡劣須轉飛馬尼拉，後來飛機四具引擎中的兩具著火，失事墜入中國海。機上三十六位乘客中有七人喪生，其餘生還乘客的救生筏在海上漂流了三十小時後，才被美國船救起，住院就醫兩個星期後，盛樹珩和朱翹仙終於到達香港[7]，在等待美國簽證的大約一個月期間，父母親歡迎他們住在我們樓下空置的單位，和我們一起用餐，我當時六歲非常喜歡聽他們的事。他們取得赴美簽證後，便回上海預備赴美。

在一九四八年至一九四九年間，有許多來自國內的親友借住利行，不知當時是因香港住屋短缺，或只是暫住，曾經有三戶人家在同一時期住在我們樓下的單位。利行的孩子都很歡喜能有更多的玩伴，但由大人的談話內容，讓我意識到國內動盪不安局面的嚴重性，也了解這群新玩伴的友誼只是暫時性的。我也很清楚他們在我們家擁擠不堪的居住環境，看到人們因戰亂被迫離鄉背井，總是很難過。

母親的姐姐瑤珠姨媽帶著六個孩子，由上海逃至香港後，便暫住我們樓下，當時這個單位有三個家庭借住。姨丈鄺兆祁是個資深工程師，仍想留在國內出一份力，所以未隨同家人來港。一九五〇

因我戰時多病，常引起中耳炎，父母親約在四〇年代末，發現我聽覺有問題。父親認識一位國內知名的眼、耳、鼻、喉科專家陳翼平醫生，大約父親在牛津期間，當時國內許多有牌照的醫生，僅可在香港政府醫務署工作，但不得行醫[c]。他請教我失聰的問題，他診斷後發現我左耳膜穿孔，所以聽覺受損。陳醫生在我耳內放了一片特殊的薄紙代替耳膜，並敷上藥膏，促進耳膜再生，在他悉心治療之下，我的耳膜終於長好，但我覺得兩耳聽覺還是有差別。父親非常焦急的定期帶我在放學後去看陳醫生。陳醫生在我耳內發現我左耳膜穿孔，所以聽覺受損。父親非常信任他的醫術，便向他學後去看陳醫生。

年時，他覺得國內局勢已漸穩定，便來香港接家人回上海。因韓戰問題，為避免正值兵役年齡的長子被送到戰場當「砲灰」，所以他們將長子留下與我們同住，可是不到兩年時間，他們其他的孩子又一個個的逃回香港。

另一家是陳氏夫婦和四個孩子。陳是前文提過的律師朋友，她與父親同時在二〇年代，於英國求學相識，她在英國讀法律，並受訓成為律師，夫家是國內的政要。我對她印象最深的不只她是位幹練的律師，而是她手飛快，可在一天之內針織好一件衣服，最神奇的是甚至午睡時，她的手也可以不停的織衣服。

第三個家庭就是父親在廣州工作時的上司劉紀文一家，帶著太太和孩子同住利行。劉太太美麗優雅，善長書畫，他們一家住利行時，我每天放學後，都去樓下看她作畫，她知道我有興趣，就教我研墨上色、用毛筆，不知不覺中，我已坐在她桌旁，她開始教我畫畫了。劉太太告訴母親，我很有藝術天份，應該學繪畫。

一九四九年中國共產黨在中國成立中華人民共和國，國民黨在蔣介石帶領下撤退至台灣。

房屋問題

戰後父親不僅透過政府，更加上自己個人的力量幫助香港市民。一九四六年父親被推選為太平紳士，職責為在太平紳士法庭裡做法官，解決像違規設攤小販等這類案情不重的案件。一九四九年英國政府為表揚父親對香港社會的貢獻，尤其在擔任穀米統制官時期的表現，特別頒發大英帝國官佐OBE勳章。父親在一九五三年成為市政局議員之後，立刻大聲疾呼政府重視屋荒問題，他呼籲大企業與政府合作為員工與建廉價屋宇，並提供合理利率的分期付款方式購屋，由此亦可增進僱主與僱員之間的良好關係。同時他也提出大眾對公共衛生缺乏認識，建議政府印製簡明的宣傳單，教育民眾(8)。

屋荒危機嚴重影響公共衛生，窮人多半住在木屋，甚至露天而居，或向舊樓業主租用天台搭建木

屋。這些居民居住環境惡劣，連廁所和自來水都沒有⁽⁹⁾。

一九五三年聖誕節，香港木屋區一場大火燒傷五萬三千人，政府方察覺香港總人口有三分之一為無家可歸的難民，解決他們的住屋問題，使他們融入社會實在刻不容緩。於是便開始策劃龐大的徙置計劃，供給廉價而較安全的房屋，清除違章建築的寮屋。但政府的整建計劃永遠無法趕上難民增長的速度。

一九六一年，父親以非官守立法局議員身份，在立法局會議中批評政府工作效率太低。政府在一九五九年宣佈計劃徙置七萬五千人至政府公屋，但根據父親所得資料顯示；至一九六一年二月時，僅三萬二千四百三十二人獲得徙置。他催促政府簡化作業程序，加速徙置木屋居民，優先供應公屋給月入港幣三百元以下的市民⁽¹⁰⁾。

直到一九八○年代，山坡的違章建築木屋漸由政府的多層公屋取代。這些難民得到安置後，大部份成為香港工業化的中堅份子。

難民與工業

一九五○年至一九五三年韓戰期間，聯合國向中國禁運，對香港轉運貿易打擊甚大，所幸一些難民不僅為香港帶入大量資金，同時也注入工業技術的知識。根據統計，這段時期移民在香港投入約港幣數億元的資金，同時在一九四七年至一九四九年，有二百多家上海的公司行號，轉在香港註冊。

香港當地的工業在中國東北工業家推動之下，令香港日趨工業化並建立起國際銷售網⁽¹¹⁾。香港本島缺乏天然資源，大量難民的到來，令香港技術性及知識性的人力資源不虞匱乏。香港的成衣業多數皆由這些新移民開創，設立工廠，造就了大量就業機會。五○年代開始，即可見到愈來愈多「香港製造」的商品，漸而取代四○年代末期「日本製造」的商標。為使香港在國際商場上更具競爭力，對科技及各類人材的需要更顯迫切。

愈來愈多的工廠與建後，香港的社會結構也起了重要的變化，傳統中國式的住家女傭逐漸消失。

原本這些婦女皆來自珠江三角洲的絲坊區，她們在村莊附近的紡絲廠工作，當經濟蕭條工廠結束後，就紛紛遷至廣州、澳門和香港。這些不幸的女工多為文盲或半文盲，唯一生路即為幫傭，其中很多人一世做「梳起」，精神上互相安慰，有時經濟上亦互相支持。她們從不修剪頭髮，都將長髮編辮梳起，年紀較大的就在腦後梳髻，我很喜歡看她們用市場買的木刨花油，整理她們的頭髮，令髮絲光亮清爽。

香港工廠如雨後春筍般成立，勞工需求也大為增加，吸引了大批原本做女傭無特殊技能的年輕女工，加入勞力市場，華人女子不願再為人幫傭。年輕人在工廠打工，可以和自己家人生活在自己的空間，只有年紀較大的女傭寧願繼續留在服務多年的僱主家。政府津貼的公共屋宇，提高許多市民的生活素質。家庭幫傭的勞力市場，則由香港僱傭介紹所帶入的菲律賓籍及後期的泰國籍女傭所取代，至一九七〇年代，香港的家庭幫傭，幾乎全來自東南亞國家。

從公眾場合開始聽到上海話，加上街頭飄溢的上海炸臭豆腐味，令我真正感到香港在變。有錢人由中國逃至香港時，總是儘其所能的將值錢細軟帶出，據我所知，在香港常有人將手邊的珠寶變賣求現，作為設工廠或其他營生的資本。後來幾年有位我們叫「上海婆」的珠寶商，常來我們家向母親兜售她手上客人託賣的特別首飾。她身材圓胖，來的時候常穿件很普通的鬆身旗袍，但內衣裡縫有各種不同的暗袋，我每次都是用無比欽羨的眼光，看她解開旗袍紐扣，然後由各個暗袋中拿出最精美的首飾。我總是盼望上海婆能在我放學回家後才來，有時我運氣好的話，剛好她晚來，我就可以湊熱鬧。見她獨來獨往的帶如此多的貴重物品，不禁擔心她的安危，但想想亦非我所該問的問題。

難民與教育

父

親開始積極參與四邑工商總會〔祖居同鄉所組成的團體〕、灣仔街坊福利會〔社區互助團體〕、東華醫院〔貧民醫院〕和保良局〔保護婦孺組織〕等草根階層團體的義務工作。他投入大量時間為窮困市民籌募冬衣、舉辦一般義診、免費醫牙、提供學雜費全免的小學教育，更對貧苦民眾捐贈國人非常重視的棺木。加上父親對教育的熱心，他經常應邀參加學校的頒獎及新校開幕典禮，這些多數為難民而設的華人學校，需要像父親這類的人士提昇他們的校譽。父親一生對需要他幫助的人，總是竭盡所能的給予協助。

戰後香港學校情況一片混亂，許多校舍都被摧毀或嚴重受損而無法使用。中國難民大量移入後[12]香港校舍極為短缺，任何可使用的建築物都充當課室。在一九四六年至一九四八年的學年中，我共換了四間學校，其中兩間很短時間即不存在。

五〇年代香港主教何明華(Rev.R.O.Hall)牧師為難民子弟成立勞工子弟學校，但香港殖民地政府懷疑這些學校宣傳共產主義[13]及灌輸反英思想，便關閉了數間學校，有時還將教師遞解出境[14]。一九五三年教育法例及附屬條文規定，禁止學校有任何政治活動，包括討論中國當前之政治，及香港殖民地政策。

政府實施三班制上課制度，同一校舍分早班、午班、及夜班三批師生使用。一九五二年時我哥哥和姐姐已去英國讀書，我和弟弟很幸運的在聖保羅男女中學，編在早上八點開始上課的早班。

我後來才知道伍英才一家當年就是因為香港缺糧和學制混亂，決定繼續留在環境好得多的加拿大。

第六章

美好的年代

戰

戰爭結束至一九五○年代初期我們一直住在利行，那段歲月，對我來說是多采多姿的。利行孩子多，從不缺玩伴，我最愛在園中自由自在的玩耍，吊在樹桿上採水果，或在雞棚趕雞，我的膝蓋經常是傷痕累累，腿上滿是蚊虫叮咬留下的斑斑點點。園中叢樹開花飄來的陣陣香氣，最令我陶醉，花開時，母親鬢髮中常插有幾朵香花。我也喜歡聽夏天的蟬叫，現要我只要聞到茉莉花香，或聽到知了叫，就會憶起我無憂無慮的快樂童年。

我們這群孩子在院中用幾塊板子搭了一個屬於我們的小「俱樂部」，裡面有幾張長椅和木凳，最重要的設備是一個小炭爐。每個星期六晚上，所有的孩子就聚在俱樂部講故事、烤蕃薯吃。有一次姐姐在學校考了第一名，便為我們的周末俱樂部向祖母討賞，當晚祖母便要廚房做了一隻太爺雞，送到「俱樂部」請我們吃。一群孩子當中數我年紀最小，所以只有在一旁聽、看的份，雖然每次都非常興奮，可以和大伙人盡興的玩到任何時間，但聽完大孩子的鬼故事，散場時，大孩子總是會邊叫著「鬼來追我們啦！」然後一呼而散，偏偏我又跑不快，一定落在最後。

有一晚我半夜醒來，看到一個長髮白衣的女人身影從我們房間移動到洗手間，我第一個念頭閃過，既然屋內沒有橫死的冤魂，我們就不會受到傷害。就是母親說戰時利行沒有死過人，便自我安慰的告訴自己，既然屋內沒有橫死的冤魂，我們就不會受到傷害。

另一晚我又看到一個白色的女人身影，站在我和姐姐的床中間，起初還以為是女傭，便坐起來查看，當我看到她仍在熟睡時，嚇得我動也不能動，叫又叫不出，只見那白色身影越移越近，走向姐姐的

62

床，用長長的手指甲觸摸她的蚊帳。我就一直告訴自己，她不會傷害我們的，因為我們從未做過虧心事，後來我就昏睡過去了。第二天早上在我詢問之下，發現女傭並未在半夜起來弄過姐姐的蚊帳，但我不想增添父母親無謂的煩惱，所以從未對他們提起此事。

直到今日我仍無法解釋我所見到的影像，但記憶卻依舊是如此鮮明。

我們住在山坡上的利行四周樹林環繞，有許多野鳥，但父親仍喜歡在家中養鳥。我們養過鸚鵡和幾隻金絲雀，父親常為鳥換水、餵穀食，籠中還放有一塊墨魚軟骨。父親最喜歡一早聽掛在陽台的鳥唱歌，有時還會引來林中的野鳥一同唱。我們的廚子也常在廚房後面餵來訪的黑鳥。有一清晨，我被父親對著窗外的喝斥聲吵醒，我從窗口望去，只見一男子腋下各挾著一隻雞，由利行山坡奔向灣仔，一看就知道他是爬進園中雞舍的偷雞賊，他剛要逃走時被父親發現。

那幾年香港有許多人吃不飽，我們的廚子常將廚房剩下的菜飯分給他們。有些專收破爛的男人，常定期挑著扁擔來我們家收購舊瓶罐，這是戰後香港資源循環再生的方法。

父親每天很早起床，母親則相反，所以我們常和父親一起吃早餐，他先將深咖啡色濃厚的魚肝油放在我們面前，每人吃一湯匙，然後一定要看著我們吃早餐時，吞下丙種維他命和鈣片。他一直保持著英國習慣，早飯吃醃肉或醃青魚加蛋，若廚子早去市場買到魚的話，我就吃片煎魚。

父親早上心情最好，是他每天最好的時光，香港學校八點即開始，他喜歡自己開車送我們上學，然後一早去辦公室，甚至比打雜工人還更早到，我問他為什麼不要司機送我們，他說：「阿莫住九龍，我不想要他一早過來接我，他可直接去寫字樓向我取車，然後開回家給媽媽用。」但我認為父親是喜歡自己開車送我們上學。

在我童年的記憶中，雖然父親嚴肅而守舊，但他是我們的支柱，極受大家的敬愛。我幼年時非常沉靜，對周遭的事物聆聽吸收，我想父親從來不知道我對他的景仰有多深。我才幾歲大時就知道自己有和父親一樣的剛強個性，有一次我才五歲，父親堅持我一定要吃完午飯才可離開餐桌，但我不餓，就頑強的坐了幾個鐘頭不肯繼續再吃，最後父親只好讓步。從那次以後，父親才接受我的硬脾

氣，知道我對自己的事一定要能自己作主。

幼年時我話很少，而是聽的時候多。我們在家都用廣東話交談，唯有在晚餐時，父母親不想傭人知道他們的談話內容，多用英文交談。為了要了解父母親說些什麼，我就加緊學英文，非常用心的訓練自己的聽力，結果在未說英文之前我已經聽得懂了。

此時大家都知道我好查根究底，母親被我問煩的時候說，她只要對我略提某人，我就要知道全盤細節，甚至人家肚腸的長相都要知道）。

姐姐於一九四七年在拔萃女書院寄宿，父母親見她在外住校非常愉快，便決定將我也送去，但我每星期日返校時就哭哭啼啼，不肯回去，父母親只好將我轉到聖保羅男女中學上午的三年班就讀。

我的學校經常有表格須要填寫，其中一欄是父親職業，我多半填上「工程師」，但後來覺得似乎不妥，因為父親做這麼多不同的事，而且我知道他決非以做工程師為生。有一天我便決定要一問究竟，到底他的職業欄應該填什麼，他想了一下才說：「就寫公司董事好了。」

利家在南灣有幢小屋子，夏天我們去游泳時常用來更衣。當時我們家的汽車是由司機阿莫開的，但父親喜歡在週末自己開車帶我們去南灣游泳，平日也一定親自送我們去學校。香港的夏天又濕又熱，令我們常長瘡癬，父親說海水能治瘡癬。每次去南灣游泳，經過南邊曲折山路時，總讓我想起趴在中國銀行卡車上逃難的那段路，然後就必定暈車，一路上父親要為我停下來好幾次。

有一天我們在南灣游泳時，父親問我喜不喜歡在南灣有幢我們自己的房子，令我非常興奮。但他擔心此區太過偏遠，治安會有問題，幾年以後他才改變初衷。

一九四六年時，我感覺到家中有一股新生命的滋長，一九四七年五月我弟弟志剛便來到人間。

休閒出海

父

父親熱愛陽光和清新的空氣，一九四七年他經濟情況許可後，便買下第一艘名為天鵝號的遊艇，父親一生共有四艘遊艇；其他三艘分別是五月花、富都及亞特蘭大號。我最喜歡坐船出海，後來成了我們生活的一部份。父親常在周末帶著我們出海，有時會去香港仔的水上海鮮畫舫吃飯，但後來香港仔海水污染嚴重，父親就不許我們再去那裡的餐館吃飯。

父親說香港外島水域有海盜，所以從不讓我們在船上過夜，但拗不過我們的苦苦相求，終於將船停在銅鑼灣避風塘內，讓我們過了一晚。當晚船伕為我們在水面上點了盞燈，大家還捉到好多墨魚帶回家給正在坐月的母親。

那時香港尚未有人口過擠和空氣污染問題，仲夏日落景最美。我每次在海上看日落時，總是想將雲彩形狀烙在腦海裡，因為那時我還小，遊完船河天黑回家時，已不支睡著，要父親抱我上床睡覺，我要第二天一早起來，將日落晚霞在我水彩畫中描繪出來。父母親非常珍惜我的作品，和喜愛我欣賞大自然美的天性。

坐船出海是父親最喜歡的休閒活動，在船上家人可享天倫之樂遠離塵囂。我們小時候父親很少在船上招待朋友，因為父母親出海的時光是屬於家人的，經常只請親人及我們的同學一起出海。

香港早期很少人有私人遊艇，所以我們能去到許多未受污染的海灘，那時海水清朗沙灘潔淨，可將挖到的貝蛤帶回家吃。我們在一般人無法來到的島嶼，可以觀察並觸摸到不同的海洋生物，我曾經摸過一條小章魚，及在淺水地方看到小鯝沙魚徐徐遊過，出海時在我們船邊還見過海馬，我也曾用手帕捉到透明的海蝦。我們的船伕都是住在香港海邊遊艇仔的水上蛋家人，由這些人之中我們學到很多海洋生物的名稱和生態。

父親是個非常有公德心的人，當他讓我們盡情在海灘玩耍的時候，他就和船伕一起清理海灘的垃圾，收集棄置的瓶罐和尖銳的石塊。我因耳疾，始終無法學會游泳，但在淺水的海灘我自己學會了

游泳，我一定要將頭抬高過水面，否則很容易得中耳炎。退潮時我喜歡守在岸邊看著沖上沙灘的有

趣小生物，我即使現在我們去海邊，還是喜歡等海水退潮。

記得有一次我們的船靠在一個有很多水母的海灣，這些有像雞爪般的毒水母對人體有害，父親便

要船伕儘量的將水母撈到岸上，牠們在太陽之下就融化成水。

夏天因陽光炙烈，我們都在午後出海喝下午茶，有時也在船上吃晚飯。遊畢回到港口時，水面被

萬家燈火倒映得燦爛燦爛，我依然記得那種帶有鹹味的海風輕拂在面上的感覺，這些珍貴的時光都

是我最美好的回憶。現在新增的填海地皮令香港海灣狹窄，及航行交通擁擠不堪，以往風貌已不復

有。

冬季我們就早上開船，中午在外野餐，飯後休息片刻就在外島徒步遊覽。在這些小島上我們見到

非常簡陋的墓穴，和子孫為先人撿骨的骨罈。我們也見過百年以上殘破老屋及蕃薯田，這是島上原

有漁民、農民和種香木外銷中國大陸的工人居住的。看到這些村民生活的情況，令我驚嘆不已，世

代相傳至今，他們的生活毫無改變，也未受香港發展影響。我們多半在傍晚轉涼之前返航。直到現

在，若我們冬季返港的話，我還是喜歡去外島走走。

在這些小島上，週年都可看見漁船傍晚返航，有一次我們在岸邊時，一個漁人向父親兜售狀如半

開扇的一種干貝，蛋家人稱它沙叉，我很驚訝的在他打開的干貝殼內發現有小珍珠，漁人告訴我

們，這些有珍珠的貝類是他從海底採集干貝肉時撈起來的，但失望的是父親什麼也沒買。

在海上我們最愛用漁線釣魚，常釣到色彩鮮艷的魚類，但我父母就不釣魚。對我們釣上的各種

魚類，總有問不完的問題討教船伕，而學到不少海洋生物的知識。有幾次在海上遇到漁船靠近我們

遊艇售賣活魚，從他們打開的船艙中可見到許多色彩鮮艷的活魚，父母親會買一兩條回家吃晚飯。

我最喜歡一九五○年代中我們的第三艘遊艇富都號，因為它夠大，我可以和同學、堂兄弟姐妹和

叔叔姑姐，一起在船上野餐。四個孩子中我交遊最廣，對這類戶外活動也最有興趣。船上孩子多的

時候，四位船伕為照顧我們忙得團團轉，孩子游泳時又要警告他們躲避水母，有一次一個親戚的孩

子正從船邊游泳扶梯爬出水面時，被一隻藍色水母的黃觸鬚碰了一下，立刻中毒，必須緊急送醫治

利行和大屋

療。

行家中客廳窗外景觀很美，可見山坡及瀑布，其中一個的瀑布下方，有人用石塊堆積成小池，夏天時街頭孩子常去池中戲水，雖然我們不准下去，但我喜歡看他們玩。

祖父在大屋園中遍植木瓜、龍眼、番石榴、枇杷、芒果、黃皮和荔枝等果樹。孩子最喜歡從樹上採水果吃，木瓜成熟時，因樹幹太直太高爬不上去，我們就在木瓜樹下鋪件舊雨衣，再用長竹桿將成熟的木瓜挑下來，大家立刻就地大吃起來。我們這些孩子在園中蕩鞦韆、溜滑梯、騎單車，和踩二叔為我們做的高蹺，還常在噴水魚池中撈蝌蚪、看金魚，大孩子可在園中籃球場打球。

偶爾，我們會去大屋向祖母請安，她總是很嚴肅的坐在同一張椅子上。有時也會和大屋持槍的錫克警衛南星聊天，他還給我們看過他捉到的蛇。傍晚工人四處找我們回家洗澡時，我們就躲在祖父在園中造的假山山洞裡。

利家人住利行和大屋時，大家走的很近，我們常去向二祖母、四祖母，及幾位叔叔、姑姐請安。大屋中有供奉祖先牌位的神台，特殊節日時我們會去祭拜。但二祖母和四祖母在她們自己家中，都設有佛堂供奉菩薩，我們比較常去二祖母處，因為她是父親的親生母親，看到她對信仰的虔誠，和一種自然流露的平和寧靜，令我心神嚮往。我也最喜歡看她咕嚕咕嚕的抽水煙，然後吐出嬝嬝餘煙。二祖母每天一定在上午和下午固定時間，在自己佛堂內，換上褐色拜佛布袍來燒香拜佛，她跪在佛像前，口裡唸著佛經，手中捻著佛珠，她拜佛唸經時全神貫注，不知我們常在她身後調皮搗蛋做鬼臉。

二祖母樂天知命，我從未聽過她有任何抱怨，與家人和睦相處從無糾紛，提起祖父時總是充滿尊敬的口吻。身材瘦小的二祖母，以堅定樂觀的天性，得到全家人的敬重，祖母去世後，她便成為家

中的大家長。

每逢父親農曆生日時，二祖母一定不假人手，親自在院中用乾稻草，古法慢火燜一道芋頭鴨給父親吃，這是父親童年最愛吃的鄉下菜。後來在五〇年代由利行搬到嘉蘭大廈後，她就改在較為現代化的廚房做這道菜。

一九四八年及一九四九年時，父親被選為第四及五屆的亞洲及遠東地區經濟委員會香港代表，五〇年代初，又擔任許多政府不同委員會的委員，同時亦是市政局議員。因他在政府和工商界的社會關係，父親常須設宴招待各方朋友，所以母親是個非常忙碌的女主人，我們雖住利行，但宴客都在大屋，我記得那時父母親穿戴整齊，由利行走下花園去大屋的樣子。雖然宴會菜餚都是酒樓預備，但母親仍須細心安排菜單、鮮花、客人名單、安排座次，及擺設佈置等細節。父親在社交圈有句名言：「客散主人安」，父母親舉辦的宴會都以早聚早散聞名。

五〇年代初時，大屋一直是我們的生活的重心焦點所在，所有重要的家庭團聚、聖誕宴會和婚禮，都在大屋大廳舉行。農曆年初一，女孩子都要穿上不是紅即粉紅的棉袍，我還要戴上小金耳環和手鐲，跟隨父母親去向祖母拜年。然後在大年初二，穿同樣的新衣去外祖父母家拜年，與母親的家人團聚。中國人喜歡代表吉祥的紅色，所以我幼年的衣服不是紅就是粉紅色，令我日後對紅和粉紅色的衣服非常有排斥感，差不多在四十年後，我才再穿粉紅色衣物，但還是不穿紅色。

外祖母偶爾而來利行看我們時，就住在我們樓下空置的單位，因他們住九龍，當時過海不甚方便。

有一天我放學回家，剛好外祖母由利舞台看完愛路扶連（Error Flynn）的戰爭片回來，有點頭痛，便向一位工人索冰袋敷頭，當年才六十多歲的外祖母就因中風去世。這是我生平第一次經歷失去親人，在我心目中她永遠是慈祥美麗的外祖母。

僕人和小販

當時香港富有的家庭都有大批的僕人，包括有廚子、洗衫婦、保姆、一個或兩個做一般家務的僕人，另外還有幾個園丁和一位司機。二祖母一直有個小女孩「妹仔」在她身邊，中國窮苦人家無法養育子女時，常將年幼女兒送給有錢人家做「妹仔」。依照中國舊時的習俗，「妹仔」的薪酬多交給她的父母，但兒子決不送人。「妹仔」到新家學做家事，以換取食宿，長大後，她的主人必須為她找個人家嫁出去，但也常有「妹仔」遭受虐待事件發生。二祖母的「妹仔」除了做輕微家務之外，也為她按摩。

雖然父親自始一直反對「妹仔」制度，但從未干涉他母親，直到戰後香港政府禁止私有「妹仔」制度之後，父親才出面要二祖母遣散她的「妹仔」。我不清楚二祖母有否將「妹仔」嫁出去，但我猜想多半是送她回家，因為她只是個小孩子。在我們自己家中每個工人都有支薪，所以我對這個風俗不甚了解。我一直以為只因僕人年紀小，所以才叫「妹仔」。

有一天我放學後，一位父母親朋友的「妹仔」即將嫁到美國，所以來我們家辭行。她告訴母親她正在學英文，做赴美準備。我聽後才開始對「妹仔」習俗多些了解。

我注意到父親在日常生活中，對他周圍的人十分關心，經常與手下員工交談，幫助不同的人。每天我都可以看到他對待我們身邊的員工，從無一句重話，只有體諒和關懷，總是盡量想辦法改善他們生活，有時甚至員工能有更好的發展須離開我們，不再為我們工作。

我弟弟嬰兒時有個保姆叫阿南，有一天她發現自己吐血，沮喪地要自殺。母親帶她看過醫生後，發現她患有肺結核，父親便負擔費用讓她在醫院住了一段時間，並讓她長期接受治療。阿南病癒後，阿南請求父親幫她做個小生意，結婚後生了幾個孩子。五〇年代初恩平路上的嘉蘭大廈剛落成不久，父親便在嘉蘭大廈靠街面，行人來往的樓梯間旁，給了她一個攤位賣拖鞋和書報雜誌，生意不錯。從那時開始她就要免費送我們全家她賣的東西，因為她拒不收錢，我們只好告訴她家人不看她賣的這類書報雜誌，但她堅稱拖鞋總可派上用場，所以就硬將拖鞋塞給我們。父

親去世後母親搬離崇明大廈時，我還見過阿南一面，崇明大廈就在她擺攤位的嘉蘭大廈對面。

我們家在一九五一年搬到使館大廈後，有個男工叫阿文，父親覺得阿文天資聰穎，應該繼續讀書充實自己，便送他去夜校讀英文，後來學製圖，阿文也只好缺課。有時父母親在家中舉行宴會那天正逢阿文須要上課或考試，但若父母親實在需要他幫手，阿文也只好缺課。我記得他去上課時，常穿著父親給他的西裝和領帶，儀表非常整齊。阿文還會用母親的英文食譜學英文，能做出很好吃的橙味鬆軟蛋糕。阿文唸完製圖課程後，就離開我們家另謀高就。

一九六〇年代末，有一次我們回香港時，見到家中的新廚子阿吳，她是我們從前所住崇明大廈的清潔工。父親見她工作非常勤奮，便要她來我們家學做廚房家務。阿吳後來在我們家工作多年，中間有時因和母親有些意見不和而曾經中斷過，但最後總是會回來工作。對我和我們的孩子來說，她就像自己家人一樣。她在我們家工作期間，父親還幫她們夫婦買了一間公寓，讓他們不愁住處可安心工作。父親去世阿吳退休後，她覺得對父親的恩德難以回報，在母親晚年時阿吳還回來照顧她。最後一次在一九九六年十月母親的追思禮拜中，我還見到阿吳。

父親雖然稱得上是有錢人，但他身上永遠只有少許零錢。李樂君是在七〇年代和八〇年代初期，為父親工作的秘書，大家都稱她李姑娘。她說若扒手要偷父親的口袋，那才真是白費心機！但身上沒錢有時總是不方便，李姑娘記得有一次父親在希慎道上的辦公大廈前，見到一個水果攤販，便想向買他幾個梨，但身上沒錢，上到辦公室後就要李姑娘去為他買幾個梨帶回家。李姑娘便差辦公室的小雜工下去買，他對小販說：「我是大老闆利先生派我來的」，嚇得違規設攤的小販連忙說：「我馬上就走」。後來當小販聽小雜工說父親只是要向他買幾個梨時，立刻要免費贈送，但父親定下規矩決不受禮，所以原本十元買八個梨，結果小販給了二十個(二)。父親對梨價完全不知，還以是公平交易呢。

使館大廈

當年逃至香港暫住利行的親友，在五〇年代初時都相繼離開，此時我們家正預備遷至位於希慎道上的使館大廈新居，使館大廈是利氏家族的第一幢大廈。

我們搬進使館大廈前，父親常將大樓設計圖帶回家研究，我們住頂樓兩層，有全層的屋頂花園，由母親親自設計佈置，父母親常在香港大街小巷，搜購各種有趣的裝飾品和古董，用來裝潢新居，他們非常興奮從此不必再去大屋請客，可在自己家中招待朋友。

大樓頂層設有大水塔儲水，每當大廈輪水時，便先將水輸送至水塔內，大廈住客就可免受水壓不夠無水之苦，我知道父親不只是為我們自己方便，同時也是為其他住戶著想。日後我們家族其他的大廈都沿用這個設計。父親對利家建造的建築物非常引以為榮，這些大廈不但設想週全而且堅厚牢固，颱風來襲時分毫無損，不像許多其他高樓遇狂風暴雨時常發生塌樓危險。我一位姓程的同學家離我們家最近，父親也常接她上學，接了她再去大屋門口接阿煥，她是祖母廚子的女兒，在聖心學校讀書。

搬進使館大廈後，父親一如以往早上自己開車送我們上學，順路也送其他學生。

我的生活在搬進使館大廈後有了極大的轉變，沒有花園讓我嬉戲玩耍，我變得非常用功讀書。如同多數的香港學生一樣，我也有個家庭教師，陳小姐每天放學後來教我數學。所有學科中除了數學之外，其他科目幾乎是不可能得八十分以上，所以為提高我的平均分數，我必須要在三項數學科目考試拿滿分。

我中學第一年的校長Bobby Kotewall小姐，在學年成績揭曉後當天晚上打電話告訴母親，我得了全班四十名學生第一名的好消息，令母親聽後興奮的整晚睡不著覺。聖保羅男女中學素以學業高水準聞名，能得第一實非易事，我認為陳小姐的功勞很大。其中有一位老師在第二年問我：「以妳的家庭背景，我真不明白妳這麼用功做什麼！」這句話到現在還有人問我。

父親對我的表現非常欣慰，還特別在家中設謝師宴，請我的老師吃中飯。我的美術老師送了一幅很大的國畫給父母親，是他自己所作的桃花，色調與我們家淺藍色的飯廳十分協調。父母親非常欣賞這幅畫，直到母親去世前一直掛在飯廳。

搬到使館大廈後，我就開始學國畫，而且學得非常投入，暑假時每天早上都去上國畫課。我第一位老師是香港很有名的畫家鮑少游，住的離我們不遠，所以我常自己走過去上課。我也學過鋼琴和聲樂，但聲樂只學了一年，因為我發現自己音域不夠廣，雖然我還是很喜歡唱歌，但沒有繼續學下去。所有的課餘活動中，繪畫還是我的最愛。十三、四歲時，我整天埋頭苦讀，毫無興趣出去玩樂，開時就是畫畫。我臥房內另外有長畫檯與書桌完全分開，所以我的畫具紙筆永遠在我手邊，不必為做功課而移開我的畫具。在七〇年左右，父親找到一些我初學作畫的作品，還特別寄來多倫多給我。

搬到使館的頭幾年，我和哥哥常在課後或周末去南華體育場騎單車、放風箏，但令人洩氣的是我老是無法讓風箏飛起來，大概只有一次成功的飛起了風箏。夏天將盡時我們自己做捕蟲網，在住處對面利園部份夷平的山坡上，捉到很多大蜻蜓。有一年過中國新年，哥哥將炮竹放在玻璃瓶內燃放，像炸彈一般爆炸開。

住希慎道使館大廈期間，對面的利園山逐漸在我眼前消失，只見山坡一天天的變低，男女工人不斷的將砂石泥土，由山坡一擔一擔的挑下，倒在卡車運走。偶爾會聽到炸藥開山的爆炸聲，父親珍藏了許多在炸開的山石中所發現的天然水晶，他將幾塊大的水晶配上雕花木座，部份送人之後，其餘自己留下。

開闢利園山時還發生了在山坡挖到觀音像的趣事，為忌觸犯神明，無人敢移動這尊神像，令工程停頓，所以只好請和尚尼姑到工地燒香誦經，然後挑選黃道吉日，經他們做好各種法事準備工作之後，才很正式的將這尊觀音像移至新界的一座廟宇供奉，這樣利園開山工程才得以繼續。

開山期間還有一口古鐘出土，根據鐘上日期記載，此鐘是約在二百多年前嘉慶元年時，一戶盧姓農家為還神謝恩，將這刻有「風調雨順，國泰民安」的古鐘捐獻給當地廟宇。父親對這口數百斤重

的鎮山古鐘非常引以為榮，並特別訂製巨型的紫檀雕花木架懸掛此鐘，此後便成了我們客廳最主要的陳列品。

住進使館大廈後，我就可以看到父母親在宴客時如何招待朋友，宴會都在樓上舉行，臥房全在樓下。父母親請客時，都是酒樓廚子來我們家做中式酒席，酒樓將爐灶鍋盤等廚房器具，全搬來我們樓上的宴客用廚房〔平日做飯的廚房在樓下〕。做準備工夫及烹調。放學後我喜歡去廚房看看菜式，若菜單內有冬瓜盅的話，湯內的菜蔬都精雕成各種不同的魚、鳥和蝴蝶形狀，然後再去看母親的鮮花擺飾，決定明天要畫的題材。就寢之前我最愛躲在中國屏風後面，看著燭光下閃閃發光的銀燭台和清亮的水晶，杯觥交錯間聽大人的談笑。宴客時母親一定用最美的中國鈎花檯布和餐巾，中式宴會就排三圓檯每桌八人，西式宴會〔中國食物西式上菜〕就用二十四人的長檯。我們家請客只吃中餐，父親的猶太朋友，因為只能吃合猶太教律潔淨的食物，所以他們都在家中先吃過晚餐才來我們家參加晚宴。

在那幾年父母親請客時，我常見到國偉三叔和三嬸來我們家，國偉三叔是父親的堂弟，當時在恒生銀行任職，父親對他非常看重，認為他極有發展潛力，所以盡量利用機會，介紹他多結識自己的朋友。時至今日國偉三叔已是爵士，為香港社會的知名人士，不但擁有許多其他銜頭，亦是恒生銀行現任的董事長。

熟知父親的人都知道他的作風，他從不看電影，最令母親失望的是，他也不跳舞。若有任何公司的董事會需要與明星周旋的話，他決不加入。他從不賭錢，我們家平日不許打麻將，母親只有一年一次在她生日的時候，才可以和她的姐妹打麻將。父親熱愛他的工作，他唯一的休閒活動就是坐船出海享受大自然。

有一次父親一位生意朋友開的五月花舞廳開幕，邀請父親參加開幕酒會，父親對這類應酬從不參加，但樹源叔公一定要拉父親同去。去到見舞廳設在二樓，只有電扶梯可上，結果父親上了電扶梯到二樓，轉頭就搭電扶梯下樓出來，這樣就表示他已參加過了酒會[2]。

我們搬到使館大廈後，每年的家族聖誕團聚都在我們家舉行，雖只限近親，但人數也超過一百，

每個孩子和男女青少年都有禮物，同時也會預備幾份禮物給大人抽獎。我最有趣參與預備各種聖誕禮物，其中包括不少日本玩具。

一九五三年聖誕我們沒有在家請客，因為父母親應父親老友「泰國米王」馬祿臣的邀請，帶著我和弟弟一起，坐馬家由香港返回泰國的商船去曼谷，這是我初次坐船旅遊，那真是一個奇妙美好的旅程。我們有自己的私人艙房，並與丹麥船長及他的副手同檯用餐。看到海上的飛魚在我們船邊滑躍而過，令我雀躍不已。

在船上有一天清早，父親叫我們起來看船駛入曼谷方向的海灣，旭日初昇，兩岸水邊叢林繁密，只見曼谷廟宇的輪廓，出現在橙黃色天空的背景中，然後再見一個火紅的光球由廟宇後面冉冉升起，不禁驚嘆造物的神奇了。

在泰國我們住進東方酒店，在河邊的餐廳用餐時，餐桌上都置有蚊香驅蚊，日後旅館改建，便將餐廳由室外改為室內。馬家也數次招待我們去他們家和上酒店用餐。我覺得泰國的青年到十八歲時，便須服兵役，或出家做幾年和尚，是很明智的政策，因為不是每個青年都喜歡接受軍事訓練。

在泰國時，我們還被邀請去曼谷的美國大使館看「綜合大電影」，這是我們首次看到用三部最新的七十釐米放映機，同時在三個弧形銀幕放映電影。父母親並帶我們參觀了蘭花養殖園、稻田，和坐船遊覽參觀兩邊河岸泰族人的生活情形。

離開泰國之前，父親覺得大家都玩得如此愉快，便想順道再去新加坡玩幾天，但我不依。理由是一月份回去時，學校立刻就有考試，我須要回去讀書，父親只好接受我的理由，全體打道回府。

第七章

邁向種族和諧：香港鄉村俱樂部

父

親永遠無法忘記在一九二七年，他二十二歲由英國返港時，只因他是華人，而被拒加入香港會的恥辱，香港會在十九世紀末期之前稱為香港英國會。日後香港會反邀父親入會，但為父親所拒，我年紀稍長後很能體會父親當時的感受。

一九五〇年代有一天我放學回家時，被引見兩位訪客，他們是葛量洪總督及夫人。葛量洪夫人是位非常友善的美國人，她說我長得很像父親，他們告辭之前來我房間說再見時，夫人又覺得我像母親，然後她說：「聽我亂說些什麼？我想妳長得像爸爸也像媽媽。」他們走了之後，父親對我說：「在學校別提這件事，因為總督的身份不可以在中國人家做客的。」我心中一直有疑惑，在這塊我們以此為家的地方，畢竟我們還是屬於二等公民。

多元種族俱樂部

父

親與幾位有同樣理念的朋友，於戰後非常積極的籌劃在香港成立一個多元種族化的家庭社交俱樂部。直到六〇年代以前，香港的社交俱樂部都是以種族、國籍及宗教信仰來區分，如香港英國會即是香港會的前身，後來又有中國會、猶太會、葡萄牙人的西洋會、德國會及美國會，另外一些例外的團體僅為體育或特殊目的而設。

75

十五年來在父親及他的友人共同努力之下，才有多元種族俱樂部的組成，他們包括香港匯豐銀行的法律顧問瓊斯(J. R. Jones)、怡和洋行大班藍道(D. F. Landale)。我小時候就見過藍道，他是父親的老朋友，曾請我們去過他在匯豐銀行大廈頂樓的住處，在一九四○年代末時，藍道曾向香港會及石澳鄉村俱樂部請求以二百元會費讓華人加入成為會員，但未得批准[1]。藍道在一九五六年退休後，由巴頓(Hugh D. M. Barton)接任，繼續共同努力促成此多元種族俱樂部。

一九四七年時父親和瓊斯將此會的初步籌劃書交給布政司麥道軻(D. M. MacDougall)，由於麥道軻頗能接受多元種族俱樂部的設會宗旨，故與政府交涉相當順利，並選中交通便利的南朗山作為俱樂部會址。祖父去世時曾大力支持父親的匯豐銀行總經理Sir Arthur Morse，加上父親和其他數位人士與麥道軻舉行非正式會議，列出一百五十萬元的建會預算。瓊斯並發出信函給各國領事館代表、銀行主席及國際人士闡釋此俱樂部的宗旨和初步方案的大綱。

興建俱樂部計劃在此非正式小組工作之下順利進行，一九四八年六月於香港匯豐銀行會議室開會，研討政府所提以年租七千二百元，將七公畝半的臨海地區，撥租給俱樂部，為期二十一年的提案。

一九四五年舉行大會，一部份非正式小組的委員不在香港，或在度假中，故委員的組成有所變更。此次會議將原名國際俱樂部，改為香港鄉村俱樂部。有趣的是，會議中有五十六位不同國籍社團代表，其中僅有父親和羅文惠兩位為華人代表，並由他們二人代表華人入會的意願，會議中又成立三個附屬委員會；法律、財務及建築委員會。財務委員會透過層面較廣的籌募委員會，得到各公司行號及私人認捐，籌募到兩百萬元的建會經費。

一九四九年共產黨在中國成立中華人民共和國之後，香港人普遍覺得前途未卜，但俱樂部與政府之間仍持續協商。直到一九五○年韓戰爆發，聯合國對香港載貨禁運，俱樂部委員決定將所有進展工作全部暫停。

一九五一年五月，俱樂部委員會去函香港政府，請求政府對俱樂部預定土地仍予保留，以待時機成熟。此時麥道軻已非布政司，政府覆信中告知俱樂部委員會，政府不可能無限期保留預定土地，若

有其他單位同時申請該地，政府將公開拍賣。針對此意外的通牒書，父親與瓊斯、羅文惠及 G. L. Wilson 立刻組團，與布政司 R. J. Nicoll 會談，會後同意將預定土地保留至一九五二年一月，其後每半年再由瓊斯向政府口頭報告俱樂部動向，同時所有工作暫停。

到一九五○年代末期，鄉村俱樂部的計劃仍無改變，一九五八年五月，署理布政司 E. B. Teesdale 再度警告俱樂部之預定土地將不再無限期保留，必須由俱樂部的贊助人提交建會具體方案，但俱樂部贊助會員的反應並不熱衷，令建會計劃瀕臨流產邊緣。

一九五九年一月政府再次降下最後通牒，限在四月一日前遞交具體方案，否則俱樂部將喪失會址預定地。於是父親及瓊斯便請教羅兵咸律師行的會計師 Sidney Gordon，和羅文錦律師樓的律師簡悅強，商討與建俱樂部之可行性。會議中一致同意應繼續促成建立此俱樂部，尤其來自中國富有的難民增加後，確有必要成立俱樂部供會員使用。瓊斯立刻召集以前臨時小組的委員，成立新的十人委員會，由於瓊斯新任政府薪俸調整委員會委員職務繁忙，故由巴頓出任召集人，三叔為秘書。

一九五九年五月鄉村俱樂部成立聯合組織委員會，包括五位華人、三位英國人、兩位美國人，及葡萄牙、荷蘭、法國、北歐、瑞士及義大利代表團各一人。並由巴頓、瓊斯及父親組成代表團觀見香港總督，請求支持。結果政府同意將南朗山五又四分之一英畝土地，以年租十元一畝，租給鄉村俱樂部，但須保證地上建築物的費用為一百萬元。土地問題解決後，委員會以發行債券方式籌募所需資金，每一債券五千元，至一九六○年二月時，基金已達目標。年底俱樂部正式組成公司，共售出四百二十張無息債券，債券持有人即為俱樂部首批基本會員。此後俱樂部一切興建工作，在利家友人甘洺工程師的監督下順利進行。

父親為香港成立多元種族俱樂部的夢想，終於在一九六二年實現，當時雖然建築工程尚未完全竣工，但因認為牛年開張較來年虎年為吉，所以挑選一月二十九日正式開幕。鄉村俱樂部由首席按察司何瑾爵士(Sir Michael Hogan)親臨開幕，致辭中說到：

這個俱樂部使得各種不同國籍社團人士，在他們習慣的俱樂部氣氛下，輕鬆愉快的聚集在舒

邁向種族和諧

適的環境⋯⋯這也是各國籍、社團人士相聚交換意見、發表理念、友善辯論的場所⋯⋯我深信鄉村俱樂部必能促進香港未來社會更為鞏固安定。[2]

俱樂部工程於二月完工，正式開放給會員使用。九月份時首批組織委員之一 Jerry O'Donnell，提出舉辦由全球八個城市提供的二十款最新潮流的服裝表演，並邀請母親和巴頓夫人組織婦女委員會，推展服裝表演，於是便成為鄉村俱樂部的首屆娛樂委員會[3]。

父

親堅信所有種族應和平共處，鄉村俱樂部特殊之處即是它的多元文化種族的會員結構，亦是此俱樂部創會的主要宗旨，入會章程中規定，普通會員及初級會員均按國籍比例分配；美籍百分之十、英籍百分之二十、華籍半數、其他國籍百分之二十，因當時仍存有反日情結，所以在最後一組又須再訂配額，以維持俱樂部真正多元種族之特性[4]。會長一年一任，首任會長為巴頓，一九六三年至一九六四年第二任會長由父親擔任。

一九六五年時，瓊斯、巴頓和父親被提名為永遠名譽會員，父親去世後，由母親繼承父親的會員資格。在致贈永遠名譽會員資格給瓊斯時，當時的會長利國偉三叔說：

瓊斯博士對鄉村俱樂部的貢獻是無法衡量的，若沒有他專注投入的熱心努力，今天我們不可能有這個國際化的俱樂部。

瓊斯致答辭時提到父親是：

由最初期的建築委員會開始我們即密切合作，銘澤兄努力將俱樂部奠下健全的基礎，邁向成功，成為今日大家所見的事實。(5)

俱樂部開幕後成為香港家庭社交生活的一大部份，這個俱樂部為父親帶來許多喜悅和榮耀。雖然在創辦初期的十五年因發展過速，俱樂部財務一直虧損。我們常在俱樂部餐廳享用美味的中、西式的午餐和晚餐，一家人都喜歡這個俱樂部樸實無華、賓至如歸的氣氛，和許多其他香港居民一樣，它成了我們的第二個家。

有一年聖誕節我們回香港時，長子偉雄才三歲，他覺得非常奇怪為什麼多倫多和香港鄉村俱樂部都有聖誕老人，而香港的聖誕老人卻是女人嗓子！又一年學校放春假我們帶孩子回香港，正巧是復活節，他們永遠不會忘記俱樂部舉辦的復活節慶祝活動中的魔術表演和尋找復活蛋。

七〇年代俱樂部開始接受公司企業會員，業務開始轉虧為盈，收入增加後，俱樂部得以重新裝修美化。雖然此時香港亦有其他新俱樂部成立，但鄉村俱樂部所具備的純樸友善及多元國籍的特質，加上各種康樂設施、游泳池、兒童遊樂場及出色的兒童活動、成人社交節目，再加上可供家庭聚餐及正式宴會的餐廳等優良條件，令此俱樂部成為有條件人士熱衷加入的俱樂部。後來俱樂部經由專業人士管理，業務更加興盛。到一九八〇年代時，公司行號須要輪候繳交百萬元的會費加入成為會員，令父親感到非常欣慰。

俱樂部晨泳

大家都知道父親每天清早五點左右便去俱樂部晨泳，俱樂部一早就特別開放，讓他一人獨自晨泳。我們回港探親時，父親晨泳完畢一定趕回來和我們一起用早餐，雖然在這樣的行程下，他還是可以最早到辦公室。

有一天父親在去晨泳途中，被警察攔截做例行檢查，要父親出示每位香港居民都應有的身份證，

但父親從未想到要申請過身份證，多數的香港人都認識父親。我想父親若不是自己開著一部德國福士的高而富小車，而是坐有司機駕駛的豪華車，警察大概不會攔他。不過到了辦公室，父親告訴秘書李姑娘這件事後，要李姑娘立刻為他申請身份證，政府還特別開例不需父親本人親自去申請。

父親在晨泳途中，每天還是順路接幾個住在附近村內，須自己走路上學的貧苦學童，他認得好幾個孩子和他們的父母。有一天早上，一個父親經常送上學的孩子不在，但孩子的爸爸在守候父親，請求父親幫助他病重的妻子。父親就立刻送他們去醫院，並安排孩子的母親受到妥善的照顧。牛奶公司的主席及大股東是父親好友周錫年爵士，香港置地的主席也是父親好友渣甸集團首腦John Keswick。亨利知道香港置地公司想要父親幫忙收購牛奶公司。牛奶公司的主席晨泳的機會，央求父親幫忙。父親在池中游泳，他就在池邊跑前跑後的試圖說服父親出面幫忙。總算亨利的努力能有回報，收購任務圓滿達成。香港置地公司及牛奶公司在一九七二年十二月合併[6]。此後大家都常笑亨利有個好澤叔，幫他收購了牛奶公司[7]。

一九七二年香港置地的主席也是父親好友渣甸集團首腦John Keswick的姪子亨利賈士域(Henry Keswick)。亨利很難與父親約時間在辦公室見面，便利用父親在俱樂部

第八章

利氏家族企業

戰後重整家族事業困難重重、進展緩慢，因家中許多地契證件在戰爭中遺失。父親和他戰後第一個秘書江蕙蘭〔後來和父親堂弟結婚，成為我們的嘉驥四嬸〕，常一起去政府田土註冊處找文件正本，希慎置業有限公司名下，另一部份又在代表祖父後裔的利綽餘堂公司名下[1]。

八叔公〔祖父堂弟〕在田土註冊處上班，幫了不少忙。最麻煩的是祖父購買地產時，部份置在祖母及利希慎置業有限公司名下，另一部份又在代表祖父後裔的利綽餘堂公司名下[2]。

因戰爭的破壞，利家許多物業亟待修葺，有些古老的舊樓甚至沒有抽水馬桶衛生設備。戰後政府限制房東不得將屋租提高超過戰前的水準，有些業主所收租金僅能勉強支付稅金，令許多業主無力修葺物業，我們有些舊樓的單位僅收月租港幣二十元。而且在日本佔領香港時期，有些租客離開香港逃至中國之後，空置單位被他人強佔，當時流行多次租用及多層分租，所以合法與非法租客混淆不清難以分辨[2]。

在屋租限制下的唯一受惠者是，交付戰前租金而以現時租價租給新三房客的二房東，及在物價平均上漲百分之十至十二後，仍享受舊樓低租做生意的店家。

戰前建造的舊樓問題直到一九五〇年代中期才得以解決，一九五六年三月十九日，父親被選為香港業主聯會主席，因為利家擁有大批戰前舊樓，對這方面的困難甚為了解，可代表此類業主發表意見。為求對業主及所有租客公平起見，父親對政府請求准許業主加租[3]。

利家的家族公司利希慎置業有限公司，在一九四六年時搬至一幢叫做亞歷山大行的舊樓，由我們稱

為徐叔的徐鏡波管理。我特別記得這幢舊樓的地板總是吱嘎作響。所有利氏兄弟在世時，都在同一地方一起工作。有時放學後我去寫字樓等父親一起回家時，最喜歡玩打字機。漢釗哥印像最深的是，三叔的寫字間窗口有冷氣機，在戰後這是非常稀有先進的。

當年利家有兩家租務公司；一家是利綽餘堂，專收祖母名下產業的租金，另一家是利東，負責為利希慎置業有限公司收租[4]。定昌堂弟是律師，由一九八〇年代初開始成為家族企業的董事及總經理，他告訴我，戰後多年家族公司業務及決策均以舊式的口說或字據為憑，所有憑據早已不復存在。他後來費了很多心血去搜尋公司的舊文件、地契、公司會議紀錄或物業買賣合約，但成效不大[5]。

七〇年代初時，利氏兄弟決定改變傳統經營家族事業的保守風格[6]。經好友Hon. J.D. Clague介紹父親與一位興建九龍重慶大廈的著名建築商陳德泰認識。陳德泰建議由利希慎置業有限公司提供建地，投資者提供所需資金，以此投資合作的關係，在銅鑼灣地區建造希慎道一號及禮頓中心兩幢新廈，陳德泰本人亦作小額投資[7]。一九七〇年與利建設有限公司正式成立。

在此計劃發展之前，由於利、林兩家為世交，所以所有利家名下的戰前舊樓全為林家的聯益建築公司建造，至七〇年代初期開始家族企業才將工程對外招標。公司既有新的作風，就須加入新血，才能有企業化的經營。利氏兄弟認為最適合的人選就是二叔長子，利家的第一個孫子漢釗，一九七六年時他正在美國無線電公司（RCA）工作，四叔便要他返港為家族公司效勞。當時漢釗堂哥四十多歲，已有家室，他同意返港工作後，妻子玉蟬則留在美國照顧孩子，以免他們在美國的教育中斷。

利舞台

利舞台在一九四六年重新營業，袁耀鴻再度出任民樂公司總經理，經理為董梓君。戰後吳慶塘仍在新加坡華僑聯合銀行工作，即將調去上海分行，但父親說服吳慶塘，認為他為利家工作更有前途，吳便返回香港成為利舞台戲院的經理。利舞台重新裝璜後，有最好的銀幕和燈光設備，還有

舒適的坐椅⑻。

電視尚未問世之前，利家孩子最大的享受就是星期天早上去利舞台欣賞卡通片和看三傻電影。去戲院時一定坐最好的B號包廂保留座位，我們很少去其他的戲院看戲，因為利舞台放映的都是最好的首輪片子，有時我也和其他家人去利舞台看美國出品的電影，但那時英文程度不夠，除了泰山和西部牛仔電影之外，其他都看不太懂。當時粵語片漸次流行，但都是些戰爭悲情片，我覺得看戲是一種娛樂，不喜歡看哭哭啼啼的悲劇，所以就不再看粵語片。那時我注意到父親從不看電影，因他對工作更有興趣。

一九四八年倫敦電影公司要求民樂公司成為中國的代理，於是民樂公司總經理袁耀鴻和利舞台經理吳慶塘，帶著倫敦電影公司的《月宮寶盒》、《鵑血忠魂》、《四羽毛》及《伏象神童》四部極受歡迎的大製作，去上海試探市場行情。但結果非常令人失望，上海的戲院根本不知道這些電影在世界各地有多賣座，二人甚至連盤纏都未賺到⑼。可是他們在上海遇到名製片人夏雲瑚和導演蔡楚生，他們很想和利家建立商業關係，後來將他們製作導演的《一江春水向東流》，和《八千里路雲和月》送到利舞台放映，這些描述戰時國人生活及批評國民政府的悲劇片，在香港非常賣座。雖然這兩部電影的製作人及導演都親共，但在文化大革命中，二人都遇害。⑽

在袁耀鴻與吳慶塘離開上海不久之後，該地就被共產黨解放。

五〇年代中至六〇年代中，最出名的仙鳳鳴粵劇團經常在利舞台演出，粵劇當時極受市民喜愛及政府的推動。但後來中國大戲在利舞台的演出逐漸減少之後，戲院便成為來自世界各國藝術團體的表演場地。我最喜歡的是Xavier Cougat 和 Abby Lane的拉丁美洲舞團，經常也有魔術表演及舉辦國際選美比賽。利園酒店於七〇年代初期落成之後，經常有選美活動，母親的姐妹最喜歡去利園酒店看各方佳麗。八〇年末時，四叔與我有一天經過利舞台，他告訴我那年的國際華裔小姐來自安大略省的士嘉堡市，我告訴他那次的安省華裔小姐選美，是由士嘉堡市的華商會主辦，而我正是評審委員之一。

父親安排外祖父黃茂霖八十多歲時仍在民樂公司做會計，只為讓他保持忙碌有事可做，外祖父在

辦公室時大家都非常照顧他，近九十歲時頭腦仍非常清楚，直到九十二歲辭世[11]。

發展地產

缺

乏平坦土地，一直是香港建築發展業長久以來不斷面對的難題，我們利家亦是如此。若我們計劃在利園山的山地建造更多的物業，不但須先夷平山地，還須先經政府批准，才能將開闢山地的砂石泥土棄置於指定地點。第二次世界大戰之前，利園山夷平一小部份之後，將砂石運至北角填海，然後再從政府手中買回所填的新生地，建了兩間工廠，一間是鐵釘廠，一間是國光油漆廠[13]。鐵釘廠後來賣給另一位中國製造商，國光油漆廠在一九四八年為太古收購[12]，成立國光漆廠[13]。太古公司以公司股份支付利家，做為收購漆廠的交換條件，令利氏家族在日後成為太古的主要股東之一，並與太古集團建立良好的合作關係。四叔曾任太古工業的董事，三叔亦成為太古旗下國泰航空企業的董事[14]。

戰後利希慎置業有限公司的首次地產發展，仍是開闢利園山的山地，香港政府准許將開山砂石運至柴灣及香港仔。將利園山夷為平地之後，即須開拓馬路，便將主要道路以祖父名，稱為希慎道，其他道路則以廣東鄉下祖祠及鄰近鄉村為中心的四邑為名，分別是新寧道、新會道、開平道及恩平道。另外有白沙道，以明代著名學者陳白沙為名，他是祖居所在的新會人，及啟超道，是以世紀初的新會著名學者梁啟超為名，當然還有利園山道。這些道路日後都交由政府使用。

記得在五〇年代時，我們剛由利行搬至希慎道上的使館大廈，有一天早上父親開車送我上學的途中，由開平道轉向希慎道上時，遇到一個男子慢吞吞的走過馬路，父親是個很沒有耐性的人，便對他說：「走快點啦！」那男子說：「我愛走多久就走多久，又不是你的路！」父親回答：「正是我的路！」

為了籌措新建物業的資金，家族出售了部份十分殘舊的樓宇和排屋。戰後由家族企業興建的第一

座公寓大廈，是位於希慎道南面的新寧樓，新寧樓是香港第一幢單位住戶為獨立業主的公寓大廈，佔了一幢單位住戶為獨立業主的公寓大廈〔15〕。建築物為馬蹄形，短的一面朝希慎道。初期香港人尚未有購置公寓的觀念，部份面向希慎道的單位便賣給由利希慎置業有限公司及上海商業銀行合股的光利公司，用來經營有五十二間房間的小型旅館，即新寧招待所。父親是光利公司的主席，三叔、徐鏡波、朱汝堂及上海商業銀行的王昌林分別擔任董事〔16〕。

新寧招待所於一九四九年開幕，由吳慶塘任經理，招待所開幕時正逢共產黨接掌中國政權，招待所業務繁忙。許多上海的工商界要人逃至香港之後，便暫住新寧招待所〔17〕，所以招待所業務繁忙。招待所的香檳廳更成了新寧的招牌，是五○年代香港人氣最旺的地方。每星期三晚上，客人可以隨著麗的呼聲廣播電台〔18〕的Three Bubbles音樂輕歌曼舞，成了香港夜生活的著名場所。香檳廳的客人必須服裝整齊，男士須打領帶，我記得五○年代時，報章提過一件香檳廳拒絕讓一位牧師入場的趣事，因為他穿著的牧師裝只有領圈沒打領帶。後來亦有海蒂樂瑪（Hedy Lamarr）、奇勒基寶（Clark Gable）、愛娃嘉娜（Ava Gardner）、威廉荷頓（William Holden）和烈打希和芙（Rita Hayworth）等國際明星光顧過香檳廳。對遊客來說，若未去香檳廳等於沒到過香港〔19〕。

利家的下一個工程即是在希慎道上的使館大廈，這是家族擁有的第一幢大廈，完工之後我們家、五叔家和三祖母，便相繼搬入使館大廈。位於希慎道和恩平道交叉口的嘉蘭大廈竣工後，住在利行的親人也陸續住進嘉蘭大廈。

利行就又像祖父在世時一樣，全部出租給外人。利氏家族當時有個不成文的規定，就是祖父的妻、妾、子女可在自家的產業免費選擇自己喜歡的住處，也因著這個原因家人可就近相聚一處，這個傳統到我們第三代就沒有再繼續下去。

利園山夷平之後，利家在一九五四年又蓋了嘉蘭大廈和崇明大廈，這兩座新樓，離我們住的使館大廈僅十數步之隔，我們周末若不坐船出海，父親就會走到這兩座新廈的頂層，查看施工情形。

五○年代時我最喜歡去的地方，就是利舞台、新寧招待所的香檳廳，和戰後利家擁有的士巴汽水廠。我們去汽水廠時，不但可以很起勁的看汽水製造裝瓶過程，還可以盡情的喝各種飲料。那時有

一種葡萄飲料銷路最好[20]，但我最喜歡的是櫻桃口味的紅色飲品，後來我才知道這種飲料只是糖水加色素。

一九五三年七叔由波士頓大學畢業回香港，便和三叔買下士巴飲料有限公司的大部股權，然後成立聯合汽水廠有限公司，此後希慎置業有限公司在士巴飲料僅有名義上的乾股。一九五五年聯合汽水廠得到玉泉汽水的連鎖代理權，一年後又得到七喜及另一家日本啤酒的代理，家族的孩子仍繼續受歡迎去飲料廠，還可自己挑選喜歡的汽水送到家中。七叔時常自己坐在送貨車上跟著送貨，他的美國作風令本地人看得頗不順眼[21]。我還記得七叔公司的貨車，在聖保羅男女學校上課中間休息時間，免費送七喜汽水給學生喝，這真是個很好的市場推銷方法。七叔後來在飲料界非常成功，他將7-Up命名為七喜之後，所有中國的喜慶宴會為討吉利，都喜歡用七喜。

利園酒店

利園山在五〇年代末期完全夷為平地，此時有位蜂農是家中鄉下友人，在利園山養蜂採蜜，他擔心一旦土地為建築物佔據時，他將無處可養殖蜜蜂，所以求助於利氏兄弟，他們便准許他在祖父堂弟利樹源名下位於沙田的一塊土地上繼續養蜂[22]。

第一期工程即是後來的利園酒店，於一九六四年開工，原本計劃建造住宅及出租辦公室大廈，一至六樓租給香港政府的醫療和教育部門，街面租給店家營業。後來因為中國文化大革命及香港一九六七年的暴動，住宅部份完全停工。直到一九六〇年代末期，由於附近隧道完成，加上當時香港旅館房間短缺，家族才決定繼續建造旅館。擁有九百間房間的旅館全部工程終於在一九七一年年底完竣[23]。

利園酒店是私人公司，除了利希慎置業有限公司為主要股東之外，其他股份屬於太古國泰企業、匯豐銀行、香港置地、大昌貿易集團和一家丹麥公司。又因利氏家族與太古集團的關係密切，便邀請太古主席H.J.C.Browne擔任利園酒店的第一任主席[24]，其後即為三叔任酒店主席，在三叔猝然逝

世後，就由父親接任主席遺缺。父親由上任開始即積極參與酒店各項業務，他並透過私人關係，由中國天津特別訂製酒店前廳的地毯，同時因為父親與日本社團的關係，日本旅遊團來香港時多半在利園酒店住宿。

當時利園酒店是香港少數幾家具有國際水準的酒店，初期與洲際酒店[25]企業的連鎖旅館合作。多年來利園酒店以在銅鑼灣便利的地點，成為亞洲旅客最喜歡住的酒店。酒店落成之後，香港地圖又再一次的呈現「利園」二字。

後來母親年事漸高，覺得在家宴客太過傷神，所以自從利園酒店開幕後，父母親便只在利園舉行宴會請客。利園酒店內有幾家不同的餐廳，但父母親最喜歡的是中餐部的彩虹廳，他們請客時多半用私人房〔有可坐二十四人的圓桌〕，或是包下整個餐廳。父母親對利園酒店餐廳的水準十分驕傲，父親常說利園的北京烤鴨水準全港第一，甚至比北京本地的烤鴨還要好吃。父親喜歡對客人介紹來自中國的特別菜，他們在彩虹廳招待過來自世界各地的朋友。

利園酒店完工後，所有利園山的土地皆已開發。希慎道旁所種的洋紫荊，就是現在香港特別行政區的代表花，用廣東四邑為名的街道兩旁，則種植一種開黃花的樹木。父親曾非常自豪的指給我看這些花木，因為這些樹不僅是在我們冬天回香港時才開花，而且也是父親特別安排由華南移植來香港的。

父親和漢釗

漢釗哥返回香港時，家族公司辦公地點正遷移至新近完工的希慎道一號，他開始由公司基層學習企業經營，和商業大廈的租務管理。雖然三叔預備將漢釗哥安置在二十二樓工作，可同時監管同一層樓工作的員工，但父親將漢釗哥的寫字間設在二十一樓的邊間，與其他叔叔一起工作，由他的寫字間可俯視禮頓中心的工程進展，以便實際監督[26]。父親又將他自己在家族建築所負責的監視產業工程進度的任務，都交付給漢釗哥。

大家都知道父親是個很沒有耐性的人，叔侄二人每天利用一起喝咖啡的時間，由漢釗哥利用一起喝咖啡的時間，由漢釗哥做

「不超過十五分鐘」的報告。父親必須知道不同工程的進度，若漢釗哥有任何困難的話，父親就利用他各種不同的關係，多半可在半個鐘頭之內為他解決(27)。漢釗哥返港後，父親建議他加入鄉村俱樂部，雖然等候入會名單很長，但因父親的創會會員身份，他姪兒的加入不成問題。漢釗哥非常感激父親當年介紹他認識許多父親的朋友，像葉謀遵和姚剛等人(28)，日後對他事業助益極大。

父親和漢釗哥二人常在星期日坐船出海，母親七〇年代末時對出海已無甚興趣，所以很少同行。但若我們當中有人在香港的話，她還是喜歡一同出海。父親此時已不喜歡太晚在外逗留，所以下午四點以前一定回到皇后碼頭。父親一心要培植漢釗哥成為未來利氏家族眾多企業的領導人。

〔花旗銀行〕商量合作發展此地的可能性，但未有任何結果。此時這塊地的四周都已大廈林立，唯獨一九七八年，利希慎置業有限公司收到一項政府非強制命令的指令；在利氏家族名下位於軒尼詩道上的空地應予使用。利家兄弟從未急於使用這塊土地的原因，其實只是因為大家都忙，實在沒有時間處理這件事。漢釗哥回港後發展這塊空地即成為他的責任，並負責監管與利建設有限公司名下，在怡和街上興利中心各種工程進展。此發展計劃仍為利希慎置業有限公司與其他投資人合作興建。這塊土地空置，香港市民都在懷疑利氏兄弟不使用這高價空地的原因，其實只是因為大家都忙，實在沒有時間處理這件事。一九七六年，三叔曾和萬國寶通銀行

當興利中心破土之後，漢釗哥每天必赴工地查看，甚至在星期日出海野餐回來都要去視察，有時教授和負責地基的包工非常困擾，馬奇是香港大學退休的工程教授。父親對地基工程進度的拖延非常不耐，每位工作人員包括漢釗哥在內，都被父親催促得暈頭轉向，所以漢釗哥對父親的例行周日晨間咖啡會報完畢後，就會打電話給馬奇教授查問進度。日後他笑著對我說：「地基工程挖不到底層就是挖不到，怎樣向人追逼也快不了啊！」

有一天，馬奇教授決定和甘洺工程公司的結構工程師Stanley Weber，一起去地基底層查看狀況，他們勘查之後終於點頭認可大廈地基工程，令大家都鬆了口氣。漢釗哥說：「馬奇教授說可

以，那就行了！」

利氏兄弟對設計圖的頂樓和底層有不同意見。四叔原本要將底層建為大戲和國樂演出場所，但大家認為不合經濟效益，便將藍圖交給漢釗哥重新策劃，以滿足各兄弟的要求。他決定將戲院預定的空間改為停車場，原先地下停車場位置改為零售業出攤位。又經過多次討論之後，終於同意將頂樓兩層保留，專租給私人俱樂部，後來由香港日本人俱樂部租下。在執行家族事業時，利氏兄弟常有不同意見，但問題一定在家族內部解決，對外則是同一陣線(30)。興利中心於一九八一年落成。

家族事業的下一步計劃是將新寧招待所和新寧樓重建為新寧中心。新寧招待所是個小型旅館，入口在希慎道上，後方則是有六十間公寓單位的大廈，每個公寓單位的業主皆是聯合地產的股東，他們對重建計劃書內容有不同意見及問題，結果須用投票方式表決，才能定案。漢釗哥表示這是利希慎置業有限公司創業七十四年以來〔祖父於一九二四年一月創辦此公司〕，唯一一次須以投票方式決定政策，原因是新寧樓有太多外間股東。新寧中心由貝聿銘負責工程設計，於一九八○年動工。

股票上市公司

由於禮頓中心、希慎道一號、興利中心、新寧中心和新寧樓的產業分別由不同的外界投資者，及利希慎置業有限公司持有，而組成不同股份持有的公司架構。為求合併統一起見，利氏兄弟便決定將七○年代成立的興利公司，在一九八一年改組為希慎興業有限公司(31)，在香港證券交易所市場公開上市，八月份有五億普通股發行，父親為公司主席，漢釗哥及四叔另組委員會研究細節。漢釗哥對父親的咖啡工作晨報，成了每天的例行公事(32)。

獲多利公司(Wardley Limited)是家族企業的往來銀行代表，建議希慎興業有限公司除了租務之外，應有更多其他地產發展買賣計劃，以吸引更多投資。此項建議是將利希慎置業有限公司名下，位於堅尼地道七十四至八十六號的祖宅大屋(33)、利行及四周花園佔地，轉至希慎興業有限公司名下並無現金可購買利希慎置業有限公司名下但希慎興業有限公司重新發展。並由仲量行對這片地產重新估價，

公司的這些產業，於是便做出以希慎興業有限公司接收這批土地的安排。希慎興業有限公司接收這批土地後，在一九八五年將此地發展為竹林苑豪華綜合大廈區，共有三百四十五個公寓單位。母親在父親去世後，和許多家族成員相繼搬入新廈。

希慎興業有限公司股票在一九八一年上市時，每股面值一元，但後來股市不振跌至三十九分。部份原因是公司股東之一陳德泰去世後，他的兒子決定拋售手上所有希慎興業的股票，令公司股值下跌不少。身為公司主席的父親和總經理漢釗哥，都深感責任的重大和憂慮，父親公開請求股東對公司繼續保持信心，勿輕易出售公司股票，並保證股值一定會再回升。時間證明父親的看法是正確的。

一九八○年代初，父親和漢釗哥坐亞特蘭大號遊艇出海，告訴他：「不要希望每個人都讚美你，若沒有人說你壞話，你已經做得不錯了。」漢釗哥對父親這些充滿智慧的訓勉，永遠牢記在心。父親在一九八三年逝世後，由四叔接任主席數年，然後由漢釗哥[34]繼任至今。

八○年代初時香港開始面臨經濟嚴重衰退，我記得回港時耳聞目睹是一片悲觀論調，除了我們家，父親仍是對香港前途充滿信心。這段時期正是中、英雙方為香港回歸中國問題作為期數年的談判期間。由八○年代中期開始，希慎興業有限公司不僅在香港，也在中國、新加坡及舊金山投資發展地產。至九○年代初，香港股票逐漸回升，市場開始復甦，但父親卻再也無法見證這一切了。

一九九四年時，希慎興業有限公司與恒生銀行合作發展嘉蘭中心，公司股票跳升至三十二元一股。在香港歷史最久的華人地產公司，利希慎置業有限公司控制下的希慎興業有限公司商譽極高，被評為東南亞十大地產公司之一。公司保守穩健的作風，及對高價位租客的吸引力，令希慎興業有限公司在地產界有「精品店」的美譽[35]，父親在世的話，對今天公司的成就應該非常驕傲。雖然希慎興業有限公司股值亦有下跌，但公司盈利仍保持穩定成長，遠景繼續看好。

香港股市在一九九七年底時，受亞洲金融風暴影響普遍受挫。

第九章

吾家有女初長成

父母親在一九五四年計劃由使館大廈搬至希慎道上，家族新造的崇明大廈頂層和樓下半層的樓面，於是我們在一年後遷入新居。

祖母的喪禮

一九五六年初祖母開始病重，同年初夏於醫院病逝，享年七十六歲。家人為她舉行了一個盛大的傳統佛教喪禮。因天氣炎熱，祖母棺木須放在冰上，停柩於大屋觀音池旁七七四十九日，並在觀音池旁的竹園搭起大竹棚，內設靈堂，右方坐男家眷，女眷則坐左方，子孫輩輪流換上黑袍或白袍守靈。每天放學後我就換上作為孫女兒穿的白袍，在棚內靈堂與家人一起坐在臨時搭建舖有草蓆的地板上，吃很簡單的素齋晚餐。

尾七將盡，家人請了成群的和尚尼姑來替祖母打齋誦經超渡，我想他們大概來自不同的宗派寺院，因他們穿著不同的袍子。出殯那天，儀式過程共數小時，喪禮過後全體家人返回大屋。出殯那天，當我正站在大廳凝視掛在後牆中央祖母的相片時，突然間我看到有隻蝴蝶飛進來停在祖母相片上，然後飛出陽台轉眼就不見了。以後，他的靈魂會化為飛鳥或蝴蝶顯靈，當我正站在大廳凝視掛在後牆中央祖母的相片時，突然間我看到有隻蝴蝶飛進來停在祖母相片上，然後飛出陽台轉眼就不見了。

出殯當晚全體家人一起吃晚飯，然後在陽台燒紙紮的房屋、僕人、金銀元寶，還有一部紙車給祖母

在陰間享用。其中最重要的是一座紙橋，沒有橋她就過不了對岸的世界。這些東西被熊熊烈火化為灰燼時我正看得入神，五姑丈簡悅慶走過來對我說：「我想阿嬤去了美國，妳看那紙車的駕駛盤是在左邊的哩！」

當晚我們家族一起在大屋吃飯，共有好幾桌親人，我記得母親和幾位姑姐那晚都穿素服，表示祖母入土後，家人進入另一階段的服孝期。

幾天以後，所有兒子在晚飯後都要回到大屋等祖母回靈，他們在大屋內外走了一大圈，讓祖母的靈魂知道兒子在迎接她。在花園時有人開玩笑說，千萬不可隨地解手，因為靈魂是無所不在的。父親此時出來說話，不許家族成員反對漢釗哥成婚，表示若有任何人反對的話，就要在香港為漢釗哥提供一份同樣好的工作機會，於是漢釗哥得以順利結婚，婚後在美國一住就是二十年。

記得祖母去世時漢釗哥正預備去美國結婚，但照中國習俗，子孫為祖母守孝期間不得辦喜事。漢釗哥的未婚妻黃玉嬋是華裔美國公民，他們結婚後漢釗哥才可在美國居留工作，而時間緊迫，他急須離港赴美向公司報到。

父親和我的英國教育

父

親在英國所受的教育和經驗令他終生受益，他要自己的子女能同樣受惠，所以一九五〇年代開始時，已將哥哥和姐姐送到英國求學，因我個性不同，父親將我留在家中。直到我十五歲時，才同意父親的決定去英國讀書。

一九五六年父母親在啟德機場送我上機。政府早在一九四〇年末即開始討論為啟德場建新跑道，但至五〇年代此計劃仍未定案。當時的啟德機場非常簡陋，僅有一道閘門供旅客出入[二]。

當年我和姐姐及另一友人李國寶[二]一起搭機去英國讀書。姐姐和李國寶是暑假結束再度返英，而我則是初次離家。

在飛機降落之前，我一直無法想像聞名於世倫敦大霧的景像，傍晚到達倫敦時，只見一片迷茫整個城市都在霧中，濃厚的黃煙霧令我透不過氣。父親的老朋友利安，坐著由緬甸司機阿永開的班特利豪華座車來接我們，我們三人在利叔夫婦家中住了幾天，他們家在倫敦市郊的蘇瑞市，庭園環境特非常優美。有一次在利叔的餐廳，我想嚐試菜單上叫做「雜碎」的一道菜，但餐廳侍應生不肯給我，他說這道菜不能賣給中國人，原來雜碎就是剩菜大雜燴的意思。

當時因姐姐在英國南部維德島沙克林的上谷女子中學(Upper Chine School)讀書，我在一九五六年至一九五八年之間，也在此校讀書。這是一間限制非常嚴格的私立女校，規模不大，全校學生僅二百人左右，從中學八年級到十三年級，師資極為優秀。程度好的學生可編入特別班，我的數學課班制最小，全班僅有我和另外一位泰國來的學生。

學校沿上谷河而建，其實這條河只是條小溪，校園環境優美，有十位全職園丁維修，夏季對外開放。春暖花開時溪邊至校園內開滿了水仙花，暑期班時校園內可見各種不同的玫瑰，玫瑰花一直可開至秋天。風和日麗時我們還可在戶外上課，冬天則是灰暗濕冷很不好過。

我在上谷女校時由九年班跳升至十一班。因為我原本計劃入牛津讀大學，所以必須一次考完六項普通初級的必修科，我第一年就修六科初級科目和高級中文，第二年修的科目更多，還得全班第一名，父母親對我的成績表現非常欣慰，但我自己卻一點也不快樂。

我並非不喜歡這間學校，而是對英國公校制度覺得厭煩。因我本身是個非常能自律，而且在藝術方面需要有所發揮的人，這樣的教育制度對我完全不適合。我最不喜歡別人命令我何時、何日、做何事，我一定要有自己的時間和空間，現在六至八個女孩住同一房間，根本不可能有任何隱私。在家時，我從不需要父母親催促我上床，現在要按時熄燈就寢。總之吃飯、睡覺、寫家信、洗澡沖涼都要規定時間〔學校規定周日可洗三次，周末隨意，所以我一周洗五次，不像在家可天天洗〕，甚至幾乎到了連呼吸時間都有規定的地步，因為不論氣溫多低，我們都須出外活動，下午又一定要運動，我對體育最沒有興趣，所以下午就和幾個也不喜歡運動的中東國家的女孩一起散步。

由於校舍沒有暖氣設備，我總是覺得飢寒交迫，因為宿舍規定不准關窗睡覺，天冷時雪花都會飄

進屋內，睡覺時我總是穿幾層厚厚的衣服，再蓋九張毛毯，加上腳下還要有個暖水壺。父親為了要我每天有足夠的新鮮水果可吃，特別安排我下課時去廚房取兩個蘋果。他也知道我經常覺得吃不飽，還要吉百利（Cadbury）公司每學期送許多巧克力餅乾給我，但學校只准學生在星期六下午和星期日才能吃校外食物，這是我一生中最胖的時期，而且手腳長滿了凍瘡。

我很不贊成學校只收女生，覺得女校的環境非常不自然，很多無聊的事在男、女同校的環境就不會發生。所以無論我功課再好，我多喜歡學校的老師，我還是覺得不屬於這種環境。

母親在一九五七年春天來英國看我們，她先去英國諾定咸看我的哥哥。她第一次發現哥哥精神有些不正常，但在學校似乎沒有人注意到，母親要他去看心理醫生，從此我父母親的生活就不再也不同以往。

我對哥哥的病情一直不甚了解，因為他對英國的公校教育制度極有信心。事。我在上谷女校第二年時，知道哥哥住在倫敦郊區醫院就醫，那年聖誕節，我在學校的家政課做了生平唯一的聖誕蛋糕後，和一位住在英國的堂姑姐，帶著蛋糕去醫院看哥哥。見到哥哥時，覺得我們孩提時兄妹的親近在漸漸的消失，他的病症令他對家人有排斥感，病情時好時壞，有幾年還不錯。多年以後我才知道哥哥有先天性的精神分裂症，存在於百分之一的兒童中，潛伏至十幾二十歲時發作。

在上谷女校的第二年，我寫信回家稟告父母親，我年底即回香港聖保羅男女中學讀中學最後一年，在信中我沒有給父母親任何理由，因為我不要他們改變我的決定，當年我是個非常任性的孩子。

父親非常失望，因為他對英國的公校教育制度極有信心。任何外人看來我的行為是一種失敗的表現，但我用成績來表現我的決心，我回港第二年又得全班第一，不但修足許多普通級的學分，而且還以高分通過中級數學測試。

一九五八年夏天我回到香港的初期，父親對我自做主張離開英國仍舊非常不悅，所以不大理睬我，我想他也知道我不會依照他的計劃去英國讀大學。在聖保羅男女中學最後一年時，我的人生方

麥基爾大學，結婚成家

一九五九年八月母親帶我來到加拿大，一如以往由父親安排旅程，我們先到西岸的洛磯山脈。母親的表姐林美娥和她丈夫伍英才，邀請我們去渥太華他們家住幾天，但因我們想先去看尼亞加拉大瀑布，所以伍英才和他兒子衛權便來多倫多機場接機，在多倫多停留期間，由他們開車帶我們

向有所轉變，我決定不照英國上谷中學老師為我安排的計劃進大學讀數學〔母親一直認為以我優異的成績應該讀法律，倒是父親從未表示過意見〕，我要改讀文科歷史。由於我從理科轉文科，加上學制的改變，我必須在一年之內讀完兩年的課程，才能參加大學入學考試。於是我向舊同學借筆記，在一年之內追上兩年的進度，但因時間緊迫，我的成績並不如以前理想。

一九五八年姐姐進牛津大學讀醫，此時六叔剛由美國普林斯頓大學得博士學位回港，他建議我既然不願回英國讀書，不如申請美國大學，但父親反對，他堅持他的孩子決不受美國教育，我從不知父親反美的原因。於是我就申請了兩間加拿大的大學，一間是滿地可的麥基爾大學，另一間是多倫多大學，然後父親為我決定去麥基爾大學就讀。

回到香港後我就專心讀書，對香港周遭所發生的事全然不知，課後除了坐船出海，就在屋頂花園讀書。父親在我們離家出外讀書後，身邊只有志剛弟一個孩子，尤其沒有我在一旁招兵買馬邀朋友上船，父親也沒有興趣和太多人出海野餐，就換了一艘比富都號小一些的亞特蘭大號遊艇。何寧是我們家最後一位看管遊艇的船工。為我們工作超過二十年。為調劑讀書緊張的情緒，我又開始畫水彩畫，並專畫臉孔。

在回港的同一年，我要求父母親不要再叫我May，而用我正式在學校的Vivienne。母親說：

「現在要我們改口太晚了，反正妳到了加拿大也沒有人知道我們叫妳May，人家只知妳是Vivienne。」

在成長過程中，我為自己做了許多決定。

去看尼亞加拉瀑布，然後再一起去渥太華幾天。母親和我再由渥太華飛到滿地可，待我在麥基爾大學宿舍安頓好之後，母親就去紐約轉英國看哥哥和姐姐，再回香港。

我進入麥基爾大學讀二年級，此時衛權也正在同校讀醫科最後一年。在麥基爾讀書的幾年極為愉快，但因我忙於和衛權交往，學校成績並不很理想，但那時讀書成績不是我最在乎的事。母親對這件事頗為不悅，因為她對我的將來另有安排，父親倒不反對我和衛權戀愛，因為他欣賞有才華的人。

一九六一年，衛權寫信去香港正式向我父親提親，但父親認為我仍在大學讀書，一切尚言之過早。同年底我就告訴父母親，我二十一歲大學畢業後預備結婚的計劃。父母親知道我自小雖然個性剛強，但很有理性。父親頗能接受衛權，但母親卻十分失望，幾年都不理睬我，她不明白我為什麼要選擇一個「窮家子」。我知道金錢不能換到真愛和快樂，所以不同意母親的看法，在當時短短的二十年中，我已看過許多有錢人痛苦的婚姻，我決不加入他們的行列。正如衛權自己所說，除了他的專業和才幹之外，他一無所有，但對我來說這就夠了，我要嫁一個我自己愛的人，父親對這點非常了解。

由於母親不贊成這門親事，對我的婚禮全不理會，這時我一面讀書考期終考，一面預備婚禮，另外衛權和我還須找地方住。為了方便父親遠道而來參加我的畢業典禮和婚禮，所以這兩件大事必須在數日之內同時舉行。於是在兩個星期之內，我旋風式的過二十一歲生日、大學畢業、又要舉行我們的婚禮。畢業典禮過後，父親問我怎麼只拿到普通榮譽而不是一級榮譽，他真不明白我過去幾個月來所承受的壓力有多大，但也很感激他相信我有能力可有更好的成績。

我們結婚那年，衛權正在滿地可的麥基爾大學做燒傷研究和教解剖學，同時攻讀外科碩士學位，次年進入麥基爾大學整型外科開始接受訓練。一九六四年衛權得到Molson研究獎學金，去英國Middlesex以整型外科研究中心知名的維能(Vernon)山醫院受訓一年，我也同時在倫敦大學的考古學系讀書。衛權在七月一日開始於維能山醫院工作之前，我們只用二十五元一天的旅費，駕車在歐

洲中部四處遊覽，對我們二人來說這是美好的一年。

在英國時我們常去倫敦探望志翀大哥，那時他已婚並有個兒子。一九六五年春天，我和衛權坐郵輪的普通艙去地中海遊覽，並在復活節時開車去蘇格蘭和威爾斯。當時父母親也正在英國，我也去向他們請安，還帶著一束紅玫瑰花給母親，但她對我仍是不甚睬，反而父親說話很多。母親對我敵對的態度，令父親非常尷尬，父親的體貼我實在非常感激。

那年夏天我和衛權回到加拿大滿地可，衛權繼續在滿地可總醫院受訓。九月時長子偉雄出世，次年滿地可正在積極預備一九六七年世界博覽會，魁北克省開始有獨立分離主義的運動。

一九六七年對我們來說是非常重要的一年。當時衛權正在參加院士考試，魁北克省開始有分化危機，滿地可街頭及許多信箱內都有炸彈爆炸的恐怖事件。雖然當時麥基爾大學已聘衛權為初級醫療人員，但因為魁北克省政局不穩，所以在衛權收到安大略省士嘉堡總醫院的整型外科部駐院醫師聘書後，我們便舉家遷到安大略省。

母親在一九六八年二月經過一次輕微心臟病之後，便聽從醫生囑咐出外旅遊調劑心情，母親原本就計劃去美國和加拿大溫哥華探訪親友，她便利用這個機會，帶表哥的女兒陳之昭去美國讀書。母親患心臟病後對我的態度大有改變，她在溫哥華時要我過去與她見面，我便在夏天帶著兩歲半的偉雄去溫哥華拜見母親。母親對我態度的軟化，令父親心境舒暢許多，從此以後，父母親每年都會來加拿大看我們。

父母親來多倫多看我們的時候，父親對多倫多市區到處都有公園，及住宅區區內繁茂的樹木，非常欣賞。父親熱愛大自然，常說香港人口稠密的地區植樹太少。他知道我熱衷園藝，對我提過他的好朋友羅富齊爵士(Sir Evelyn de Rothschild)也有同好。

父母親在一九七〇年來多倫多看我們時，我們的租屋在一鎮屋型社區內，衛權當時是士嘉堡總醫院中唯一沒有自置房子的醫生。父親覺得偉雄及一九六九年出世的俊雄正在成長，這間住屋不夠大，應該要一幢有院子的房子。但我心目中，對我憧憬的房屋有很特別的構想，因孩子們的藝術薰陶對我來說十分重要，我要有一間美術室與廚房相連，但市面上的房子根本沒有這樣的隔間，唯一

的方法是儲備足夠建屋費用自建。我從未想過向父母親開口，但父親非常慷慨地願意幫助我們，讓我們在早已預購的土地上開始自建住宅。

一九七二年春天我們搬入新屋後，父母親便來多倫多。父親見到我們超大的客廳，便要像他為利園酒店大廳所訂製的天津地毯一樣，也特別要為我們的客廳訂製一張天津地毯。但是他說地毯製造加上運送過程，至少要等一年的時間，或者我願意選擇兩塊地毯雙併式用的話，馬上就有現貨可運來多倫多，但我寧可等。後來我還收到寄來的地毯圖樣讓我挑選，至於地毯的顏色，是特別照我由雜誌中剪下花卉的色版訂做，色調與客廳壁磚相襯。父親也讓我挑選一張普通尺碼的地毯，來配襯我們藍色的飯廳。我們果真在一年之後收到地毯，但等待的確是值得的。父親對我們實在是關愛，要如此費心的送地毯給我們。

一九七二年志剛弟弟由香港中文大學畢業，父親便培植他接受國際財經訓練，安排他去日內瓦、紐約華爾街、最後一站去東京，在山一證券公司及富士銀行實習。富士銀行總裁吉岡義之與父親是朋友[3]，這是弟弟大好的學習機會。

當時弟弟已婚，並有一子。他們由日內瓦赴紐約的途中，特別來多倫多探訪我們，大家相處得非常愉快。說也奇怪，弟弟在那次探訪時對我說：「二家姐，我不會活得太長，或者最多只有十五年，但在這之前，我一定要有一番轟轟烈烈的作為！」，雖然那時他過胖，但臨離開香港之前的健康檢查報告顯示他一切正常。

志剛一家到紐約不久，父親就打電話告訴我志剛在紐約去世的消息，當時他才二十五歲。衛權和我立刻飛去紐約，父親則獨自一人由香港前來料理弟弟的後事，母親沒有同行。

原來志剛去世當天正和朋友於午餐時間在外走路，突然倒地不起。所有在紐約的利氏親戚接到消息後，都前來安慰我們，幫助父親料理志剛後事，在堪色斯大學任教的六叔也特別趕來。我和志剛一向姐弟情深，但我的悲慟又如何能與父親的喪子椎心之痛，或妙玲弟婦喪夫的悲傷相比，幸好他們的嬰兒稚子尚不懂事，不知什麼是人間慘事。

父親辦完志剛後事，便帶著承武孫和妙玲次媳回香港，負起照顧承武未來的責任，由那時開始，

與父親同遊中國

一

一九七八年秋天我對父親提起，想和衛權帶孩子回中國看看。那時除了中國政府安排的團體之外，中國觀光尚未對外開放。我們在父親事先經由北京安排之下，去渥太華的中國大使館取得

提供了他與母親維繫美滿長久的婚姻秘訣是，「偶爾吵吵小架！」

慶祝酒會在利園酒店舉行，當晚父母親都非常愉快，賓客都是至親好友，慶祝蛋糕上綴滿了金色的蘭花。父親致詞時說到，五十年前他和母親在利園結婚時，就是站在現在他所站的地方，所不同的是，一九二八年的利園高高在利園山上，現在重建的利園酒店已在夷平的地面上了。同時父親也

一九七八年二月是父母親金婚紀念日，父親並不想要什麼特別儀式，他本人連自己生日都不慶祝，他不喜歡麻煩人。但四叔堅持這是值得紀念的日子，要利家全體一起慶祝，令母親非常高興。

因為金婚紀念日是在二月，只有我和幼子迪雄能回去慶賀，兩個大孩子須要上學，由衛權留在家中照顧他們。

一九七六年聖誕節回去時，父親招待我們一家坐Rasasayang號郵輪，由新加坡去峇里島旅遊。使得偉雄、俊雄和一九七一年出世的迪雄都興奮不已，以為上了電視節目中的愛之船，這是他們第一次坐郵輪旅行。我們住新加坡期間，父親沒有為我們訂最好的文華酒店，因為酒店老闆是父親的朋友，若知道是父親訂房間的話，一定不肯收費。

我們每年必返港探親，在一九七六年我去時，父親帶承武去他的辦公室，看著承武向公司裡一位擅長中國書法的梁小姐學寫毛筆字。承武稍長，他們祖孫二人每星期六早上必在一起，父親帶承武去他的愛之船，這是他們親保證，香港在一九九七年主權移交後，一切維持現狀，五十年不變，所以父親覺得可放心繼續投資及照常經營他的的企業。

七〇年代初期我已開始注意到香港的主權問題，父親來加拿大看我們時，提起中國領導人對父他既是承武的嚴父亦是承武的慈祖。

了中國的簽證。

父親為我們安排了一個非常愉快的旅程，我們先回香港過聖誕節，再坐火車進大陸。那時只要一過邊界，立刻可以覺得是兩個全然不同的世界，一下子由高樓大廈滿街汽車，轉為田野和單車。政府人員在廣州火車站安排我們辦理入境清關手續，然後有位導遊一路照顧我們整個行程。

我們由廣州飛抵北京，然後一路往南走，參觀了所有主要名勝及非觀光區的小地方。這次行程中，我們與母親的表哥陳耀真教授和他太太毛文書見面（四），他特別為我們安排參觀北京城外平常不對外開放的整型外科醫院。衛權非常訝異國內的醫生在這般簡陋的設備環境中，能有如此高的水準。這是我第一我們在北京中央醫院還看到用針灸麻醉動手術，及其他各種不同的中國傳統醫療方法。這是我第一次在手術房內，看到正在進行扁桃腺切除的病人，還能清醒的和護士交談，覺得非常驚奇。那時國人都穿毛

我們去了長城和紫禁城，然後到杭州和桂林，每到一個地方都留下深刻的印像。我注裝，彼此稱同志，也沒有現代化的旅館，住的地方清早無水可用，我們都在一般的飯堂吃飯。我注意到在共產黨統治下，星期天早上必有自由市場，人們可自由交易（五）。

當我們抵達桂林時，二子俊雄開始生病，衛權診斷是得了猩紅熱，馬上給他服下抗生素。在桂林的最後一天俊雄已覺得舒服許多，便和我們一起四處遊覽，然後我們在除夕由桂林飛回廣州與父親會面。

因父親的關係，我們在廣州期間成了廣州市政府的貴賓，特別安排住在政要所住的賓館。因為孩子想放炮仗，父親便帶我們坐小巴士上街找炮仗，結果炮仗沒買到，倒是參觀了廣州市區。父親還指給我看在一九三〇年代，他在廣州市政府工作時參與興建的一座歐式橋樑。

當晚因廣東省省長不在廣州，便由副省長請我們在賓館餐廳晚餐，令我上了一課就是；世上任何國家的官方宴飲，包括貧窮的共產國家在內，水準都不會差。

父親計劃第二天一早和我們一家人坐車去嘉寮村祖祠，所以只有在飯後才有時間帶我看看賓館的花園。我們原本預備全家一起和他散步，但俊雄說他無法走路，因為他的膝蓋已開始腫脹，衛權便抱他回房休息，只有我一人和父親在園中散步。

我回房時見俊雄所服的抗生素不起作用，又開始發燒，便立刻找醫生，結果這位女醫生建議我們送孩子去醫院驗血。衛權便抱著俊雄，我們一起跑到醫院，俊雄一眼瞥見醫院急診室的情況，就要求「不要留我在這裡」，當然我們也不會將他留在那樣的醫院。因為是新年除夕，醫院的化驗室休息兩天無人值班，我當機立斷決定立刻帶俊雄回香港。

回到賓館時父親早已就寢，我便去他房間叫醒他：「爸爸，我要馬上帶俊雄回香港，你可不可以儘快幫我找頭班飛機的機票？」父親知道我必有理由做此決定，所以也不多問醫院的情形。只說：「明天是新年，大概會很難」，我說：「那末找部車，我們馬上開車回香港」，「那更麻煩，路上情況不好再加上邊界的檢查站，我更難安排你們一路順利回香港，讓我先想想辦法再說。明天嘉寮村還有人等著我去，偉雄和迪雄可以跟我去，因為他的名字附在我的護照上，所以他一定要隨我們回香港。」但可惜迪雄沒有單獨護照，不能跟父親去，因為他只帶一個孩子回香港時才住自己家中，否則都住利園酒店，免得為父母親及家中工人帶來不便」，利園酒店就在父親住處對面。父親做完這些安排後才再回房休息。

父親為我們做安排的時候，我和衛權開始收拾行李。一位政府官員告訴我，第二天早上五點他可以送我們去機場，但不能保證飛香港的頭班機能否有四個機位給我們，不過他會儘量想辦法。此時父親亦與母親聯絡，要她通知七叔的小兒科醫生朋友過來看俊雄，因為過年期間幾乎沒有私家醫生願意出診。父親同時聯絡香港機場準備輪椅，及要利園酒店派車接我們回酒店，免得為父母親及家中工人帶來不便。

第二天我們一早即起床，賓館廚房還為我們預備了豐盛的早餐，但我們心焦得一點胃口都沒有。一切照父親的安排回到利園酒店，母親打電話過來告訴我們醫院方面七叔已安排妥當，然後七叔說他已派司機來接我們。和父親及偉雄分手後，我們幸好能坐到頭班機，在二十五分鐘後就回到香港。一切照父親的安排回到香港。去養和醫院的急診室，他會在醫院等我們。

七叔在養和醫院為我們介紹了一位在美國受訓，醫術非常好的小兒科醫生，他確定俊雄是得了猩紅熱，必須繼續服用較高單位的抗生素數日。養和醫院到現在都屬貴族醫院，收費高昂，所以當七叔告訴我醫藥費「全免」，他已和醫院結清帳單時，我們都不知道說什麼才好。我和他的關係一直很

特別，他像我的朋友而非長輩叔叔，他只比衛權年長十歲。回港當天下午俊雄已舒服許多，第二天已經可以和我們一起去利舞台看電影了。

這一切使我感到我和父親的個性是多麼相像，我們不必多說一字，彼此即能互相了解對方。我知道當時換了我在父親的處境下，我也會做同樣的安排。

此時父親帶著偉雄在新會祖祠，即衛權家的祖祠，令偉雄受到畢生難忘貴賓式的款待。父親原本亦要帶我們全家去離新會不遠也是四邑之一的新寧，他覺得讓孩子對父母雙方的祖先都有所認識，是件非常有意義的事。到了新寧，偉雄雄去了新寧，現在雖然我們不能前去，但父親還是單獨帶偉沒有想到村民會送禮物給他們，其中還有活生生的雞。

偉雄回到香港對我們描述他在中國的見聞時，他說：「公公帶我去一間炮竹廠，他們任我在外面儘放炮仗；在發電廠水壩河邊的大榕樹上有上千的白鷺；我還和公公去泡溫泉，在溫泉煮蛋。但是和公公同房睡就很麻煩，他睡覺時打鼾好大聲！」

父親非常高興見到俊雄康復不少，看偉雄玩得如此開心，便對俊雄說：「下次公公帶你返鄉下。」

父親在中國時，心境總是非常愉快。

第十章

由動亂至改革：對高等教育的遠見

香港社會在一九五〇年代分為親共、親國民黨，及親英與其他不同的派系，因為我們在家從不談政治，所以我無從知道父母親的政治傾向。中國政府對香港態度較為軟化之後，在一九五六年，中、港邊界應民眾需要再度開放，內陸中國居民只要有回鄉證，即可自由進入香港。由二月至九月，共有六萬多人由大陸來港滯留不歸[二]，令水荒問題更加嚴重，於是迫使香港政府又將邊界封鎖。同年我去英國求學不久，國民黨在慶祝雙十國慶時，與支持共產黨的市民及反英殖民政府派民眾發生暴動鬥爭。暴動持續數日，英方調動英軍武力鎮暴後才平息，暴動中有數十人喪生，數千人被逮捕入獄或被驅逐出境。那段時間我已開始懂事，對此時政府法規有所了解，並影響我對香港殖民地政府的態度。

香港政府通過一連串的法律加緊控制人口，並有權查封觸犯政治條例的報社，將出版人以政治罪名判罪入獄。條文規定組成任何社團，均須經警務處處長批准，街頭超過九人以上並無關係人士之集會均屬犯罪行為。在這些規定之下，市民只要不企圖計劃推翻殖民政權，仍有某些程度的自由。

中國在六〇年代所經歷的恐怖文化大革命〔一九六六年至一九七六年〕，波及香港之後引起政治和社會的騷亂和暴動，當時局勢令市民驚恐不已。但對社會不滿的示威行動，則有正面效應，引致日後社會革新。

103

一九六七年香港暴動

一九六五年九月毛澤東開始積極整肅異己份子，導至發生文化大革命。國內年輕人可任意攻擊批判文化及學習方式，最令人痛心的是對國內亟需的學者人才大肆蹂躪摧殘。一九六六年夏天八支紅衛兵隊伍，總數一千五百萬青年在天安門廣場會師。一九六六年八月二十二日，紅衛兵藉口英人在香港有暴力行為，開始攻打英國駐北京大使館，將大使館閘門攻破，投擲汽油罐，令大使館起火燃燒，結果須由周恩來總理下令調派公安武警和人民解放軍，才將英國大使館外交人員救出。

國內的文化大革命並未能阻礙父母親在六〇年代去中國旅行，他們在新華社秘書何銘思陪同下去到重慶，重遊戰時他們住過的地方。正當父親對何銘思敘述他在重慶的往事時，他們被成群的紅衛兵包圍，令何思銘驚恐不已。所幸這些紅衛兵並沒有什麼行動[1]，他們只是對父母親感到好奇，因為父母親雖然在外表衣著上已盡量做當地人的裝扮，但他們看來仍是與眾有異。

一九六六年香港一群年輕人反對渡輪加價，作出平和抗議行動，引發心懷不滿的勞工階級青年對社會上不平等而無出路的積怨，演變成一連數日的暴動。後來須調動用警察武力，才能制止暴動，其中有一輕年人遇害，許多人被捕及一名示威者事後自殺身亡。除此之外，國內局勢的動盪不安，亦波及香港。

工廠工潮在一九六七年演變成共產黨學校學生反政府的示威，及零星的學生及工人暴力行動。有些香港共產黨或自命為紅衛兵的恐怖份子，在家中自製俗稱為「菠蘿」的土製炸彈，置於公眾場合造成騷動，有些是真炸彈，曾炸死數人，有些只是假炸彈[3]。吳慶塘當時任香港文華酒店的副總經理，他說那時雖然酒店照常營業，但幾乎生意全無。警方直到夏天才開始採取行動，對共產黨的商店、工會及學校進行突擊搜捕[4]，搜捕行動中有數人死亡，多人被捕。在這些動亂期間有數百個社區團體，公開表示支持香港政府和反對共產黨。

加拿大籍的Ruth Hayhoe[5]在香港親眼目睹一名共產黨員，被他自己的炸彈炸傷。在寄給她住英

國的母親的家信中，形容這些土製炸彈是「小而無害的」。她也提到在她任教的協恩中學所遭受到的困難，她說有位四年級的學生在學校佈告欄內張貼公開信，指責英國政府的「奴化教育」政策，[協恩中學是基督教教會學校]還在校外懸掛一面紅旗。學生受校方譴責後態度非常蠻橫不服，並將她父親帶到學校與校方理論，她父親甚至怒摑班導師。一九六七年的香港社會，彌漫著一片騷動不安的氣氛⑹。

香港街頭發生暴民對公車投擲石塊及毆打司機事件後，倫敦保險協會命令香港保險公司取消所有的暴動險。九龍巴士公司總經理在與太古集團保險公司經理姚剛見面時，請求該公司勿取消巴士的暴動險，以防萬一發生暴動時對司機能有所補償⑺。更有人散佈謠言稱紅衛兵正向香港進軍，造成香港居民人心惶惶，開始囤積糧食，將商店貨架物品搶購一空。那年夏天父母親正在歐洲旅遊，坊間便流傳，像利銘澤夫婦這種人物都已離開香港，香港局勢必更加惡化，父母親聽到這消息後，立刻返回香港以正視聽。

父親覺得此刻他有責任在香港盡一份力量，為香港請求中國政府勿再煽動群眾，或許能有所幫助。父親的朋友姬達(Jack Cater)當時是香港政府的保安司，在情況最混亂的時候每天都到父親的辦公室向父親求助⑻。後來父親便請新華社社長梁威林及《大公報》發行人費彝民，代向周恩來請求勿讓暴動在香港蔓延下去⑼。事實上，當時香港的暴動和中國並無太大關係，後來周恩來總理特別指示香港新華社，在香港的立場要維持不變。

此時香港的情勢，令母親憶起一九四一年香港淪陷時的恐怖景象，她非常驚怕，但父親卻毫無畏懼，他決不考慮離開香港，他願用生命來保護這塊土地。父親於是率先發表公開談話安撫人心，並指責共產黨的行動對香港社會造成動盪混亂的現象⑽。

但此時中國大陸的局面更趨惡化，任何人都有受紅衛兵批鬥的可能。母親的表哥陳耀真教授和他太太毛文書教授二人都是眼科專家，文革時被紅衛兵當眾辱罵、毆打、趕出家門，他們的莫須有罪名就是知識份子，成份不好，尤其陳耀真更是美國哈普金斯醫學院出來的醫生。幸好他們總算苟存性命，下放他方，直到七〇年代初，父母親才輾轉找到他們夫婦二人。一九七八年底我們在北京和

社會改革

香港一九六六年的暴動，令香港政府在教育上增加三倍經費，使年輕人有更多機會受教育，並改善公共屋宇、健康醫療制度和社會福利。一九六七年，殖民地政府覺悟到不能只靠十九世紀的中、英條約來維持一個合法政府的威信，而須靠政府的施政及投入社會才能贏得民心。

由大陸逃來香港的難民子女，在一九七○年代時均已長大成人。一九七一年人口調查顯示，香港本土出生人口首次佔香港總人口的大多數。老一輩的難民在香港去世後，亦葬在香港，令他們的子孫對香港開始有了歸屬感。那些在五○及六○年代，為香港工商業起飛貢獻過心力的人，現在開始可以享受他們半生辛勞的成果。

政府在支持教育制度方面的改善，令許多文盲父母的子女有機會受到基本的高中教育。並在一九六九年開始，政府設有獎助學金制度，使家境清貧的子弟在香港能有讀本地大學的機會，值得給予機會接受教育的子弟，會對社會經濟做出更多貢獻，及對香港有歸屬感。香港人醒覺到他們不但是土生土長的香港人，亦對香港付出心力，使香港有今天的成就，便開始對政府作出非政治性，而是改善經濟及社會的要求。

這段期間不斷有大學生、教師、社工、傳教士、護士及工會人士組成的罷工和抗議活動。這些活動基本上都十分理性和守秩序，他們非常自制的藉罷工行動來表達一些有意義的信息，但同時也觸

陳教授夫婦見面時，陳教授還給我看他在文化大革命期間，藏起來的一頂法國扁呢帽和一雙西式皮鞋，那時他若被紅衛兵發現這些所謂資本主義的東西，他們夫婦二人怕早就沒命了。

當紅衛兵像蝗蟲般啃蝕中國大陸時，香港海面常見有大陸飄流過來的死屍[二]。死狀之慘令香港居民極為憂慮和恐懼，只因家家都有親人留在國內。

幸而後來香港局勢逐漸好轉，一九六九年初已大致恢復正常。

犯了非法聚會的條例。罷工活動中有極少數的暴力事件，起因皆是由於警方過於干涉而引起[12]。經過多次靜坐示威和公開論壇討論，及在社區團體均廣泛支持此提案下，政府終於同意在大多數政府行政及管理事務方面，可用中文〔粵語〕表達。

香港貪污行為素來猖獗。直至七〇年代，方由大學生及宗教團體代表，組織成千上萬的市民在街頭示威抗議，矛頭直指警務處人員及其他政府機構。一九七三年總督麥理浩任命高等法院克爾法官(Sir Alastair Blair Kerr)，為主持調查皇家[13]香港警務處總警司葛柏(Peter Godbur)案件的一人調查委員會委員。葛柏因涉嫌貪污遭停職調查時逃離香港。克爾的兩份調查報告，加上後來社會大眾群情洶湧，導致政府在一九七四年二月成立了廉政專員公署，由姬達(Jack Cater)任此新部門的長官。葛柏後來由英國遞解回香港受審[14]。當時還有許多其他警官被控，亦有不少人辭職，警務處被迫重新改組。後來廉政專員公署訂定：公務人員受禮為犯法行為。

基督教工業委員會及若干教會團體在整個七〇年代不斷組織勞工抗議示威，在共產黨及國民黨的勢力之外發展了無政治背景的工運，促使政府修改勞工條例。繼護士罷工之後小學教師罷工成功，在香港組成了教師工會。白領階層及藍領階層的工會紛紛成立，對政府當局的專制權力正面挑戰。在香港的遮打公園、維多利亞公園、政府大廈前的廣場及督憲府門前，都是大家熟知的公眾集會場所。雖然政府明令禁止在公眾場所非法集會，但社團申請集會亦逐漸減少，到後來甚至警察還保護遊行示威者的安全，及遊行時為他們指揮交通，讓示威群眾向政府當局呈遞請願書[15]。

政府在群眾示威後，做了相當大的讓步。在此過程中，香港社會及政府雙方結構都更加鞏固，香港政府一改其殖民方式作風，對民眾在教育及語言方面的要求較為順應，政府部門的服務提高，社會公正亦有改進。擁有最高權力的殖民地政府，在七〇年代初期的行政運作方面有了極大的改變。

父母親認為從七〇年代開始，香港總督只屬外交官身份，再不能使香港市民唯命是從了。

父親和教育

父

親畢業生對教育熱衷支持，一九六九年以前香港在高等教育方面一直未設有獎學金，時常有家境清貧的子弟考入大學，但無力支付學雜費，而向私人求助。父親接到這類信件，他總是放在衣袋中，隨時提醒自己抽時間處理，父親會先查閱這些學生的成績紀錄，若是值得幫助的好學生，父親便會在經濟上資助他們學費、食宿費用及零用錢。父親在晚年時，為防自己有任何不測，常在一年前就預先支付所有的費用，幫助這些學生讀書[16]。

有些學生曾說過，父親是香港唯一不怕麻煩給他們回信的富人。父親對這些學生從不要求回報，有些受父親幫助過的學生日後非常有成就，他們對父親的幫助永誌在心。父親在為青年教育方面所付出的心力，全不受個人因素的左右，他本人是基督徒，但他一樣熱心去主持孔聖堂中學的開幕典禮。父親對創辦旺角勞工子弟學校這類教育機構最為熱心，更大力支持籌募建校基金的活動[17]。

陳之昭是母親表兄妹陳耀真和毛文書的女兒之一，文化大革命時她同一位中山大學醫科同學，由大陸坐船和其他難民一起逃到香港。她和母親聯絡上之後，我父母親就負責照顧她生活起居和教育，父親還送她去美國學英文，後來再進入哈普金斯醫學院讀醫。陳之昭初到美國讀書時須用英文由頭學起，她能和她父親當年一樣，在哈普金斯醫學院讀完眼睛專科，實非易事。她現在是美國馬利蘭州貝西斯大的國家眼科研究所的免疫病理科主任[18]。

父親的秘書胡太太在一九七〇年代初退休，父親屬意利氏企業旗下的華利貿易公司工作的李樂君，來做他的私人秘書。李姑娘告訴我父親要用她的原因，是她在工作空閒時不像其他的秘書小姐只看些八卦畫報，父親去華利貿易公司，時常見她在讀書，但父親不知李姑娘是在準備國外大學入學托福（TOEFL）〔以英語為外國語言的測驗〕考試。那時李姑娘才十九歲，她覺得年紀太小不夠經驗，但父親告訴她將來可在他身邊學到很多新事物，才讓她有信心開始為父親工作。李姑娘說她連生病都不敢缺，父親喜歡見人進修充實自己，所以要李姑娘去香港大學夜校讀英文。

課，因為憑父親與大學的關係，她缺一堂課父親都會知道。她剛開始為父親工作的頭三個月，因情緒緊張經常失眠，多年來做父親的秘書，因他的直脾氣，令李姑娘常掉眼淚，但她也知道父親的批評都是善意。李姑娘對自己的英文電話會話能力很沒有信心，但在父親的辦公室又非常需要，所以第二年父親便經香港大學安排送她去英國牛津大學，讀六個星期的英文暑期班。暑期班在七月才開始，但父親早在一月份就付清全部費用。李姑娘在英國時由她妹妹暫代父親秘書的職位。

父親一直樂意幫助有意向學的清貧子弟讀書。有一位學生叫譚麗芬，當時正在英國拿兩年獎學金讀大學。她寫信告訴父親，想進香港大學讀醫，但家境不許可。經父親查證她確是獎學金學生，父親就資助她完成學業，譚後來成為一位婦產科醫生。父親去世後，經由他生前所建立的各種關係，譚還幫李樂君的先生找到一份工作。

譚麗芬目前是香港衛生署助理署長，在一九九七年至一九九八年香港盛行家禽流行性感冒，與中國協商進口健康雞隻來香港的負責人即是譚麗芬。

李姑娘非常了解父親的為人，她不但每天在工作上和父親相處，同時父親的支票也經她開出。她告訴我：「你父親要我按月開出八百元的支票，給一位得了肺結核的看更子女讀書，至於他所資助的每個大學生，都是在一年前就預付所有費用。」

李姑娘後來嫁給父親老朋友亦是利氏企業職員徐鏡波的兒子。七〇年代後期李姑娘有了家庭，父親不出海時，就把遊艇借給李姑娘和她的丈夫與孩子使用。

高等教育

二

次世界大戰結束後，中國的內戰接踵而來，大量中國難民(19)湧入香港，對教育需求極大，尤其在高等教育方面更為迫切。

在六〇年代中期，香港僅有一所大學。香港大學於一九一一年創立，創校的目的是作為中、英學

術交流中心，以推進中、英了解及友好關係，換言之，非為香港社會大眾而設。太平洋戰爭之前，這所大學只是學習西方文化的一個前哨站，學生多來自東南亞、中國及香港。一九四六年時，為維持英國在遠東地區的地位與聲望，確有必要重組此大學。一九四八年父親好友賴廉士成為大學校長，父親亦加入大學校務委員會為委員。

一九五〇年調查報告，認為香港大學應反映香港本地社會需要，而非僅為維持英國聯邦在遠東的地位。

由於國內時局不穩，一些國際學術機構撤離，國際文化活動中斷，令香港在中西文化交流的作用上更顯重要。

香港工業化產生對高等教育的需要，難民人口中有大量國內中學生無法回到國內繼續升學，須在香港繼續學業。但在香港大學學位不足，又採用英語教學，中文中學的學生，能進入大學的機會非常微渺。

港督葛量洪委任一特別委員會，負責檢討高等教育問題。委員會發表的《賈士域報告書》，受邀對香港大學發展提出意見。在他們發表的《曾寧士、盧根報告書》中，主張香港大學仍應維持以英語為授課語言的大學，他們二人認為政府只須在中文中學與英文大學之間填補缺口，即可銜接中文中學畢業生進入大學，於是便有金文泰中學特別二年制的設立，但因受惠學生不多，未能解決問題。

一九五三年，英國大學行政管理專家曾寧士（Ivor Jennings）和盧根（Douglas Logan），受邀對香港大學發展提出意見。政府便立刻撥款給予香港大學在一九五二至一九五三學年開設中文課程，但在校董會卻遭否決。校董深恐開辦中文課程之後，最終會使大學有所改變，而且認為香港大學在戰後當急之務應在鞏固其地位方面，而非發展新方向。

(Keswick)，是第一份公開文件，提議香港高等教育必須適應香港市民需要，並建議香港大學仍應是本港唯一頒授學位的學府。政府便立刻撥款給予香港大學在一九五二至一九五三學年開設中文課程，但在校董會卻遭否決。

香港的教育制度一直是分開中、英文教學，英文學校的學生有小學至大學的完整體制，而中文學校畢業生進入大學，於是便有金文泰中學特別二年制的設立，但因受惠學生不多，未能解決問題。

依照中國國民黨政府制訂的學制，用上海出版的教科書，同時香港的中文學校多與廣州的學校有聯校則止於高中。在一九四九年前，香港中文中學畢業學生可去中國繼續升學，因香港中文學校完全

繫。但自中華人民共和國成立後，香港學生便無法前去升學，加重教育制度負擔。尤其在大量中國難民學生流入香港後，問題更加嚴重。

來自中國難民中有富辦學經驗的學者，便在香港承擔起新的挑戰。這些學者和專業人士之中，有些人是以發揚中國文化和培育知識青年為己任的教育理念興學，但亦有為求謀生，開始以設備簡陋和租來的課室，創辦起所謂「難民學校」或稱「流亡書院」。根據香港政府在一九五二年的調查，共有三十多所這類學校，程度及課程長短參差不齊。有九所程度較高的機構開設四年制文、商課程，其中新亞[20]、崇基和聯合書院前身的院校，成為日後香港中文大學的基本成員書院。這些書院全有賴於國際友人的支持得以維持，如崇基書院建校得到基督教會大力援助，另外在香港聖公會會督何明華不斷的奔走努力爭取之下，政府終於同意在馬料水撥地建校，成為日後香港中文大學重要的資產。

到了一九五六年，這三所書院所頒授的學位已獲歐、美許多大學承認，有些大學甚至還對傑出的書院畢業生提供獎學金。但是在香港，書院畢業生的學歷在公職就業或職業訓練時卻全不獲政府承認。三所書院屬私人機構，財務上完全沒有政府的資助，但卻受教育署及一九五二年教育條例管轄。所以在一九五六年，三所書院聯合向政府爭取香港政府的資助與承認。

三所書院的代表經過協商之後，雅禮(Yale-in Asia)協會駐新亞書院代表兼董事郎家恒(Charles Long)，於一九五六年八月十六日向教育司高詩雅(D.J.S. Crozier)，提出建議書。指出私立院校不應被規範於一九五二年教育法例，因該法例只適用於香港的中小學。政府應另外訂立具有大學程度的大專學院法例。再者，作為香港教育制度中的一部份，院校不能全靠外國機構、教會或私人資助，香港政府一定要負起提供基本設備與經費的支持。他又提到在現行教育制度之下，僅有香港大學是唯一頒授學位的學術機構，令上千的優秀學生選擇往外地及台灣升學，造成未來領導人材的流失。建議書結論並稱，無法與香港大學獲同等地位的專上院校，亦很難對大學教育作出最佳貢獻，因此專上院校必須獲得頒授學位的資格。這份文件成為政府創立香港中文大學的第一批公文檔案。

一九五六年一月教育署副教育司毛勤（L. G. Morgan），在討論如何解決香港學生升學問題時，提到根據觀察結果，政府每年津貼香港大學八百萬元經費，給予英文中學學生升學，卻極少或毫無資助，令中文中學深感不平。毛勤在同年十月的另一份備忘錄中，舉出五項不同辦法，以應付中文中學學生的全盤需要，其中最具意義的是提到「建立一所具有自己的大學條例和擁有頒授學位資格的中文大學」[21]。但備忘錄結論仍強調以加強現有香港大學的發展以配合社會需要才是最佳的辦法。一九五六年十月，香港的擁護國民黨人士，和親共人士衝突，發生流血暴動，令香港政府覺醒不可再忽視市民對更多大專教育的要求[22]。一九五七年一月崇基、新亞及聯合三所「流亡書院」代表在教育署開會，聖公會會督何明華和雅禮協會駐新亞書院代表朗家恒亦同時出席，為香港中文大學建校之路邁進，但未能達成任何決定。三院隨即在二月成立香港中文專上學校協會，為香港中文大學建校之路邁進。經過多次會議協商之後，一九五八年八月各方代表終於同意在香港成立一所新的大學。

一所新大學

一九五九年六月二日香港政府正式宣佈，將成立一所以中文為主要授課語言的新大學。港督柏立基（Sir Robert Black）聘請多年來擔任牛津大學歷史系教授及導師富爾敦爵士（Sir John Fulton）為顧問〔他也曾是父親及歷任港督柏立基，和麥理浩Sir Murray Maclehose的老師〕，於一九六〇年三月呈交港督。在此份報告書中他指出學術自由、大學自主、研究工作和結合中、西文化，對形成新大學的基本特性尤為重要[23]。

馬臨教授在一九七八年至一九八七年任香港中文大學校長，他認為後來被封勳爵的富爾敦爵士，應該是香港中文大學的催生功臣。又因父親與富爾敦爵士的私交甚篤，父親曾親自赴英國富爾敦退休所住的約克郡，與他當面談及香港中文大學，令富爾敦對未來的香港中文大學有更多的了解。父親在這方面非常有說服力[24]。

三所書院在此之前的發展經驗，多源自中國及早期與美國大學的關係，但缺乏英國方面的經驗與聯繫。此時富爾敦爵士便為香港中文大學帶來英國牛津、威爾斯及塞撒斯三所不同大學的發展運作經驗。《富爾敦報告書》完成後，隨即委任由二十人組成的大學臨時校董會，主席由關祖堯擔任，父親是副主席。校董會在短時間內即決定將大學命名為「香港中文大學」，父親同時亦被任命為校園計劃及建設委員會和大學投標管理委員會的主席。由此時開始，直到父親去世，父親為香港中文大學在建校及成長過程中，付出無限精力和心血。父親對香港中文大學的情感一如他自己的子女，馬臨教授對我說過，若沒有父親對香港中文大學所做的各種貢獻，香港中文大學不可能有今天的成就[25]。

在校董會向政府極力爭取之下，政府終於同意將位於馬料水[26]，毗連崇基書院，面積達三百英畝，風景優美的大幅土地，撥給香港中文大學作為建校及將來擴充校舍之用。一九六三年九月，香港中文大學條例在立法局通過，大學成立典禮在同年十月十七日，由香港總督柏立基以大學監督身份親臨主持。

一九六四年十月九日首次大學投標管理委員會會議在公爵大廈父親的辦公室舉行。這些會議後來繼續在父親不同地點的辦公室舉行，直到一九七七年才改到利園酒店開會。一九八三年父親去世之前，他一直在香港中文大學的這個委員會及校董會服務。

監管與建大學校舍的職務，對身為土木工程師的父親極為適合，工作任務非常重大，整個建校計劃就如同在一片須先將山地夷平的土地上，建築一個小型的市區一樣。山石泥土運到對面吐露港的船灣淡水湖工地，做建壩工程之用[27]。除原有的崇基書院校舍之外，委員會須在全無道路及下水道的新生地上，策劃與建校舍細節。在一九六六年的會議紀錄中提到，因無法確定政府是否在未來兩年內有由沙田淨水廠舖設水管來校園的計劃，所以校園廁所衛生設備須用海水。另外在一九六七年會議紀錄中亦建議，因部份山坡地斜度太大，無法舖植草皮，須立刻在斜坡地種植樹木以保持水

土。

香港中文大學非常得益於父親在香港政府的人際關係，能請到父親友人司徒惠為大學的建築師，另外又請船灣工程公司的工程師為香港中文大學工作。建校初期，父親還請司徒惠去世界最好的大學觀摩，司徒惠在一九六○年代中開始設計香港中文大學建築之前，曾走訪了十五所世界上最著名也最美麗的大學校園[28]。

父親身為香港中文大學校董會的副主席，一年須主持一、兩次校董會。父親主持的會議向來以速戰速決聞名，而且絕對準時開會，會議過程極少超過四十五分鐘。一次會議中一位校董遲到十分鐘，等他坐下來開會時，他的會議部份已經結束了[29]。

一九八三年初，父親想要試驗製造一種用來釀造中國米酒，亦作中藥用的生酵母。他便請教馬臨教授在香港中文大學化驗室製作這生酵母的可能性，結果父親非常高興試驗成功，並計劃在家中自行試驗發酵。他對不同的醫藥一直深感興趣。

父親對香港中文大學的前途極為關心，在父親的遺囑中，對待香港中文大學就如同他的子女一樣。父親去世後，母親繼續對香港中文大學熱心支持，也將香港中文大學視如自己兒女一樣。利氏家族中亦有其他成員，受父親影響對香港中文大學慷慨資助。祖父時期的藝術品中，我最欣賞的是一座長毛巨象的象牙雕刻，整座象牙上有雕工精美的三國演義故事，這件珍貴的藝術品，現在正巍巍然的在香港中文大學文物館陳列。

母親在父親去世不久，便在香港中文大學醫學院外科科學部設立利銘澤金牌獎，獎勵成績最優異的應居畢業生，以紀念父親。

一九八七年九月，香港中文大學舉行一項命名典禮，將大學科學館演講大樓命名為「銘澤樓」，

但不辭辛勞的為香港中文大學與政府交涉，完成校舍的興建，同時對大學基金亦做出巨額的捐獻。父親對香港中文大學最具體的信心表現，就是讓志剛弟在香港中文大學就讀直至畢業。弟弟初入大學時住學校宿舍，他告訴父親學校的床墊不很舒服，結果父親將宿舍所有床墊全部換新！

鐘，等他坐下來開會時，他的會議部份已經結束了[29]。

父母親來多探望我們時，常聽父親談到設立香港中文大學對香港華人居民的重要性。父親不

以紀念父親生前對香港社會及香港中文大學的卓越貢獻。一九八八年十月香港中文大學因母親在公益慈善方面的熱心，及對香港中文大學的繼續支持，給她特別頒贈榮譽博士學位。

第十一章

日本關係

第二次世界大戰結束後，日本人在香港創業顯然有極大困難。父親雖然在戰時曾參與抗日工作，但他認為日子太平後，大家都應不再計較過去。父親的遠見是，日本在戰後不久的將來經濟必會蓬勃，所以父親希望與日本建立長遠的良好關係，為香港人帶來繁榮。

一位在東京早稻田大學唸書的華人學者，創立了一個屬於學術研討性質的逍遙會[1]。月會每次都是十二人一桌聚餐晚宴，事後父親必會再回請他們。日本人對父親極為敬重，任何日本商人包括日本總領事在內，到達香港之後，必先對父親做禮貌上的拜訪以示尊敬[2]。

當日本人俱樂部於一九五五年在香港創會時，父親是最先願意提供協助的人士之一[3]。日本人俱樂部原本設於海港酒店，共有一百〇六個企業及私人會員，一九九六年十一月時會員已增加至二萬五千個，俱樂部除了餐廳設施之外，尚有中、英文班、娃娃製作班、國畫及書法班等活動[4]。日本人俱樂部在香港發展史上，會址多設在利氏家族的物業內[5]。由七〇年代開始，父母親每年定期在利園酒店宴請所有在香港發展的日本企業人士，介紹他們與中國商界認識，促進雙方交流。

六〇年代末期，日本財經機構為求生存，必須與香港的商界巨頭結合，在香港設立分公司。曾有多家日本企業邀請父親入股[6]，但父親立場是一概不參與，唯獨教育方面是例外。

日本學校

父

親為日僑子弟在香港建立日本學校出力不少。父親協助日本學校申請到外人在港經營外國學校的政府許可，及取得教育署、工務局的認可，通過衛生、防火條例。根據日本駐香港總事對日本政府的報告中表示，香港日本學校若沒有父親的大力襄助，建校過程將會困難而冗長。

父親獲悉日本學校建校計劃時，建議將校址設在希慎道上利氏家族的崇明大廈內，因設在該廈的香港教育署預備遷移至對街即將完工的利園酒店出租樓面內[7]，但因當時日本學校的籌備建校委員會尚未組成而作罷[8]。

利希慎置業有限公司的租務向由五叔管理，當時有許多人表示有意承租香港教育署遷出後的空間，但父親執意堅持將空樓保留給未付分毫租金及訂金的日本學校。在樓面空置半年之後，至一九六六年一月，日本政府才撥出香港日本學校建校預算，此時香港日本學校才有能力支付租金，至一九六六年五月十日，香港日本學校[9]正式開課，校舍設在希慎道崇明大廈[10]二樓和三樓，及簽訂租約。開學第二天，五叔即到學校去見藤田一郎校長，遵照父親的指示，將一月至三月的租金退回校方。學校每個人對父親的慷慨大度都覺得難以置信[11]。

父親對日本學校的發展極為關切，經常對藤田一郎校長提出不同的建議。學校後來在嶺英商場擴充課室[12]，一九七六年一月二十四日，日本學校小學部在藍塘道正式開課，學校繼續擴展後又將初中部設在寶馬山道，於一九八二年十月二十三日開始上課。日本學校各校的開幕典禮，父親都被邀請為出席貴賓。在寶馬山中學部開學儀式中，校長藤田一郎對來賓和師生面前發表演說時，特別提到他與父親之間的珍貴友誼，及對父親的感激，更介紹父親是「香港日本學校的大恩人」[13]。

一九六九年三月十二日，父親受日本天皇賜封勳三等瑞寶章，是日本在一八八八年所創的第三級最高榮譽勳章[14]，授勳典禮於寶珊道二十四號，日本駐香港總領事岡田晃官邸舉行。父親對這枚日本勳章感到非常光榮，雖然英女皇在幾年之後才准許父親佩戴這枚日本勳章，及使用勳銜，並規定

在使用勳銜時必須用全銜，以免和他的英國勳銜混淆不清[15]。

中國與日本之間

日

本政府在一九六〇年代亟欲與中國重建外交關係，便交由駐港總領事進行籌劃，此時日本駐香港總領事是岡田晃，由於無法直接與中國官方聯繫，便交由駐港總領事進行籌劃，此時日本駐香港總領事是岡田晃，與父親頗有交情。在岡田晃的《水鳥外交秘話》著書中，提到他們夫婦二人在一九六九年八月十七日，接受我父母親邀請坐船出海時，他和父親討論到中、日之間重新建立邦交的可能性。當時父親表示願意循他在北京朋友，周恩來和廖承志的渠道，來做橋樑工作。

一九七一年九月十日，駐港總領事岡田晃在日本與日本首相佐藤見面，商討中、日關係的問題。日本首相明確指示岡田晃須注意下列事項：日本同意視台灣為中國一省的看法；同時日本不反對中國加入聯合國；但認為中國應停止干涉日本內政，並聲明雖然日本同意台灣在聯合國席位僅是臨時性，但亦不會贊成在短時間內要求台灣退出聯合國；及日本政府須知道今後進行中、日邦交正常化應走的方向，因為至目前為止，中國全不接受日本官方代表訪問。日本首相希望岡田晃經由他在北京完成此任務。由於此事在香港進行與北京作適當的接觸，首相更准許岡田晃必要時赴北京完成此任務。由於此事在日本外交事務上事關重大，所以岡田晃可以越過外交部直接向首相報告。

身負重任的岡田晃總領事於九月十日返回香港，原本可求助於和他交情很深的一位周恩來在南開大學的同學唐炳源，但不幸唐炳源在六月十七日去世。憑父親與中國的關係，及與岡田晃個人的私交，他認為父親是在中間促成此事的最佳人選。但不巧父親離港外出數星期，岡田晃便求助於恒生銀行關係而相識，但與中國官方往來則全經由父親[16]。國偉三叔與岡田晃第二天見面後，立刻將岡田晃介紹給父親的好友《大公報》發行人費彝民，請他代將日本政府的意向傳達至北京。

九月十六日，周恩來總理接見了來華訪問的日本國會代表川崎秀，會面時周恩來表示；在日本同

意承認中華人民共和國是唯一合法的政府，並接受台灣是中國一省的原則下，中國歡迎日本官方代表來華訪問。岡田晃相信北京方面的迅速反應，必和國偉三叔與岡田晃在九月十七日會面時，他表示在香港的中國官員，與岡田晃會面無問題，但正式與日本外交部會談，那就要看北京政府的決定。他提議佐藤首相親自提出建議，經非官方的日本訪客赴北京送交周恩來。九月二十日岡田晃向首相辦公室作電話報告時，得知佐藤首相尚未考慮致私函給周恩來。

九月二十一日，香港盛傳毛澤東因病逝世，為此取消十月一日的國慶活動，加上又有報導，日本政府會在聯合國大會上，提出「中國代表權問題」。由於這些形勢的變化，岡田晃懷疑中國政府方面能否在九月二十三日以前作出答覆。

一九七一年九月二十二日晚上，岡田晃接到國偉三叔的緊急電話，稱北京因突發重大事件亟需處理，無法與日本政府代表會面，商談雙方關係正常化的事宜，希望岡田晃能諒解。後來才知所指的突發事件是林彪事件。

林彪發起印製小紅皮書「毛語錄」，又在一九六五年發行「人民戰爭萬歲」的小冊，鼓吹中國只要動員落後國家的民眾，就像毛澤東動員中國貧農一樣，便可征服全世界。一九六九年四月舉行的共產黨第九次全國代表大會中，林彪被提名為唯一的副主席，及毛澤東正式接班人。林彪和妻子葉群在一九七○年四月時也許已經感覺到毛澤東對他們的態度有所轉變，而開始秘密進行反叛毛澤東的計劃[17]。

一九七一年九月十四日清晨，蒙古外交部召見中國駐烏蘭巴托大使，告知一架中國飛機（載有林彪夫婦和兒子林立果），闖入蒙古領空，在前一天清晨二時墜毀。中國方面將此消息封鎖數月，外國傳媒至一年以後才獲悉，甚至在一九七二年春天時，日本媒體仍繼續報導林彪，一似他仍在世[18]。

國偉三叔在一九七一年十月八日詢問岡田晃是否願意在十月二十五日的澳大利亞國慶酒會上，與《大公報》發行人費彝民非正式會面。酒會見面時費彝民向岡田晃證實國偉三叔為中、日關係所說及所做的一切，但由於情勢變化，請日方耐心等待來自北京的進一步指示。同一天，在十月二十五日

聯合國通過決議，承認中國政府有聯合國代表權，日本支持台灣的提案遭到否決。國偉三叔相信若非因為林彪事件，使岡田晃無法在駐香港總領事任內，完成中、日復交的任務，否則岡田晃一定可以成為二次大戰後，中、日恢復邦交的首任日本駐華大使[19]。

山一證券

一九六〇年代時，父親再度和牛津求學時期一起打拳的同學小池厚之助是山一證券家族的長子[20]，及日本山一證券的主席。一九六四年山一證券因財務困難，求助於日本興業銀行帶頭的各日本主要銀行，小池厚之助便再向日本銀行及中央銀行求援。

一九七〇年初山一證券財務好轉後，想要在香港設立分公司。因父親與該公司前任主席小池厚之助的關係，山一證券的主管便帶著小池厚之助的信函拜訪父親，請求父親幫助山一在香港開業。當時小池厚之助為表示對山一管理不善負責而辭職的遭遇，促起父親同情之念，他憶起當年祖父遇害後，家中財務困難的日子。現在他的好友亦是家中長子繼承父業，需要幫助的時候，父親便表示，若他本人加入香港山一證券能對他的好友有所幫助的話，他會樂意去做。並立刻對公司建議與數位可能成為董事和股東的人士聯繫[21]。

山一國際〔香港〕有限公司在一九七一年七月正式營業，日高輝為主席，父親是副主席[22]，小池厚之助則是名譽顧問。父親為公司帶入許多具影響力的人士成為董事，並介紹許多重要的顧客。山一國際〔香港〕有限公司訂於八月十六日在香港文華酒店舉行開幕酒會，那天氣候惡劣風球高掛，渡輪已在傍晚停航。幸好風雨並未阻礙貴賓的來臨，有許多社會知名人士出席，山一公司認為是因父親的情面，來賓才會風雨無阻的捧場[23]。

121 築橋

白石信一[24]是山一國際〔香港〕有限公司[25]的業務經理，負責拓展香港業務，常與父親會面，報告東京股市行情和香港公司業務。父親見到公司在香港穩定成長，感到十分欣慰。小池厚之助每年都會參加七月在香港舉行的股東大會，父親總是非常高興能與他見面。白石信一說晚宴時父親招呼小池厚之助夫婦最多，雖則日高輝才是「大老闆」[26]。

山一證券公司在一九八二年時計劃成為獨資公司，便請教父親向山一國際〔香港〕有限公司股東買回所有在外股份的可能性，父親一本他樂於助人的性格，便承擔下這個任務，開始進行向公司的香港股東及董事，買回山一國際〔香港〕有限公司的股份，使山一成為獨資公司，令日本山一的股東和董事對父親感激不已[27]。

母親告訴我銅鑼灣一帶因父親的日本朋友開設的商業機構而繁榮起來。銅鑼灣是祖父早年購買的銅鑼灣山地，後來利氏子孫繼續發展地產土地，也是大多數利氏家族成員，包括我們家在內，於五〇至八〇年代居住的地方。銅鑼灣吸引了許多日本企業在此投資，日本第一家百貨公司大九百貨公司便於一九六〇年十一月在此設連鎖店。由於需要一位中國經理與日本管理配合，父親便介紹了一位能說日文的台灣朋友劉火炎擔任這個職位[28]。日本崇光百貨也在一九八五年五月於銅鑼灣開第一家商店，後來在香港各地都設有分店。另外尚有以高級貨品著名的三越百貨店、日本人俱樂部及日本商會都設在此區。

這些公司在香港開業時，父親總是大力支持，他為三越〔香港〕百貨公司開幕剪綵後，三越集團主席岡田茂在給父親的感謝信中說：

• • • 本人堅信是由於閣下的人品和情面，本公司在香港推展業務活動中，才能有如此眾多的社會賢達和知名人士出席支持，在此致上本人最深的謝意。[29]

八〇年代時，日本投資已成香港經濟主力，為香港帶來繁榮，父親當年與日本所建立的良好關係，對此有相當大的幫助。

一九九七年日本第四大證券交易公司的山一證券公司，受亞洲金融風暴影響不幸破產。香港的山一國際〔香港〕有限公司，則以公司淨值港幣八千八百萬元的售價賣給台灣的京華證券體系[30]，在當時經濟不景的情況下，山一的顧問皆認為售價甚為理想。京華證券體系肯投資買下山一國際〔香港〕有限公司，是想利用山一的國際金融地位以開展中國大陸的業務，公司新名稱為京華山一證券公司。

山一前副總裁白石信一在給我的信中寫到：

山一國際〔香港〕有限公司過去幾年在經營有關中國方面的股票，亦十分活躍。[31]

當年幸得令尊大人和府上諸位親人的大力相助，山一國際〔香港〕有限公司才能在一九七一年開始於香港營業。過去二十七年中，山一國際〔香港〕有限公司不僅在香港，同時在亞洲地區建立起良好的商譽，公司財務健全並有精幹敬業的員工。

以目前的情況，對父親非常可告慰的是，在京華證券體系的承購協議書中，同意所有一百二十一位山一國際〔香港〕有限公司的員工，得以保留原有職位[32]。

第十二章

愛國華人

中國的領導人稱父親是愛國者，表示父親對中國政府的忠誠。但我認為父親的愛國思想有不同的意義，他愛的是中國人民，不論他們在什麼政府統治之下。

父親年輕時寫給母校的一封信，已表示身以中國人為榮，並對國事非常關心。我在四〇年代末時年事稍長，漸能觀察父親平日為人作風，他一直是盡其所能的減輕中國和香港人民所受的苦難，他雖然單獨一人，但他相信總會有影響。

母親有一次提起她初遇父親時，父親說英語帶有牛津口音，但後來〔我懂英文以後〕卻帶中國口音。母親相信他是故意改掉的，大多數人必會以帶有牛津口音的英語炫耀，一輩子不會改，但父親不同。父親素以香港為榮，多年來他曾自費安排英國牛津的學生來香港實地學習，拓展他們的經驗[二]。

父親對政治的冷漠，令他在助人方面更為有力。父親與中國領導人的友誼，常令人誤以為他是共產黨員，他總是說：「我不是共產黨員，就算我想入黨的話也沒資格，因為我是個資本家。」

第二次世界大戰之後，蔣介石國民黨與毛澤東共產黨在國內展開如火如荼的內戰。父親此時便退居香港，認為香港是中國人的地方，只是暫時由英國管轄。他相信在香港一樣可以為民服務，改善大眾生活。所以由那時開始，他便專心香港事務，但從未忘記他在中國的根，只是在等適當的時機再為中國效力。

每年的十月一日是中華人民共和國國慶，在一九五〇年代時，父親是第一位，也是唯一的一位，受

123

解決水荒

香

香港難民人口不斷增加，水荒問題日趨嚴重。當時香港用水全靠水庫積存雨季帶來的雨水供應，初期是一日供水數小時，後來隔日限時供水，最後每三日供水一次，六○年代初期雨水稀少，造成香港嚴重的水荒危機。

香港有困難時，父親總是一如以往當為己責。他常在報章呼籲民眾節約用水。不斷公開地向市民解釋制水原因，和政府正盡全力解決水荒問題[3]。事實上，唯一能夠解決水荒的主要辦法就是由中國取水供應香港，由於北京當局不承認英國在香港的合法關係，不肯和倫敦方面商討有關香港的問題，所以香港只能經由在港華人與中國交涉供水問題。當時在香港僅有父親能與中國政府高層人士溝通，所以與中方協商的責任，便落在父親的肩上。

香港新華通訊社在一九四七年設立，是中國駐香港的非官方領事館，五○年代初由父親好友梁威林任社長。香港向中國的取水事件便由梁威林居中，和港方代表周竣年及父親，與中國政府代表第一書記陶鑄及廣東省省長陳郁開始協商[4]。

一九六三年五月，周恩來總理允許香港運水輪船每日進出珠江取水，同時中國政府為永久解決香港用水問題，下令相關部門著手研究由廣東東江取水運至香港的可行性。一九六三年五月三十一日父親再度公開呼籲民眾節約用水，並對父親當時非常深入的參與討論向中國取水的方法，在各方積極設法解決用水問題的同時，大家都擔心香港水庫即將乾涸無水可用。父親解釋由大陸運水不但困難重重，而且僅是暫時救急終非長久之計。他也提到正和中國協商，為民眾解釋由大陸運水不但困難無水可用。

邀參加慶祝國慶的香港〔非共產黨〕人士[2]。父親多半都會參加，因為他覺得他不但應珍惜與中國領導人的友誼，同時也認為他與中國政要的特殊關係，能為香港居民帶來福祉。香港在各方面都仰賴中國，中國不僅是香港的貨物集散地，同時在食物及飲水方面無一不靠中國供給。

香港永久性的解決缺水問題[5]。

香港在六○年代初期水荒問題極為嚴重，政府宣佈由一九六三年六月一日起，在人口稠密的地區，僅可每四日供水四小時，人口較少的地區，每四日供水三小時[6]。

香港政府終於在一九六四年四月二十三日，和廣東水利局達成協議，正式簽訂供水協定。由東江引水至深圳水庫的水管工程立刻動工[7]，完工之後可對香港輸送用水。《華僑日報》在一九六五年一月訪問父親，談到父親對新年的展望時，父親除了祝賀市民新年萬事如意之外，也希望東江引水至香港的工程能如期在三月一日順利完工[8]。

工程於一九六五年一月完工，三月開始對香港供水。由每年六千萬立方米[9]開始，到夏天時香港三分之二的總用水量，皆由東江引進[10]。深圳供水典禮中，父母親是僅有的香港人士，周竣年爵士原本亦想參加，但未得英方許可[11]，但卻無人能阻父親前去深圳。

一九六七年暴動令中國對香港供水受到影響，原本中國同意香港水務署要求，在十月一日至次年六月三十日之間，對香港供水一百五十億加侖，外加十八億加侖，但在六月初時，香港已用罄中國同意的供水量。香港希望中國在七月份能額外供水二十萬加侖，但中國在六月二十八日仍遲遲未能答覆。於是工務局局長Michael Wright決定在中國未答覆之前，由六月初開始每日供水八小時，至六月二十九日起隔日僅供水四小時[12]。根據當時香港與中國的供水協議，要到十月一日才再度開始對香港供水。

香港水荒在一九六七年七月時更加嚴重，政府由七月十三日開始，每四日只供水四小時[13]。沒有人知道中國不理會香港請求增加供水的真正原因，只能臆測中國當時忙於應付文化大革命混亂，而無暇顧及香港市民的需求。

到一九六○年代末期生活才逐漸恢復正常，後來又相繼增建兩期由東江引水至香港的工程，第一期由一九七六年開始至一九七八年完工，第二期一九八一年開工，將供水量增加到一年六億六千萬立方米[14]，為香港居民永久解決了民生用水問題。

香港與中國之間

父母問題

親與中國的特殊關係在六〇年代引起部份人士的妒忌和猜疑。雖然父親曾為香港出力解決用水問題[15]，但有些人批評父親在協商過程中，偏袒中方利益[16]。香港殖民政府需要中國支持時就要父親幫忙，但又希望父親和中國保持距離。可是父親絕不會背棄在中國友誼深遠的朋友，所以父親和戴麟趾(David Trench)總督〔任期1964年至1971年〕經常意見不和有衝突。水荒嚴重時，若非中國在緊要關頭伸出援手，為香港解決供水問題，香港根本已不適居住。

父親認為中國人只要中國方面准許入境，就有權去中國探親訪友，無論如何他是個有自由的人，所以當殖民政府禁止父親回國甚至母親返鄉探親，父親的盛怒可想而知。父親一開始就看不起戴麟趾，認為他根本不夠資格做香港總督[17]，他相信戴麟趾既要利用中國人，但又對中國人很差，令父親對他極為反感。李國寶當時與父親每星期至少見面一次，日後他告訴我，父親當時雖屬親英，卻無法忍受殖民政府對中國人的侮蔑，在多次爭執後，父親憤而辭去所有香港政府義務工作的職務[18]。

此時大家都公認父親是下一位被英女王封為爵士的人選，母親還特別選購了一個非常美麗的青花花瓶，上面繪有引喻福、祿、壽的鹿、松及一隻獼猴捧著桃子，來慶祝這件事，豈知父親回來竟告訴母親他已辭職的消息。

一九六五年六月十三日父母親由非洲東岸的馬達加斯加返港時，有幾位非官守立法議員在機場接機，由簡悅強交給父親一份政府接受他辭職的信函[19]。一九六六年時父親已辭去所有香港義務性的公職，他的辭職表示今後他的所做所為不須得到香港政府認可，但並不表示父親不再為香港民眾服務，從此以後他只代表自己而非香港政府。

後來東亞銀行的李國寶赴倫敦，問及有關人士有為什麼父親對香港社會曾作多方貢獻而未被封爵的原因，竟是香港殖民地政府某些官員，將父親列入黑名單之內[20]。

父親與中國建立良好關係，並不只是因為父親知道香港終須回到中國，他希望能先為主權順利移交做好鋪路工作。父親曾多次告訴我：「主權移交過程必須在平和及互利的情況下進行，絕不可涉及武力。」北京領導人深知父親的誠意，非常尊重父親。父親深信應由港人治港，香港的將來絕不能單靠英國或中國[21]。可惜父親無法親眼見到香港主權和平轉移。

父親和國偉三叔似乎是香港最先知道鄧小平對香港一國兩制，及香港保持五十年不變政策的人士。在七○年代初，父親和國偉三叔一起去中國時，某政要召父親入室，告知一些特別消息。父親對國偉三叔說：「國偉，你也進來，我要你聽聽談話內容。[22]」當時中國政要對父親保證香港主權移交後，一切維持現狀不變。

父母親在七○年代初來多倫多探望我們時，父親曾和我談到中國問題。他認為在過去的兩個世紀中國已受夠苦難，二十一世紀是屬於中國人的，而我一定可以見到中國再富強起來。我才發現他對中國及中國人民的關切有多深。

父親一直認為中國與香港政府和市民關係歧見太深，一九八二年六月父親在德國法蘭克福的國際會議中，對香港經濟機會的演講中說到：

中、港政府之間的關係，無可置疑的存在緊張情況，表面看來比實際的嚴重。這大都由於殖民政府以前官員的淺見和倫敦殖民部政策。但香港市民與中國政府的關係卻並非如此。

這段話是指一九六○年代的情形，後來父親又提到一九七○年代總督麥理浩所作的改善：

在總督任期內，因他獨到長遠的眼光，和治事的能力，令中國與香港的關係開始有了顯著的改進。[23]

中國關係

對父親來說，七〇年代是他致力為香港與中國政府之間做橋樑工作的日子。他與殖民地政府關係決裂後，政府再也不能批評父親言行。當年香港商人根本不願進入中國旅遊或投資，事實上，中國是港商避而不去的地方。

父親為香港主權交接能順利進行，認為雙方需要對話。為了促進香港與中國雙方的交流，父親每年春節都會舉辦春茗，邀請願意與中國接觸，認識中方代表的工商界領袖，政府要員和父親自己的外國友人參加。因父親在香港的人際關係，受邀者幾乎都會出席，如此一來雙方便能開始交往，繼續使所有人獲益。

新華社亦十分願意與香港工商界及立法、行政兩局議員多接觸，當時的新華社社長梁威林日後告訴我：「若由我發帖邀請這些人，沒有人會到，但你爸爸出面就不同了，大家都會來。」[24]父親每年春節在利園酒店舉辦的春茗，就像香港名人集會，後來成為香港一年一度的社交盛事。

父親的春茗只請男賓，女眷不在邀請之內，但女性議員仍被邀請。父親的秘書李姑娘在會場招呼賓客入座後，宴席開始之前即須離場。一本名流雜誌中有段花邊新聞報導，說父親有位外籍友人初到香港受邀參加春茗，帶了妻子一起赴宴，到了利園酒店才知僅有男客可參加宴席，連忙將太太送回旅館，再獨自回到會場[25]。

有一年我們回香港時，正逢父親舉辦春茗，但只有衛權可去，父親便要我當晚帶孩子們去利舞台看魔術表演，因為我不能參加。雖然父親認為春茗是男人的宴會，但他去世後卻由從未出席過春茗的母親出面擔任榮譽主席，繼續數年舉辦春茗，父親有知的話不知作何感想！

父親也和其他中國人一樣常回鄉下故居祖祠。嘉寮村是戰後父親最先著手幫助的地方，他見到幼年和祖父坐船運送曾祖父遺體經過的舊橋已破損不堪，便捐造新橋。我們在九〇年代回去時，一到嘉寮村，村民就急著帶我們去看這座他們非常引以為榮的新橋樑。

我們同時也參觀了父親和銘洽二叔合資贈建的新校舍及學童遊樂場，另外還有一家父親幫助村民開創的小型製帽廠，廠房是一間十分整潔光亮的大房間。日後我們再次返回嘉寮村時，這家製帽廠已開始兼做海外名牌帽子，村民對他們的成就非常驕傲。

一九九二年，新會市政當局特別頒贈新會榮譽市民金鑰給母親，以紀念父親對故鄉的貢獻。由於曾祖父早年由開平移居新會，開平在一九九三年亦對母親頒贈金鑰。

多年來父親和他的弟弟都一本國人飲水思源的傳統，在故鄉興建醫院，並對祖祠故居新會出錢出力。

父母親在一九七八年來多倫多時，對我們提到許多新疆、甘肅旅行的趣聞。並給我們一些相片留念，我最喜歡的是父親騎單峰駱駝的一張。在新疆自治區的烏魯木齊時，當地族長以貴賓宴席款待父母親一行人，他們第一次吃到新鮮的髮菜。髮菜是中國人在年節為討其名吉利而常用的吉祥菜，族長為了要對遠道因為音近廣州話的「發財」，一般人都不知髮菜是一種沙漠植物，還以為是海產。母親說：「當我看見而來父母親表示歡迎的誠意，特別準備了一道當地最名貴的上菜，就是羊眼。盆中羊頭的那對眼睛瞪著我看的時候，我已經要作嘔了！」

因父母親常去中國旅遊，所以父親對中國的見聞非常廣博。新華社的何銘思常陪同他們進入中國訪問，他說父親在旅途中，對大城市發展及鄉村僻野的各種大小事情都充滿興趣。

一九七七年他們遠赴中國西北部旅遊甘肅省及新疆維吾爾自治區，次年一月父親還在香港華商銀行公會作《祖國西北行》[26]的演講，放映上百張的彩色風景及劉家峽水電站的幻燈片，甚至還展示了他由新疆戈壁沙漠帶回的石塊。父親對特殊的石頭非常欣賞，他對喜愛的事物有感染性的狂熱。

在文化交流方面父親亦曾出力推廣。一九六八年，在河北省滿城出土的西漢〔公元前二〇六年至公元二十四年〕劉勝墓[27]，內有中山靖王后竇綰的「金縷玉衣」，及其他在一九六九年甘肅武威東漢墓出土的銅奔馬，即一般人稱為「踏燕飛馬」、鍍金銅宮燈和秦陵將軍俑等古物[28]安排在香港展出。便請父親協助統籌展覽，父親得到霍英東同意將展覽場地設在星光行，並安排保險、警衛安全及售票等事宜。展覽規模相當龐大，共佔地三層，參觀民眾反應非常熱烈。此次中國歷代文物國寶能在香港首《大公報》長約一百八十八公分。

次展出深具意義，令殖民地市民對中國的歷史和文化留下深刻印象[29]。中國官方時常經由香港新華社在年節時將一些特別的禮物，像香港市面買不到的中國特產水果，和春節的牡丹花、金桔樹和小蜜柑送給父親表示敬意，父親對中國送他的禮物覺得非常榮幸。父親去世後，中國官方仍繼續送禮物給母親。

七〇年代有一天李姑娘接到香港新華社的電話，用廣東話說有「一粒荔枝」特別由中國運來香港給父親，要李姑娘派部大車去取，她不明白為什麼要用大車去取一粒荔枝。李姑娘誤以為新華社的人用俗語將「粒」字的發音改為近「籮」字的發音，但她還是派了大車去取，結果取回一大籮的荔枝。原來音近「粒」字發音的「籮」年輕人已不大用[30]，所以把李姑娘搞糊塗了，這是她一輩子也不會忘記的笑話。那天所有公司同仁都有分食到荔枝。

父親一生中助人無數，常有人送禮到家中或寫字樓。其中有一兩位對父親的成就非常妒忌，故意送鐘給父親，令李姑娘非常反感，因為國人送禮最忌送鐘，廣東民俗「送鐘」有咒人早死之意。但父親毫不迷信，他說「如果他們要送鐘給我，也沒什麼不好。[31]」

父親是戰後香港首位經常赴中國旅遊的知名人士，以父親的名氣，當年國內有許多青年男子自稱是父親的兒子，但他們不知報章上提到父親訪問大陸時，母親都有同行，同時也必有中國官員陪同隨行。父親對這類無聊流言全不理會，〔同樣地，國內也有許多年青女子自稱是母親的乾女兒，因為她們無法說是母親的親生女兒，只好自認是乾女兒〕辦公室員工每次聽到有人要向父親歸宗認祖時，都當笑話談論。樹源叔公和公司同仁都認為若是妄指別人的話還有可信度，但這些人想要與父親扯上關係的話，就應事先做些調查工作再開口[32]。

父親和香港太古集團的姚剛在七〇年代時成為好朋友[33]，雖然父親身為利氏家族企業的主席，而且利氏家族與太古集團在一九四八年開始就建立了良好的商業關係，但父親和姚剛是在一九七二年，姚剛成為共濟會〔美生會〕分會主席之後，才開始成為好友。在共濟會的會議中，他們二人經常坐在一起，每年一月在日本舉行的共濟會會議他們也常一起出席，父親開始對他產生信任，在私事和公事上常請姚剛參與。

姚剛在中國工作多年，有豐富的經歷和良好的人際關係，加上他能說多種中國方言，每當父親有國內的朋友訪問香港時，任何飯局聚餐，父親總是要姚剛一起參加。正因如此姚剛得以結識多位來港做非官式訪問的官員，如廣東省省長、副總理及各部門的首長等[34]。父親樂於利用他和中國領導人的特殊關係，幫助各方人士的熱心，令姚剛非常欽佩。

一九七八年中國對外開放投資，中國政府便邀請太古集團訪問北京。太古集團由一八〇〇年代開始在中國即有業務，當公司宣佈駐中國代表人選時，父親堅持應由姚剛代表駐中國，但父親認為有姚剛居中對雙方都有益處，所以姚剛還是去了北京。

一九八一年有一天父親打電話給姚剛，要姚剛在下星期三騰出整天時間，幫父親接待一位由中國來香港訪問的部長，父親並要姚剛為這位北京來訪有工程學識背景的部長，安排計劃當日訪問行程。那天早上八點三十分，漢剑哥也同在利園酒店，父親為姚剛介紹認識了當時是電子工業部部長的江澤民，父親對姚剛說：「姚剛，好好招呼這位客人，他是個前途不可限量的人。」姚剛帶江澤民參觀機場設施，特別是太古集團的國泰航空公司飛機維修部門，及政府在九龍興建的廉價屋宇。父親認為姚剛與江澤民都來自上海，有許多共同話題，是接待江澤民的最佳人選。江澤民由香港結束訪問返國後，即出任上海市市長，在一九四八年時，是魏建議姚剛去英國為太古集團工作。江澤民成為黨總書記，魏鳴一成了中國國際信託投資公司泰富集團的主席[35]。姚剛深信父親是個有遠見的人，和許多其他人一樣，都認為父親對人的觀察力極有眼光。

麥理浩總督是第一位接受中國邀請，訪問北京及華西的香港總督。當時父母親正在新華社社長王匡[37]陪同下前往海南島旅遊，為了要讓父母親能參加通車典禮，還特別派專機來海南島接父母親前往廣州。但當時風大，飛機被迫由北轉西。在訪問結束時，並赴廣州出席廣九鐵路直通車[36]通車典禮。副部長魏鳴一，與姚剛是北京大學的同室校友，在一九四八年時，二人就財經方面問題交換不少意見。後來才知道江澤民的江澤民特別感到興趣。姚剛並以豐盛的午宴款待江澤民，二人就財經方面問題交換不少意見。

飛至肇慶，然後再從肇慶趕赴廣州[38]。通車典禮對父親意義重大，它代表中、英雙方誠意溝通的重要開端[39]。

父親不但為中國及香港建立良好關係，亦將企業觸角延伸至歐洲及日本，如英國倫敦的羅富齊銀行、丹麥的摩勒集團及日本的山一證券公司。在香港投資的外商，後來亦相繼赴中國投資。父親在忙於經營企業及開展新事業的同時，他的聲望也不斷提升。父親認為與人交往相識之後，便有可能成為生意的夥伴，當中國在七〇年代末開放外人投資時，父親便率先回應投資與中國合作。

父親在一九七〇年代時，不但已得到香港社會各階層人士和政府官員的尊敬與信賴，中國領導人對父親亦是敬重有加。國際上都稱他是香港的「決策性人物」之一[40]。此時香港政府在順應民意方面所做的改善，令父親非常欣慰，這些改善可為將來和平的主權移交，莫下良好的基礎。在這段非常重要的年月裡，他不但為中、港雙方設立了商業的橋樑，亦為香港未來政府的基礎架構做了極大的努力。

當時各界都認為父親是一九九七年七月一日香港回歸中國後，最理想的特區首長人選。每當我聽到這種說辭時，我總是提醒對方，一九九七年時父親將年達九十二歲了。

我認為父親以七十八歲高齡，仍能像三十五歲的壯年人一樣有活力的工作，是因為他充滿了不同的理想，永遠想要開始新的計劃。一九八〇年代初，父親又在中國進行了兩項新計劃，一是將廣州國際長途電話系統現代化，及在深圳、廣州之間舖設雙軌鐵路，可惜父親臨終之前未能見到這些計劃實現[41]。

中國在一九八二年一月首次在貿易上超過日本成為香港最大的物資供應國家。父親相信中、港貿易增加後，更須改善中國本身的運輸系統：

為應付日漸增加的中、港貿易，中國廣東與香港之間的交通勢必須要改善，以加速貨物的輸送，減低運送及處理成本。應第一優先建立廣州至深圳的鐵路，而且必須是雙軌鐵路，連接九龍。香港是南中國海岸唯一有現代化設施的深水港，加上日後往返香港與廣州兩地的貨櫃

花園酒店

中

國開放外人投資時，為表示對中國政府的信心，父親率先回應。那時國內旅館水準落後，他計劃要在中國建造一間最大、最華麗的現代化旅館。

中國共產黨在一九七○年代尚未有與外人投資合作經驗，父親是首位外人在國內投資，政府繁文縟節加上冗長無謂的會商，非常影響工程進度，令投資成本不斷增高。

父親原本計劃在北京興建新酒店，但中方建議將酒店建在海南島，父親認為參與合作計劃的中方人員，缺乏經營企業的概念。七○年代的海南島，尚未有足夠的基本設施，來承受如此龐大的計劃。

父親後來決定在廣州離火車站不遠，廠商前來貿易展覽會場頗為方便的黃金地段選擇建地。結果選定在廣州空防重地白雲山飛機場附近，與建花園酒店。中國官方便向父親提出，花園酒店須在屋頂裝置高射炮，及地下須有防空壕的要求。父親向當時的中央軍事委員會副主席楊尚昆，就北京的要求多次耐心協商，後來北京方面終於同意放棄，但仍堅持酒店須有自己的緊急發電設施，直到今日仍是非常必要的設施。

花園酒店﹝香港﹞有限公司成立後，便與廣州嶺南置業公司在一九八○年三月二十八日簽訂﹝43﹞合作協議﹝44﹞，在位於廣州白雲賓館南方，環市東路青菜崗，原為菜圃佔地五萬二千六百平方公尺的的

我們家在一九八五年回廣州參加花園酒店開幕典禮時，我能毫無困難的由旅館房間直接打電話回加拿大多倫多，與未能同來廣州的兒子通話，令我非常感動。

數量增多，所以海上交通運輸應儘速改為鐵路，由較為便捷及運費較低的雙軌鐵路輸送，將使香港、中國及全世界都可受惠。﹝42﹞

土地上建造廣州花園酒店[45]。花園酒店由廣州珠江外資工程公司分兩期工程建造，第一期工程一千三百房間，第二期九百四十間，旅館房間每間造價約五萬美元[46]。整個計劃包括旅館、會議中心及公寓大樓。

父親經由友人及銀行籌措與建花園酒店的資金，除父親本人為主要股東外，並有許多友人支持他。另外在姚剛遊說之下，太古集團亦一反公司投資的原則做了小股東。直到今日仍和利氏家族不同企業保持密切聯繫的丹麥摩勒公司，當年也因父親的關係，成為花園酒店股東之一。此計劃外資總投資額為港幣七億元[47]。

我仍記得父親談論這個計劃時的興奮和期盼，他說花園酒店落成開幕時，不但將是中國首間五星級最大的觀光旅館，同時也是世界上最美、最大的旅館之一，這是他給中國的獻禮。一九八○年十二月二十七日，由楊尚昆為花園酒店破土奠基，父親在奠基典禮中表示，希望花園酒店能為中國的現代化盡一份微薄的力量[48]。

花園酒店的建築師是父親友人司徒惠，他亦是香港中文大學的設計建築師。在最初的設計圖中，中國資方要求全部旅館房間皆為一式的雙人房[49]，引起不同的爭議。父親希望將來花園酒店落成後吳慶塘父子能負責管理，他們父子二人認為一個現代化的酒店，應具備有大小不同功能的旅館房間，同時他們覺得酒店附近無甚風景，因此酒店頂樓不適合設旋轉餐廳。這些歧見令工程進度頗受影響，後來雙方終於達成協議，將旅館房間重新設計，具有不同大小的房間，並增添套房以應市場需要，但旋轉餐廳仍照原計劃進行。此次爭議，導致吳慶塘父子和資方意見不合，雙方產生惡感[50]。

一九八三年初因財務管理不善，酒店建費不斷追加。建造過程中所發生的各種問題，令父親精神壓力很大[51]。父親在七月去世後，北京方面便要求母親擔任花園酒店〔香港〕有限公司的主席[52]，新任的香港新華社社長許家屯出面宴請所有中國資方代表和母親共餐後，母親同意出任主席，承擔解決花園酒店財務危機的重任。雖然太古集團僅是小股東，但仍由姚剛出面幫助解決困難，他應允解決花園酒店中方代表，在太古可派稽核員赴中國查帳的條件下，太古將再代為籌措足夠資金。但太古

的稽核人員發現帳目根本無從查起，因為這一億美金的支出，居然全無紀錄可循。雖然如此，為了要使酒店工程能繼續起見，仍要求原有投資者追加投資金額，並非只是因為中方的要求，而亦是為紀念父親對此計劃所付出的心血。太古集團首先再增加投資金額，同時表示若有任何股東不願繼續投資，差額皆由太古取代。並將現任花園酒店會計師停職，然後酒店才逐漸步向完工的階段[53]。

一九八四年十月二十八日，花園酒店開放營業，主要租客有美國及日本的領事館[54]，領事官邸則設在同屬花園酒店建築的公寓大樓內[55]。父母親的老友緒方鈴子亦在花園酒店內，成立聯絡日本政府和商務的辦事處，後來到一九八八年時，她一直在東京為花園酒店推展業務。

花園酒店於一九八五年八月二十八日正式舉行盛大開幕典禮，邀請來賓在酒店作客三天。我們特別飛回香港與家人一起赴廣州慶祝，當時由香港赴廣州的直通車許多車廂都被來賓包下，其實慶祝活動從香港火車站就已開始了。

到達酒店時，我們受到貴賓式的歡迎，正如我所料，花園酒店是一座雄偉壯觀而華麗酒店。看到母親優雅地站在台上以國語致辭時，我非常為母親驕傲，多麼希望父親也能在場與我們分享這一切。

一九八九年六四天安門事件之後，全國經濟都受影響，花園酒店業務亦受牽連，全無收入可支付銀行貸款的利息[56]，面臨被銀行接收的命運。母親決定親赴北京請求支援，計劃正式拜訪國家主席楊尚昆，他是一個很切實際的人，而且對我父母親非常尊重。

一九九〇年初，母親在新華社一位高級官員陪同下，正式與國家主席楊尚昆會面，楊並在釣魚台設晚宴款待母親[57]。母親對楊尚昆表示，花園酒店的股東在走投無路的情況下，逼不得已只有請中國政府接收，或關門結束營業。楊尚昆對母親說：「利太太，請放心，花園酒店決不會關門的。」

母親返港後一個月，中國銀行通知花園酒店〔香港〕有限公司，表示銀行願意以無抵押信用方式，貸款美金二千五百萬元給花園酒店，母親的「救亡」任務算是圓滿達成。所幸花園酒店業務後來逐漸回復正常，故未動用這筆貸款，日後在短短幾年之內，所有其他貸款亦全部還清[58]。

父親晚年時，有人問他為何將錢放在只有四厘利息的中國銀行，而不放在其他利息較高的金融機構，父親說：「我不會將錢提取出來的，中國是我的國家」[59]。

第十三章

生意人

父親對利姓的解釋是「勝利的利，利益的利」[1]，而父親也的確具備贏家的心智。其實父親根本稱不上是個「成功」的生意人，真正的生意人凡事皆以利為出發點，人們常說以父親的條件應該有更多的財富，但父親不同，他是個有社會良知的生意人，他的的出發點是人的福祉為先，獲利其次。他認為金錢應用在社會大眾，而非貪圖個人享受。一九七五年《南華早報》Berta Manson 在她的「企業王國創造者」的系列專題報導，引述父親在專訪時，非常遺憾的表示，香港富有的大企業「對香港社會廣大的貧窮青年做得太少」[2]。

香港有許多做投機生意一夕致富的人[3]，父親對這種事最為憎恨。因為他們不但搞亂經濟，提高物價，還使一般市民生活更加困難，他認為投機份子是社會禍亂的根源。雖然利氏家族在香港擁有大批產業，但每當房價飛漲時，父親是躊躇不前，因為如此一來居住問題將成為社會大眾無力負擔的民生支出[4]。父親在許多公開場合，發表反對屋價上漲的談話，而且對他自己的言論，絕對言行一致。

非投機性的投資，對父親來說才是成功企業的首要條件，他認為「公司一定要有堅固的基礎及長遠的計劃⋯⋯在長期漸進式的穩定發展中，才能有最佳的改進」[5]，在一九八二年的演講中：他說

這些商業活動〔投機〕也許會令少數人致富，但並不能對整個社會帶來財富，也對全民提供很少就業機會。高投機性的活動性質在新「香港秩序」中將無法獲益。[6]

137

這也是我從父親身上學到的經驗。鑽營投機生意的人，能在一朝之間致富，但也能在一夕之間一無所有，而累及許多無辜受害者。父親認為投資應該是投資在民眾，為社會提供工作機會，及提高市民生活水準。現在的年輕人聽到這種論調，必認為早已不合潮流，但我認為這才是健全社會的基礎。

香港購買樓宇的方式，直到現在仍和世界其他地方不太相同，市民必須通宵不睡漏夜排隊搶頭籌，取得號碼才有機會購買。父親常將他自己的理念灌輸給別人，李姑娘說在七〇年代時，有一天父親在辦公室對員工說，任何人若想買新地盤的公寓樓宇，他可向他熟識的地產發展商幫他們拿到前面的號碼，可有機會先買，但必須保證樓宇是買來自用，而非炒樓花。李姑娘說：「雖然我喪失了炒樓花賺些錢的機會，但我不敢背著你爸爸去做這事！」

父親買東西時從不討價還價，他覺得每個人都有權討生活，若覺得價錢太高可以不買。我記得有一年過中國年，和父親及幾位他們的朋友一起去逛年宵市場，母親的一位朋友想買些桃花[7]回家，便向花販還價，結果被父親勸止，他認為應該讓這些小生意人在過年時多賺錢。

大家都知道父親是個一絲不苟的人，他每著手開始一個計劃，一定事必躬親的去完成。身為許多企業的主席，公司的年度報告其實並非父親的責任，但父親必自修正逐字評讀後才可付印[8]。父親有太多事業的構想及廣泛的社會關係，他只對生意交涉及開創過程最為熱衷，對公司運作營業及細節並無太大興趣。所以有時會誤信管理階層，令公司營業虧損[9]。父親生性耿直，他以為手下處事態度應該與他一致，當他相信一個人的時候，任何人的忠告提示都不會動搖父親的信任，此時最令母親感到無助難過，因為她是旁觀者清，但又無力改變。

戰後除了利氏兄弟的企業外，父親也自己另創事業，像九龍的士公司就不很成功。父親也許是香港第一位買入賓士柴油引擎汽車，做出租汽車的人。但後來因管理不善，在過海隧道完工之後便將公司出售[10]。

雖然父親可以利用很多關係賺大錢，可是我常聽他說，他一點也不想做香港的首富，乍聽起來真不像是生意人的論調。他生性儉省，金錢對他個人來說並無太大意義，就像其他許多利家人一樣，

父親從不穿過份奢華的衣著，也不開最名貴的座車。記得他曾告訴我，勞斯萊斯汽車公司剛來香港對父親推銷時，他說：「我買不起這種奢侈品」，他寧願開他那部福士的高爾富小車。但是父親又會毫不吝嗇的，買最昂貴的首飾珠寶給母親，這也許是他唯一肯花錢的地方。

一九六〇年三月，父親帶領香港貿易訪問團赴西非考察，返港時對香港製造商在貨品包裝、價格、尺碼及市場推銷上，做了若干建議；譬如鞋類包裝紙盒應予改進，因鼠類經常咬壞用漿糊黏製的紙盒；瓷器運送時應裝在有填充物保護的容器內以防破損；服裝尺碼應標準化等。並對廠家因品質低劣而喪失貿易機會感到惋惜，他相信香港貨品在品質改進後，價格可與日本貨看齊，因為市場對港貨需求極大。又建議所有香港製造商，應聯合印製商品目錄冊，令買家對商品能一目了然，容易訂貨[二]。

父親於一九六三年八月應香港政府邀請，組團赴德國法蘭克福參加國際貿易會議。又因德國政府已邀請父親赴德國訪問在先，父親便安排同時在德國開會及訪問。父親第一站到達倫敦時，接到聖詹姆士皇宮送交父親一份信函，邀請父親於七月二十四日（星期三）赴白金漢宮接受英女皇賜封大英帝國司令CBE勳章。因為此次母親未能同行，父親便邀請了Jack上校及Tom Churchill少將兩位友人同赴白金漢宮觀禮，由於事出突然父親全無準備，只得穿租來的大禮服接受勳銜。

父親常喜歡去歐洲旅行，同年夏天他由倫敦飛去丹麥的阿本若，探訪老朋友Jebsens，然後去他們在羅木島的別墅。那時母親留在家中聽到父親在冰冷的海峽游泳時，她說父親大概還以為自己很年輕。然後由另一友人從羅木島開車送父親去德國漢堡，再由兩位德國官方嚮導帶領參觀各大城市。結束德國訪問之後，父親便飛往維也納與國偉三叔會合，考察奧地利的水力發電廠。最後在八月底父親再率團赴法蘭克福參加會議，父親對觀摩學習新的事物從不感到厭倦。

香港的小型工業在六〇年代如雨後春筍般的興起，對業主來說，工廠用地是一大困難。父親在一九六三年三月，代表小型工廠業主在立法局會議中替他們請願，反對政府強制收回工廠用地售給發展商。父親在議會中強調，這些工廠業主既然由政府手中合法取得牌照開工，就應受到保護，政府須標賣工廠用地時，政府若須徵用工廠的土地，就應先為廠家另覓新址，以合理的租金租給廠家。政府須通

知廠方讓他們有同等機會參加競投。他反對大型工廠併吞小廠的做法，並強調保護這些勤奮工作的工廠業主的重要性，因為他們是香港社會的基層骨幹[12]。

那段期間父親對外國資金多投資外地而不來香港，引以為憂。他在一九六三年向立法局提議廢除徵收遺產稅，以吸引更多公司在香港設立，政府可由此獲得大量稅收，比起政府在一九六三年僅收到二千萬元的遺產稅相比較，後者實微不足道[13]。可惜他的建議未被採納。

為香港帶來嶄新的產品。為紀念新工廠的設立，董事會每年資助十名坪洲學童，在坪洲兩所學校免費就讀[14]。香港鋼管公司採用最好的原料，鋼鐵為日本製鐵株式會社供應，又向八幡製鐵所進口滾筒鋼索捲。父親去世時公司仍正常營業，後來公司才轉讓出售。

父親生意雖多，但從未減少研究解決工程難題的興趣，父親在戰後不久就建議政府由跑馬地至香港仔興建過山隧道，當時根據父親估計建築費約港幣一百多萬元，但政府不感興趣。若干年後此隧道依然需要興建，但造價已高出許多[15]。

一九六四年立法局討論英軍在香港石崗及新界地區興建軍事建築案時，父親提出在設計這些建築物，應考慮到日後僅少量修繕，即可轉為公眾圖書館、學校或政府辦公室等民事用途，令將來這些建築物由英國歸還中國香港政府時〔港人治港〕，仍為有使用價值的建築物[16]。由此可見，父親早已開始為香港做一九九七年主權移交的準備，亦不願浪費資源。

一九六四年父親在我們所住的崇明大廈屋頂，造了一個太陽能熱水器。他在一張大帆布上放置六條直徑六吋的黑水管，經過黑水管吸收太陽的熱能，使熱水器內的水成為可用的熱水。這座香港首次建造的太陽能熱水器，材料費僅一百元，香港傳媒對此都有廣泛報導，雖然試驗成功，但從未用做商業用途。[17]

父親除了幫助其他廠家，本身亦參與工業活動，一九六四年父親在香港離島坪洲成立香港鋼管公司，十二月二十一日由Hon. D. R. Holmes主持開幕儀式，父親充滿自信的表示，新成立的工廠將

新隧道

從一九五五年開始，政府與民間就不斷公開研討與建跨海大橋，或海底隧道，以改善香港、九龍之間交通問題的可能性。跨海大橋會受氣候影響，尤其在颱風季節安全堪慮，而海底隧道工程牽涉問題又太過複雜，且建費更高。經多年研究討論結果，香港政府終於在一九六三年五月，推翻跨海大橋的設想，全力集中促建海底隧道[18]。

香港與九龍之間有海底隧道後，車輛便無須在油麻地汽車渡輪排隊候船渡海，到了對岸再坐的士。我們家只有在特別家庭聚餐或新年時才駕車上船渡海。那時若用渡輪載車過海，至少費時一日，所以市民如非必要都是搭渡輪過海。

一九六三年初，父親與會德豐船務有限公司的馬登(George Marden)及嘉道理，為興建香港與九龍之間的海底隧道，共組維多利亞城市發展有限公司[19]，一九六四年一月將計劃藍圖送交政司和官產及測量部[20]。但雙線道隧道行人及汽車均可通行，後來又改為香港隧道有限公司。原本計劃為到一九六五年八月十一日，香港政府通過海底隧道工程議案時，將隧道改為車輛專用，不受颱風影響二十四小時全天候開放。工程預算為港幣二億一千萬元，下年秋季即可動工，香港政府擁有四分之一新隧道的所有權[21]。

香港政府批准海底隧道興建工程之後，父親積極的向英國商業投資銀行籌措到大部份的資金[22]，六〇年代香港經濟不景，投資意願不高，僅有父親、利希慎置業公司、馬登家族和嘉道理家族為海底隧道最初的投資者。父親曾嘗試說服油麻地渡輪公司加入投資，因該公司未來營業將受新隧道的影響，但公司主席劉定國反對，直到今天這個決定仍令他引為憾事[23]。

在公司籌組過程中，父親曾拜訪《大公報》發行人費彝民，徵詢與建海底隧道時機的意見，我相信父親所指的是政治時機。費彝民告訴父親，香港絕對需要此隧道以解決交通問題，便利市民。並對父親保證香港穩定的政局將會長期維持[24]。

父母親在七〇年代初來多倫多時，父親就對我說過建造海底隧道的種種困難。尤其在初期很難說服香港政府給予財務支持，但當法國政府表示有興趣提供資金時，香港政府又立刻改變態度表示有意加入。

監督隧道工程亦成了父親的任務。雖然漢釗哥日後對我說：「今天建造海底隧道易如煲鴨湯」[25]，但在六〇年代仍是一件浩大艱巨的工程，父親所學是土木工程，當第一節沉箱沉下海底時，父親便邀請費彝民至工地參觀，在隧道開放通車的前夕，父親又請費彝民與他經海底隧道由香港驅車至九龍。父親並沿途對他解釋通風空氣循環系統，及防海水滲透等工程方面的技術問題[26]。費對父親的全程參與每個細節，一絲不苟的治事精神非常佩服。父親對海底隧道的實現非常自傲。

一九七二年八月二日海底隧道正式通車後，香港、九龍之間的交通有了極大的改革[27]，駕車渡海不再是件令人頭疼的大事，油麻地渡輪等候過海的車輛長龍已成歷史。但初期海底隧道營業並不十分理想，因為每次使用隧道須付費五元，但使用過的人都喜歡它的方便，加上也沒有其他的方法能開車過海。後來港幣兌英磅匯率十分有利，貸款很快還清，公司也開始有豐厚的利潤[28]。

海底隧道通車不久我們回到香港時，堂兄妹便帶我們由九龍開車至香港，其中一位堂妹對我說：「每次我們付五元隧道費時，其中兩元就進了你爸爸的口袋！」我相信她是太過誇大其辭了。

電話公司

一九六二年香港電話公司主席H.R.M. Clenland，邀請父親擔任電話公司董事，後來在一九六五年父親成為公司主席[29]。

一九六〇年代香港電話系統頗為落後，一九六六年全港只有三十萬條電話線，平均百人之中僅八人有電話，有六萬人申請排隊等候電話。於是父親便決定擴展公司業務，在香港不同地方增建電話

接收站，預備將電話線增加至一百八十萬條。電話公司又在東南亞海底舖設電纜，以改善通訊品質，同時在技術及管理方面增聘人手，應付日漸增加的需要。同年公司宣佈利潤已增至港幣二千九百萬元(30)。

父親一向對德國機器深具信心，所以決定採購德國電訊設備，來改進香港電話系統。當時Jardine Fleming(31)建議父親用瑞士法郎採購，豈知後來法郎兌港幣巨幅升值，令購買成本非常昂貴，但父親仍堅持電話費不漲。此次採購引起不少爭議，也令父親倍受責難。李國寶的父親李福樹亦是電話公司董事之一，認為是誤信不當的建議，而導致錯誤的決定(32)。

一九六九年時因大眾迫切需要，香港電話線已增加至五十萬條，即每一百人中有十二點四五人有一條通話線，為亞洲除日本外第二高電話佔有率的城市。待衛星通訊系統在同年裝置完工後，香港的國際電話系統品質大為改善。一九七○年公司最重要的工程即是將荔枝角訊號站收發器電腦化，屆時將成為世界上最先進的電子通訊作業系統，服務範圍可由香港遍佈至新界。公司技術部門有兩千員工接受訓練，並送四名工程師赴英國，六名員工至德國慕尼黑接受技術訓練。電話公司並在官塘開始與建員工訓練中心，預計一九七一年四月完工使用(33)。

父親擔任電話公司主席期間，發現管理部門問題很多，又傳聞公司有員工受賄，甚至總經理梅爾(Charles Male)都有涉嫌(34)。當今的鄧蓮如女男爵亦是政府調查電話公司管理不當的委員之一，但是由於涉案主嫌梅爾早已走避南非，而香港與南非之間無引渡條例，無法將他送返香港接受問話，此案也只有不了了之(35)。

此時父親的辦公室在太子大廈二十五樓，電話公司設在四樓，兩個辦公室之間因政府派員調查案情，受到不斷的打擾，令父親不勝其煩。

後來父親便請他的朋友姬達(Jack Cater)(36)出任電話公司總經理，但總督麥理浩同時需要姬達掌管一九七四年創立的廉政專員公署。父親衡量輕重之下，覺得公職比電話公司更為重要，便另請F.L.Walker擔任總經理。

當香港電話公司風波平息，一切情況正常後，父親便向電話公司提出辭呈。他對費彝民表示過，

香港市民遲早有一日會明白，他對改善香港電話系統所做的一切（37）。

煤氣公司

一九六四年父親成為香港中華煤氣有限公司有史以來第一位華人主席。該公司於一八六二年成立，對香港供應煤氣照明。一九七五年由渣甸集團控制的香港電燈公司欲收購香港中華煤氣公司，但為父親所拒。後來此收購與反收購事件演變成為極為引人注目的商業戰。父親形容港燈的收購企圖是「大魚吃小魚」的做法（38）。他不斷在報章及公開場合，勸諭煤氣公司股東拒絕香港電燈公司收購建議，勿將手中股票出售，父親並宣稱根據香港電燈公司帳目顯示，該公司已預伏向股東套取現金，以應付日後龐大開支對股東有不利做法的趨勢。雖然中華煤氣公司規模遠不及香港電燈，但父親卻能以公司穩定健全的財務和豐厚的利潤，令股東對公司更具信心（39）。

除此之外，父親與和記集團大班J.D. Claque，和著名股票經紀人Noel Croucher兩位公司董事多次會商對策。他們在對勸諭客戶拒絕將中華煤氣股票售予香港電燈方面，付出極大心力（40）。八月二十日父親及各公司董事成功的防止了港燈收購行動。

中華煤氣公司原本在英國註冊成立，一九八二年時父親決定將公司註冊由英國遷回香港，成為香港公司，轉移註冊時公司二千二百三十八位股東中僅有二人在倫敦登記。事前父親曾對股東解釋，將公司註冊由英國轉移香港的目的，是為使公司免受在英國公司法例處理之不利，尤其英國在一九七三年加入歐洲經濟聯盟後，公司管制法更為嚴厲。這些法例主要是為在英國營業的公司而設，實不適用於只在香港營業的公司。此次公司轉移註冊斬斷英國聯系，共花費港幣一百二十萬元。移交特別儀式在新寧大廈漢釗哥的辦公室舉行，此後香港中華煤氣有限公司終於完全成為香港公司。為紀念公司轉移註冊成功，全體員工均獲頒贈一面一安士重的金幣，公司並對香港大學、香港中文大學及香港理工學院，各贈港幣二十五萬元補助金（41）。香港中華煤氣公司一九八〇年的盈利為港幣三千九百萬元，六年之後躍升至二億三千五百萬元。

公司成立一百二十五年後，終於成為香港主要能源供應機構，煤氣已不再只是富人使用的燃料，而成為香港市民每日的民生必需品。

父親在七〇年代開始，就進行經由海底埋管工程，將中國的天然煤氣運來香港使用。但當時因受安全及工程困難的影響，此項計劃可惜未能在父親有生之年實現[42]。

父親去世後，中華煤氣公司與中國海洋石油總公司主席秦文彩，在一九八五年簽訂備忘錄，同意在不久的將來[43]對香港供應天然氣，為香港帶來廉價的天然氣能源。

羅富齊銀行

羅富齊（Rothschild）銀行早已計劃在香港成立分行，並邀請父親做香港分行的創辦董事，一九七三年三月正式成立香港羅富齊銀行。一九七四年一月父親被任命為銀行副主席，大家都不明白這家猶太銀行請父親幫忙的原因，香港甚至還謠傳父親一定受過猶太割禮。事實上，是因為銀行需要一位有聲望的香港知名人士領導，雖然羅富齊是主席，但因他不長住香港，父親便常須主持銀行許多會議，二人成了非常要好的朋友，他認為父親實際上是香港羅富齊銀行的首位主席。

父親擔任銀行副主席期間〔一九七四年至一九七八年〕，曾介紹許多生意機會給銀行，並協助聘用香港本地的行政主管人員。在羅富齊給我的信中，他提到父親還非常熱心的為銀行大門區額題了以下的字句：

> 生財有道　致力金融
> 業羅萬彙　四海匯通
> 資金富厚　營利至公
> 輔導經濟　資商惠工

齊心合眾　駿業興隆[44]

七九年給父親的信中寫到：

‧‧‧‧欣見閣下領導有方，令本公司香港分行業績斐然，實不勝感激。

‧‧‧‧再次多謝閣下各方協助，及對本人的厚愛‧‧‧。[45]

丹麥關係

一九六○年代父親與丹麥的摩勒集團開始合作，該公司並與許多利氏家族的企業有業務往來，雙方合作關係日漸穩固後，更對父親多項計劃投資。父親後來與這位丹麥公司的主席私交甚篤。

這公司是摩勒父子於一九○四年在丹麥斯文堡創立，原本為一間船務公司。一九六五年老摩勒逝世後，便由兒子將公司發展成為國際化的大企業，旗下擁有運輸船隻、油輪、在丹麥領域的北海鑽油台、鋼鐵造船塢、貨櫃工業、航空業、歐洲汽車的引擎風扇皮帶及剎車護片廠，醫療器材的製造和銷售、文件資料處理的供應和銷售、及丹麥第二大的超級市場連鎖店，及其他多項商業的龐大企業。

當丹麥摩勒公司的執行董事喬金生（Per Jorgensen）於一九七七年八月到達香港時，與父親一見如故。那時這家丹麥公司已與利氏家族企業有三項合作計劃，分別是利園酒店、希慎道一號和禮頓大廈兩座商業大廈。喬金生說他初到香港時，尚未有足夠的國際商業經驗，父親對他各方面都非常照顧，並將他帶進香港複雜的企業環境，學習經營管理。父親的坦誠相助，及充滿活力現代化有效率的處事方法，令他佩服不已[46]。

我們家與丹麥摩勒家族友誼日深後，父母親在一九八二年七月特別赴丹麥訪問，喬金生夫婦多日

相陪擔任導遊。喬金生告訴我，父親是個興緻極高的遊客，因為他對對新鮮事物充滿好奇又有興趣，加上精力充沛，參觀不同城堡時總是有問不完的問題。後來在一九八二年年底時，摩勒公司主席還帶著女兒來香港探望我們家人[47]，正巧我與衛權也在香港，很榮幸的能在晚宴中和他們見面。

摩勒公司後來繼續對父親的企業大力支持，如利園酒店、希慎興業有限公司及花園酒店〔香港〕有限公司等。喬金生後來並成為希慎興業有限公司初期的董事之一。

航運公司

父

親與在日本建造許多貨船的香港維達航業有限公司有間接的關係，該公司旗下的輪船皆以「大」字排名，如大鷹、大玉等，大玉是以母親名字瑤壁命名，壁為玉的通稱。

維達航業公司為母親姪女李廓靈愛的夫家李平山所有，因家族關係，李家便要求父親當公司主席，父親在七〇年代協助此公司成為股票公開上市的公司。

多年來公司營運成績蒸蒸日上，父母親曾多次赴日本參加此航運公司的新輪船下水典禮。後來李平山病重，在逝世前要求父親應允照顧他兩個即將繼承家族事業的兒子。很不幸的在李平山逝世後，他的兩個兒子將他們所繼承的航運公司，以一筆他們認為相當高的價錢，賣給一位在馬來西亞出生的生意人陳松青手下的佳寧投資集團。事實上，大部份的售價是用佳寧投資集團的股票支付。

由於父親對航運公司轉售過程全不知情，當事人事前又未與父親協商，父親便決定與此公司斷絕一切關係，將手中公司股權全部出售。也幸好如此，因為維達航業有限公司發生財務問題，拖垮了李家。原因是雖然維達航業公司已出售轉手，但李平山生前對銀行的個人擔保仍由兩個兒子承擔[48]。一九八三年購得維達航業有限公司的佳寧投資集團倒閉事件，成為香港有史以來最大的商業醜聞。馬來西亞銀行界的 Lorrain Osman 及陳松青被控詐騙馬來西亞裕民財務公司港幣六十億元〔美金七億六千九百萬元〕，馬來西亞裕民財務是馬來西亞裕民銀行的附屬機構，此銀行是馬來西亞

的第二大銀行(49)。

加拿大關係

一九八二年六月，父親在德國法蘭克福的演說中曾說：

本人深信香港在中國開發石油計劃中，可在各方面提供支援。香港對中國的重要性實不容置疑，但我們也不可否認香港須仰賴中國才能生存的事實。將來中國沿海的石油和天然氣能使工業國家的供求平衡嗎？(50)

七〇年代末期，加拿大卡格利的Ranger石油公司，希望能與父親合作共組公司在中國勘採石油，但為父親所拒。後來這家公司便向英國的商業銀行倫敦漢堡斯(Hambros)銀行求助，經由銀行與姚剛的關係和父親連繫，計劃成立石油公司在南中國海取得石油開採權。當時大家都認為南中國海域有蘊藏豐富的石油，姚剛認為這是非常好的建議，便與父親聯絡，他們二人認為這項計劃將對中國極有助益。

倫敦Cazenove公司(51)的合夥伙人Victor Lampson，在漢堡斯銀行董事David Lewis陪同下，在希慎道一號的利希慎置業有限公司會議室，參加由父親召開的會議。會中父親同意他們所提的計劃，投資一百萬美元，並在一九八一年成為加華石油有限公司的主席，姚剛為董事之一，另外尚有許多其他投資人，包括父親的香港朋友在內。

父親一直深信中國沿海有蘊藏豐富的石油未被開發，一九八一年底或一九八二年初這家公司在南中國海開始探勘石油時，已有七家外國石油公司在黃海及海南島附近的南中國海同時探勘石油。父親說「這是中國四大現代化中，最重要的一個環節。」(52)

一九八一年至一九八四年間，父親投資的石油公司在南中國海共鑽了三十五口井，但都未發現石油。後來全球石油價格下跌，Ranger公司便買回所有公司股份，將器材設備拍賣，最後加華石油有限公司被迫清盤結束營業。直到一九九七年六月為止，尚未有一家石油公司能在南中國海成功的開採到石油，當年加華石油有限公司的石油勘採計劃，完全是依照最初Ranger公司的地質礦藏報告進行[53]。

一九八一年時香港已由中國進口百分之二十的石油產品，父親相信當中國的石油開採成功，石油源源湧出時，將對世界經濟造成極大的影響[54]。雖然父親逝世時加華石油有限公司勘採石油計劃仍未成功，但父親一直深信中國沿海必有石油蘊藏。

第十四章

共濟會：終身的承諾

在我的記憶中，我在家的時候父親好像總是要去共濟會（美生會）開會，這些會議對我充滿神秘感，因為共濟會是一個會員關係密切的男性社團，直到近年才較為公開。

共濟會是一個以發揚友愛和慈善為道德規範的組織，不只在金錢方面，精神上各會員亦互相勵志真誠以待，全不涉及政治，事實上，共濟會在其會址內嚴禁討論政治[1]。大家基於共同的理念、情誼，將全世界的會員結合在一起。許多人都誤以為香港共濟會的會員非富即貴，其實任何二十一歲以上之正直男性公民皆可申請入會。共濟會會員之間皆以兄弟互稱，新會員入會時即傳授「盡己之責，為世典範」[2]的思想，並以履行修身律己的會旨為榮。

慈善助人為共濟會基本宗旨，共濟會在世界各地幫助經營醫院、照顧殘障、失明人士、精神病患及不良於行的人。並創辦安老院、設立獎助學金、學術研究基金，及會員在各人居住地做各類社區服務。

有些學者在研究共濟會起源時，發現可遠溯至聖經中的伊甸園、中國帝王、甚至日本天皇。在遠東關於東方源流有兩種版本；一是認為中國民間的秘密會社，其習例與共濟會有許多相似的地方，其次是中國帝王為確使天命攸歸所舉行儒家祭祀儀式，與共濟會亦有相當密切的關係[3]。

當今共濟會起源自建造歐洲大教堂的石匠，他們組成石匠團體，以選自教堂建築藝術的中古世紀歷史傳說，融入聖經和民間故事，然後發展演變成一套全球適用的綜合集會儀式。共濟會大分會在歐、美迅速開創後，儀式更為統一化。短短的四十年後，已擴展至遠東。共濟會於一八〇〇年代早期在香港開

150

始創會，一八四五年成立皇家蘇士分會，其分會泄蘭分會，亦於十八個月之後成立。

父親留英期間其監護人邱吉爾曾邀他入共濟會，父親對共濟會以發揚友愛、慈善與真誠的會旨十分認同。若非祖父遽逝，父親很可能已加入阿波羅大學第三五七分會[4]。

一九二九年父親加入香港共濟會第三六六六大學分會。共濟會為富經驗的一般分會會員，設有一個所謂較高階級的頭銜，太平洋戰爭爆發之前，父親已成為香港及遠東區共濟會的區總監。

中日戰爭期間我們住重慶時，父親是個極為熱心的會員，積極參加第二〇一三號原本在廣州集會的華南分會的復會工作，同時父親亦是美國加州大分會設於重慶的堅毅支會的客座會員，雖然兩個支會會址設於同一個城市內，僅數哩之隔，但卻位於水急無橋的長江兩岸。漲潮時水位可在數小時之內上漲四十呎，所以每參加一次會議往返路程都須費時整日[5]。

太平洋戰爭後，父親回到香港仍繼續熱衷共濟會活動。一九五〇年時他成為南華〔由重慶遷來〕和康馬克兩個支會的總監，一九五一年又任大學支會的第一首席位。當時位於堅尼地道一號的泄蘭堂正在興建，雖然共濟會地區工程總監督只是象徵性的職位，但父親仍是一本他治事的認真態度，每天都去工地以土木工程師的身份視察施工進展[6]。新的泄蘭堂大廳經常有人吹風笛，使我開始喜愛優美動聽的風笛奏樂。

一九六一年四月，英國共濟會大總監士加堡伯爵，任命父親為共濟會在遠東及香港地區的區總監。共濟會在地理轄區上，將以前的香港及南華區改為香港、遠東地區，以便將日本共濟會區包括在同一地區之內。當時日本僅剩下一個支會，直接受命於不屬其支會的英國倫敦聯合分會。〔共濟會於一八七〇年代在日本創辦分會，一九六〇年代時僅存日昇支會。〕

日本支會屬於父親的共濟會轄區之後，父親每年一月必去神戶參加他們的會員入會典禮，典禮後的宴席間，父親總是神情極為愉快。他的熱心連帶的影響到其他香港的會員，他們不顧日本一月寒冷的天氣，也相繼加入日本之旅，幾年之後會員妻子亦被邀參加。到父親逝世時，赴日人數已增加

至二十人，神戶之旅成為香港共濟會會員的年度大事[7]。他也和蘇格蘭區總監一起參加過神戶分會莊嚴美麗的克比堂獻堂典禮。

父親的新職位令他承擔至少需二十年才能解決的日本橫濱共濟會堂，及其四周空地產權的棘手問題。這塊土地原屬太平洋戰爭前在橫濱活動的六個英國特定團體所有，但後來即未再使用過。曾經使用過該會堂的一些駐日軍隊中的蘇格蘭支會會員及新會員，非常擔心以後可能失去聚會場所，但又無經濟能力可購買這塊價格已一減再減的土地。

一九八二年終於以非常和諧的方式，解決了日本橫濱會址的產權問題。土地賣給橫濱市發展成為公園後，將賣地所得大部份資金，交由蘇格蘭支會東星第六四〇號做為購買新會址之用。其餘金額則在香港大學及香港中文大學設立基金，提供研究共濟會獎助學金，由英國分會監管[8]。父親畢生注重教育，加上他和這兩所大學關係特別密切，這問題能如此圓滿的解決，使父親個人深感滿意。

雖然父親屬於英國行會，但他也是在香港的其他轄區支會的固定客座會員。愛爾蘭的大總監，對父親頒贈榮譽資深會員資格，後來又成為蘇格蘭大分會的榮譽副區總監。

父親擔任共濟會區總監達二十一年，在此期間父親對共濟會奉獻出無限心力。香港地區共有十四個分會，及四個附屬支會，父親每年一定親自出席這些不同單位的入會典禮及年會，從未缺席過。這些會議通常在十月及次年四月之間舉行，會議日期都特別安排父親在香港，或他可由外地趕回開會的時間召開。

父親任區總監時，陶喬(George Todkill)擔任儀式組長多年，他說父親是個很容易共事的人，因為他總是知道自己要做什麼。而且父親極為守時，開會時他一定在晚上六點二十分踏入會堂，六點三十分時已開始主持會議分發任務。父親吩咐陶喬在十點二十分時，不論有任何人正在發言，一定要結束會議。當會眾站立舉杯道別時，陶喬就送父親上車，其他會員仍繼續在會場交談，但父親習慣早睡早起，所以總是先離開。

有人臆測父親曾計劃過共濟會在中國復會，有幾次父親在共濟會的泄蘭堂以私人午宴款待來訪的中國友人，若對方話題涉及共濟會時，父親便會向他們解釋不涉及政治的會旨，及引導參觀會議廳。

父親在中國旅遊時，曾在華南看了四個共濟會的舊會址，但他非常謹慎的不讓人誤解他有收回會址的意圖。父親並讓中國政府有機會參閱有關共濟會正確的歷史及會旨資料[9]，提供正確的相關資料極為重要，一九七四年時有一本刊物對中國讀者報導稱，共濟會香港分會是香港外籍人士三合會的幫會組織，並將共濟會與中國的秘密幫會相提並論，使外界誤解共濟會是幫會組織，並稱共濟會是「白人的國際三合會」[10]。

父親逝世後，香港逐漸接近一九九七年香港主權回歸中國的日期，對於中國政府是否允許共濟會這類社團，在香港繼續存在是個未知數。姚剛特別就此問題赴北京徵詢意見，並對北京當局強調父親自少年開始即屬共濟會會員。結果港、澳辦事處對姚剛保證，只要會員遵守香港特別行政區的基本法，香港共濟會在一九九七年之後仍可繼續活動，所有會議仍准許以英語進行。由於舊日的共濟會給外人的印像是個秘密組織，中國方面則希望共濟會日後活動能較為公開，尤其在社會工作及慈善事業方面。共濟會會議儀式中，須對當地政府宣誓效忠，所以在一九九七年七月一日之後，將不再對英國君主政權致敬，而改向對中國政府效忠[11]。

第十五章

高瞻遠矚

八〇年代初中，英雙方為香港主權問題開始談判，當時香港經濟正走下坡，民眾對未來都缺乏信心，決定移民，許多市民皆做移民加拿大、美國、澳洲及紐西蘭的打算。市面上有句大家常說的話就是，「做過一次難民之後，我們不想再做難民。」移民外國成了熱門話題，甚至還有專為可能會移民的人而編撰發行的書刊[1]。

由統計數字上分析，中國和香港的遠景相當看好。一九七七年至一九八二年之間，中國出口至香港的貿易額為港幣二百九十五億一千萬元，增幅為百分之三十二，而中國進口香港貨品數額亦增加百分之一百八十七。中國進口額大增的原因是香港中華電力公司對廣東省增加供應電力所致。中國近期的現代化計劃已使香港再度成為貨物轉口集散地[2]。

一九八一年香港政府舉行地方選舉，是邁向較有代表性方式政府的第一步。因為當時英國政府正準備與中國談判香港未來問題，所以覺得有必要讓香港民眾在地方事務上，較有表達意見的力量。

我們家則一切如常，不受任何影響，父親對中國及香港未來的信心十足，絲毫不受動搖。他對「一國兩制」的觀點是：

……這個結果表示國際關係的新方向，而此新關係是基於雙方政府的互相尊重，並應以所有政府及當地人民福祉做為根本條件。

154

他對一九九七年七月一日以後的展望是：

對中國來說，香港對中國的現代化過程在一九九七之後的許多年，仍會舉足輕重，自由企業在社會公正下得以維持，不致受緩慢工作態度而拖累[3]。

父親相信香港居民仍會一如以往勤奮工作。父親指出有些人說中國靠香港套入大量外匯，但香港若無中國又將如何自處[4]？香港依賴中國供應最重要的水和食物及廉價勞工，他不明白人們為何如此漠視香港須靠中國才能存在的事實。

香港與上海同為國際商港，二者之間常互相競爭及比較，在一九四九年中華人民共和國建國之前，上海一直是中國最主要的貿易中心。香港商界非常關切，在一九九七年主權移交中國之後，上海是否有取代香港的地位，成為中國首位商業中心及通往中國門戶的可能。父親在一九八二年發表談話中表示：

由於香港不受外匯管制及低稅的制度，也是融資的主要中心，為了永遠保持香港比其他如上海等地區優越的地位，我們必須時時投注所有資源，增強財務結構基礎及工業科技。[5]

父親認為由Edward Du Cann為首的英國國會代表，在一九八二年接受中國政府邀請訪問北京時，居然建議中國政府應就香港問題與倫敦開始「協商」，是件很荒謬的事[6]。加上英方妄想中國繼續簽定這個根本不平等的條約，是完全不切實際的想法。事實上，中華人民共和國從未承認在一八四二年所簽訂的南京條約，在一八六○年及一八九八年的北京條約，中國已聲言將如期收回香港及九龍主權，當時未見英方有任何正式反對。父親認為當時雙方政府都認同香港是中國領土的一部份，暫由英國管轄至一九九七年七月一日為止[7]。

父親相信香港的未來一部份須靠香港居民自身的努力，若香港能繼續保持生產力量，對中國及世

界經濟產生特殊效益，才能在一九九七年之前有合理實際與理性解決問題的共識。主權問題應以雙方經濟，而非靠武力或政治意識，甚或國際法的基礎來考慮。最重要的是使香港能永久保持獨立的經濟現況，成為世界的金融中心，再將現代科技知識引進中國。所以香港現行的法律及商業慣例都應延續，港幣亦應保持自由兌換[8]。

父親對未來的香港政府，有以下的進言：

日後香港可在新成立的管理委員會之下，成立一個由現行制度改善修正的新政府。香港在中國旗幟下成為「特區」，管理委員會的領導人可三、四年一任，由中、英人士輪流擔任。政府的任何改變與修正都應該在一九九七年之前，以漸進和緩方式進行，避免臨時突變所帶來的衝擊⋯⋯在立法局全體新議員選出之前，可由數位指定議員繼續運作，成為數年的臨時過渡措施⋯⋯而公務人員架構亦應在謹慎策劃之中，盡量維持現狀[9]。

在法律方面，父親建議目前全世界所承認的香港法律，在一九九七年之後在中國同意之下應繼續沿用。最終上訴法庭應設在香港，而非北京或倫敦，在中、英及香港同意下，可特別安排由英國樞密院的法官擔任新的職位，繼續協助香港[10]。

在財經方面，父親認為香港已在外匯基金及儲備受限於殖民地的英幣規定下而引起的災難中得到教訓。香港在一九七二年基金多元化之後，已成為世界第三大的金融中心。一九八二年時他說：

本人認為中國領導人提到保持香港現狀時，應將香港所有的優勢全力保存。香港外匯基金在一九九七年時，不應轉至倫敦或北京，而應保留在香港本地，或香港認可的任何其他地方，才可永久保持港幣的獨立性。使得國際商業界對香港加強信心。[11]

心靈祥和

道理勳爵在一九八一年七月十四日寫給父親的信中提到：

回顧戰後不久的香港及看到今天的光景，我深信目前的成果，是來自如同閣下及府上各位親人及一般有信心及進取心的市民努力，實令人由衷欽佩。

敬祝賢伉儷身體健康、福壽雙全，並盼與閣下友誼長存。

父親在一九八二年決定不再坐船出海，便將亞特蘭大號遊艇送給看船工友何寧，讓他將賣船所得用來退休養老，父親希望何寧在他有生之年能安享退休生活[12]，何寧在我們家工作多年，看著利家兒孫長大[13]。那年我們回港探望父母親時，我簡直不能相信父親會放棄這艘他最心愛的遊艇，但我不知道他是因為心臟血管硬化，醫生囑他不應繼續游泳。

父親與二祖母即他自己的生母，有許多相似的地方，令父親非常引以為傲。我常聽他很驕傲的稱讚二祖母，說她雖然年事已高，但思路卻依然清晰敏捷。我想父親一定以為自己也可像二祖母一樣高壽。一九八三年二月一日父親寫給嘉道理的信中說到：

多年來都能定時收到府上果園的柑橘，實在是盛情可感。

家母即將九十八歲，身體健朗，篤信佛教，每年此時都期盼能將府上柑橘擺置神台供奉，她每天仍打四圈麻將當做運動……

一九八三年一天早上，母親見父親面帶微笑便問他原因，父親說他夢到祖母在對他呼喚。

父親的老朋友廖承志在一九八三年初夏去世，父親是香港唯一受邀赴北京參加喪禮的人。廖承志不只是父親的好朋友，亦是他所尊重的人，所以父親一定要親赴北京致唁。費彝民在一九八三年六月二十六日，在北京所住的酒店頂樓與父親見面時，費彝民要寫些東西但身邊無筆，便向父親借用，用後稱讚父親的筆很好用。分手時又怎能料到這一別竟是永訣[14]。那年夏天北京特別炎熱，氣溫高達華氏一百度，父親搭機回港途中誤點數小時，加上機場又無冷氣，父親只覺透不過氣，呼吸非常困難。

由北京回來之後父親就身體不適，醫生診斷後立刻要他進聖保祿醫院。醫院辦理入院手續要二千元保證金，父親無現金支付，只好打電話給秘書李姑娘，要她回家向母親取錢，並嚴禁李姑娘將他入院的消息告訴任何人，甚至包括他自己的幾位弟弟[15]。當天在利希慎置業有限公司工作的利家兄弟，對父親的行蹤都覺得極不尋常，因為父親從沒有一天不上班，李姑娘只能托詞說父親有事。後來醫院的主管Sir Albert Rodrigues巡房時看到父親，消息才傳到利家兄弟，第二天大家都責怪李姑娘不應對他們隱瞞事實。

醫生囑咐父親要靜心休養，這對父親來說幾乎是件不可能的事。母親還請了一位特別護士照顧他，但父親卻將護士辭退。父親僅准許極少數人可以知道他入院，他自認很快即可出院回家，甚至不許母親告訴我們這個消息，因為父親最討厭別人為他大驚小怪，他對自己的病痛從不在意。兒女在父親去世之後才知道他因病入過醫院。

新華社社長許家屯和副社長李儲文，在七月二日去醫院探望父親。他們是極少數父親住院期間所見的人。當天父親正吵著要出院回家，母親便要許家屯幫忙相勸父親多在醫院休養幾天。許家屯與李儲文進到病房時，見到父親已起床坐在椅子上接待他們，父親說他沒什麼毛病只是大家太過緊張罷了[16]。在醫院住了三天之後，父親就心煩氣燥的急於出院，他向主治醫生攤牌，對醫師宣稱若再不讓他出院回家的話，他就自己走出醫院。當時是七月五日早上，他仍須用氧氣輔助呼吸。

七月五日當天在利園酒店已安排舉行午宴，歡送水務署署長Tucker退休，由於請帖早已發出，若父親仍在醫院的話，就安排由中華煤氣公司的總秘書代父親主持午宴，後來父親既已出院就堅持

自己主持。他並在餐前要李姑娘將需要他簽字的支票帶到利園酒店給他，李姑娘覺得父親面色不大好，而且說話較為遲鈍。她回到公司對仍在公司做事的家驥四嬸提起此事，家驥四嬸說：「他想出院的話，沒有人能阻擋！」

七月六日早上，父親一如往常在小餐間吃完早餐，預備穿衣出門上班，突然倒地不起，待救護車將他送到醫院時已告不治，與世長辭。

李姑娘家位於父母親所住的崇明大廈對面，當她經過崇明大廈返公司時，我們家中司機兼守衛阿力對李姑娘說：「利先生走了」，李姑娘一時未能會意，再問他：「走到那裡？」阿力不禁眼紅的哭了起來。李姑娘實在不能相信這個消息，後來她神情恍惚漫無目的走在街上，碰到漢釗哥剛從崇明大廈的嘉蓮大廈走出，她問漢釗哥她該做什麼，漢釗哥說：「先回寫字樓再說」。李姑娘在幾個月之後甚至仍不能接受父親去世的事實，總覺得他會回來。她望著窗外以為會像以前一樣，在下午還可以看到父親回家用完中飯，從街上走回公司的情景[17]。一位朋友在七月六日早上坐的士時，司機告訴她香港剛失去了一位好人，一問之下才知道他所指的是我父親。

七月六日晚上七時，姚剛由加州洛杉磯返達香港機場，他的司機告訴他這個消息時，他非常震驚的說：「那我現在怎麼辦？我所有的中國關係都沒有了！」[18]

七月五日晚上，我正在加拿大多倫多家中用完晚飯[19]，接到七叔的電話告訴我父親去世的消息。

我驚駭得腦海一片空白，簡直不能相信我所聽到的事實，我們完全不知父親入過醫院，而且每個人都理所當然的認為，父親會永遠在我們身邊。

電訊由世界各地排山倒海而來，其中有中國國家主席李先念，及楊尚昆、習仲勛、谷牧、余秋里、姬鵬飛、經普椿、廖夢醒等中國國家領導人，紛紛致電慰問。中文報章對不同人士的電訊的內容均有廣泛報導。

七月某日，《大公報》費彝民的辦公室收到三支與他在北京酒店向父親借用同樣的筆，原來是父親生前囑咐秘書送交費彝民的。費彝民見到這三支筆時真是感慨萬千，父親在病中還如此體貼入微，記得這些小事[20]。

由於父親是共濟會遠東及香港地區的區總監，共濟會在七月十八日在香港聖約翰大教堂為父親舉行追悼會。因為衛權須要返回多倫多照料他的病人，所以長子偉雄特別飛來香港代表衛權參加這個追悼會。母親要家中女眷全部穿黑旗袍，所有男孫輩穿黑西裝，不知家中親人如何找到這些裁縫，能在四十八小時之內趕製出這批孝服。

追悼會那天烈日高照，非常炎熱，教堂內坐滿了人。Justice Cons致詞時頌揚父親一生以發揚共濟會宗旨助人濟世美德為目標。在共濟會區總監任內，將現有慈善基金籌募及施賑制度，重新規劃，將這責任交給父親奉獻心力最多的地區慈善會。他不只是成功的企業家還具有多方才華，更是一位宅心仁厚的慈善家，能啟發他人同心為善。共濟會儀式中，父親最喜歡讀的經句是，門徒保羅歌頌慈善為懷的讚美詩[21]。他並形容父親為人親切和藹，深得身邊所有人的敬愛，他的領導能力和靜默的權威更能提昇他人的信心及熱誠。父親從不吝於誇讚他人的好處，可是若發現對方未盡全力時，又會毫不遲疑的加以批評。但父親對屬下一向是體恤和關懷[22]。

十月八日，日本神戶的共濟會會員在聖安德魯飛翔天使禮拜堂，為父親舉行另外一次的追悼會，會中並特別宣讀神戶市長官崎辰雄所致的電唁。副總監督海福納（Christopher Haffner）致頌詞時，提到父親對神戶日昇分會的特別照顧。神戶分會是率先響應父親為紀念英國總會成立二百五十周年，捐贈醫學研究獎助學金的分會。海福納亦提及父親與中國領導人物的特殊關係，父親是國家主席李念第一位接見的香港市民。更說到父親對一九九七年香港問題實際解決方法的見解，最令人深思緬懷[23]。

李姑娘為父親工作超過十二年，所知甚多，而且與外界人際關係很好，所以父親去世後有許多人願以高薪聘用她，但李姑娘全不接受，她覺得沒有人能取代像父親這樣的上司。她珍藏了一小張我提到父親面帶笑容的相片，她認為是父親相片中最好的一張，還保留了一些她替父親寫的中文書信影本，她說這些都是極有感情的紀念品，後來她非常慷慨地將這些珍藏全部交給我，作為此書的參考資料。李姑娘說父親不是完美無瑕的聖人，但他仁慈善良，忠直誠懇，而且永遠是位謙謙君子。

父親去世的消息連續在中英報章、電視及廣播中廣泛報導，為防二祖母知道真相，父親的妹妹立

刻將二祖母常看的電視機切斷電源，偽稱電視故障，由於她不識字，報章雜誌則不必擔心。二祖母在晚年極少出門，親人及家中僕人都受囑不得對她提及此事。以後幾年每當二祖母詢問父親未前來向她請安的原因時，母親總是找藉口支吾以對，過了一段時期，她就不再追問。我們相信她心中明白，只是不願證實心中的恐懼而已。

父親的遺願是將他的骨灰灑在香港海灣，但母親很守舊的執意不肯，因為她死後要葬在父親身邊。

父親生前人人都尊稱他為「澤哥」，許多人都深切的懷念他。寫此書時，每個人都極為熱心的幫助我，因為他們對父親仍充滿了敬愛與感激。有人稱他是「偉人」、「好朋友」甚至「傳奇人物」，亦有人很惋惜的認為，父親的死對香港主權問題的中、英談判是一大打擊。

從父親的喪禮可得到證實，甚至他的死，都在替中國與香港之間建立橋樑，為雙方帶來和平與繁榮。

結語

周恩來總理遺孀鄧穎超女士為對我父親表示敬意，特別提名母親為中國人民政治協商會議的香港代表。

母親常說：「雖然妳父親性急又古板，但他對我這樣好，我實在沒有什麼可說他的。」母親在父親一生中一直是他最關愛的，父親本性寬厚大度，每做任何事業投資，一定自動將半數置於母親名下。父親誠實耿直的性格令母親對他完全仰賴，母親對任何重大事情的決定及難題，甚至家中應付帳單及她旅遊行程，全由父親處理安排。母親總認為自己會比父親早走，所以父親的遽逝令她不只悲慟萬分，頓時失去生活重心，而且對父親置她不顧撒手而去覺得非常刺傷，使她接連數月都須靠鎮靜劑過日。年紀七十四歲的母親，還是盡了她的全力繼續走她該走的路。

我多麼希望父親在世時，能有多些時間與他在一起，又多麼希望能再向他多問些問題，但我也和其他人一樣，以為父親會長久的在我們身邊。父親所作的榜樣，使我學到許多事情，並將盡我所能以父親作為我待人處世的準則。對父親的關愛我將永誌在心，並以一顆感恩的心來承受他留給我們的名聲，身為他的女兒，我感到非常榮幸。

利銘澤生平事業摘要

一九二七年　牛津大學畢業：文學士
一九三二年　牛津大學：文科碩士
一九四六年　太平紳士
一九四六年至一九四八年　穀米糧食統制處處長
一九四九年　大英帝國官佐勳章（O. B. E.）
一九四八年至一九四九年　第四、五屆亞洲及遠東地區經濟委員會會議香港代表
一九六○年　香港赴西非貿易訪問團團長
一九六三年　香港赴德國法蘭克福貿易訪問團團長
一九六三年　大英帝國司令勳章（C. B. E.）
一九六四年　香港大學榮譽法學博士
一九六四年　香港中文大學榮譽法學博士
一九六九年　日本三等瑞寶勳章

香港政府委任各局議員及委員會委員：

一九四九年　稅務委員會委員
一九五三年至一九六○年　市政局議員
一九五三年　薪俸調整委員會委員
一九五四年至一九六○年　特別房屋調查委員會委員
一九五二年至一九五九年　公務員敍用委員會委員
一九五三年至一九五九年　建築條例委員會委員

164

一九五五年　空運牌照局委員
一九五九年至一九六五年　立法局議員
一九六一年至一九六六年　行政局議員
一九六二年至一九六五年　反貪污諮詢委員會委員
一九六○年至一九六五年　漁業發展及貸款委員會委員
一九六一年至一九六六年　高等教育委員會委員

共濟會：
一九六一年至一九八三年　香港、華南共濟基金信託委員會主席
　　　　　　　　　　　　香港及遠東地區區總監

香港大學：
一九四八年　開始擔任大學校董
一九五四年　開始擔任校務委員會委員

香港中文大學：
一九六三年至一九八三年　校董會副主席
一九六三年至一九八三年　校園計劃及建設委員會主席
一九六三年至一九八三年　大學投標管理委員會主席
一九六三年至一九八三年　榮譽學位委員會委員

董事會主席：
聯合地產有限公司
加華石油有限公司
國光漆廠有限公司
花園酒店〔香港〕有限公司
源和洋酒行
維達航業有限公司
香港中華煤氣公司
香港電話有限公司
香港鋼管有限公司
希慎興業有限公司
民樂公司
九龍的士有限公司
光利公司
利園酒店
利希慎置業有限公司
興華半導體工業有限公司
華利貿易公司

副主席：
香港羅富齊銀行
山一國際〔香港〕有限公司

166

董事：

香港華商銀行公會

東亞銀行

亞洲航業有限公司

香港建屋貸款有限公司

香港置地及代理有限公司

香港信託有限公司

香港紡織有限公司

會德豐船務有限公司

及其他公司

其他：

香港業主聯會主席

香港鄉村俱樂部會長

南華體育會會長

四邑工商總會會長及永遠名譽會長

灣仔街坊福利會會長

華商會名譽會員

中國工程師學會香港分會永遠名譽會員

香港鄉村俱樂部永遠名譽會員

香港日本人俱樂部永遠名譽會員

僑港新會商會終身董事

167

香港總商會會員〔一九六〇年至一九六八年〕
保良局永遠董事局董事〔一九五九年至一九六〇年〕
保良局副主席〔一九六〇年至一九六六年〕

168

利銘澤的弟妹：

二叔－銘洽

三叔－孝和〔榮根〕，Harold

四叔－榮森，J. S.

五叔－榮傑

六叔－榮康，J. K.

七叔－榮達

二姑姐－舜華，Doris

三姑姐－舜英，Ansie

四姑姐－舜琹，Joyce

五姑姐－舜賢，Dione

六姑姐－舜豪，Amy

七姑姐－舜儀，Diana

八姑姐－舜娥，Vivien

169

註釋

永別

1. 一九八三年七月七日Hong Kong Standard《香港虎報》刊載
2. 一九八三年七月七日，七月十二日《南華早報》刊載

第一章

1. 父親的弟妹皆以叔或姑姐排行序稱呼
2. 中國南方的鄉村，亦是利氏家族祖祠所在。國人宗親觀念極重，相信父親必深以此二位同鄉為榮。
3. 一九二一年七月三十一日《子褒學校年報》第五頁及第七頁
4. 一九九七年十月十七日Percy O'Brien信函
5. 一九七四年英國倫敦出版V.H.H. Green所著A History of Oxford第一百八十八頁及一百八十九頁
6. 一九九七年十月十七日Percy O'Brien信函
7. 一九九七年十月三十日Percy O'Brien信函
8. 一九九七年十月三十日Percy O'Brien信函
9. 一九九七年十月十七日Percy O'Brien信函
10. 白石信一所譯小池厚之助在一九七一年九月七日，於山一證券公司內部發行雙月刊之文章。

170

第二章

1. 一九九七年四月招黃瑤芬及胡黃瑤芝於加拿大溫哥華口述

2. 一九九七年四月胡黃瑤芝於溫哥華口述

3. 一九三四年香港出版張蓮覺〔何東夫人〕所著《名山遊記》第一百〇五頁

4. 一九九七年六月香港訪問曾於黃埔船塢工作的George Todkill，並提供一九三一年父親在工地監工的相片。

5. 一九九六年一月利漢釗於香港口述

6. 一九九七年四月招黃瑤芬及胡黃瑤芝於溫哥華口述

7. 一九三九年上海出版Chungshee H. Liu所著Hainan, The Island and the People

8. 錄自一九三九年香港出版王少平所著《菲島瓊崖印象記》第八十一頁，王亦是父親在海南牧場的投資人之一。

9. 王少平《菲島瓊崖印象記》第六十六頁及六十七頁

10. 王少平《菲島瓊崖印象記》第六十九頁

11. 王少平《菲島瓊崖印象記》第八十一頁

12. 王少平《菲島瓊崖印象記》第八十九頁及九十頁

13. 一九九六年一月在香港訪問，經常陪同我父母親入中國的前香港新華社秘書何銘思。

14. 包括中國資源委員會技術室主任及曾任台灣交通部部長的沈怡、資源委員會副主任委員錢昌照、及資源委員會採購室主任蔣平伯等人，以上資料由吳慶塘於一九九五年春在多倫多提供。

15. 為留德工程師，以採用Omega機械儀器建立火車精準時刻聞名，極獲蔣介石重用。

16. 一九九五年春吳慶塘於加拿大多倫多口述

17. 一九九五年春吳慶塘於多倫多口述

第三章

1. 一九九五年香港出版謝永光所著《香港抗日風雲錄》第七十二頁及七十三頁
2. 一九六〇年英國倫敦出版 Tim Carew 所著 The Fall of Hong Kong 第二十六頁及二十七頁
3. 一九九五年香港出版謝永光所著《香港抗日風雲錄》第九十六頁
4. 一九八〇年加拿大多倫多出版 Ferguson, Ted 所著 Desperate Siege: The Battle of Hong Kong 第

五頁

5. Ferguson 所著 Desperate Siege 第六頁及七頁
6. 一九七五年香港出版 Sir Selwyn Selwyn-Clarke 所著 Footprints: The Memoirs of Sir Selwyn

Selwyn-Clarke 第五十八頁

7. 一九九六年一月譚徐靈輝於多倫多口述，戰時譚為防空隊員。
8. 一九九六年十一月伍英才於多倫多口述
9. Ferguson 所著 Desperate Siege 第七頁
10. 國民黨左派領導人廖仲愷之子
11. 一九九六年十一月前香港新華社社長梁威林於廣州口述
12. 一九九六年一月前香港新華社秘書何銘思於香港口述
13. Selwyn-Clarke 所著 Footprints: The Memoirs of Sir Selwyn Selwyn-Clarke 第六十四頁
14. 當時未婚，以本名 Elizabeth Teng 工作

18. 一九九七年六月香港電話訪問姬達爵士
19. 一九九五年春吳慶塘於多倫多口述
20. 一九九五年夏吳慶塘於多倫多口述

15. 一九九六年一月譚葆和於多倫多口述

16. 一九九六年一月譚葆和於多倫多口述

17. 一九八二年香港出版David Faure所著Saikung, The Making of the District and its Experience During World War II, 錄自Journal of the Hong Kong Branch of the Asiatic Society亞洲學會香港分會學報第二十二冊中的一百八十四頁及一百八十五頁。

18. 一九九六年十一月伍英才於多倫多口述

19. Selwyn-Clarke所著Footprints: The Memoirs of Sir Selwyn Selwyn-Clarke第六十五頁

20. 伍家在香港淪陷及日本投降後的全部經歷，由伍英才於一九九六年十一月於多倫多口述。

21. 一九九六年一月譚葆和於多倫多口述

22. 他願繼續留在香港為市民提供醫療服務，但被某些人指控為奸細，日後為日軍拘禁。

23. 一九九六年一月譚葆和於多倫多口述

24. 一九九三年香港出版《活躍在香港——港九大隊西貢地區抗日實錄》書中，江水所撰「護送何香凝、廖承志母子倆的經過」章節中第二十二至二十六頁。

25. 一九九三年香港出版《活躍在香江》章節第二十及二十一頁。

26. 一九八一年香港出版Edwin Ride所著B.A.A.G., Hong Kong Resistance, 1942-1945第二十七頁，註二，第十七頁、第二十九頁及註十七。

27. 汪背棄蔣在重慶所設政府後，自行在南京另設偽政府。

28. Edwin Ride所著B.A.A.G.第三十一頁至四十四頁

29. Col. L. T. Ride於一九四六年，對英國政府所寫關於華南不同組織的報告。

30. 一九九五年春吳慶塘於多倫多口述

31. 一九九六年十一月梁威林於廣州口述

32. 一九九六年一月何銘思於香港口述

第四章

1. Sir Selwyn-Clarke所著Footprints: The Memories of Sir Selwyn-Clarke第六十九頁
2. 一九九五年一月譚葆和於多倫多口述
3. 一九九七年二月利漢輝於加大拿大溫哥華口述
4. 一九九六年十月利漢釗於香港口述
5. 一九九六年十月利漢釗於香港口述
6. 一九九六年十一月伍英才於多倫多口述
7. 一九九六年一月利漢釗於香港口述
8. 一九九六年十一月伍英才於多倫多口述
9. 一九九六年十月利漢釗於香港口述
10. 用絲不用棉，較普通棉被輕暖。
11. 由貴州至桂林
12. 凌鴻勛、石志仁、侯家源、袁夢鴻
13. 父親從未加入任何政治黨派
14. 此職位由二姑丈鄭觀成指派，永光煤炭行最大客戶為鐵路局，所以生意極為穩定，鄭的姪子譚乃亮為會計，與吳慶塘同住公司附近的竹泥屋內。
15. 一九九五年春吳慶塘於多倫多口述
16. 吳慶塘亦有參與此建築物的監工
17. 一九九五年春吳慶塘於多倫多口述

18. 一九九五年春吳慶塘於多倫多提及，當年非常高興能有免費火車通行證。吳因喜好打乒乓球頗受鐵路局員工歡迎，經常打球時間多過鐵路監工時間，乒乓球為當時少有的娛樂活動之一。

19. 國華銀行總經理，為國內及海外華僑界極具影響力的財經人物。

20. 新加坡華僑銀行主席

21. 新加坡華僑銀行總經理

22. 一九九五年春吳慶塘於多倫多口述

23. 一九九六年一月利漢釗於香港口述

24. 一九九六年一月利漢釗於香港口述

25. 三叔曾任董事

26. 一九九七年十月香港盛樹珩信函

27. 一九九五年春吳慶塘於多倫多口述

28. 一九九七年四月招黃瑤芬於溫哥華口述

29. 一九九六年一月利漢釗於香港口述

第五章

1. 每五日取白米一斤四兩、麵粉一斤及青豆半斤，一斤等於一點三二磅；一兩等於一點三三安士。

2. 刊載於一九四六年至一九四八年《華僑日報》

3. 一九九五年春吳慶塘於多倫多表示，當年任何人在此職位皆可發大財，但父親從不為自己圖利。

4. 一九九六年一月利江蕙蘭於香港口述

5. 非大英帝國聯邦受訓醫生不得在香港行醫

6. 一九六三年盛樹珩與利家重建友誼，任職香港文華酒店為營業部總管，妻子為朱貴思。

7. 一九九七年十月十四日盛樹珩香港來函

8. 一九五一年七月二日、七日、十二日、二十三日，一九五一年八月九日，一九五一年十一月五日，一九五二年二月二十三日，一九五二年四月一日、十五日、二十七日，一九五二年六月十六日，一九五二年七月十二日、十五日、十九日、二十日、二十九日，一九五三年一月十日、十六日，一九五三年三月十五日、三十一日，一九五三年五月十日、十七日、三十一日《華僑日報》

9. 一九五三年六月二日《華僑日報》

10. 一九六一年三月二十三日《華僑日報》

11. 一九四一年時香港四分之一勞力人口服務於工業生產

12. 日本投降時人口為五十萬人，一九四九年時多達二百萬人。

13. 一九四九年一間專在中國及東南亞吸收黨員的共產黨學校被迫關閉，至一九六七年時香港政府極少關閉學校，但對學校「顛覆」活動則定期監察。

14. 一九六五年香港出版Alexander Grantham葛量洪總督所著Via Ports第一百十五頁

第六章

1. 一九九五年四月李樂君於加州洛杉磯口述，李為父親生前最後任用的秘書。

2. 一九九五年四月李樂君於加州洛杉磯口述

第七章

1. 一九九二年香港出版 Heady, Sue 所著《香港鄉村俱樂部》第二頁
2. 《香港鄉村俱樂部》第十三及十四頁
3. 《香港鄉村俱樂部》第七十九頁
4. 《香港鄉村俱樂部》第十六及十七頁
5. 《香港鄉村俱樂部》第二十頁
6. 一九七二年十二月十四日《香港虎報》
7. 一九九六年一月利漢釗於香港口述

第八章

1. 一九九六年一月利江蕙蘭於香港口述
2. 一九九六年一月利江蕙蘭於香港口述
3. 一九五六年七月三十一日《華僑日報》
4. 一九九六年一月利榮森於香港口述
5. 一九九六年一月利定昌於香港口述
6. 一九九六年十一月利漢釗於香港口述
7. 利漢釗一九九六年十一月於香港表示，約為百分之五至百分之十。
8. 一九九七年二月吳慶塘於多倫多口述
9. 一九九七年二月吳慶塘於多倫多口述
10. 一九九七年二月吳慶塘於多倫多口述

11. 一九九六年一月利江蕙蘭於香港口述

12. 太古集團於一八一六年在英國成立，公司於一八六七年一月一日在上海設立Butterfield &
Swire Co.，對中國進口棉花及棉布，並由中國出口絲和茶。一八七二年成立中國航運公司
(C.N.Co.)，第二次世界大戰後，太古將中國公司總部移至香港。一九四六年七月成立Swire
and Maclaine有限公司經營進出口業，又在一九四七年六月成立Taikoo Wharf and Godown公
司。一九四八年時太古取得國泰航空公司的大部股權，公司業務廣及製造、工業工程、飲料、
地產、保險、農業、及零售業。

13. 一九四八年十月十九日於香港註冊

14. 公司於一九四八年成立

15. 一九九七年二月吳慶塘於多倫多表示，這是香港當時地產交易及商業法的一大改革，並自此帶
動香港幾十年後的經濟發展。

16. 一九九五年春吳慶塘於多倫多口述。

17. 我深信與香港上海商業銀行的關係對此極有影響

18. 香港的商業有線電台

19. 一九九五年春吳慶塘於多倫多口述

20. 一九九七年二月利有璇於溫哥華口述

21. 一九九六年十一月利漢釗在香港表示：當年香港的老闆決不會坐公司的送貨車。

22. 日後家族在一九九○年代將土地出售

23. 利乾於一九九八年一月由香港提供此資料

24. 一九九六年一月利漢釗於香港口述

25. 利乾於一九九八年一月由香港提供此資料

26. 一九九六年十一月利漢釗於香港口述）
27. 一九九六年一月利漢釗於香港口述。
28. 一九九六年一月利漢釗於香港口述。
29. 香港在一九七三年受世界石油危機影響股市價格大跌，導致經濟衰退至一九七六年止。
30. 一九九六年十一月利漢釗於香港口述。
31. 一九七〇年十月成立的私人有限公司，名為興利建設有限公司，屬一九二三年所組的利希慎置業有限公司名下。
32. 父親為公司初期董事會的董事長，陳斌、胡法光、Michael Jebsen、Per Jorgensen、郭得勝、利漢釗、利榮森、利國偉、Ian Robert Anderson及葉謀遵為董事。
33. 總面積為80,881平方呎，祖父當年是以祖母、父親、銘洽二叔、孝和三叔和榮森四叔的名義購置這些產業，全賴利氏家人將產業歸至家族公司利希慎置業有限公司名下，令所有家族成員得以受益。事實上祖母在世時，已將她名下的產業全部歸所有子女名下。
34. 一九九七年底，身兼其他職位的利漢釗，被推選為香港聯合交易所有限公司主席。
35. 一九九六年一月利漢釗於香港口述。

第九章

1. 原本計劃在新界屏山興建新機場，但香港殖民地政府覺得，飛機若在屏山起飛降落勢必在中國領空飛繞而過，因在五〇年代時曾有民機被擊落。啟德機場增建的新跑道可供最大客機起降，跑道用地伸入九龍灣內，直到一九五〇年代末期，這條新跑道才告完工使用。
2. 目前是東亞銀行主席及總裁
3. 一九九七年三月白石信一由日本提供資料

4. 由一九七〇年開始，他們即為中國高級國家領導人的眼科醫生，包括鄧小平在內。

5. 中國全面禁止自由交易二十年後，在一九七八年才開始有自由市場。

第十章

1. 一九六五年香港出版Alexander Grantham葛量洪總督所著Via Ports第一百八十八及一百八十九頁

2. 一九九六年一月何銘思於香港口述

3. 一九九五年春吳慶塘於多倫多口述

4. Ruth Hayhoe於一九六七年七月十七日寫給她母親的家書

5. 一九九七年被選為香港教育學院院長，同時亦是多倫多大學安省教育學院比較教育學教授。

6. 一九六七年十月二十八日Ruth Hayhoe家書

7. 一九九七年六月姚剛在香港說；當年他的職位僅是初級經理，對正在香港的太古主席Sir Adrian Swire表示，政治暴動不至於有太嚴重的財物損失，同時在道義上，公司不應在客戶最需幫助的時候背棄他們。由於香港太古對此事有權可自行做主，太古便決定對客戶續保暴動險，結果公司不但分文未損，還贏得社會大眾的信心。

8. 一九九六年一月利江蕙蘭於香港口述

9. 一九九六年十一月於廣州，對一九八三年七月十六日費彝民在《大公報》發表之「緬懷利銘澤」

10. 一九九六年十一月李國寶於香港口述

11. 一九六八年七月三日Ruth Hayhoe家書

12. 多倫多大學、約克大學聯合亞太研究所資料；一九九七年五月陸鴻基教授於亞洲人權與民主訪問梁威林。

13. 會議中發表的The Rise of a Civil Society in Hong Kong第十六頁及十七頁。

14. 一九九七年六月姬達爵士Sir Jack Cater，在香港表示；香港警察在一九六七年暴動之後才冠上「皇家」二字。

15. 陸鴻基教授所著The Rise of a Civil Society in Hong Kong
第十八頁

16. 一九九七年八月由Lady Cater提供屬於姬達爵士Sir Jack Cater的資料

17. 一九九五年四月李樂君於洛杉磯口述

18. 一九九七年一月二十九日《大公報》

19. 一九九七年十月陳之昭醫生於馬利蘭州巴爾地摩口述

20. 在一九四五年及一九四九年之間人口增加四倍

21. 一九九四年香港出版，由吳倫霓霞所編的《邁進中的香港中文大學》The Quest for Excellence

22. 《邁進中的香港中文大學》The Quest for Excellence第二十頁及二十一頁

23. 《邁進中的香港中文大學》The Quest for Excellence第二十五頁

24. 一九九七年六月馬臨教授於香港口述

25. 一九九七年六月馬臨教授於香港口述

26. 一九五一年十月由基督教會代表組成

27. 香港中文大學投標管理委員會陳尹璇提供的一九六四年至一九八三年投標管理委員會會議紀錄

28. 一九九七年六月馬臨教授於香港口述

29. 一九九七年六月馬臨教授於香港口述

20. 後來與耶魯大學有聯系

第十一章

1. 一九九七年六月緒方鈴子於香港口述

2. 一九九七年六月緒方鈴子於香港口述

3. 日本駐港總領事於一九六八年對日本政府的績效報告

4. 一九六九年香港日本商會離開香港日本人俱樂部，另組辦事處

5. 一九九七年六月香港日本人俱樂部事務局長吉岡義之於香港口述

6. 日本山一證券白石信一於一九九七年三月所提供的資料

7. 後者日後遷入對街新完工的利園酒店

8. 一九六五年十月二日成立

9. 一九七五年日本學校在藍塘道157號自購產業

10. 特別來賓為父親、日本總領事遠藤又男、教育署副署長、簡悅強為中國人代表及馮秉芬爵士。後者說服香港政府准許香港日本學校得以用日本學制授課。

11. 藤田一郎於一九八六年五月十日所撰「香港日本人學校開校二十周年特刊」第十九頁，由吉岡義之譯為英文，原文載於 Phoenix Publication 第十三期。

12. 一九九四年拆除，重建為嘉蘭中心的一部份

13. 藤田一郎的「香港日本人學校開校二十周年特刊」

14. 勳章上飾有碎鏡及一圈寶石，還有階級較高的勳章才有的金稜線，資料由吉岡義之一九九七年八月於香港提供。

15. 一九八八年香港出版，由 Christopher Haffner 為紀念我父親所寫的 The Craft in the East。

16. 一九九六年十月利國偉爵士於香港口述

17. 此時杭州的七〇四計劃〔一九七〇年四月〕正剛開始，此計劃是興建一所佔地五十英畝可防核

子武器的地下軍事基地。地面上兩幢華麗的建築物分別屬於毛澤東和林彪所有，這計劃開始時或許並沒有圖謀囚禁毛澤東做人質的意圖，但此建築完工後確實可作此用途。一九七〇年毛澤東在廬山推翻了林彪欲宣稱毛為「全世界最偉大的天才」，神化毛澤東為傀儡領袖的企圖，林彪此時心中明白必須開始進行第五七一隱喻「武裝起義」的計劃。

林彪欲推翻毛澤東的密謀，約在一九七一年春天於蘇州開始策劃，當時林彪夫婦與二十六歲的兒子林立果正在蘇州度假，全部行動是由林立果指揮。根據官方報導，原本計劃是先佯裝行刺毛澤東，然後林彪假作「營救」毛澤東，中立了周恩來、江青、康生及其他軍事領袖。但因林人手不夠，此計劃未能成功。又有另一計劃，在毛澤東搭乘特別列車在中國中南部巡視時，伺機進行暗殺。林彪在一九五九年取代彭德懷為國防部長，空軍是他計劃叛變的主力。毛聽到風聲後，當即改變行程，急速經過上海，於九月十二日早上到達北京。九月十一日林彪及葉群正在北京以東約一百三十英哩的北戴河海邊等候消息，當晚得知行刺計劃失敗後，葉群立刻收拾行李，其中有英、中和蘇、中兩本字典。同日下午五時林立果搭乘屬林彪專用，編號二五六號的三叉式引擎飛機，由北京飛到北戴河。機上三名飛行人員於九月六日受命，預備翌日早上七時起飛，九月十二日晚上周恩來接到八四三一情報單位密報，林彪、葉群及林立果有潛逃出國的跡象後，便立刻改變當日行程，延期接見日本訪問團。周恩來在三十分鐘之內下令禁止全國飛機起飛，尤其是林彪的三叉式專用機。一種說法是，此時周恩來還做勢打電話至北戴河，向林家三口問安，使他們明白事跡敗露，毛、周二人都已察覺到他們的陰謀。半夜時，三名機員被命令預備隨時待命起飛，機上除林家三人之外，尚有其他三名乘客。當時毛澤東正在中南海的室內游泳池游泳，他建議趁飛機還在中國領空時，派軍機擊落，但據聞毛澤東只回應「聽其自然」。一九九三年紐約出版Harrison E.

18.
一九八三年東京出版岡田晃所著《外交水鳥秘話》第一四九至一六一頁。由香港恒生銀行職員
Salisbury所著The New Emperors第二百八十四頁至三百〇三頁

19. 一九九六年十月利國偉爵士於香港口述
譯為中文。
20. 於一八九七年創立
21. 白石信一於一九九七年三月所提供的資料。當山一國際〔香港〕有限公司成立時，白石信一是香港的業務經理為森下茂樹下屬。
22. 一九八二年九月之前山一國際〔香港〕有限公司股權全部屬於山一證券公司
23. 白石信一於一九九七年二月所提供的資料
24. 寫此書時他身為日本四大證券公司之一的山一證券公司副主席
25. 一九七一年和一九七三年之間
26. 白石信一於一九九七年三月由日本大阪所提供的資料
27. 白石信一於一九九七年三月由日本大阪所提供的資料
28. 一九九七年六月緒方鈴子於香港口述
29. 一九八一年九月三日三越百貨店主席岡田茂給我父親的信函。三越百貨店於一六七三年創立，並在一九○四年組成公司。
30. 根據一九九七年十二月二十二日Asian Economic News，京華證券體系公司為台灣企業家沈慶京所有。
31. 一九九八年一月十一日白石信一的信函
32. 一九九七年十二月二十二日Asian Ecomonic News

第十二章

1. 一九八八年香港出版Christopher Haffner所著The Craft in the East第四百二十二頁

在此同時香港繼續建造世界最好的水庫，並將海水淡化處理使用。

2. 一九九七年六月姚剛於香港口述

3. 一九九六年十一月梁威林於廣州口述

4. 一九六三年五月及六月《大公報》

5. 一九六三年五月三十一日《大公報》

6. 一九六四年四月二十三日《大公報》

7. 一九六五年一月三日《華僑日報》

8. 一立方米約等於二百二十加侖

9. 一九六五年四月二十一日《大公報》

10. 一九九六年十一月梁威林於廣州口述

11. 一九九六年六月二十八日《香港虎報》

12. 一九六七年七月十三日《香港虎報》

13. 一立方米約等於二百二十加侖

14. 一九八三年七月八日 Times

15. 一九九六年十一月李國寶於香港口述

16. 一九九六年一月利江蕙蘭於香港口述，利江蕙蘭在利希慎置業有限公司任秘書至六十五歲退休，父親每日放工都順路送她回家，在車上常會告訴她一些平日不談的公司機密。

17. 立法局議員、行政局議員、反貪污諮詢委員會委員及漁業發展貸款委員會委員

18. 一九九六年十一月李國寶於香港口述

19. 一九六五年六月十四日《華僑日報》

20. 一九九六年十一月李國寶於香港口述

21. 一九八三年七月十六日費彝民於《華僑日報》所撰「緬懷利銘澤」

22. 一九九六年一月利國偉爵士於香港口述，透露此消息的中國政要因仍在世不便提及真實姓名。

23. 父親於一九八二年六月十四日及十五日，在德國法蘭克福Gravenbruch-Kempinski Hotel所發表的On the Importance of Hong Kong to China演講內容。

24. 一九九六年十一月梁威林於廣州口述

25. 一九七九年一月《名流月刊》第二十四頁

26. 一九七八年一月十一日《大公報》

27. 一九七七年十一月二十七日馬臨教授信函

28. 一九七八年三月二十四日《大公報》

29. 一九七七年六月馬臨教授於香港口述

30. 中國年輕人常不分「n」與「l」發音，令字義混淆不清

31. 一九九五年四月李樂君於洛杉磯口述

32. 一九九五年四月李樂君於洛杉磯口述

33. 姚剛於一九四八年大學畢業後即加入太古集團的上海辦事處工作，後來成為首位獲送至英國接受實習訓練的本地人，通常此機會僅保留給牛津畢業生。一九五一年韓戰爆發後，太古不願再派專家至中國，便詢問姚回中國的意願，結果以二十二、三歲的年齡，姚剛成為太古在中國的保險業經理，總部設於上海，在天津、青島、漢口、廈門及汕頭皆有分公司。一九五三年時他覺得太古在中國前途不明，提議太古自中國撤退，太古便接受他的建議撤出中國，姚剛在一九五三年聖誕節抵達香港。他退休之前兼太古集團六個輔屬企業的主席。

34. 一九九七年六月姚剛於香港口述

35. 中國國際信託投資公司為北京政府最具實力的國際公司，海內外共有二十間分公司，員工兩萬六千人，資產美金五億元以上。海外發展方向集中於開發天然資源及通訊事業；如在華盛頓西

36. 雅圖所有的森林產業，成為美國西北部的木材主要供應商。其他企業亦有中華電力公司、港龍航空、香港電訊、貿易，及大多在香港、澳門及中國的地產業。公司股票在香港證券交易所正式上市。姚剛於一九九七年六月在香港表示；因他與魏的私人友誼是「太古與中國國際信託投資公司關係密切的原因，促使二者有許多合作企業」。

37. 旅客可由香港上車直赴廣州辦理入境手續，不必在邊境接受檢查。

38. 一九九六年十一月王匡於廣州口述

39. 利銘澤所發表的 On the Importance of Hong Kong to China 演講

40. 美國銀行副總裁 H.A. Washcheck 於一九八〇年九月四日致父親的信函

41. 費彝民於一九八三年七月十六日在《大公報》所撰「緬懷利銘澤」

42. 費彝民「緬懷利銘澤」

43. 合約規定中國在十五年之後擁有旅館所有權，但後來延長至二十年。

44. 附屬條約於一九八三年五月三日簽署

45. 合約中稱花園賓館

46. 一九八〇年三月二十八日，花園酒店〔香港〕有限公司與廣州嶺南置業公司，簽訂廣州花園賓館的工程及經營合作合約。

47. 一九八三年五月三日，花園酒店〔香港〕有限公司與廣州嶺南置業公司，簽訂廣州花園賓館的工程及經營合作附屬合約。

48. 一九八〇年十二月二十七日《大公報》

49. 一九九五年春吳慶塘於多倫多表示，當時是中方代表堅持此設計。

50. 一九九五年春吳慶塘於多倫多口述

51. 姚剛於一九九七年六月於香港表示；完工時造價超出預算百分之八十，為港幣十五億元。

52. 她因而成為廣州花園酒店董事局的副主席

53. 一九九七年六月姚剛於香港口述

54. 父親計劃在東京設立聯絡處，由緒方鈴子負責。

55. 一九九七年六月緒方鈴子於香港表示；當時雖然美國領事館已遷出，僅將文化中心留在花園酒店，但日本領事館仍未有遷移打算。

56. 港幣七億元

57. 為中國政府在北京的賓館專招待達官顯要，因古代君王於內宮釣魚而命名為釣魚台。

58. 一九九七年六月姚剛於香港口述

59. 一九九五年春李樂君於洛杉磯口述

第十三章

1. 一九七五年十月二十六日《南華早報》Berta Manson 所撰 Empire Builders 的系列報導

2. 一九七五年十月二十六日《南華早報》

3. 這是香港在一九七〇年代初期出現的社會現象，導致一九七三年的經濟衰退。

4. 一九七二年一月一日《大公報》

5. 一九七五年十月二十六日《南華早報》

6. 一九八二年六月十四日及十五日，利銘澤於德國法蘭克福經濟會議中，所發表的 On the Importance of Hong Kong to China 演講詞。

7. 一如西方家庭的聖誕樹，國人在農曆年時家中常擺飾桃花，盼能在年初一開花為來年帶來好運。

8. 一九九五年春李樂君於洛杉磯口述

9. 一九九六年十月利漢釗於香港口述

10. 一九九六年十月利漢釗於香港口述

11. 一九六○年四月一日《華僑日報》

12. 一九六三年三月十九日《華僑日報》

13. 一九六三年三月十九日《華僑日報》

14. 香港鋼管有限公司開幕致辭

15. 一九九六年一月利江蕙蘭於香港口述

16. 一九六四年八月二十日《大公報》

17. 一九七九年八月《名流月刊》第二十四頁

18. 一九五五年、一九五六年、一九五九年、一九六○年、一九六一年、一九六二年、一九六三年

《大公報》

19. 一九六三年一月二日及四月《大公報》

20. 維多利亞城市發展公司秘書在一九六四年一月六日給父親的信函

21. 一九六五年六月二十四日《大公報》

22. 一九九六年一月利漢釗於香港口述

23. 一九九六年一月利漢釗於香港口述

24. 中國政府並不打算將國內不穩定的局面波及香港

25. 一九九六年利漢釗於香港表示，香港第三條過海隧道可在一九九七年完成。

26. 一九八三年七月十六日費彝民於《大公報》所撰「緬懷利銘澤」

27. 這亦是香港市區革命性的改變，將香港及九龍聯合為一個大城市。

28. 一九九六年一月利漢釗於香港口述

29. 直到一九七五年十二月G. R. Ross接任之前，父親仍為主席。

30. 一九六七年三月三十一日《華僑日報》

31. Jardine Fleming & Company Limited是香港第一間商業銀行，於一九七〇年成立，Jardine Matheson Holdings Limited及Robert Fleming Holdings Limited共為股東。

32. 一九六六年十一月李國寶於香港口述

33. 一九七〇年三月三十一日《華僑日報》

34. 一九五〇年代及一九六〇年代時，由於電話線路嚴重短缺，電話公司受賄猖獗，甚至還有黑市行情。

35. 一九九七年六月於香港電話訪問姬達爵士

36. 姬達爵士是香港戰後的軍方高層人員，那時與父親相識並成為好友。他於一九七三年十月至一九七八年十月任職於香港廉政專員公署為廉政專員，繼任職布政司，日後獲封爵位。

37. 費彞民所撰「緬懷利銘澤」

38. 一九七五年七月二十九日《大公報》

39. 一九七五年七月及八月《大公報》

40. 利漢釗於一九九七年八月由香港所提供的資料

41. 一九九七年香港出版Robin Hutcheon所著The Blue Flame

42. 一九八三年七月十六日費彞民所撰「緬懷利銘澤」

43. Robin Hutcheon所著The Blue Flame

44. 一九九七年六月十一日Sir Evelyn de Rothschild由倫敦致父親信函

45. 一九七九年十二月四日Sir Evelyn de Rothschild由倫敦致父親信函

46. 一九九七年六月Per Jorgensen由哥本哈根所提供的資料
47. 一九九七年六月Per Jorgensen由哥本哈根所提供的資料
48. 一九九七年四月利廓靈愛於溫哥華口述
49. 一九九三年七月八日利廓靈愛於溫哥華口述
50. 利銘澤On the Importance of Hong Kong to China演講詞
51. 姚剛一九九八年二月香港提供資料顯示；這家英國倫敦公司是英國唯一的獨資大證券公司，在過去三十年中，公司在世界十一個金融中心皆設有分公司，香港分行於一九七四年創立。員工一千多人分佈全球，業務範圍為企業金融、工業經紀及資金管理。
52. 一九八一年八月四日《大公報》
53. 一九九七年四月林達光教授於溫哥華口述，一九八〇年代林為澳門東亞大學校長。一九九七年六月姚剛於香港口述，林教授與姚剛皆為加華石油有限公司董事。
54. 利銘澤On the Importance of Hong Kong to China演講詞

第十四章

1. 一九八八年香港出版Christopher Haffner所著The Craft in the East前言
2. Haffner所著The Craft in the East前言
3. Haffner所著The Craft in the East前言
4. Haffner所著The Craft in the East第四百二十二頁
5. Haffner所著The Craft in the East第四百二十二頁
6. Haffner所著The Craft in the East第四百二十二頁
7. Haffner所著The Craft in the East第四百二十五頁

第十五章

1. 一九八〇年代初北美經濟萎縮導致香港移民潮暫緩，但一九八六年許家屯的反對香港自由選舉言論及北美經濟好轉，又興起移民熱。

2. 一九八二年六月十四日及十五日利銘澤於德國法蘭克福Gravenbruch-Kempinski Hotel經濟會議中所發表的 On the Importance of Hong Kong to China 演講詞。

3. 利銘澤 On the Importance of Hong Kong to China 演講詞

4. 利銘澤 On the Importance of Hong Kong to China 演講詞

5. 利銘澤 On the Importance of Hong Kong to China 演講詞

6. 英國及中國駐聯合國代表，在一九七一年聯合國會議中同意，將香港由聯合國的殖民地名單中刪除，香港問題將由兩國雙方談判。

7. 利銘澤 On the Importance of Hong Kong to China 演講詞

8. 利銘澤 On the Importance of Hong Kong to China 演講詞

9. 利銘澤 On the Importance of Hong Kong to China 演講詞

10. 利銘澤 On the Importance of Hong Kong to China 演講詞

11. 香港政府在一九九七年之後應走的方向，在父親的 On the Importance of Hong Kong to China 演講詞中有發表意見。

8. Haffner所著The Craft in the East第四百二十二頁

9. Haffner所著The Craft in the East第四百二十四頁

10. Haffner所著The Craft in the East第三百六十二頁至三百六十四頁

11. 共濟會地區副區總監姚剛弟兄提供的一九九七年春季共濟會遠東及香港地區分會通訊錄。

12. 我在一九九七年六月回香港時，曾見到買下亞特蘭大號的船主的兄弟叫阿明，他是Deacon & Co. 主席R.G.Ross的船工，他告訴我亞特蘭大號有幾年成為供人出海野餐的出租船隻。何寧日後在為專為富人照顧遊艇的年輕船工圈中頗受尊重，並成了他們的大阿哥。

13. 他來我們家工作時，哥哥和姐姐已赴英國讀書。

14. 一九八三年七月十六日費彝民在《大公報》所撰「緬懷利銘澤」。

15. 一九九四年春李樂君於洛杉磯口述。

16. 一九九三年香港出版許家屯所著《許家屯回憶錄》第四十三頁。

17. 一九九五年春李樂君於洛杉磯口述。

18. 一九九七年六月姚剛於香港口述。

19. 香港與多倫多夏季因日光節約時間相差十二小時。

20. 費彝民所撰「緬懷利銘澤」。

21. 一九八八年香港出版Christopher Haffner所著The Craft in the East第四百二十四頁及四百二十五頁。

22. Haffner所著The Craft in the East第四百二十四頁。

23. Haffner所著The Craft in the East第四百二十四頁。